JOURNALISM

NOT JUST A TEXTBOOK ...

Check out the extensive FREE online resources to support your study

Free interactive eBook	Author tutorials	Journal articles	Useful weblinks

Find out more at
https://study.sagepub.com/harcup

Use your interactive eBook on your smartphone, tablet, laptop or computer to:

| Hightlight and take notes | Watch author tutorials | Read journal articles | Find links and examples of journalism in action |

At the end of each chapter, the video icon takes you into Tony's office where he will tackle a common problem in journalism practice and give you step-by-step ideas on how to solve it.

SAGE was founded in 1965 by Sara Miller McCune to support the dissemination of usable knowledge by publishing innovative and high-quality research and teaching content. Today, we publish more than 750 journals, including those of more than 300 learned societies, more than 800 new books per year, and a growing range of library products including archives, data, case studies, reports, conference highlights, and video. SAGE remains majority-owned by our founder, and after Sara's lifetime will become owned by a charitable trust that secures our continued independence.

Los Angeles | London | Washington DC | New Delhi | Singapore

JOURNALISM

PRINCIPLES AND PRACTICE

---- 3rd edition

TONY HARCUP

Los Angeles | London | New Delhi
Singapore | Washington DC

Los Angeles | London | New Delhi
Singapore | Washington DC

SAGE Publications Ltd
1 Oliver's Yard
55 City Road
London EC1Y 1SP

SAGE Publications Inc.
2455 Teller Road
Thousand Oaks, California 91320

SAGE Publications India Pvt Ltd
B 1/I 1 Mohan Cooperative Industrial Area
Mathura Road
New Delhi 110 044

SAGE Publications Asia-Pacific Pte Ltd
3 Church Street
#10-04 Samsung Hub
Singapore 049483

Editor: Mila Steele
Assistant editor: James Piper
Production editor: Imogen Roome
Proofreader: Leigh C. Timmins
Indexer: Adam Pozner
Marketing manager: Michael Ainsley
Cover design: Jen Crisp
Typeset by: C&M Digitals (P) Ltd, Chennai, India
Printed and bound by CPI Group (UK) Ltd,
Croydon, CR0 4YY

© Tony Harcup 2015

First edition published 2004

Reprinted 2005 (twice), 2006, 2007, 2008 (twice)

Second edition published 2009. Reprinted 2009, 2011, 2012, 2013

Library of Congress Control Number: 2014948965

British Library Cataloguing in Publication data

A catalogue record for this book is available from the British Library

ISBN 978-1-4462-7408-8
ISBN 978-1-4462-7409-5 (pbk)
ISBN 978-1-4739-3033-9 (pbk and eBook)

At SAGE we take sustainability seriously. Most of our products are printed in the UK using FSC papers and boards. When we print overseas we ensure sustainable papers are used as measured by the Egmont grading system. We undertake an annual audit to monitor our sustainability.

In memory of my mum, Beth, and my dad, Fred.

CONTENTS

LIST OF BOXES

ACKNOWLEDGEMENTS

Thanks to all the journalists, students, teachers and friends who have helped in one way or another over the years, whether you realise it or not. Special thanks to all the interviewees for giving your time and your stories, and to Julia Hall and Mila Steele for believing in this book.

PREFACE TO THE THIRD EDITION

This book can be used as a textbook and a "how to" guide, although I hope it also offers much more. The idea is to introduce the voices of a range of practising journalists, as well as scholars from the field of journalism studies and beyond, and get them to talk to each other. Chapters can be read in a number of ways: by reading the left-hand side *practice* section first, followed by the more theoretical section; by reversing the order; or by flitting between the two, following the bold words in the initial text to the relevant accompanying *principles* entries. This will provide useful preparation for the journalistic art of keeping an eye on a number of things at once, and should also mean that the book will repay repeated visits.

Many things have changed in the world of journalism since the second edition appeared, perhaps most notably the explosion in the use of social media that was merely hinted at back then. The other has been the whole Leveson saga. Social media and ethics are embedded in every chapter, but this third edition also sees the addition of two new chapters to help contextualise more fully the principles and practices involved. Other new additions for this edition include a scenario (*What would you do?*) at the end of every chapter to help readers think through the complexities and implications of what they have just read, plus three top tips on what to read next.

Each chapter has been fully revised and updated and every word has been reviewed, with many fresh insights being added courtesy of a number of new interviews. As a result, this third edition comprises around 50 per cent new material. It has grown in size in the process, prompting a slight reorganisation (and re-titling) of some chapters, with a new division into three themed sections: *What is journalism?* (Chapters 1 to 7); *How to do journalism* (Chapters 8 to 12); and *What now for journalism?* (Chapters 13 to 15). As before, each chapter includes a guide to useful further reading.

For the benefit of anyone unfamiliar with the Harvard style of academic referencing, when you see something like this in the text (Bloggs, 2015: 10) it means that you can easily find out the source by turning to the alphabetical list of references at the back and looking up the name Bloggs, followed by the year of publication, in this case 2015. The number 10 in the above example refers to the page number in the original source. Bloggs is a hypothetical example, by the way.

Also listed in the references are all those journalists interviewed for this book, whether for the first, second or third editions. Sadly, two of the original interviewees are no longer with us. Paul Foot died at the age of 66 in July 2004, not long after publication of the first edition, and his funeral was attended by an estimated 2,000 people (Ingrams, 2005: 6). The Paul Foot Award is awarded in his memory each year, and two winners of the award have now been interviewed for this book: Deborah Wain and Andrew Norfolk.

Brian Whittle, who started out on a local paper as a 17-year-old, was a very different type of journalist from the Oxford-educated Foot. But, although they may have had different backgrounds and attitudes, they were both cracking reporters and were equally generous with their time, willingly discussing their craft with me for the benefit of future generations of journalists. When I later bumped into Brian at a press do, he told me he had finally got around to reading the book and had enjoyed it – rather to his surprise, I suspected. Not long afterwards, in December 2005, he collapsed and died at a party held to mark the departure of the *Express* and *Star* national titles from Manchester. As former colleague Peter Reece (2005) commented: "It was fitting that he was in the company of journalists, for tabloid ink ran through Brian's veins." He was aged just 59.

Neither Paul Foot nor Brian Whittle lived long enough to be able to send a tweet, even if they had been so inclined. But the fact that so many of their thoughts quoted in these pages remain as pertinent today as when they were spoken suggests that the fundamental principles and practices of journalism might not have been transformed quite as much as some people think.

GUIDED TOUR OF THE BOOK AND INTERACTIVE EBOOK

MORE THAN JUST A BOOK ...

As well as two new chapters on **An Ethical Approach to Journalism**, and **Engaging with the Audience and Social Media**, the third edition of *Journalism* includes a FREE interactive eBook, providing students with on-the-go access to a wealth of digital resources.

WHAT MAKES THE EBOOK INTERACTIVE?

Each chapter contains interactive icons which link to the following extra resources:

 A new journalism scenario video for every chapter and three additional introductory videos for each part of the book

 Further reading, including SAGE journal articles to help you explore further

 Useful weblinks, such as reports, guidelines and YouTube videos

HOW DO I ACCESS THE INTERACTIVE EBOOK?

Go to the inside front cover of your book to find your unique code, and follow the step-by-step instructions to redeem your free interactive eBook! You can find out more about using your interactive eBook at https://study.sagepub.com/harcup

- The unique code provided on the inside front cover of this book gives you 24 months FREE access to an eBook via VitalSource Bookshelf®
- Access the book from your desktop, laptop, tablet or smartphone
- Click on the icons to access the extra resources
- Make notes and highlights that automatically sync across your devices.

PART ONE

WHAT IS JOURNALISM?

People make their own history but not under circumstances of their own choosing, as someone once said (Karl Marx, actually). So it is with journalism. *Part One* of this book explores scholarly and practitioner accounts of journalism in the context of the real life conditions under which journalists operate: that includes looking at the aspirations and actions of individuals as well as the constraints that can limit journalistic autonomy. The concept of ethics is introduced here and will be a recurring theme throughout the book. The seven chapters comprising *Part One* examine some of the key roles played by journalists as news-gatherers, witnesses, reporters, investigators and entertainers, the last of which is often overlooked in the academic literature. Journalism can be fun and there is nothing wrong with that. But it can also be harrowing, as the interview with Andrew Norfolk (Chapter 6) makes clear. Together this blend of light and dark is what makes the cocktail of journalism so intoxicating, and the opening chapters of this book describe and discuss the necessary ingredients. The aim is to help readers not only produce better quality journalism, but also to understand journalism better.

PART 1 VIDEO

CHAPTER 1

THE WHO, WHAT, WHERE, WHEN, WHY AND HOW OF JOURNALISM

"Journalism, like acting and prostitution, is not a profession but a vocation", declared former *Times* journalist Louis Heren (1973 [1996]: 187–188) in his memoirs. Rather more recently, Sharon Marshall described former colleagues on assorted redtop tabloids as almost all "mad, drunken, immoral, sex-crazed chancers". And those were just their good points, judging by her confession that "deep down I love every double-crossing, slippery, two-faced little one of them" (Marshall, 2010: 269). We can see something of the mythology of journalism at work in these two comments about both the weighty and the popular press. There's a tendency among journalists to see themselves as slightly roguish, verging on the disreputable: ever-present members of society's awkward squad, except when they are sucking up to the editor, proprietor or proprietor's spouse. As Andrew Marr puts it in his own memoir:

> Journalism is a chaotic form of earning, ragged at the edges, full of snakes, con artists and even the occasional misunderstood martyr. It doesn't have an accepted career structure, necessary entry requirement or an effective system of self-policing. Outside organised crime, it is the most powerful and enjoyable of the anti-professions.
> (Marr, 2005: 3)

That phrase "outside organised crime" pre-dated the revelations of organised criminality at (and closure of) the *News of the World*, of course, but the point still stands that journalism can be powerful and infuriating and full of contradictions. Journalists routinely juggle complex intellectual, legal, commercial and ethical issues every day, simultaneously and at high speed, all while giving the impression of being little deeper than a puddle. And it can be fun.

COMMUNICATION

The basic questions of journalism highlighted in the title of this chapter – Who? What? Where? When? Why? How? – are echoed in an early model of the mass communication process, formulated by Harold Lasswell in 1948. For Lasswell, analysis of the media begins with the question: "Who says what to whom, through what channel and with what effect?" (McQuail, 2000: 52–53). This has been termed a "transmission" model of communication because it is essentially one way, from sender to receiver. This and later versions of the transmission model have been challenged in recent decades as too simplistic, too linear, too mono-directional to explain the complexities of communication. It has been argued that an "active audience" can filter messages through our own experiences and understandings, sometimes producing readings "against the grain", or even suggesting multiple meanings. Increasingly, too, audiences are contributing to journalism directly via social media and user-generated content. The ways in which journalists engage with the audience on social media are considered in detail in Chapter 14 but also crop up throughout the book.

> **"Journalism largely consists in saying 'Lord Jones Dead' to people who never knew that Lord Jones was alive."**
> *GK Chesterton.*

JOURNALISM

Journalists may indeed inform society about itself, but such a formulation falls far short of an adequate definition. Journalism is defined by Denis McQuail as "paid writing (and the audiovisual equivalent) for public media with reference to actual and ongoing events of public relevance" (McQuail, 2000: 340). Like all such definitions, this raises many questions – Can journalism never be unpaid? Can media be other than public? Who decides what is of public relevance? – but it remains a reasonable starting point for

In western, liberal democracies, at least, each of us is at liberty to commit acts of journalism if we so choose. That is because journalism is a trade, or a craft, rather than a "proper" profession along the lines of medicine or the law. It's not complete liberty hall – in Chapter 2 we will consider some of the constraints that limit the behaviour and autonomy of journalists – but it does mean that journalists are not required to seek anyone's permission to practise journalism. That, in turn, means that nobody can be denied permission to practise journalism, even if they turn out to be a con artist or a sex-crazed chancer.

So what is it all for? Journalism is a form of **communication** based on asking, and answering, the questions Who? What? Where? When? Why? How? Journalism is also a job. Journalists need to pay their rents or mortgages and feed their kids, and they have been known to refer to their workplaces as "word factories". Yet being a journalist is not the same as working in other types of factory because journalists play a *social* role that goes beyond the production of commodities to sell in the marketplace. Imperfect though it might be, **journalism** informs society about itself and makes public that which would otherwise be private. Journalists have been described as a **fourth estate** of the realm, the eyes-and-ears of the people, acting in the **public interest**. Rather an important job, you might think, but "the people" don't always agree.

Public opinion polls routinely remind journalists that we vie for bottom place with politicians and estate agents in the league table of trustworthiness; that has been the case since long before the 21st century phone-hacking scandal and Leveson inquiry into press ethics. Such attitudes have become all too familiar to Jemima Kiss, who explains:

> It seems pretty much anyone outside the industry takes a sharp intake of breath when you say you're a journalist, which means I often feel the need to say, "I'm not *that* kind of journalist." The assumption is the cliché of a ruthless, doorstepping tabloid hack, I suspect, the type perpetuated in cheesy TV dramas.

Yet despite this image problem, a never-ending stream of bright young and not-so-young people are eager to

> **"Most of journalism, and all of the interesting part, is a disreputable, erratic business which, if properly conducted, serves a reputable end."**
> *Max Hastings.*

any analysis of the principles and practices of journalism. McQuail goes on to differentiate between different types of journalism: "prestige" (or quality) journalism, tabloid journalism, local journalism, specialist journalism, "new" (personal and committed) journalism, civic journalism, development journalism, investigative journalism, journalism of record, advocacy journalism, alternative journalism and gossip journalism (McQuail, 2000: 340).

Such differentiation is rejected by David Randall, who recognises only the division between *good* and *bad* journalism:

> The bad is practised by those who rush faster to judgement than they do to find out, indulge themselves rather than the reader, write between the lines rather than on them, write and think in the dead terms of the formula, stereotype and cliché, regard accuracy as a bonus and exaggeration as a tool and prefer vagueness to precision, comment to information and cynicism to ideals. The good is intelligent, entertaining, reliably informative, properly set in context, honest in intent and effect, expressed in fresh language and serves no cause but the discernible truth. Whatever the audience. Whatever the culture. Whatever the language. Whatever the circumstances. (Randall, 2011: viii)

Whether it is as simple as that is a question we will explore further in this and subsequent chapters. For now, let's stick with defining journalism as:

> A set of practices through which information is found out and communicated, often involving making public what would otherwise be private, and which is typically published or broadcast in a format such as a newspaper, magazine, bulletin, documentary, website, or blog. Journalism entails discovering or uncovering fresh, topical, factual material and making it publicly available, but it goes beyond that to include amplifying, contextualising, or commenting on facts and comments that have already been made public . . . (Harcup, 2014a: 148)

FOURTH ESTATE

The notion of the press as a "fourth estate of the realm" – alongside the Lords, the House of Commons, and the established Church – appears to have first been used by become journalists. Why? Because it can be one of the most exciting jobs around. You go into work not necessarily knowing what you are going to be doing that day. You get the chance to meet powerful people, interesting people, inspiring people, heroes, villains and victims. You get the chance to ask stupid questions; to be one of the first to know something and to tell the world about it; to indulge a passion for writing, maybe to travel, maybe to become an expert in a particular field; to seek truth and campaign for justice; or, if that's your thing, to hang out with celebrities.

Then there's the thrill of seeing your byline or watching your own footage; and the odd experience of hearing your voice on a piece of audio. You can watch people share and discuss it on social media – or not, as the case may be. You can then do it all over again. And again. Little wonder, perhaps, that so many people are prepared to make sacrifices for a career in journalism. Sacrifices such as paying for your own training before even being considered for a job, unless you are either extremely lucky or are the offspring of a powerful figure in the industry; then being paid less than many of the people whose own complaints about low pay might make news stories. It was more than a century ago that journalists staged the first strike in the history of the National Union of Journalists, when they walked out of the *York Herald* in 1911 to protest against working hours and conditions that were described as being reminiscent of Charles Dickens' *Nicholas Nickleby* (Mansfield, 1943: 159; Gopsill and Neale, 2007: 84–85). For many journalists relatively little has changed since then apart from the technology. If your priorities are a secure job with decent pay and predictable hours, you'd be better off looking elsewhere. The pay of most journalists, particularly those just starting out and particularly those working in the local or regional media, is nothing short of shameful. As one trainee reporter put it more than a decade ago:

> **"Start-off pay is abysmal and if they are lucky it will move on to disgraceful after a year, and by the end of the training it will be only just short of appalling."**
> *Sean Dooley.*

> Young people with a strong enough passion for writing will suffer low wages for the chance to work in journalism. But it is a disgrace to the industry as a whole that they should have to. The industry cynically manipulates our ambition. (Quoted in Journalism Training Forum, 2002: 57)

Edmund Burke in the 18th century. Recalling this usage in 1840, in what is believed to be the first time it appeared in print, Thomas Carlyle had no doubt of its meaning:

> Burke said there were three estates in parliament; but, in the reporters' gallery yonder, there sat a fourth estate more important far than they all. It is not a figure of speech, or a witty saying; it is a literal fact, very momentous to us in these times. Literature is our parliament too. Printing, which comes necessarily out of writing, I say often, is equivalent to democracy: invent writing, democracy is inevitable. (Carlyle, 1840: 194)

Ideas about democracy and a free press have to a large extent grown alongside each other and come together in the concept of the fourth estate. Although initially referring specifically to the parliamentary press gallery, the term has become a more general label for journalism, locating journalists in the quasi-constitutional role of "watchdog" on the workings of government. This is central to the liberal concept of press freedom, as Tom O'Malley notes:

> At the centre of this theory was the idea that the press played a central, if unofficial, role in the constitution. A diverse press helped to inform the public of issues. It could, through the articulation of public opinion, guide, and act as a check on, government. . . . The press could only fulfil this function if it were free from pre-publication censorship and were independent of the government. (O'Malley, 1997: 127)

PUBLIC INTEREST

The concept of the public interest is much used in debates about journalism but it has not proved easy to define. For former *News of the World* journalist Paul McMullan, the public interest simply means what people are interested in, as he told the Leveson inquiry:

> I mean, circulation defines what is the public interest. I see no distinction between what the public is interested in and the public interest. Surely they're clever enough to make a decision whether or not they want to put their hand in their pocket and bring out a pound and buy it. I don't see it's the job – our job or anybody else – to force the public to be able to choose that you must read this, you can't read that. (McMullan, 2011)

And that was long before the financial crisis that began in 2007–08, since when wage rates – and freelance fees – have declined even further in comparison with the cost of living.

JOURNALISM OR CHURNALISM?

Some wannabe journalists *are* put off when they discover the awful truth about pay. Others become disillusioned by work experience in newsrooms, observing that too many journalists seem to be chained to their desks in a culture of "presenteeism", processing copy and checking things out – if at all – on the telephone, online or via social media. It was when he was working as a business journalist with BBC Scotland that Waseem Zakir came up with the word **churnalism** to describe too much of today's newsroom activity:

> Ten or 15 years ago you would go out and find your own stories and it was proactive journalism. It's become reactive now. You get copy coming in on the wires and reporters churn it out, processing stuff and maybe adding the odd local quote.
>
> It's affecting every newsroom in the country and reporters are becoming churnalists.

It is true that an ever-increasing workload may reduce the chances of doing the very things that made journalism seem so attractive in the first place. On top of all that, young journalists have to listen to more experienced hacks grumbling that "it wasn't like this in my day". The old-timers may have a point, but even the journalists of 100 years ago looked back fondly on a supposed "golden age" of journalism circa 1870 (Tunstall, 2002: 238).

Even when disabused of romantic illusions about travelling the world on huge expense accounts, pausing between drinks to jot down the occasional note, large numbers of people are attracted by the fact that journalism remains an occupation in which no two days are exactly the same and where the big story may be only a phone call away. And by the fact that journalism *matters*. Many journalists around the world pay with their lives precisely because journalism matters, as we shall see in Chapter 2.

> **"Some of my most memorable pieces have been interviewing ordinary people in extraordinary situations."**
> *Cathy Newman.*

It would be fair to say that McMullan has been something of a lone voice, at least in public, in defining the public interest in such a way. The public interest will be considered in more depth later in this book, particularly in Chapters 2 and 13.

PAUL MCMULLAN
VIDEO AND
TRANSCRIPT

CHURNALISM

As far as I can tell, the portmanteau word "churnalism" was first published in the original edition of this book way back in 2004, credited to Waseem Zakir; so it is worth keeping in mind that, when he refers to "10 or 15 years ago", that would now be more like 25 years ago. Churnalism later took on a new life when Nick Davies (2008: 56) referred to "what some now call 'churnalism'" in his book *Flat Earth News*, having been informed of the term by one of my ex-students who was helping with his research. Since then countless academics, journalists and other commentators have told us without checking that Davies himself coined the term; he did not, nor did he ever claim to have done so. The funny thing is that most of those erroneously crediting him with the coinage have done so in the very process of criticising journalists for recycling material without checking. The word "ironic" is both overused and frequently misused, but it might just fit here.

Churnalism, meanwhile, is alive and well in the digital age, judging by a recent study of public relations in the field of science, which quoted a press officer explaining how it works: "You send out a press release and it gets picked up by a newswire and you can see it on 80 different websites. And for me it's brilliant" (Williams and Gajevic, 2013: 516).

PUBLIC SPHERE

The idea of the public sphere rests on the existence of a space in which informed citizens can engage with one another in debate and critical reflection; hence its relevance to discussions of the media. Jürgen Habermas traces the rise of the public sphere in Europe in the late 17th and early 18th centuries and argues that increasing commercialisation led subsequently to the decline of the public sphere and the press as a space that enabled "the people to reflect critically upon itself and on the practices of the state" (Stevenson, 2002: 49). Today, according to this analysis, such reasoned public discussion has been

Explanations of *how* and *why* journalism matters depend, like so many things, on *who* is speaking. Journalism is variously said to form part of a **public sphere**, to support a **free press** or to inculcate us with the **ideology** of the ruling class. Journalism is probably all those things and more because there is not really just *one* journalism.

WHAT'S IN THIS BOOK?

Individual journalists have their own tales to tell, their own beliefs about what they do, their own reasons for pursuing a career in whatever field of journalism they work in. For each edition of this book I have interviewed a range of journalists from different generations, different backgrounds and different media, some of them several times. Their comments are taken from these interviews unless otherwise indicated. Here are just some of those you will hear from in subsequent chapters:

- Carla Buzasi, founding editor-in-chief of the online-only *Huffington Post UK*, who previously worked on the digital side of magazines such as *Glamour*, *Marie Claire* and *Vogue*. Carla ran the *Huffington Post*'s UK operation from its launch in July 2011 (in the same week that saw the closure of the country's biggest-selling newspaper, the *News of the World*) until leaving to become global chief content officer for the fashion trend forecaster WGSN in 2014. She tweets as @carlabuzasi.

- Lindsay Eastwood, for many years a staff reporter on ITV Yorkshire's *Calendar* news programme, for which she still free-lances. After working on her local newspaper (the *Craven Herald*) straight after leaving school, she moved to the *Watford Observer* and worked shifts on the nationals before returning north to the *Yorkshire Evening Post*. Lindsay later switched to news and documentary television and now also teaches journalism as well as tweeting as @lindsayeastwood.

> **"Reporters are becoming churnalists."**
> *Waseem Zakir.*

- Paul Foot joined the *Daily Mirror* after university and also worked on the *Daily Record* in Glasgow before moving on to *Private Eye* and then *Socialist Worker.* He left when he was offered his own page

replaced by "the progressive privatisation of the citizenry and the trivialisation . . . of questions of public concern" (Stevenson, 2002: 50). But, in turn, Habermas has been accused of idealising "a bygone and elitist form of political life" (McQuail, 2000: 158). As with many topics introduced in this chapter, this is not the last you will read of the public sphere.

FREE PRESS

Editors and owners alike are often heard extolling the virtues of a "free press", a liberal model based on the idea that everyone is free to publish a newspaper without having to be licensed by those in power. Hence the strength of feeling and rhetoric around the Leveson Report of 2012 and subsequent discussions about a royal charter to oversee self-regulation of the UK press. Although publishers must act within the constraints of laws ranging from defamation to phone-hacking, they do not have to submit to censorship in advance nor does anyone except broadcasters need to seek anyone's permission to publish. Through the democracy of the free market, so the argument goes, we get the press we both desire and deserve. However, this concept of a press selflessly serving the public does not go unchallenged. Colin Sparks, for example, points to an increasing concentration of ownership and to economic barriers on entry, keeping out competitors. He argues:

> Newspapers in Britain are first and foremost businesses. They do not exist to report the news, to act as watchdogs for the public, to be a check on the doings of govern-ment, to defend the ordinary citizen against abuses of power, to unearth scandals or to do any of the other fine and noble things that are sometimes claimed for the press. They exist to make money, just as any other business does. To the extent that they discharge any of their public functions, they do so in order to succeed as businesses. (Sparks, 1999: 45–46)

For Sparks, a truly free press – presenting objective information and a range of informed opinions while acting as a public forum – is actually "an impossibility in a free market" (Sparks, 1999: 59).

IDEOLOGY

By ideology is meant "some organised belief system or set of values that is disseminated or reinforced by communication" in the *Daily Mirror*, but eventually fell foul of the post-Maxwell regime at the paper and returned to his spiritual home at the *Eye*. When he was interviewed for this book he was on the staff of the magazine as well as being a columnist for the *Guardian* newspaper and a freelance contributor to a range of other publications. He died shortly after the first edition appeared in 2004, but is commemorated every year in the Paul Foot Award for Investigative Journalism (see Chapter 6).

THE PAUL FOOT
AWARD

- Sarah Hartley is a freelance journalist and the former head of online editorial at MEN Media in Manchester, where she helped run a converged editorial operation across print, TV, radio and the web. Sarah started out as a trainee on the weekly *Leamington Spa Observer* and later became news editor of the *Northern Echo* newspaper. She switched to the *Echo*'s website before moving to the *Manchester Evening News* online operation and, later, to the world of freelancing where she now blogs about journalism and other topics at www.sarahhartley. me.uk/ and tweets as @foodiesarah.

- Jemima Kiss is head of technology at the *Guardian*, which she joined in 2006 initially as an online new media reporter. She did not train as a journalist but studied fine art at college before working at the Brighton Media Centre, where she helped develop the centre's website. Jemima began writing freelance technology-based features for websites produced by a company based at the centre before becoming a full-time journalist for www.journalism.co.uk in 2003, writing about the digital publishing industry. She mostly learned on the job but was also sent on several short training courses about writing for the web and media law. She tweets as @jemimakiss.

> **"The heroes of journalism are reporters."**
> *David Randall.*

- Neal Mann is multimedia innovations editor at the *Wall Street Journal* in New York, having trained as a broadcast journalist before working at *Sky News* as researcher, field producer, deputy news editor and digital news editor. After leaving *Sky* he went to the *WSJ*, initially as social media editor. He describes the multimedia innovations editor job as "looking

(McQuail, 2000: 497). Marxists believe that a ruling-class ideology is propagated throughout western, capitalist societies with the help of the mass media. Ideology may be slippery and contested, but it is argued that the principle remains essentially as expounded by Karl Marx and Friedrich Engels more than 160 years ago:

> The ideas of the ruling class are in every epoch the ruling ideas: ie, the class which is the ruling material force of society, is at the same time its ruling intellectual force. The class which has the means of material production at its disposal, has control at the same time over the means of mental production, so that thereby, generally speaking, the ideas of those who lack the means of mental production are subject to it. The ruling ideas are nothing more than the ideal expression of the dominant material relationships, the dominant material relationships grasped as ideas . . . (Marx and Engels, [1846] 1965: 61)

Ideological power has been described as "the power to signify events in a particular way", although ideology is also "a site of struggle" between competing definitions (Hall, 1982: 69–70). To illustrate the point, Stuart Hall refers to media coverage of industrial action in the UK public sector:

> [One] of the key turning-points in the ideological struggle was the way the revolt of the lower-paid public-service workers against inflation, in the "Winter of Discontent" of 1978–9, was successfully signified, not as a defence of eroded living standards and differentials, but as a callous and inhuman exercise of overweening "trade-union power", directed against the defenceless sick, aged, dying and indeed the dead but unburied "members of the ordinary public". (Hall, 1982: 83)

Viewed from this perspective, the "news values" employed by journalists in the selection and construction of stories can be seen not as the neutral expression of professional practice, but as ideologically loaded (Hall et al, 1978: 54). Thus, for all the apparent diversity of the media, and taking into account various exceptions, the routines and practices of journalists *tend to* privilege the explanations of the powerful and to foreclose discussion before it strays too far beyond the boundaries of the dominant ideology (Hall et al, 1978: 118).

at how we can change the way we do journalism, to deliver content to the audience on a variety of different platforms, and create experiences". He has also spent time in Sydney, having been seconded to help News Corp Australia do something similar there. Neal tweets as @fieldproducer.

- Jane Merrick is political editor of the *Independent on Sunday* and a columnist on the *Independent*, having previously worked for the *Daily Mail*, the Mercury news agency in Liverpool, and the Press Association (for whom she was working when interviewed for this book). She tweets as @janemerrick23.

- Cathy Newman presents *Channel 4 News* but also reports on many stories herself as well as conducting investigations for the *Dispatches* current affairs programme. Before switching to television in 2006, initially as a political correspondent, she worked for the *Independent* and *Financial Times*, specialising first in media, then in politics. As well as appearing on screen, Cathy is a regular blogger (including for the *Telegraph*) and helped create the *Factcheck* blog on the C4News website. She tweets as @cathynewman.

- Andrew Norfolk is chief investigations reporter for the *Times*, having previously worked for the *Evening News* in Scarborough and then the *Yorkshire Post*, where he was a member of a team that exposed the "Donnygate" corruption scandal. In 2014 he was named Journalist of the Year in the British Journalism Awards, following his Paul Foot Award two years earlier, for a lengthy investigation into the reluctance of police and care agencies to protect vulnerable young girls in Rochdale, Rotherham and elsewhere from being groomed for sexual exploitation. His series of *Times* stories prompted two government-ordered inquiries, a parliamentary inquiry and a new national action plan on child sexual exploitation.

- Deborah Wain also won the Paul Foot Award but from the other end of the journalistic food chain. She was not working for a well-heeled national news organisation, but for an under-resourced weekly newspaper, the *Doncaster Free Press*, when becoming the joint winner of the award in 2007 for an

An emphasis on the ideological content of journalism is frequently challenged for downplaying the agency of journalists themselves and/or for failing to take account of the complex ways in which audiences may actually "read" media texts.

AGENCY

Within the study of journalism, agency means the extent to which individual journalists can *make a difference* to media practices and content: "To have agency is defined by the ability to be able to actively intervene" (Stevenson, 2002: 226). To say that journalists have agency is not to deny that they operate in a world of constraints (see Chapter 2), nor to ignore the political and economic pressures to replace journalism with churnalism and/or user-generated content; it is to argue that structural forces do not totally determine all the actions of individuals. Yet many academic critics of the media seem to allow little room for agency and to downplay the role of journalists, preferring to concentrate on structural or market issues, as Angela Phillips (2015: 139) points out. Take Sparks' explanation for the "lurid, sensational and sometimes offensive material" he finds in much of the media:

> "The business of the press is disclosure."
> *John Thaddeus Delane.*

> None of these elements can be traced to the shortcomings of individuals. Newspaper proprietors may be, in the main, bullying reactionary bigots who force their editors to print politically biased material. But even if they were self-denying liberal paragons, it would still make sense for editors to act in the same way, because that is the best business model available to them. Again, editors and journalists may well be moral defectives with no sense of their responsibility to society and to the people upon whose lives they so pruriently report. But even if they were saintly ascetics, it would still make sense for them to publish the same sorts of material, because that is what best secures the competitive position of their newspapers. (Sparks, 1999: 59)

Little sense there of the flesh-and-blood journalists we will hear from in these pages. Yet if journalism matters – as is argued in this book – then the actions of individual journalists must matter too.

investigation into a local further education college. Deborah had gone into journalism straight from school, starting out on the *Matlock Mercury*. Then, after a stint on the *Derby Evening Telegraph*, she went to university to study drama and fine arts. She has now left the *Free Press* but continues to write, including dramas for BBC Radio Four.

- Martin Wainwright was for many years the northern editor of the *Guardian*, having previously worked for the London *Evening Standard*. He retired in 2013, but not before building the *Northerner* blog into a lively presence on the *Guardian* website. He continues to make occasional BBC radio programmes about how grim it's not up north and he tweets as @ mswainwright.

> **"All human life is there."**
> *Old* News of the World *motto.*

- Brian Whittle started on the weekly *Harrogate Herald* at the age of 17 and went on to work for the Bradford *Telegraph and Argus*, the *Northern Echo*, the *Sun*, the *Daily Sketch*, the *Sunday People*, the *National Enquirer* and the *Daily Star* before launching his successful Cavendish Press news agency in Manchester. Brian died in 2005, but the agency lives on.

Among the other journalists featured in this book from time to time are Trevor Gibbons of BBC online; David Helliwell, who was interviewed while assistant editor of the *Yorkshire Evening Post*; consumer affairs reporter Kevin Peachey, who was interviewed while working for the *Nottingham Evening Post*; and Abul Taher, a former news editor of *Eastern Eye* who was interviewed while working for the *Sunday Times*.

Another presence felt throughout this book will be that of the author. As a journalist for the best part of four decades now, I have first-hand experience of working for a range of media large and small, mainstream and alternative. As a long-standing member of the National Union of Journalists, I have engaged with the ethics and social role of journalism as well as the industrial issues that impact upon the working conditions of journalists, including staffing and pay. As someone who now teaches on vocational courses accredited by the National Council for the Training of Journalists (NCTJ) along with the Broadcast Journalism Training Council (BJTC) and the Professional Publishers Association

(formerly the PTC), I have first-hand experience of practical journalism training. And as someone who has tried my hand at research, I am aware of the insights that can be achieved by academic scholarship about, critical engagement with, and reflection upon the principles and practices of journalism.

However, I am also aware of the gap of understanding that too often separates those who *study* media from those who *produce* media. In the UK, as Richard Keeble (2006: 260) notes with regret, "mutual suspicion persists between the press and academia. . . . Scepticism about the value of theoretical studies for aspiring reporters remains widespread". Similarly, in the USA, Barbie Zelizer highlights this disconnection:

> As a former journalist who gradually made her way from wire-service reporting to the academy I am continually wrestling with how best to approach journalism from a scholarly point of view. When I arrived at the university – "freshly expert" from the world of journalism – I felt like I'd entered a parallel universe. Nothing I had read as a graduate student reflected the working world I had just left. . . . My discomfort was shared by many other journalists I knew, who felt uneasy with the journalism scholarship that was fervently putting their world under a microscope. (Zelizer, 2004: 2–3)

Under a microscope is perhaps not the most comfortable place to be, which might explain why so many who earn their livings within the media in general and journalism in particular feel the need to either ignore or attack those looking down the lens. As David Walker (2000: 236–237) notes, "The academic literature of sociology, media studies or cognate disciplines nowadays goes almost entirely unread by journalists". Many journalists seem happy to cover stories about the work of academic researchers on a vast range of subjects, from the health effects of drinking coffee to the psychology of sexual attraction, but when journalism itself comes under scrutiny, such academic study is suddenly deemed to be a waste of time and money. "It's difficult to think of another field . . . in which practitioners believe that the study of what they do is irrelevant to their practice", observe Simon Frith and Peter Meech (2007: 141 and 144): "If journalists look at university journalism courses and find evidence that academics simply don't understand the realities of journalism, so academics look at journalists' accounts of themselves and find evidence of a striking amount of myth-making."

The press "is fearful of being dissected", in the words of one national newspaper reporter (Journalism Training Forum, 2002: 46). Yet surely there are *some* insights to be gained from such dissection and from what has been described as "the melding of theory and practice in a judicious mix of skills and experience along with scholarly study" (Errigo and Franklin, 2004: 46)? I believe there are, and I think that journalists and academics alike have something useful to contribute to the process of understanding; that is why I wrote this book. The aim is to help bridge the conceptual divide between those journalists (practitioners) who feel academics have little to teach them, and those academics whose focus on theory is in danger of denying journalists any degree of autonomy (or **agency**). This book makes explicit some of these different ways of exploring the principles and practices of journalism. In a dialogic approach, each chapter begins from a practitioner viewpoint but includes a parallel analysis from a more academic perspective. These two ways of seeing are not to be read in isolation, as each engages in dialogue with the other; they talk to each other, as do the best journalists and the best scholars.

This book does not attempt to go into too many of the specifics of, for example, being a foreign correspondent, a war correspondent, a celebrity blogger, a courtroom tweeter, a sub, a sports reporter, a showbiz diarist, a presenter, a motoring correspondent, or most of the other specialisms that all have their own rules and folklore; that is because the fundamentals of journalism must be grasped before more specialised roles can be carried out effectively or understood at more than a superficial level. The experience of Edward Behr rings a bell that echoes down the years. As a young reporter, Behr went to work for the Reuters agency in Paris:

> In London, Agence France-Presse (AFP) correspondents rewrote Reuters' copy, as fast as they could, and the finished product ended up as part of the AFP news service. In Paris we shamelessly rewrote Agence France-Presse copy, serving it up as Reuters' fare. All over the world lesser news agencies were writing up *their* versions of Reuters' stories and serving them up as authentic Indian, Spanish, or Brazilian news agency stories. Somewhere, at the bottom of this inverted pyramid, someone was getting a story at first hand. But who was he, and how did he set about it? (Behr, 1992: 72)

He may not be a "he", of course, but it is this reporter who will be the focus throughout this book: the reporter who goes out, whether physically or virtually or both, and gets a story at first hand.

JOURNALISM EDUCATION

This book is designed to help readers produce such reporting, with a necessary emphasis on the basics. Therefore, many of the practices discussed here will be those that developed originally within print journalism in general, and newspapers

JOURNALISM EDUCATION

in particular, because they remain a solid foundation for a career in journalism that today embraces online, television, radio, magazine, mobile and other formats. The practical emphasis will be on the *core* journalistic skills that will be part of any good training course covering journalism in any – or all – media. Such skills cannot be allowed to diminish in importance, even if too many media organisations have in recent years made themselves dazed and confused by trying to leap aboard every passing technological bandwagon, even before they have a clue where it might take them. "There is no possibility of standing still," argues media commentator Roy Greenslade (2008), because "what is state-of-the-art today will be old hat by tomorrow".

This title goes beyond practical instruction in skills to encourage understanding of, and critical reflection upon, our practice. Media employers have been accused of wanting cheap young journalists to be schooled in the routines of work through "basic skills, relevant knowledge and an unquestioning attitude", unencumbered by engagement with ideas from critical theory (Curran, 2000: 42). The book is certainly aimed at supporting students and

JOURNALISM AS AN ACADEMIC DISCIPLINE

<table>
<tr><td>"Get it right. Get it fast. But get it right."
Old Press Association motto.</td></tr>
</table>

trainee journalists in the acquisition and application of reporting and writing skills to complement the other necessary elements of journalism training, such as shorthand, media law, and knowledge of public affairs. Yet, at the same time, it will introduce and engage with some of the more academic analysis that aids our understanding of how journalism works. To this end, the book is aimed at supporting *journalism studies* as well as *journalism training*. Taken together, the two elements can be said to constitute *journalism education* (Bromley, 1997: 339). By asking Why journalists do certain things – as well as the Who, What, Where, When and How – the study of journalism can offer insights that complement journalism training and encourage a questioning attitude and a more reflective practice.

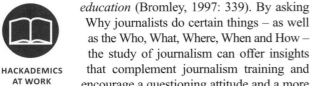

HACKADEMICS AT WORK

Much of the material discussed in these pages may be seen as culturally and historically specific to the UK in the second decade of the 21st century, but there will be many points of wider relevance. Each chapter will raise questions that could form the basis of individual reflection and/or group discussion. Each chapter also suggests further readings that, together with the references listed in the extensive bibliography, will provide a wealth of stimulating material to encourage further exploration of the issues discussed

here. The ethics of journalism, highlighted so publicly during the Leveson inquiry, will be addressed specifically in Chapters 2 and 13. However, because ethical issues have implications for *all* aspects of journalistic practice, questions about ethical issues will also be raised at appropriate points throughout the text, just as ethical issues crop up throughout a journalist's working life – often when least expected.

Journalism is sometimes said, usually by journalists to their critics, to be merely a mirror that reflects society. It is also sometimes said, not so much by journalists, to be a distorting mirror. Clearly journalism cannot be a simple *reflection* of everyday reality because it is both selective and organised (up to a point). As Walter Lippmann observed as long ago as 1922, reporting is not "the simple recovery of obvious facts" because facts "do not spontaneously take a shape in which they can be known. They must be given a shape by somebody" (quoted in McNair, 2000: 71). That's where journalists come in. Journalism is not simply fact-gathering. It involves dealing with sources, selecting information and opinion, and telling stories – all within the framework of the constraints, routines, principles, practices and ethics that will be discussed in the following chapters.

THE LEVESON REPORT

SUMMARY

Journalism is not simply another product but a process of communication, although not necessarily a one-way or linear process. Journalism is said to play a social role in informing society about itself, yet there is a gap of knowledge and understanding between vocational journalism training and academic journalism study. This book will describe the practices of practitioners, while engaging with the principles that inform both practice and analysis. A number of concepts introduced in this chapter will reappear at various points throughout this book.

QUESTIONS

If journalism is not a profession, what is it?
What role does journalism play in society?
Why are journalists apparently so mistrusted by the public?
What skills does a good journalist need?
Why does media studies get such a bad press?

WHAT WOULD YOU DO?

You work for a news organisation that expects you personally to find, write, edit and publish around 12 stories every day; to push those stories out via social media to drive traffic to the website; and to engage with readers and others who make comments on the stories. What do you think journalists faced with such demands do, and what would you do?

HOW MIGHT YOU TACKLE THIS ISSUE?

FURTHER READING

No journalism student should be without their own copy of the *Oxford Dictionary of Journalism* (Harcup, 2014a), even if I say so myself. Then, one of the more thoughtful introductions to journalism from the perspective of a reflective practitioner is David Randall's (2011) *The Universal Journalist*, now in its fourth edition. Other useful introductions to journalism – these ones from journalists-turned-academics – include those by Sheridan Burns (2013), Keeble (2006) and Sissons (2006). The edited collection by Bromley and O'Malley (1997) includes valuable historical material that ought to be of interest to students, producers and consumers of journalism alike. McQuail (2000) is a comprehensive and largely comprehensible introduction to media and mass communication theories, while McQuail (2013) explores arguments about the importance of journalism to society. For further exploration of journalism studies scholarship, see Zelizer (2004), Wahl-Jorgensen and Hanitzsch (2009) and Phillips (2015). Further suggestions will be made at the end of every chapter.

TOP THREE TO TRY NEXT

Tony Harcup (2014a) *Oxford Dictionary of Journalism*
David Randall (2011) *The Universal Journalist* (fourth edition)
The news – from a variety of media and platforms, every day

SOURCES FOR SOUNDBITES

Chesterton, 1981: 246; Hastings, 2004; Dooley, quoted in Slattery, 2005; Newman, interview with the author; Zakir, interview with the author; Randall, 2011: 1; Delane, quoted in Wheen, 2002: xi.

CHAPTER 2

CONSTRAINTS, INFLUENCES AND ETHICS

It must count as one of 21st-century journalism's more bizarre scenes. It took place in the summer of 2013 at the headquarters of a London-based news organisation, when a pair of spooks turned up to watch an editor and colleagues use a power drill and angle grinder to destroy a number of computers. Not just any computers, but ones containing information that had been leaked by US National Security Agency whistleblower Edward Snowden. It was a supremely pointless yet hugely symbolic act, as the editor recalls:

It was hot, dusty work in the basement of the *Guardian* that Saturday, a date that surely merits some sort of footnote in any history of how, in modern democracies, governments tangle with the press. The British state had decreed that there had been "enough" debate around the material leaked in late May by the former NSA contractor Edward Snowden. If the *Guardian* refused to hand back or destroy the documents, I, as editor of the *Guardian*, could expect either an injunction or a visit by the police – it was never quite spelled out which. The state, in any event, was threatening prior restraint of reporting and discussion by the press, no matter its public interest or importance. This was par for the course in 18th century Britain, less so now. In our discussions with government officials before July 20 we had tried to impress on them that, apart from being wrong in principle, this attempt at gagging a news organisation was fruitless. There were, we told them, further copies of the Snowden material in other countries. (Rusbridger, 2013)

> "A solicitor's letter produces a spectacular effect in a newspaper office – editors put work aside, executives are summoned, anxious conferences convened."
> *Alan Watkins.*

The spooks insisted that the ritual sacrifice go ahead, after which they seemed satisfied despite the fact that reporting of the Snowden leaks duly continued via the *Guardian*'s New York office and elsewhere.

THE GUARDIAN'S SNOWDEN FILES

CONSTRAINTS

Journalism is not produced in a vacuum. Journalists work within a range of constraints and influences; structural factors that affect their output (McQuail, 2000: 244). Media theorists argue that journalists "have to make decisions at the centre of a field of different constraints, demands or attempted uses of power or influence" (McQuail, 2000: 249). These range from legal constraints and regulatory codes of practice to the less visible influence of proprietors, organisational routines, market forces, cultural bias, patriotism, professional ethos, a personal sense of ethics, and a gender, racial or class imbalance in the workforce. Further constraints – time, sources, subjectivity, audience, style, advertisers – are addressed in David Randall's suggestion that every newspaper (and, presumably, every news organisation) might consider publishing something along the lines of the following disclaimer:

This paper, and the hundreds of thousands of words it contains, has been produced in about 15 hours by a group of fallible human beings, working out of cramped offices while trying to find out about what happened in the world from people who are sometimes reluctant to tell us and, at other times, positively obstructive. Its content has been determined by a series of subjective judgements made by reporters and executives, tempered by what they know to be the editor's, owner's and readers' prejudices. Some stories appear here without essential context as this would make them less dramatic or coherent and some of the language employed has been deliberately chosen for its emotional impact, rather than its accuracy. Some features are printed solely to attract certain advertisers. (Randall, 2011: 24)

Journalists involved in publishing material that the state or other powerful forces would rather remain secret can count themselves lucky if vague official threats such as those made to the *Guardian* are the worst thing that happens to them. After the murder of photographer Luis Carlos Santiago in 2010, the Mexican newspaper *El Diario de Juarez* ran a front-page leader asking the drug cartels, as "the de facto authorities in this city", for guidance on how to stop journalists being targeted (Carroll, 2010). And in Sri Lanka, *Sunday Leader* editor Lasantha Wickrematunge even predicted his own assassination in a column written shortly before (and published shortly after) his death in 2009, in which he warned that "murder has become the primary tool whereby the state seeks to control the organs of liberty" (Wickrematunge, 2009).

LASANTHA WICKREMATUNGE'S FINAL ARTICLE

Killings, kidnappings, assaults and threats are the most brutal examples of **constraints** on the work of journalists and their effects can be pervasive. For every journalist killed, and for every dozen threatened, there may be hundreds or even thousands of journalists who – consciously or otherwise – are more likely to stick to safer stories as a consequence. This is what is meant by the phrase self-censorship.

IFJ SAFETY INFORMATION

More visible forms of censorship and constraint include the prosecution and jailing of journalists, the deportation of troublesome foreign correspondents, the banning of particular outlets, police raids on TV studios and newspaper offices, attempts to close down internet or social media connections, and the confiscation of equipment. All these things and more happen in various countries around the world in the 21st century, as journalists and fellow citizens insist on what the English poet John Milton demanded more than 370 years ago: "the liberty to know, to utter, and to argue freely according to conscience" (Milton, [1644] 2005: 101). When three *Al Jazeera* journalists were jailed for seven years just for doing their jobs in Egypt in June 2014 there were protests in many parts of the world, including in the UK, where *Channel 4 News* journalists went on air

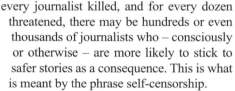

"I don't like to go into print without checking my facts."
Francis Wheen.

Journalists work in a field of conflicting loyalties, all of which have the potential to influence their work. They may feel a sense of duty towards their audience, editors, advertisers, proprietors, the law, regulatory bodies, contacts, colleagues, fellow citizens, and to themselves and their families (Frost, 2000: 61–64; Harcup, 2002b: 103). Denis McQuail highlights "the tension arising from the following oppositions at the heart of media-making":

- constraint versus autonomy;

- routine production versus creativity;

- commerce versus art;

- profit versus social purpose. (McQuail, 2000: 246)

In Chapter 1 we heard the argument that a free press (social purpose) is impossible in a free market, because market forces (profit) work against the objective of supplying the public sphere with the material required for a reasoned discourse. But market forces are not the only pressures at work: "[The] relations between media organisations and their operating environment are governed not solely by naked market forces or political power but also by unwritten social and cultural guidelines" (McQuail, 2000: 249). Even when analysed solely in economic terms, it has been pointed out that although media organisations will "naturally gravitate towards oligopoly and monopoly market structures", if unchecked this process may have a negative impact on the journalistic product which could hit sales and advertising income (Doyle, 2002: 125–126). In other words, it might sometimes make business sense to invest in quality journalism.

The constraints and influences discussed in this chapter need to be understood not as totalising systems imposing on journalists certain ways of doing things; rather, they are a range of sometimes conflicting influences, some more powerful than others and some more powerful at certain times or in certain places, with a *tendency* to influence journalists in certain ways. Constraints on journalists are subject to counter-pressures and can be negotiated and resisted as well as accepted, as we shall see throughout this book.

PROPRIETORS

Ultimately, it is the media owners who, "through their wealth, determine the style of journalism we get", with their mouths covered in symbolic black tape (Channel 4 News, 2014).

Every year the International Federation of Journalists (IFJ) and other organisations produce grim lists of journalists and media workers killed in the course of their work. There were 118 such killings during 2014 (plus another 17 accidental deaths while on assignment), including 14 in Pakistan, 12 in Syria, nine in Afghanistan, nine in Palestine, eight in Iraq, eight in Ukraine, six in Honduras and five in Mexico (IFJ, 2015). Few, if any, journalists go out of their way to become targets for killers or kidnappers, yet no journalist can be certain as to whether or not a particular story might attract unwelcome attention, and it is often journalists operating in their home countries who are most at risk, not necessarily those arriving from overseas. The threat of death may be the most extreme but it is far from being the only constraint on journalism, as this chapter explains.

THE LAW

The UK boasts of having a "free press", yet journalists' activities are constrained by hundreds of different pieces of legislation or statutory legal instruments (Petley, 1999: 143). Therefore, anybody wishing to work as a journalist in the UK really needs to study *McNae's Essential Law for Journalists* (Dodd and Hanna, 2014). Even journalists who are never sent to cover a court case and who do not intend to investigate state secrets still need to understand what the law does and doesn't allow; that includes criminal and civil law, custom and precedent, statute and statutory instruments, UK and European law, and the different rules that apply in Scotland and Northern Ireland, and all the rest.

One of the ever-present legal risks for all journalists is defamation, which, if it is written, broadcast or put online, is known as libel. It applies to *any* kind of journalism because even sports stars and fashion divas can sue too. Publishing something about somebody can be deemed to be defamatory if the statement tends to do any of the following:

- expose the person to hatred, ridicule or contempt;

- cause the person to be shunned or avoided;

argues Michael Foley (2000: 51). Media proprietors set the broad lines of policy for their organisations, and the combination of vertical and horizontal integration (synergy) may increase pressures on journalists to cross-promote other products or to keep their noses out of their company's business. The situation in public service broadcasting is more complex than in commercial media, including bureaucratic and budgetary control rather than "naked market forces"; nonetheless, public broadcasters operate in an increasingly competitive environment and are certainly not immune from market pressures (McQuail, 2000: 259–261).

In their "propaganda model" of how (US) media operate, Edward Herman and Noam Chomsky identify media owners as the first of five filters through which the wealthy and powerful are able "to filter out the news fit to print, marginalise dissent, and allow the government and dominant private interests to get their messages across" (Herman and Chomsky, 1988). The filters are:

- wealth and concentrated ownership of dominant media firms;

- advertising;

- reliance on information from the powerful;

- punitive action (flak) against transgressors;

- anti-communism. (Herman and Chomsky, 1988)

This model has been dismissed by critics as a conspiracy theory, as too mechanistic, as failing to take account of resistance. Herman counters:

> [The] filters work mainly by independent action of many individuals and organisations.... [The] propaganda model describes a decentralised and non-conspiratorial market system of control and processing. . . . We never claimed that the propaganda model explained everything or that it illustrated media omnipotence and complete effectiveness in manufacturing consent. (Herman, 2000: 102–103)

Media themselves tend not to draw attention to the potential impact of ownership structure on issues such as editorial content and diversity. Indeed, argues Robert McChesney (2000: 294–295), "The news media avoid any discussion of media structure, leaving analysis of media ownership and advertising to the business pages and the

- lower the person in the estimation of right-thinking members of society generally; or

- disparage the person in his/her business, trade, office or profession. (Dodd and Hanna, 2014: 238)

There are a number of defences open to journalists and publishers, which include that the statement can be proved to be true; that it is an honest opinion based on what are believed to be the facts; or that the statement is protected by legal privilege, for example because it is a quote from an MP's speech to parliament or the evidence of a witness in a court case. But, because of the costs involved in defending libel actions, there has sometimes been a tendency to settle actions rather than defend them in court, or even to avoid reporting allegations against individuals known to be rich and litigious enough to cause trouble. This is sometimes referred to as the "chilling effect". *Private Eye*'s Francis Wheen (2002: xi) suggests a simple way of reducing the risks of defamation, which is to check the facts – *before* publishing. That's a pretty sound starting point for any journalist.

Journalists sometimes find themselves in court not because somebody wants to extract money or an apology, but because somebody wants to know the identity of a confidential source of information. As Dodd and Hanna (2014: 404) warn, "A journalist protecting a source's identity must be ready for a long and tortuous legal battle". That's precisely what happened to Bill Goodwin after he took a phone call just three months into his first job as a trainee reporter with *The Engineer* magazine. A source told him about a company in financial difficulties. He called the firm for a response and the reply was a faxed injunction ordering the magazine not to publish anything about the company. Two days later he was in court facing an order to disclose the identity of his source or be sent to prison (Goodwin, 1996).

Goodwin refused, citing the principle enshrined in the National Union of Journalists (NUJ) code of conduct (see Chapter 13) that a journalist should protect a confidential source of information otherwise other sources might not come forward; this is another form of "chilling effect". Over the following seven years the case went before a succession of courts before he won at the European Court of Human Rights, which ruled in 1996 that an order to disclose a source could not be compatible

> "If one journalist betrays a source, others will be less willing to come forward in the future."
> **Bill Goodwin.**

trade press, where they are covered as issues that concern investors, not workers, consumers, or citizens."

ROUTINES

Journalists traditionally engage in routines, recurrent practices such as working to deadlines, keeping to word or time limits, ensuring that each edition or bulletin is exactly full, conforming to house style, making regular check calls to official sources, and covering diary jobs. If some routines have broken down as a result of 24-hour news, online journalism and social media, the result is not *no* routines – just *different* routines. That's because there is an occupational pressure on journalists to "bow to the imperative of routine news copy production" (Manning, 2001: 52). Although the unexpected may happen at any time, crises develop patterns so that, for journalists, even "the unexpected becomes the predictable" (Curran and Seaton, 1997: 276). Research has consistently found that "content is systematically and distinctively influenced by organisational routines, practices and goals rather than either personal or ideological factors" (McQuail, 2000: 244–245). Or, perhaps, rather than *only* personal or ideological factors.

ADVERTISERS

The interests of advertising can influence journalistic output, although such influence does not *normally* take the form of advertisers threatening to take their money elsewhere unless they receive favourable editorial coverage. Direct intervention by advertisers does happen occasionally, but much less often than many people would think. A far more prevalent influence is that the content patterns and style of media are matched to the consumption patterns of target audiences (McQuail, 2000: 261). Commercial media operate in a "dual product market" in which the media product sells *itself* to consumers and at the same time sells its *audience* to advertisers (Sparks, 1999: 53; Doyle, 2002: 12). Mass circulation newspapers demand a mass readership for mass advertising, while the "quality" press depend on delivering smaller target audiences for more niche advertising markets. The quest for these different audiences directly affects the journalism offered in different titles, as Colin Sparks notes:

with Article 10 of the European Convention on Human Rights unless there was an overriding requirement in the public interest (Welsh and Greenwood, 2001: 286).

Similarly, freelance journalist Robin Ackroyd fought a long and ultimately successful battle to defend the source of his *Daily Mirror* story about the treatment of Moors murderer Ian Brady in Ashworth high-security hospital. The Mersey Care NHS Trust, which runs the hospital, launched legal proceedings to force him to identify his source. During eight years of legal pressure he stood by the NUJ code of conduct and, with backing from his union, defended the principle of protecting confidential sources during a series of court cases and appeals. High Court judge Mr Justice Tugendhat ruled in Ackroyd's favour, declaring that the journalist had "a record of investigative journalism which has been authoritatively recognised, so that it would not be in the public interest that his sources should be discouraged from speaking to him where it is appropriate that they do so" (quoted in Gopsill and Neale, 2007: 280–282). Even then, the case was not over until the House of Lords refused the Mersey Care NHS Trust's application for a third appeal in 2007. Ackroyd, who had spent almost a third of his career fighting the case, said afterwards, "It's had a huge impact on my work. . . . But journalists ultimately, if they are faced with a position like this, have to make a stand as an individual and I was prepared to do that" (quoted in *Journalist*, 2007b). Such cases will continue to be fought on their individual merits as journalists resist attempts to identify confidential sources and/or to seize notes, pictures, phones and computer hard-drives.

Of course, it helps to fight a case if you know you are in one, which is why UK journalists became so concerned in 2014 when it emerged that police had been able to use the Regulation of Investigatory Powers Act (RIPA) to access the phone records of reporters and their newsdesks without their knowledge and without having to go before a judge. An angry campaign to Save Our Sources led the Home Secretary to announce a review of procedures.

Before we leave the powers of the state, let us pause and consider the Defence, Press and Broadcasting

> **"Forty years experience of 'press self-regulation' demonstrates only that the very concept is an oxymoron."**
> *Geoffrey Robertson QC.*

The popular press are under market pressure to try to reach the widest possible audiences, and thus must prioritise the kinds of material that will sell vast quantities. Quality newspapers are much less interested in maximising circulation, and are concerned to prioritise the kinds of material that will sell to particular kinds of people. . . . The products that serve the richest audience are approximations to the newspaper of democratic mythology. The others are quite different commodities. (Sparks, 1999: 53 and 59)

Meanwhile, the shift of advertising away from local newspapers has led to editorial closures and cutbacks.

PUBLIC RELATIONS

At the heart of public relations, according to Daniel Boorstin, is the "pseudo-event", which he defined in the early 1960s as something planned rather than spontaneous, arranged for the convenience of the media, with an ambiguous relation to reality (Boorstin, 1963: 22–23). For Boorstin, the pseudo-event blurs the roles of actor and audience, object and subject. For example, a politician can in effect *compose* a news story by "releasing" a speech to the media, while a journalist can *generate* an event by asking an inflammatory question (Boorstin, 1963: 40).

Since Boorstin described the rise of the pseudo-event, "public relations staffs have expanded while journalists have been shrinking, creating news media's greater editorial reliance on press officers" (Franklin, 1997: 19). Organisations ranging from local charities to multinational corporations now employ press officers who supply journalists with a stream of potential stories, comments and fillers. This process has been described as an "information subsidy" through which media organisations receive a flow of free material that will "favour those, notably business and government, best able to produce strong and effective PR material" (Lewis et al, 2008a: 2 and 18).

Press officers do not just supply information; they also play a role in controlling access. Writing in the context of music journalism, Eamonn Forde argues that the industry press officer has become increasingly powerful as a "buffer zone", gatekeeping access to artists and screening journalists along the lines of "the Hollywood approach to press management" (Forde, 2001: 36–38). For Bob Franklin, the growing power and

Advisory Committee. That's where Whitehall mandarins meet representatives of the UK media and agree to restrain coverage of sensitive military or security issues. From time to time members of the committee stir themselves to issue a Defence Advisory (DA) notice or, more commonly, to write a polite letter to editors, requesting that some matter be ignored or played down. In these days of so-called open government, the committee has its own website, which includes minutes of its meetings: www.dnotice.org.uk. The whole thing is entirely voluntary on the part of the media, operating as "an unofficial system of censorship involving public officials and senior media executives" (Curran and Seaton, 1997: 367). DA notices are, in effect, a system of *self-censorship* and are not to be confused with *self-regulation*, of which more below.

DEFENCE ADVISORY NOTICE SYSTEM

REGULATION, SELF-REGULATION AND LEVESON

Journalism on television and radio in the UK is subject to what is known as statutory regulation, whereby misdemeanours can be punished with fines and even the withdrawal of licences. Lindsay Eastwood noticed the difference in regulatory regimes as soon as she left newspapers for television:

> **"I did not come all this way not to interfere."**
> *Rupert Murdoch.*

> TV is much stricter on things like intrusion, and taste and decency. You can't have people saying "God" or "Jesus Christ" in a voxpop, because if one person complains and it's upheld, it counts. They are quite careful at *Calendar* not to upset people, whereas newspapers are not bothered so much about flak. I think the difference is you can lose your licence with TV. They can shut you down, so there's a bit more at stake really.

In contrast to the broadcast system of licences being at risk, print and online journalism has a system known as self-regulation. The Independent Press Standards Organisation (Ipso) was set up in 2014 by most of the newspaper and magazine "industry" (or, at least, by proprietors and their editors) to replace the Press Complaints Commission (PCC). The PCC had been largely discredited by its failure to get to grips with the phone-hacking scandal at the *News of the World* and, by the time Lord Justice Leveson

journalistic reliance on press officers comes at a price because "they are not detached observers and reporters of the world, but hired prize fighters, advocates and defenders of whichever sectional interest employs them" (Franklin, 1997: 20).

SOCIAL ENVIRONMENT

New recruits to journalism go through a process of "assimilation of newsroom mythology and socialisation", and those who survive learn "a way of doing things" that results in "a conformity of production and selection" (Harrison, 2000: 112–113). This professionalism "can only be recognised by fellow professionals" (McQuail, 2000: 257). Robert McChesney argues that most journalists are socialised into internalising their role as "stenographers for official sources", with the result that: "When a journalist steps outside this range of official debate to provide alternative perspectives, or to raise issues those in power prefer not to discuss, *this is no longer professional*" (McChesney, 2002: 17, my emphasis).

However, the extent to which journalism is constrained in this way is questioned by Greg McLaughlin's study of reporting the Kosovo conflict. He found that, while many reporters may have internalised Nato's frame of reference, this did not entirely determine how stories were presented, and "it would be wrong to dismiss as irrelevant the resistance of some journalists to Nato spin control" (McLaughlin, 2002a: 258). Paul Manning similarly warns of downplaying agency:

> [There] is a danger that in envisaging the practice of news journalism as a production process, shaped by bureaucratic routines and organisational imperatives, we underestimate the extent to which particular journalists *do* make a difference. (Manning, 2001: 53, emphasis in original)

If agency is a crucial consideration when discussing constraints, so too is the extent to which the social composition of the workforce influences journalistic practice. Not just the composition of the workforce but the make-up of the hierarchy, which is not always as equal as it might be. A recent study of gender and journalism still found that:

> In the traditional structures of journalism there are many junior women but still no clear path of advancement. . . . A number of exceptional

published his report into press ethics in 2012, the PCC had already announced its own demise. The PCC had been set up in 1991 by the newspaper industry itself to ward off the threat of privacy laws or broadcast-style statutory regulation. It oversaw an Editors' Code of Practice that covered journalism on newspapers, magazines and, from 2007, websites and other online output associated with newspapers and magazines – including audio and visual material. It was a voluntary arrangement with no powers to punish those who transgressed the code of practice, and it only made formal rulings on a tiny proportion of complaints. Rather than being the industry's policeman, the PCC was more like a police community support officer, resembling the police from a distance yet with little clout if challenged. However, despite its relative toothlessness, the PCC did act as some kind of constraint on the activities of journalists because editors had no desire to be embarrassed by PCC rulings, and that possibility was one factor taken into consideration when planning coverage. It also did useful work behind the scenes in advising people (such as victims or the bereaved) who suddenly found themselves subjected to media scrums and in liaising with newsdesks over issues such as whether or not the press would be welcome at a funeral. The new Ipso has been dismissed by critics as simply the PCC mark 2 despite the fact that it has the power to levy fines of up to £1 million for systematic breaches of the Editors' Code. There is some doubt whether such fines will ever happen, which no doubt will be claimed by Ipso as a sign of its success and by critics such as the Hacked Off campaign as a sign of its failure.

MEDIA OWNERS

As with self-regulation, so with concentration of ownership: big media **proprietors** are used to getting their own way. That can act as a further constraint on the journalists they employ, critics argue. That helps explain why some staff on the *Wall Street Journal* were less than keen on their title being taken over by Rupert Murdoch in 2007; they were nervous about what they had heard about his empire. About Sam Kiley, for example, who spent 11 years as a foreign correspondent on Murdoch's

individuals have achieved but this has not transformed the culture. There is a tendency to think that the argument has been won, but the concrete evidence shows a stubborn resistance to change across many western countries. (Franks, 2013: viii)

Anne Perkins asserts that, because relatively few women rise to the most senior editorial positions, "a distorted image of women's lives protrudes from the newsstands" (Perkins, 2001). But this assumption is challenged by Karen Ross, who studied women journalists in the UK:

Gender *alone* will not make a difference in changing the culture of newsrooms or in the type of news produced, inasmuch as a journalist's sex is no guarantee that she or he will either embrace sentiments that privilege equality or hold specific values and beliefs that promote a more equitable and non-oppressive practice. (Ross, 2001: 542, my emphasis)

Similarly, it may indeed be shameful that journalists in the UK are still overwhelmingly white, but can we assume that journalistic practice would be significantly altered merely by the presence of more black journalists? Or of more journalists from working-class backgrounds? Research is inconclusive, but some studies suggest that journalists owe more of their relevant attitudes and tendencies to "socialisation from the immediate work environment" than to their personal or social backgrounds (McQuail, 2000: 267–269).

Nick Stevenson sounds a cautionary note about the tendency of media theorists to "overstate the incorporating power of ideology" (Stevenson, 2002: 46). Questioning assumptions that the social background of journalists leads automatically to a middle-class perspective in their output, he argues not that class composition has *no* influence, but that there are ideological divisions and conflicts *within* classes, limiting the degree of "ideological closure" achieved by the structural dominance of journalism by white middle-class graduates (Stevenson, 2002: 33). We might also sound a cautionary note in case anybody thinks that bullying or a macho culture might only be found in the most commercial, redtop media; recent years have seen repeated allegations of bullying surface in parts of the BBC. The prevailing atmosphere within newsrooms, the extent to which dissent can survive and journalists have individual and ideological room to breathe, cannot be divorced from the existence or otherwise of an effective collective forum, argues Paul Foot in this chapter. His point is echoed by McChesney, who

Times before resigning in 2001, exasperated by reports on the Middle East conflict being framed to reflect the perceived views of the owner:

> Murdoch's executives were so scared of irritating him that, when I pulled off a little scoop by tracking, interviewing and photographing the unit in the Israeli army which killed Mohammed al-Durrah; the 12-year-old boy whose death was captured on film and became the iconic image of the conflict, I was asked to file the piece "without mentioning the dead kid". After that conversation, I was left wordless, so I quit. (Kiley, 2001)

Andrew Neil, former editor of the *Sunday Times*, describes Murdoch's normal methods of control as rather more subtle, beginning with choosing editors "like me who are generally on the same wavelength as him. . . . Then he largely left me to get on with it. But you always have to take Rupert into account" (Neil, 1996: 164). He can certainly pick them, as demonstrated by the way the editorial line of all 175 Murdoch-owned newspapers on three continents just happened to agree with his own pro-war stance leading up to the 2003 conflict in Iraq (Greenslade, 2003a).

> "Editors hire in their own image."
> *Gary Younge.*

Murdoch has long been an easy target for those who claim media owners wield too much power. But it is not only journalists taking the Murdoch shilling who feel proprietorial constraints, explicit or implicit. David Walker confesses:

> At the *Independent* I spilled much ink in editorials savaging his [Murdoch's] power and pricing strategy. But such criticism is vitiated by a lack of honesty about one's own organisation. How many *Independent* journalists, myself included, ever wrote in their own newspaper about the effects of ownership by Mirror Group Newspapers? (Walker, 2000: 241)

There is nothing new in media owners being accused of using *their* journalists to pursue certain agendas. It was in 1931 that Conservative party leader Stanley Baldwin launched his famous attack on press barons Beaverbrook and Rothermere, owners of the then hugely influential *Daily Express* and *Daily Mail* respectively:

> The newspapers attacking me are not newspapers in the ordinary sense. They are engines of propaganda for the constantly changing policies, desires,

points out that rocking the boat can be a risky business for journalists. Like Foot, he advocates "strong, progressive unions" as a bulwark to defend journalistic integrity against commercial pressures (McChesney, 2000: 61 and 301–304) as well as against bullying.

ETHICS

Within journalism the word "ethics" is often taken to refer both to ideas about right and wrong and to systems under which journalists are policed (or by which they may police themselves). Journalists may follow their own personal sense of conscience, which may be informed by cultural, political, religious, secular, philosophical, family, community or other influences. Journalists may also be required to follow ethical codes, guidelines or rules laid down by their employer and/or by regulatory bodies covering the industry in the country in which they are working; such codes may reflect or differ from their own personal sense of ethics. In addition, many journalists choose to follow the collective code of ethical conduct of a voluntary organisation, such as the National Union of Journalists (NUJ). Some of the major areas of ethical controversy include censorship, self-censorship, privacy, using material posted on social media, coverage of suicide, intrusion into grief, war reporting, bias, harassment, media scrums, stereotyping and the use of discriminatory language. However, arguably, everything a journalist does – or chooses not to do – has potential ethical implications.

PUBLIC INTEREST

The concept of the public interest is implicit and often explicit in the codes and laws that relate to journalism, argue Glenda Cooper and Stephen Whittle (2009). The Editors' Code of Practice adopted by Ipso, carried over from the PCC, allows certain forms of journalistic behaviour only in relation to stories in the public interest, and for its definition of the public interest see *Box 2.1*. The more detailed formulation in *Box 2.2* comes from Cooper and Whittle (2009: 96), who argue that investigations by journalists ought to be both "proportionate to what is being investigated and clearly targeted". The idea of the public interest will make frequent appearances throughout this book.

BOX 2.1

HOW THE EDITORS' CODE DEFINES THE PUBLIC INTEREST

1   The public interest includes, but is not confined to:

    i   Detecting or exposing crime or serious impropriety.

    ii   Protecting public health and safety.

    iii   Preventing the public from being misled by an action or statement of an individual or organisation.

2   There is a public interest in freedom of expression itself.

(Ipso, 2014)

BOX 2.2

THE PUBLIC INTEREST DEFINED

By Glenda Cooper and Stephen Whittle

- Citizens in a democratic state have an interest in having access to information about the workings of that state, of its institutions and its officials, both elected and appointed. This interest, however, is not confined to the state's institutions, but also to private corporations and to voluntary organisations which require the public's trust.

- When an individual holds an office, whether in a public institution or a private company or voluntary organisation which seeks the public's trust, it is in the public interest that that individual's public actions in pursuit of these goals be open for inspection, analysis and investigation by the news media.

- Such an individual is to be judged for his/her public acts, not private ones. In this case, "private" should be taken to mean issues to do with personal relations, personal communications, beliefs and past affiliations – always assuming these are within the law – however much these might appear to others, even to a majority, to be deviant, or immoral, or bizarre. The test is always public actions.

  - The division between private and public is rarely absolute: the person who believes in flying saucers or is conducting a sado-masochistic relationship may be a council officer or a department store manager. But the first set of beliefs or actions cannot be presumed to inform their behaviours in their job. If, in an investigation, links are shown to exist between the public and the private, then the latter is a legitimate area of inquiry by the news media. But there is no prima facie public interest in ET believers, or in sado-masochists.

(Cooper and Whittle, 2009: 97–98)

PRIVACY AND PUBLIC INTEREST

personal wishes, personal dislikes of two men. What are their methods? Their methods are direct falsehood, misrepresentations, half-truths, the alteration of the speaker's meaning by publishing a sentence apart from the context. . . . What the proprietorship of these papers is aiming at is power, and power without responsibility – the prerogative of the harlot throughout the ages. (Quoted in Griffiths, 2006: 251–252)

In 1949 Lord Beaverbrook told the Royal Commission on the Press that he ran the *Daily Express* "merely for the purpose of making propaganda and with no other motive", and in the 1980s Robert Maxwell described the *Daily Mirror* as his personal "megaphone" (Curran and Seaton, 1997: 48 and 76).

Former *Mirror* journalist Paul Foot describes such proprietorial influence on journalism as "absolutely insufferable". Yet he did suffer it in the shape of Maxwell, and he managed to produce much challenging journalism in spite of it. Foot recalls how he pinned up a list of Maxwell's business friends and, whenever he was investigating one of them, made sure he had the story copper-bottomed and "legalled" (checked by lawyers) before the subject would be approached for a comment:

> The minute you put it to him – "is this true?" – he rings Maxwell. That happened on several occasions. So you have to have the story sewn up and prepared for when Maxwell says: "Are you sure this is right?" *But we got most of the stuff published.*

For most journalists in most newsrooms, most of the time, proprietorial interference probably means little more than an editor's instruction to make sure you don't crop the owner's wife off a photograph or there'll be hell to pay. Many journalists go about their work without giving the wishes of the owner a second thought. Yet proprietors have influence not just by direct intervention. They set the tone, they decide which markets to target, they control editorial budgets, they can condemn or condone a culture of bullying, and they hire and fire the editors who are their representatives on Earth.

There are some alternative models of media ownership. The publicly owned BBC enshrines the Reithian principles of public service broadcasting (Briggs and Burke, 2002: 160–163); the *Guardian* is owned by the Scott Trust, with a strict separation between financial and editorial matters (Franklin, 1997: 98); and smaller-scale media may be run by ad-hoc groups, community organisations or workers' co-operatives (Harcup, 1994 and 2005). Journalists working for such media may escape the owner wishing to use them as a personal megaphone, but even they cannot avoid most of the other constraints discussed in this chapter.

> "How could I live with myself if I didn't write the truth?"
> *Anna Politkovskaya.*

ROUTINES

Deadlines, **routines** and the whims of the newsdesk tend to be the most prevalent everyday constraints on journalists. Routines may change as the technology changes, but there are still routines even if online journalism means that a story is never *finished* these days (was it ever really finished even in the old days?). The constant pressure to meet deadlines, including the instant deadlines of online and rolling broadcast news, teaches journalists that an average story delivered on time is usually of more value than a perfect story that arrives late. Not that the deadline is always bad news. Many journalists welcome deadlines for providing the focus, and the adrenalin rush, necessary to get the job done. Although the latest technology theoretically means that newspaper deadlines become later, in practice they have moved forward to cope with smaller staff numbers and the fact that, for economic reasons, many "local" titles are now subbed and printed many miles away from their circulation areas.

As more news organisations have become web-first – and/or Twitter-first – the role of the deadline is changing but not disappearing because journalists are adapting to the routines of audiences, as Jemima Kiss of the *Guardian* explains:

> Print deadlines are a luxury. We have multiple deadlines [online] every day, one for breaking news, ie as-soon-as-possible, then two peaks during the day: 7am to 9am is the main one and then 12 to 2pm lunchtime traffic. But that's just the UK, so we then need to time stuff for the US and Australia.

Time has always been at even more of a premium on television because of its (relatively) more cumbersome methods and routines, as Lindsay Eastwood discovered when she switched from newspapers to become a TV reporter:

> It takes so long to do everything. You've got to set up the story and organise camera crews, and it takes an hour to film a minute's worth of stuff. There's just so much faffing about and not actually doing the journalism, which I find very frustrating.

You're still getting a shot of the house while all the newspaper reporters are knocking on the doors of neighbours, and I'm saying to the cameraman, "Come on". Then you've got to get back to the studio to cut it before deadline.

Faced with a constant shortage of time, journalists make many decisions instantly, almost subliminally. News editor David Helliwell says most of the numerous press releases arriving at a newsdesk will receive just one or two seconds' attention before a journalist decides whether it might make something. Spending five minutes pondering each one in detail would quickly bring the routines of the newsroom grinding to a halt.

Time constraints can result in inaccurate journalism, believes Martin Wainwright:

You're doing stuff so quickly you don't have time to be absolutely sure about things, and more importantly the people you're talking to don't. So they will say things they believe to be true, about a developing situation, which then turn out not to be. It happened in the [Selby] rail crash when for nearly a week everybody said 13 people had been killed. The police said 13 people had been killed. In fact it now turns out to be 10. A central fact of the whole story was wrong for nearly a week, and somebody coming across a newspaper from that week and not checking a week later will not get the truth.

Lack of time may also lead to journalists falling short of professional standards, as Michael Foley notes: "Much that passes for unethical behaviour takes place because too few journalists are taking too many decisions quickly and without time to reflect. This is because proprietors have not invested in journalism" (Foley, 2000: 49–50). Maybe. But the UK national paper enjoying some of the heaviest editorial investment is the *Daily Mail*, hardly a stranger to complaints of unethical behaviour or inaccurate reporting.

Even on the squeaky-clean *Guardian*, reporters can be constrained by being sent out when somebody at head office has apparently already decided what the story is. Wainwright again:

During the foot and mouth [disease] crisis the newsdesk said to me: "Can you go shopping and see the meat panic? And we do *want* a meat panic." You're always coming up against that kind of pressure. It's a really pernicious aspect of modern journalism, that they don't trust people like myself who are here. They think they know what the story is because they've read it in the *Daily Mail* or heard it on the *Today* programme.

He adds that reporters sometimes feel pressure to deliver the goods simply because the routines of production planning mean that a large space or timeslot has been allocated in expectation of a major story:

A colleague had it with drug dealers. The story collapsed but they [still] wanted a big thing about drug dealers. The way they'd designed it and thought about it, it had to be *big*. Lots of journalists I know complain about this and say, "they're not really interested in how *I* am seeing this".

A similar point is made in a telling anecdote from John Kampfner, who recalls a Conservative party meeting he covered for the *Financial Times* during which two politicians outlined their differing views on the UK's relationship with Europe:

Both had said as much many times before, and I wrote a quiet piece. That evening, the newsdesk at the *FT*, not one usually to follow others' stories, politely enquired if I had been at the same event as my colleagues. They pointed out the screaming "Tories in meltdown" headlines. Somewhat chastened, I ratcheted up my story so as not to feel exposed. I should not have done. It was a non-story. (Kampfner, 2007)

It is not unknown for a newsdesk to put pressure on a reporter to set aside personal or ethical considerations in the pursuit of a story. Even in organisations publicly committed to following ethical codes of practice, there may be an atmosphere of *if you haven't got the story, don't bother coming back*. For example, journalists returning empty handed from "death knocks" – calls on the recently bereaved to pick up quotes and pictures – may be ridiculed for being insufficiently aggressive. A sports reporter on the *Stoke Sentinel* once lost his job after refusing to seek an interview with one of his close contacts whose son had just died (Morgan, 1999).

AUDIENCE

Traditionally, journalists knew relatively little about the ways in which their output was consumed. That is changing with technology being used to monitor the behaviour of online audiences, as Neal Mann explains:

> We have direct feedback – analytics – on how people are engaging and why they're engaging. We never had that on TV so I didn't know why people switched off: did one shot switch them off, was my scripting too slow? You wouldn't know that on TV, whereas online you can see the audience drop off as you get to a certain shot. As a result we can change the way we produce content and retain their attention.

That is a long way from the "we know what's best for you" approach that much serious journalism tended to adopt in the past. Combined with online lists of *Most Read* and *Most Shared* items, the Your Comments sections attached to stories, and conversations conducted via social media, it means there is more communication between journalist and (a section of the) audience than ever before. This is discussed further in Chapter 14.

Every now and then journalists will receive instructions or exhortations from on high to produce more aspirational human interest stories, based on the findings of surveys or focus groups of the existing or potential audience. At the same time as (supposedly) attracting new readers, such lifestyle copy – entertainment, holidays, health, consumer stories, and so on – has been used to attract (or hold on to) **advertisers**.

Journalists are typically thought of as the active ones in the relationship with their audience, but audiences are not always passive. Take the reaction to the *Sun* front page of April 19 1989, concerning the Hillsborough football disaster in which 96 Liverpool fans died. Under the banner headline THE TRUTH, the paper reported anonymous police officers accusing "drunken Liverpool fans" of stealing from the dead and attacking rescue workers. The reaction on Merseyside was based on the fact that so many people knew – via family, friends or personal experience – a different version of "the truth". There was nothing passive about this particular audience: "All over the city copies of the paper were being ripped up, trampled and spat upon … *Sun* readers in Liverpool had voted spontaneously with their feet and sales of the paper had collapsed"

(Chippindale and Horrie, 1992: 289–292). That strength of reaction was notable precisely because it was so unusual, as again in 2011 when public, social media and advertiser reaction to the revelation that a missing schoolgirl's phone had been hacked led Murdoch to close the *News of the World*, fearing it had become a "toxic" brand.

Hostile audience reaction may also act as a potential constraint on individual journalists, not just on large news organisations. The plus side is that the reporter who gets something wrong is likely to get tweets, calls, emails (or even the odd letter) from irate readers and may learn not to make that mistake again. The less positive side is that the prospect of drowning in a flood of abusive comments from the audience might dissuade some journalists from tackling particularly controversial subjects in the first place (yet another form of "chilling effect").

PUBLIC RELATIONS

"It's now a very good day to get out anything we want to bury", wrote the British government spin doctor Jo Moore in a soon-to-become notorious email sent at 2.55pm London time on September 11 2001, within an hour of the second hijacked plane hitting New York's World Trade Centre. Her memo, to senior colleagues in the Department for Transport, Local Government and the Regions (DTLR), continued with the helpful suggestion: "Councillors' expenses?" (Clement and Grice, 2001). The department's press office duly rushed out news release number 388 concerning a new system of allowances for local councillors (DTLR, 2001). As Moore predicted, the councillors' expenses story was ignored by a media concentrating on recounting the rather greater horrors of the twin towers.

When her words were leaked, Moore became something of a hate figure and subsequently lost her post. But wasn't she only doing her job? Isn't the whole **public relations** (PR) industry designed not simply to promote good news about clients but to bury bad news? Not according to the Institute of Public Relations, which promotes ethical practice and exhorts its members to "deal honestly and fairly in business with employers, employees, clients, fellow professionals, other professions and the public" (www.ipr.org.uk). Jo Moore was neither the first nor the last press officer to time the release of information to minimise coverage;

Friday afternoons and the beginning of holiday periods seem to be particularly popular times. Others prefer disguising bad news with apparently good news, so that job losses become a footnote in a piece of puffery about an apparent expansion.

It might seem odd to discuss PR within a chapter concerned largely with *constraints* on journalists. After all, the work of the PR industry is visible in the media every day, and some short-staffed newspapers are only too grateful to be stuffed full of scarcely rewritten news releases. But PR is not just about *releasing* information; it is also about *controlling* information. And controlling *access*. Many journalists have an ambivalent attitude to PR. On the one hand, they maintain they are too hard-bitten to listen to PR departments, yet they are also quick to moan about bullying by political spin doctors, demands for copy approval on behalf of celebrities, or the freezing out of journalists who don't comply (Helmore, 2001; O'Sullivan, 2001; Morgan, 2002b). Perhaps an ambivalent attitude is only natural. Although many press officers have good working relationships with journalists, based on trust and even grudging respect, the fact remains that they are *working to different agendas.*

> **"I don't believe in heroism . . . [but] freedom is not gained by kneeling or in silence."**
> *Lydia Cacho.*

COLLEAGUES

If journalists have a social role in informing society about itself, does it matter that journalists are not particularly representative of that society? Editor Jon Grubb clearly believes so:

> For too long newspaper editorial departments have been dominated by white, middle-class staff. If newspapers want to truly connect with the community they must strive to better reflect the multi-cultural nature of their audience. This issue is not just about colour. We need more journalists with working-class roots. Until papers can understand the problems, hopes, aspirations and fears of all sections of the community they will find it difficult to win their hearts and minds. (Quoted in Keeble, 2001b: 143)

Not just newspapers. Witness the prevalence of Oxbridge types at the BBC, particularly on more prestigious programmes, such as *Newsnight*. Research suggests that the **social environment** in which journalists work "does not reflect the diversity of the UK population, either in terms of ethnic mix or social background": 96 per cent of journalists are white and very few are from working-class backgrounds (Journalism Training Forum, 2002: 8). Peter Cole calls it "shameful and disgraceful" that local papers in places such as Bradford, Oldham and Burnley have so few non-white journalists (quoted in Slattery, 2002). Ethnic minority journalists are sometimes seen almost as *representatives* of the entire black community or of the Muslim community; alternatively, they may be warned against dwelling on race (Younge, 2002). White British journalists, in contrast, are not expected to represent "the white community" – even assuming there is such an entity – and are not warned off "white issues".

As well as being very white, newsrooms had a rather blokey atmosphere in the past. However, the increasing proportion of women entering journalism in recent years has resulted in a more or less even split between the sexes (Journalism Training Forum, 2002: 4). There may be more women in journalism, but they are not always in the most powerful positions, as Anne Perkins notes: "The higher up a newspaper hierarchy you travel, the fewer women there are to be seen" (Perkins, 2001).

Journalists are recruited from an even more limited pool now that so many have to pay for postgraduate journalism courses on top of huge undergraduate debt. Journalism can look like a closed door to outsiders, as only 30 per cent of journalists get their first job after seeing it publicly advertised; others approach employers on spec, are offered a job after work experience, or hear about vacancies through a range of informal means (Journalism Training Forum, 2002: 33). In the words of a Fleet Street sub:

> Newspaper journalism fosters a culture of the clique. Anyone who does not fit into the prevailing clique's clearly defined pigeon-holes tends to be viewed with suspicion and ends up being marginalised or forced out. People may be tolerated for their usefulness, but few are promoted to the hierarchy, which remains a club that promotes only those who they recognise as younger versions of themselves. (Quoted in Journalism Training Forum, 2002: 60)

The extent to which journalists internalise prevailing attitudes, and reproduce them in their work, is a matter for debate among academics and among some within journalism itself. The issue is at its most acute during times of conflict. While reporting Nato briefings in Brussels during the bombing of Serbia, *Sky News* correspondent Jake Lynch felt that most reporters had accepted the US/UK frame of reference:

> Journalists were prepared to accept the fundamental framing of the conflict which Nato was conveying, namely that this was all the fault of Slobodan Milosevic. . . . [That] was *internalised*, unexamined, by journalists . . . (Quoted in McLaughlin, 2002a: 258, my emphasis)

Independent reporter Robert Fisk was rather more blunt about his colleagues' shortcomings: "Most of the journalists at the Nato briefings were sheep. Baaaa Baaaaa! That's all it was." In turn, "mavericks" such as Fisk have been accused by fellow journalists of being more concerned with making "political points" than with straightforward reporting (quoted in McLaughlin, 2002a: 263–264).

In war or peace, journalist colleagues can constrain each other by creating an atmosphere of conformity in which anyone who is a bit different or who challenges the norm is ridiculed, bullied, forced out, marginalised or tolerated as the resident Jeremiah. But colleagues can also support individuals, whether those like Bill Goodwin, who was threatened with the power of the state, or those facing pressure to act in unethical ways. That's why Paul Foot urges journalists to band together in a trade union rather than stand alone. "You can only have an alternative to the control of the editorial hierarchy and the proprietor if you've got the discipline of being in a collective body behind you", argues Foot.

JOURNALISM AS STENOGRAPHY FOR POWER

But even collective strength is not always sufficient to protect individual journalists, as was demonstrated one Saturday afternoon in Moscow when Anna Politkovskaya took a break from her computer keyboard to go shopping for groceries. On her return she took a couple of bags up to her seventh-floor flat and went back down to collect the others from her car. It was her final journey because, as the lift doors opened at the ground floor, she was shot dead. Anna

Politkovskaya may not have been working on the afternoon of October 7 2006, but few doubt that it was her work as a journalist that prompted someone to kill her – or to order her death.

Anna Politkovskaya worked for the relatively small circulation Russian newspaper *Novaya Gazeta*, and her reports about war, terrorism and their attendant human rights abuses had earned her countless death threats. Her journalism also won praise from supporters of democracy and free speech around the world, although she was something of a marginal figure in her own country (Parfitt, 2006). Her death was shocking, yet in many ways unsurprising. She was aware of the dangers of making powerful enemies by her reporting, as her sister Elena Kudimova later recalled:

> Anna knew the risks only too well. We all begged her to stop. We begged. My parents. Her editors. Her children. But she always answered the same way: "How could I live with myself if I didn't write the truth?" (Quoted in Specter, 2007)

In 2014 five men were jailed in connection with her death, but neither her family nor her colleagues believe the full story has yet been told. Anna Politkovskaya's son Ilya said: "We will never consider the case closed unless the person or persons who ordered her killed are found and tried" (Dejevsky, 2014).

You don't have to be reporting on war or terrorism to face violence and threats, as Mexican journalist Lydia Cacho can testify. She has specialised in investigating international sex trafficking and prostitution and has described journalism as "a torch that illuminates reality, and our task is to ensure that it continues to burn thanks to professionalism, **ethics** and the will to give voice to other people" (quoted in IPI, 2010). Despite producing journalism in the **public interest** – or, rather, *because* of doing so – Cacho has suffered violence and threats, leading her temporarily to flee her own country in 2012, but not to give up her work. "I don't scare easily", she said, adding: "I'm trying to find out who did it and expose them, which is the only thing I can do" (quoted in Saner, 2012).

LYDIA CACHO AUDIO INTERVIEW

SUMMARY

The work of journalists is influenced by a range of structural factors, such as legal constraints, regulatory regimes, the system of media ownership, organisational routines, shortage of time, market forces, advertising considerations, cultural bias, patriotism, professional ethos, personal ethics, and a gender, racial or class imbalance in the workforce. Constraints and conflicting loyalties lead to claims that individuals have little influence on journalistic output, while others argue that constraints can be resisted or negotiated in pursuit of ethical journalism in the public interest.

QUESTIONS

Why do journalists guard their independence so fiercely?
Can journalists have too much information about what the audience wants?
Should journalists always protect confidential sources?
Are journalism and public relations two sides of the same coin?
Can a journalist's personal or social background influence how they do their job?

WHAT WOULD YOU DO?

You are a local newspaper reporter sent to the magistrates' court to report the day's cases. Outside the courtroom, immediately following one case involving a local woman convicted of shoplifting, you are approached by a man who says: "I know who you are and if you put any of that in the paper I'll come and break your legs." He then walks off. What do you do?

HOW MIGHT YOU TACKLE THIS ISSUE?

FURTHER READING

Nobody practising as a journalist in the UK should be without the latest *McNae* (Dodd and Hanna, 2014), which tends to be updated every two years, and anybody practising as a journalist elsewhere should seek out the equivalent tome. For detailed consideration of the public interest, see Cooper and Whittle (2009). To read what Anna Politkovskaya was working on when she was murdered, see *A Russian Diary* (2008). For a journalist's story with a happier ending, see Alan Johnston's (2007) *Kidnapped*, a gripping and inspiring account of his 114 days in captivity in Gaza. Many more everyday constraints and ethical considerations are introduced in Harcup (2007) and Frost (2011). Also highly commended is Knightley's (2004) classic study of journalism and censorship in wartime, *The First Casualty*. O'Malley and Soley (2000) offer the historical background to press regulation and self-regulation; also see Cole and Harcup (2010). For details on the Murdoch empire, see McKnight (2013) or Page (2011). McQuail (2000) reviews a range of relevant theories and research findings, and Chapter 11 is particularly useful here. Tumber (1999) includes many relevant original readings, including Herman and Chomsky on their propaganda model and Golding and Murdock on the influence of economic power. Herman and Chomsky (1988) themselves are worth reading in the original, along with Herman's (2000) later contribution to the debate. McChesney (2000) offers a detailed and passionately argued case for journalism being far too important to be left to market forces, as do the various contributors to Williams (2014a).

TOP THREE TO TRY NEXT

Mike Dodd and Mark Hanna (2014) *McNae's Essential Law for Journalists*
Edward Herman and Noam Chomsky (1988) *Manufacturing Consent*
Granville Williams (2014a) *Big Media & Internet Titans*

SOURCES FOR SOUNDBITES

Watkins, 2001: 114; Wheen, 2002: xi; Goodwin, 1996; Robertson, quoted in Foley, 2000: 44; Murdoch, quoted in Bailey and Williams, 1997: 371; Younge, quoted in Thomas, 2006; Politkovskaya, quoted in Specter, 2007; Cacho, 2009.

CHAPTER 3

WHAT IS NEWS?

Editor Kevin Ward was a satisfied man after he composed the front page splash of his *South Wales Argus* one Saturday in 2014, concerning a court case involving a local man accused of assaulting his partner and her pet. After putting the paper to bed with the headline MAN BITES DOG, Ward tweeted: "I've waited 30 years to write that headline." The headline duly went viral, among journalists and journalism students at least (*Press Gazette*, 2014).

MAN BITES DOG

"Dog bites man isn't news, man bites dog is", is an adage perhaps as old as journalism itself. Like many such sayings, it conceals as much as it reveals. True, it tells us something about the value of novelty in news stories. In the opinion of Harold Evans (2000: 215), man bites dog is not just an interesting tale, "it is also a good headline, in its own right", as was demonstrated by the *South Wales Argus*. But that is only part of the story when it comes to news, which is – still – the lifeblood of journalism. Man-bites-dog stories may be unusual but they are not quite as rare as hens' teeth. Take this headline above a dramatic must-read story in the *Times*: BEAR ATTACK SURVIVOR HAD TO EAT THE DOG THAT SAVED HIM (November 4 2013). Or this: WOMAN BITES DOG IN SAVAGE PIT BULL ATTACK (*Independent on Sunday*, June 17 2001). Replace the dog with a more exotic creature and a story can travel the world, as in this example: "Gu Gu the panda was bitten by a visitor to Beijing Zoo after attacking the drunken man for attempting to hug him" (MAN BITES PANDA, *Guardian*, September 21 2006). And, just to show that a bark can sometimes be as newsworthy as a bite, consider this account of an unusual court case that made the nationals:

A teenager who was arrested for barking at two dogs has cleared his name in court in a case that cost the

NEWS VALUES

News values have been described as "an attempt to render the daily, instinctive decisions of professional journalism tangible" (Smith and Higgins, 2013: 22). Lists of news values produced by scholars are aimed at helping to explain journalists' actions when it comes to the selection of news; the idea is not for them to be used as some kind of checklist by journalists, but for them to be used to deepen our understanding of how journalism works. To that end, the news values listed in *Box 3.1* are an attempt to update and develop an earlier taxonomy of news values produced by Norwegian academics Johan Galtung and Mari Ruge in the 1960s. Galtung and Ruge's influential list of 12 factors may be summarised as follows:

Frequency: an event that unfolds at the same or similar frequency as the news medium is more likely to be selected as news than is a social trend taking place over a long period of time.

Threshold: events have to pass a threshold before being recorded at all. After that, the greater the intensity, the more gruesome the murder, the more casualties in an accident, then the greater the impact on the perception of those responsible for news selection.

Unambiguity: the less ambiguity, the more likely an event is to become news. The more clearly an event can be understood, and interpreted without multiple meanings, the greater the chance of it being selected.

Meaningfulness: the culturally similar is likely to be selected because it fits into the news selector's frame of reference. Thus, the involvement of UK citizens will make an event in a remote country more meaningful to UK media. Similarly, news from the USA is seen as more relevant to the UK than is news from countries that are deemed to be less culturally familiar.

taxpayer £8,000. . . . Magistrates fined him £50 with £150 costs in January but the conviction has been quashed by a judge, who remarked: "The law is not an ass." (MAN WHO BARKED AT DOGS IS CLEARED IN £8,000 CASE, *Daily Telegraph*, April 28 2007)

It is the (relative) rarity of such stories – the element of novelty, of surprise – that makes them newsworthy.

There are times, however, when stories of dogs biting people are also deemed newsworthy enough for selection, usually because there are additional factors involved. Getting hold of data under the Freedom of Information Act can sometimes be enough for a story, such as these examples: "At least two Greater Manchester posties are attacked and injured by dogs every week, figures reveal" (*Mancunian Matters*, June 13 2013), and "More than 1,000 people including officers and members of the public have been bitten by police dogs in the past five years in the region" (*Wolverhampton Express & Star*, August 17 2013). Such statistics can be shocking but they do not have the same impact as an individual human interest story, especially one involving a vulnerable victim.

A powerful dog killing a tiny child is rare enough to make national TV news and newspaper front pages, but sadly is not so rare that there is ever any shortage of examples with which to update this chapter. Just one week in 2014 saw two particularly horrific stories about the deaths of babies, both of which were splashed on the UK's two most popular redtop newspapers: KILLED BY A DOG CALLED KILLER (*Daily Mirror*, February 12 2014); ANGEL KILLED BY DEVIL DOG (*Sun*, February 12 2014); 'DOG ATE MY BABY'S HEAD' (*Sun*, February 19 2014); and THE DOG'S KILLED MY 6-DAY-OLD BABY GIRL (*Daily Mirror*, February 19 2014). It is not just dog attacks on children that can make the headlines, but adult victims are most likely to be featured if there are additional noteworthy elements, as in this front-page splash: MUM-OF-FOUR KILLED BY PITBULLS WAS PREGNANT (*Daily Mirror*, December 12 2013).

> **"I can handle big news and little news, and if there's no news I'll go out and bite a dog."**
> **Charles Tatum**
> **(Ace in the Hole).**

Consonance: journalists may predict that something will happen, thus forming a mental "pre-image" of an event which in turn increases its chances of becoming news.

Unexpectedness: the most unexpected or rare events – within those that are culturally familiar and/or consonant – will generally have the greatest chance of being selected as news.

Continuity: once an event has become headline news it remains in the media spotlight for some time because it becomes familiar and therefore easier to interpret. Continuing coverage also justifies the attention an event attracted in the first place.

Composition: an event may be included as news less because of any intrinsic news value than because it fits into the overall composition or balance of a newspaper or news broadcast.

Reference to elite nations: the actions of elite nations are seen as more consequential than the actions of other nations. Definitions of elite nations will be culturally, politically and economically determined and will vary from country to country, although there may be universal agreement about the inclusion of the USA.

Reference to elite people: the actions of elite people may be seen as having more consequence than the actions of others.

Reference to persons: news has a tendency to be presented as the actions of named individuals rather than as a result of impersonal social forces.

Reference to something negative: negative news can be seen as unambiguous and consensual, generally more likely to be unexpected and often to occur over a shorter period of time than positive news. (Galtung and Ruge, 1965: 65–71; Harcup and O'Neill, 2001: 262–264)

Various additional news values have been suggested by other academics. Angela Phillips (2015: 18) argues for the inclusion of *conflict* as a news value in its own right rather than as merely one form of bad news. Allan Bell, meanwhile, adds the importance of *competition*, increasing the desire for a scoop; *co-option*, whereby a story that is only tangentially related can be presented

Not that victims necessarily have to die for a dog bite incident to become news. A Metropolitan Police apology for the way one of its dogs bit and mauled a burglary victim became a page lead in a broadsheet newspaper: ACTOR TELLS OF TERROR AT MAULING BY POLICE DOG AT HOME (*Guardian*, January 17 2014). More police dogs, this time in the USA, were the subject of a *Mail Online* story headlined: NOT COLOURBLIND: NEW REPORT SHOWS 'RACIST' LA POLICE DOGS ONLY BITE BLACKS AND LATINOS (October 12 2013). But not all dog stories are as grim as those above. How about TILL DEATH US DO BARK – MAN WEDS DOG (*Daily Mirror*, November 14 2007), for example; isn't that a headline that makes you want to read on?

THE SELECTION OF NEWS

What is it about the above events that make them news and how is it that most journalists – in UK newsrooms, anyway – would instantly have recognised them as stories worth covering and selecting? By going beyond the simplistic man-bites-dog definition to consider some of the additional elements that can turn even a dog-bites-man story into news, we begin to grasp what are called **news values**. Exhaustive debates about which stories should be covered and with what prominence tend not to be everyday occurrences in most newsrooms, partly because nothing would ever get done if every decision were discussed in detail and partly because prevailing news values are more likely to be absorbed and reproduced than challenged (Evans, 2000: 3). That does not – or should not – mean that the selection of news is an automatic or unthinking process. It just sometimes looks that way, as David Randall notes:

RESEARCH INTO NEWS VALUES

[A] lot of news judgements [are] made swiftly and surely and seemingly based on nothing more scientific than gut feeling. The process is, however, a lot more measured than that. It just appears to be instinctive because a lot of the calculations that go into deciding a story's strength have been learnt to the point where they are made very rapidly – sometimes too rapidly. (Randall, 2000: 24)

in terms of a high-profile continuing story; *predictability*, that is, events which can be pre-scheduled for journalists are more likely to be covered than those that turn up unheralded; and *prefabrication*, meaning that the existence of ready-made texts (news releases, cuttings, agency copy) will greatly increase the likelihood of something appearing in the news because journalists will be able to process the story rapidly (Bell, 1991: 158–160).

In their overview of scholarship on news values from Galtung and Ruge onwards, Helen Caple and Monika Bednarek (2013: 18–28) have grouped together definitions of news values according to the size, scale or scope of an event; the level of conflict or negativity involved; the level of positivity involved; the impact, significance or relevance of an event; timing; nearness or proximity; the degree of expectedness or consonance of an event; novelty value; the prominence or elite status of those involved; the personalisation of an event; human interest; sensationalism; factors relating to news-writing objectives; factors relating to balance of content; factors relating to the news agenda and news cycle; and external or other factors.

Yet, although the news values identified by Galtung, Ruge and others may be "predictive of a pattern" of which events will be deemed newsworthy, they cannot provide a *complete* explanation of all the irregularities of news composition (McQuail, 2000: 343). While acknowledging that a set of common understandings exists among journalists, Lewis (2006: 309) believes that any rationale for what makes a good story retains an arbitrary quality. For Golding and Elliott (1979: 114–115), stories must fit with the routines of news production as well as the expectations of the audience, and news values "are as much the resultant explanation or justification of necessary procedures as their source. . . . They represent a classic case of making a virtue out of necessity". John Richardson (2005: 174) argues that identifying something as "newsworthy" does not necessarily explain *why* it is so and, as John Hartley (1982: 79) points out, identifying news values may tell us more about *how* stories are covered than about why they were chosen in the first place.

It is also argued that most lists of news values fail to address what lies behind news values in terms of *ideology* (a concept introduced in Chapter 1). The news offers a highly selective version of events influenced by the "ideological structure" of prevalent news values, argues Stuart Hall (1973: 235). He explains:

What are these calculations about the relative merits of potential stories that can appear so instinctive to the untrained eye? They involve estimated measurements of relevance and interest to an audience – not necessarily the same thing – multiplied by perceptions of importance and then subtracting the logistical difficulties in getting the story. Identifying the factors that help journalists make such calculations may help us to answer the question "What is news?".

Editors traditionally refer to news as opening a window on the world (or as some kind of mirror), but news is mostly about what does *not* usually happen – that's why it is news. It is true, as we have seen, that dog-bites-man stories *can* become news – but most of them don't. And few news organisations would stay in business if they featured stories such as this:

> Police reported no major incidents as traffic flowed fairly smoothly along the M56 this morning. Meanwhile, patients in the casualty departments of the city's hospitals were treated without having to wait on trolleys in corridors overnight. Of the thousands of children on the streets yesterday, none was abducted. Finally, on the weather front, the Met Office said that rainfall was average for this time of year, no rivers had burst their banks, and people were going about their business with little risk of flooding and no need to be rescued by helicopter.

"For most people starting out in journalism, news is whatever the editor says it is."
Lynette Sheridan Burns.

Pretty dull stuff, yet that is the kind of thing that happens most days, indicating that news is a highly *selective* view of what happens in the world. And that selection is based on factors that can range from the tragic elements of a story to its potential comedy value.

For Randall (2000: 23), news is "fresh, unpublished, unusual and generally interesting". Up to a point. As the word itself implies, *news* contains much that is *new*, informing people about something that has just happened. But it ain't necessarily so. Some stories (the First World War, the Second World War, the Kennedy assassination, the Moors murders, the Yorkshire Ripper, the Hillsborough disaster, the Soham murders, Jimmy Savile) are always with us, it seems, with or without any new facts to report. Other stories are freshened up by telling us that so-and-so "spoke last night" or "broke their silence" about some ancient

"News values" are one of the most opaque structures of meaning in modern society. . . . Journalists speak of "the news" as if events select themselves. Further, they speak as if which is the "most significant" news story, and which "news angles" are most salient are divinely inspired. Yet of the millions of events which occur daily in the world, only a tiny proportion ever become visible as "potential news stories": and of this proportion, only a small fraction are actually produced as the day's news in the news media. We appear to be dealing, then, with a "deep structure" whose function as a selective device is un-transparent even to those who professionally most know how to operate it. (Hall, 1973: 181)

Robert McChesney gives the example of journalists' emphasis on individual events and news hooks (or pegs), meaning that "long-term public issues, like racism or suburban sprawl, tend to fall by the wayside, and there is little emphasis on providing the historical and ideological context necessary to bring public issues to life for readers" (McChesney, 2000: 49–50). Furthermore, mainstream news values tend to privilege individualism, regarding it as "natural", whereas civic or collective values are marginalised (McChesney, 2000: 110). This is what is meant when critical commentators argue that, far from being neutral, news values provide journalists with ideologically loaded "maps of meaning" used to make sense of the world for an audience (Hall et al, 1978: 54).

The news values inherent in mainstream journalism have been critiqued in theory by media commentators and academics, and in practice by those citizens who have set up their own forms of alternative media (Harcup, 2005, 2007: 49–66). Such critical thinking has also informed a set of alternative news guidelines drawn up by a group of European charitable and non-governmental organisations to encourage less ideologically loaded coverage of developing countries, although the guidelines are concerned more with selection and representation than with notions of inherent newsworthiness (see *Box 3.2*). In fact, in a lesser-quoted part of their classic study, Galtung and Ruge (1965: 84–85) themselves suggested that journalists should be encouraged to counteract prevailing news values by reporting more on long-term

BOX 3.1

NEWS VALUES

Research suggests that potential items must generally fall into one or more of these categories to be selected as news stories within mainstream media (Harcup and O'Neill, 2001: 279):

- The power elite
  Stories concerning powerful individuals, organisations or institutions.
- Celebrity
  Stories concerning people who are already famous.
- Entertainment
  Stories concerning sex, showbusiness, human interest, animals, an unfolding drama, or offering opportunities for humorous treatment, entertaining photographs or witty headlines.
- Surprise
  Stories with an element of surprise and/or contrast.
- Bad news
  Stories with negative overtones such as conflict or tragedy.
- Good news
  Stories with positive overtones such as rescues and cures.
- Magnitude
  Stories perceived as sufficiently significant either in the numbers of people involved or in potential impact.
- Relevance
  Stories about issues, groups and nations perceived to be relevant to the audience.
- Follow-ups
  Stories about subjects already in the news.
- Media agenda
  Stories that set or fit the news organisation's own agenda.

BOX 3.2

ALTERNATIVE NEWS VALUES

A set of guidelines has been drawn up by a group of European charitable and non-governmental organisations to challenge the ways in which developing countries are often portrayed in the news (NGO-EC Liaison Committee, 1989):

- Avoid catastrophic images in favour of describing political, structural and natural root causes and contexts.
- Preserve human dignity by providing sufficient background information on people's social, cultural, economic and environmental contexts; highlight what people are doing for themselves.
- Provide accounts by the people concerned rather than interpretations by a third party.
- Provide more frequent and more positive images of women.
- Avoid all forms of generalisation, stereotyping and discrimination.

scandal or other; or by the apparent discovery of some new information. Take the first three paragraphs of this news story published 97 years after a hanging, perhaps the ultimate example of the "delayed drop" intro:

> It is one of the most notorious cases in British legal history, the story of an apparently mild-mannered doctor who poisoned and dismembered his show-girl wife, then fled across the Atlantic with his young lover – only to be caught after a sharp-eyed captain recognised him from the newspapers.
>
> Dr Hawley Crippen was hanged in 1910, after an Old Bailey jury took just 27 minutes to find him guilty of murdering his wife, Cora, who had vanished earlier that year.
>
> Nearly a century later, research appears to show that the evidence which sent Crippen to the gallows was mistaken: the human remains discovered under his London house could not be those of Cora. (100 YEARS ON, DNA CASTS DOUBT ON CRIPPEN CASE, *Guardian*, October 17 2007)

Even older is this newspaper intro, based on a new study in a scientific journal that was published on page three of the *Times* more than 2,300 years after the death in question:

> Perhaps it was the absence of worlds to conquer that drove Alexander the Great to alcohol. Maybe the pressures on his soul from his complicated love life were salved by the demon drink. What now appears to be known for sure is that it was his love of wine that led to his death. (ALEXANDER THE GRAPE WAS JUST TOO MUCH OF A SEASONED CAMPAIGNER, *Times*, January 13 2014)

The new element on which such stories are hung is known as the "peg". Most news is much newer than the two examples given above. But many stories appearing in the national media are already a week or two old, having been passed up the journalistic food chain from the local weekly to a regional daily newspaper, possibly taking in an online news outlet, a local radio station or a regional TV news bulletin and then, maybe via a freelance news agency, on to the national stage – where the "when" of the five Ws

> **"News is anything that makes a reader say 'Gee whiz!'"**
> *Arthur MacEwen.*

issues and less on events, by including more background and contextualising information, by not shying away from complex and ambiguous issues, and by increasing coverage of non-elite people and nations.

CONSTRUCTION

As we saw in Chapter 1, Walter Lippmann argued that facts must be given a shape if they are to become news, and this is what academics mean when they refer to the *construction* or even the *manufacture* of news. It is not that facts are invented by journalists (except in rare cases), but that the process of identifying, selecting and presenting facts in a news story is a form of construction and is necessarily viewed through a "cultural prism" (Watson, 1998: 107). According to Nkosi Ndlela, the selection and construction of news represents and simplifies the world rather than reflects it (Ndlela, 2005: 3). Studies suggest that journalists frequently construct news stories within the framework of earlier stories or even through the retelling of enduring myths (Lule, 2001) or "collective narratives" (Phillips, 2007: 8–14).

However, a focus on how events and facts are constructed into news items offers only a partial explanation of the processes at work. The concept of "pseudo-events", introduced in Chapter 2, suggests that "many items of news are not 'events' at all, that is in the sense of occurrences in the real world which take place independently of the media" (Curran and Seaton, 1997: 277). Some commentators go even further in divorcing the news from real life:

> News is not out there, journalists do not report news, they produce news. They construct it, they construct facts, they construct statements and they construct a context in which these facts make sense. They reconstruct "a" reality. (Vasterman, 1995)

For Jorgen Westerstahl and Folke Johansson (1994: 71), the journalistic processes of news selection and construction are "probably as important or perhaps sometimes more important than what 'really happens'". Similarly, Joachim Friedrich Staab argues:

> [E]vents do not exist *per se* but are the result of subjective perceptions and definitions. . . . Most events do not

will be buried somewhere near the bottom in the hope that any whiff of staleness will be overlooked. The majority of local stories will not make the national media, never mind the international media, without some additional element to grab attention – stories such as the opening of a new school, the death of a child in a simple road accident, or a fire in a warehouse. That does not mean they are not news; it just means that news values are relative.

Now that we have Twitter streams, news tickers, 24-hour rolling news channels on TV and constantly updated news websites – in addition to printed newspapers, including mass circulation free distribution titles such as *Metro* – journalists have a lot more time and space to fill with news than ever before. And *fill* is exactly what they often have to do, as one admits: "The amount of air-time that they have to fill with analysing stuff, that 10–15 years ago you wouldn't have even thought about . . . has led to a change in what defines news, what is newsworthy and where hype begins and real news judgement ends" (quoted in Sugden and Tomlinson, 2007: 51). But was there ever a time when "news judgement" could be described accurately as being "real"? Was earlier in-depth reporting of a big criminal trial or parliamentary debate really any more *real* than today's coverage of a twitterstorm or a viral video?

A GOOD STORY

THEORIES OF NEWS SELECTION

If news isn't necessarily new, and if it isn't a simple reflection of reality, what exactly is it? News may be about animals, places or the weather, but it is mostly about *people*. People *doing* things. Things such as fighting, saving, killing, curing, crashing, burning, looting, robbing, rioting, stealing, stalking, trolling, kidnapping, rescuing, giving, marrying, divorcing, striking, sacking, employing, resigning, conning, suing, investigating, arresting, quizzing, freeing, loving, hating, kissing, bonking, hunting, chasing, escaping, fleeing, creating, destroying, invading, deserting, voting, leading, following, reporting, negotiating, accepting, rejecting, changing, celebrating, commemorating, inventing, making, breaking, selling, buying, treating, operating, comforting, mourning, leaving, arriving, delivering,

exist in isolation, they are interrelated and annexed to larger sequences. Employing different definitions of an event and placing it in a different context, news stories in different media dealing with the same event are likely to cover different aspects of the event and therefore put emphasis on different news factors. (Staab, 1990: 439)

NEWS FRAMES

Within journalism studies the phrase "news frames" is used to mean that journalists tend to simplify events to fit in with ways of thinking and talking that are instantly recognisable to an audience (Niblock and Machin, 2007: 196). The frame might be familiar to members of an audience not so much from personal experience as from their previous consumption of news, as Franklin (2005a: 85) observes: "When people have little direct knowledge of events, they become increasingly reliant on news media for information, but also an understanding or interpretation, of those events." Arguably, alternative forms of media can play a role in challenging the most familiar frames, just as avant-garde artists might refuse to allow their work to be constrained by a frame or even by the confines of a gallery.

MARKET-DRIVEN NEWS

Pressure to "monetise" content, combined with the existence of online news and 24-hour broadcast news channels, means that there is a commercial imperative to produce news not so much to inform a broadly-defined public sphere, but to fit "particular demographics, which can be used to locate the world of news events in the lives of particular market-segmented groups", according to the authors of a study of Independent Radio News in the UK (Niblock and Machin, 2007: 191). They found that news stories were selected as much on the basis of their perceived appeal to radio stations' target audiences – as measured by factors such as age, gender, lifestyle – as on any inherent qualities of importance or newsworthiness. This means that news is sometimes driven by market factors that are often overlooked in academic studies of news values (Niblock and Machin, 2007: 188).

GATEKEEPERS

The concept of gatekeeping is associated with a David Manning White study of how a wire editor at a US morning

ing, failing, winning, losing, searching, finding, irth, surviving, dying, burying, exhuming.

ell as doing, news can be about people *saying* things, whether in the form of tweets, speeches, announcements, publications, accusations, or replies to journalists' questions. News can also be about somebody being *set to* do something, *set to* say something, or even – surely the most postmodern of conditions – being *set to* react to somebody else who is *set to* say something. Any of the verbs listed above *may* become news if the raw ingredients have the makings of a good story for your audience. It will depend on who is doing or saying something, where, when, and in what circumstances. It will also be influenced by what other stories are around at the same time.

"News stories are what people talk about in the pub, or wherever they gather", says Brian Whittle. He should know. As the editor of a large regional news agency, his income depends on spotting stories that his customers – the regional, national and international media – will pay for. He continues:

> Six people killed in a bus crash on the M56, that's hard news. You can't get any bigger hard news story than what happened in America [the attack on the World Trade Centre on September 11 2001]. But a lot of other stories are a result of lateral thinking. When a story's been around for a few days, you're looking for where the next development will be – so good instinct will result in a good story.

Evidence of his eye for a good story can be seen in the framed front-page splashes adorning the office walls of his news agency: CATWOMAN 'SEDUCED' BOY OF 15 … PAEDOPHILE WALKS FREE … 18,000 POLICE TO FAIL DRIVING TESTS … BOY, 9, WRECKS TEACHER'S LIFE … and so on, all stories likely to pass the test of being mentioned by people chatting in the pub, gathering next to the water cooler or sharing on social media.

Somebody else who knows a thing or two about telling stories is the writer Michael Frayn, whose career has combined journalism with success as a novelist and playwright. He says: "Very deep in both journalism and fiction and life in general is the concept of a *story*. Why are some things a story and

> "News is what a chap who doesn't care much about anything wants to read. And it's only news until he's read it. After that it's dead."
>
> *Evelyn Waugh.*

newspaper selected stories for inclusion during one week in 1949. White concluded that the choices were "highly subjective" and based on the editor's own "set of experiences, attitudes and expectations" (White, 1950: 72). The gatekeeping approach has since been challenged for assuming that there is a given reality out there in the "real world" which newsgatherers will choose either to admit or exclude (McQuail, 2000: 279). A study by Walter Gieber suggested that the personal attitudes of individual journalists or gatekeepers was less significant than the mechanical and bureaucratic processes involved in producing and editing copy (Gieber, 1964: 219). For Gieber:

> News does not have an independent existence; news is a product of men [*sic*] who are members of a news-gathering (or a news-originating) bureaucracy. . . . [The] reporter's individuality is strongly tempered by extrapersonal factors. (Gieber, 1964: 223)

As Jackie Harrison (2006: 13) puts it, news is that which "is judged to be newsworthy by journalists, who exercise their news sense *within the constraints* of the news organisations within which they operate" (my emphasis).

The gatekeeping model has subsequently been developed by Pamela Shoemaker to take account of multiple levels of decision-making and wider factors:

> The individual gatekeeper has likes and dislikes, ideas about the nature of his or her job, ways of thinking about a problem, preferred decision-making strategies, and values that impinge on the decision to reject or select (and shape) a message. But the gatekeeper is not totally free to follow a personal whim; he or she must operate within the constraints of communication routines to do things this way or that. All of this also must occur within the framework of the communication organisation, which has its own priorities but also is continuously buffeted by influential forces from outside the organisation. And, of course, none of these actors – the individual, the routine, the organisation, or the social institution – can escape the fact that it is tied to and draws its sustenance from the social system. (Shoemaker, 1991: 75–76)

Individual gatekeepers may display a degree of agency but they do not operate totally autonomously, which may go some way towards explaining why studies to date tend to suggest that decisions about news selection others just a sequence of events? All journalists recognise a story, and that's why they begin to tell it, but it's very difficult to say what a story is" (quoted in Armitstead, 2002, my emphasis). In his first novel, *The Tin Men*, Frayn included the morbid results of fictional market research into what audiences want:

> The crash survey showed that people were not interested in reading about road crashes unless there were at least ten dead. A road crash with ten dead, the majority felt, was slightly less interesting than a rail crash with one dead, unless it had piquant details – the ten dead turning out to be five still virginal honeymoon couples, for example, or pedestrians mown down by the local JP on his way home from a hunt ball. A rail crash was always entertaining, with or without children's toys still lying pathetically among the wreckage. Even a rail crash on the Continent made the grade provided there were at least five dead. If it was in the United States the minimum number of dead rose to 20; in South America 100; in Africa 200; in China 500. (Frayn, [1965] 1995: 69)

It may have been a spoof but it was informed by Frayn's first-hand knowledge of the ways in which the **construction** of stories, and the placing of events within **news frames**, can render news predictable. As predictable as the annual stories about A-levels allegedly getting easier or the pictures of female tennis players showing their knickers at Wimbledon every summer.

Formulaic and predictable some output may be, but at least there is usually some connection between journalism and real events featuring real people. Contrary to popular belief, journalists who totally invent stories – as featured in the film *Shattered Glass*, for example – are very much the exception rather than the rule. Most news stories are not invented but they are constructed; that is, the raw material has to be observed, selected and processed into something recognisable to audience and colleagues alike as news. Perhaps that is why seasoned news junkies find so many stories so familiar; we have heard most stories before with just the names and places changed.

NEWS VALUES

NEWS VALUES AS IDEOLOGY?

As should already be apparent from the range of stories cited in this chapter so

are little different whether the editorial gatekeepers are male or female (Lavie and Lehman-Wilzig, 2003).

The very concept of gatekeeping is under threat from the erosion of distinctions between producer and audience brought about by online and social media, which holds out the possibility that "the roles that journalism assigned to itself in the mid-nineteenth century . . . as gatekeeper, agenda-setter and news filter, are all placed at risk when its primary sources become readily available to its audiences" (Hall, 2001: 53). However, being readily available does not mean that such primary sources will necessarily be widely accessed or understood. As Cecilia Friend and Jane Singer put it:

> Journalists can no longer be information gatekeepers in a world in which gates on information no longer exist. Yet the need for sense-makers has never been more urgent. Gatekeeping in this world is not about keeping an item out of circulation; it is about vetting items for their veracity and placing them within the broader context that is easily lost under the daily tidal wave of "new" information. (Friend and Singer, 2007: 218)

far, coming up with a foolproof definition of news is easier said than done. News values have been deconstructed by academics, but rather fewer journalists have either the time or the inclination to stand back and subject the selection process to such critical scrutiny. Veteran TV reporter John Sergeant says: "It is often distressing to argue about news stories, because usually journalists rely on instinct rather than logic" (Sergeant, 2001: 226).

Recruits to journalism tend to pick up a sense of newsworthiness and develop their "nose" for a story by consuming news and by picking up prevailing news values from more experienced colleagues. It can be a fairly subjective process. The *Guardian*'s Martin Wainwright says he measures a potential story against whether it interests him or "increasingly as I get older, would it interest my children?". These days journalists can get a clearer idea of what interests the public – well, a section of the public – because figures are available on which online stories are the most read and/or the most shared. Trying to make sense of such information (analytics) can be a bewildering process, partly because it can change by the second and partly because it is not always clear which aspects of particular stories have led to their apparent popularity.

So newsworthiness remains hard to define, but we can get a fairly good idea about how news values work by examining those stories that *do* make it into the news. One study of the UK national press (Harcup and O'Neill, 2001) suggests that, although there are exceptions to every rule, potential news items must generally satisfy one or (ideally) more of the requirements listed in *Box 3.1* to be selected as news stories. Although the list is based on a study of national newspapers, similar considerations will come into play when journalists select stories for broadcast, online and local or regional media. Let's see how they operate in practice.

THE POWER ELITE: STORIES CONCERNING POWERFUL INDIVIDUALS, ORGANISATIONS OR INSTITUTIONS

Virtually every action of the Prime Minister seems to be considered newsworthy, from cabinet reshuffles at one end of the spectrum to the width of their grin at the other. This is less so for the Prime Minister's senior colleagues and so on down the pecking order of government and opposition, through the backbenches, in diminishing order of newsworthiness. Whereas the Prime Minister's choices of clothing or holiday plans are usually enough to generate a news story, cabinet colleagues might have to make a policy announcement or a blunder to grab the headlines, while a lowly constituency MP will be of interest to the national media only if they are embroiled in some kind of scandal, row, rebellion or defection. Locally, even the most somnolent constituency MP will be considered one of the power elite, as will the leader of the council and/or a directly elected mayor, and many of their comments and actions will be reported in the local media. As with individuals, some institutions or organisations are deemed to be newsworthy because of their positions of power and/or influence – examples include Nato, the Vatican, the European Commission, the Bank of England, Oxbridge universities and Eton.

CELEBRITY: STORIES CONCERNING PEOPLE WHO ARE ALREADY FAMOUS

Celebrities are newsworthy and it has ever been thus, long before anyone had ever heard of Harry Styles or Rihanna. The evidence is the fading sign still adorning the wall of the old *Harrogate Advertiser* building in which I once worked – "List of visitors Wednesday" – which dates back to when the local paper began as little more than a weekly list of the rich and famous who came to stay in the North Yorkshire spa town over 150 years ago. However, today's journalists are often heard complaining that good stories are squeezed out by an obsession with celebs on the A, B, C, D and Z-lists. Brian Whittle dismisses many news editors as "daleks who only rate a story if it features a third-rate celebrity". He recalls one of his former news editors defining a good news story as "ordinary people doing extraordinary things", before adding with a hint of sadness: "I think some of that's been lost." Even an extremely tangential link to a celeb might push a story up the news agenda, which appears to explain why an item about a sinkhole appearing in an old military cemetery became a tabloid page lead:

> Army chiefs are desperately trying to save the remains of a soldier after his grave disappeared into a giant cavern. By coincidence, the name on his

military headstone is Private Ryan, echoing the title of the Tom Hanks Second World War movie. (SAVING PRIVATE RYAN, *Daily Mirror*, March 1 2014)

Certainly, if you come up with a story featuring somebody who is already famous, you will have a better chance of it being picked up than you would with a similar story populated entirely by "ordinary" people (aka civilians or muggles). And even a celebrity tweeting a fairly vacuous comment or mundane picture is often enough to generate coverage of a "story" that might simply not have existed in the days before social media.

ENTERTAINMENT: STORIES CONCERNING SEX, SHOWBUSINESS, HUMAN INTEREST, ANIMALS, AN UNFOLDING DRAMA, OR OFFERING OPPORTUNITIES FOR HUMOROUS TREATMENT, ENTERTAINING PHOTOGRAPHS OR WITTY HEADLINES

Editors look favourably on stories and pictures with the capacity to entertain or amuse an audience. Indeed, some stories have little else going for them, such as the one about the woman who makes miniature movie-themed costumes for her pet, which took up most of a news page in *Metro* and featured no fewer than five photographs: WHO FRAMED BENJI RABBIT? HAM ACTOR? HE PREFERS LETTUCE (*Metro*, January 17 2014). Or the piece about a Sikh man who tweeted a picture of himself standing outside a branch of the clothes shop Urban Outfitters while holding up a large letter "T" in just the right place to apparently change its name: URBAN TURBAN GOES VIRAL (*Metro*, February 5 2014). A sex angle is also popular with many editors, and court cases or employment tribunals involving sex have a greater chance of being covered than those without. Other reliable entertainment stories likely to trigger a response are those based on lists. But hard news, even tragic news, may also be judged on whether it is entertaining – not in the sense of being amusing, but of offering an unfolding drama, with plot twists featuring characters we come to know. For example, there is little suspense or drama about the dozens of children killed on our roads each year, and they receive relatively little media coverage. But

> "The construction of news simultaneously constructs for audiences a framework of interpretation as it presents the 'facts'."
>
> *Maggie Wykes.*

there is huge coverage of the intense drama attached to a police hunt for a missing child: the smiling picture, the plotting of the last movements, the release of CCTV footage, the emotional appeals, perhaps the discovery of a body, the placing of flowers with heartfelt messages, the arrest of a suspect, the howling mob outside court, even the tiny coffin at the funeral. Journalism as entertainment is discussed further in Chapter 7.

SURPRISE: STORIES WITH AN ELEMENT OF SURPRISE AND/OR CONTRAST

This is where the stories of people biting or even marrying dogs come in, along with other surprising, shocking or unusual events, ranging from the 12-year-old who becomes a mum to the one-legged man who skywalks on the wing of an aeroplane. There is also a great value placed on contrast, as in the vicar who runs off with a married woman (or man), the police child protection officer who is arrested for downloading child porn, or stories such as THIEF STEALS £240 IN LOTTERY TICKETS... BUT WINS ONLY £15 (*Metro*, January 17 2014).

BAD NEWS: STORIES WITH NEGATIVE OVERTONES SUCH AS CONFLICT OR TRAGEDY

Death, tragedy, job losses, factory closures, and falls from grace are all examples of somebody's bad news being good news for journalists, as are the horrific stories of dogs killing children discussed earlier. Sometimes journalists might almost *create* conflict by seeking hostile reaction to an incident or comment in the hope of starting – and reporting – a "row". Or, if they are really lucky, a "war of words" – with or without a community being "up in arms".

GOOD NEWS: STORIES WITH POSITIVE OVERTONES SUCH AS RESCUES AND CURES

Positive stories are far more prevalent than is suggested by the cynical claim that the only good news is bad news. Somebody somewhere always seems to be winning a dream prize, going on the trip of a lifetime, or achieving straight As with accompanying hugs when they get their exam results. People are frequently hailed as heroes for leaping into action to rescue others from burning houses or to do what one "quick-thinking" bus passenger did and steer the vehicle to safety after the driver collapsed on a steep downhill stretch: STOREMAN STEPS IN TO SAVE THE DAY ON RUNAWAY BUS (*Yorkshire Post*, November 13 2013). Miracle cures or escapes are also more common than their names suggest, and even foreign miracles can make the news in the UK, as in the following tale from California: MIRACLE IN THE DESERT – CRASH GIRL, FIVE, SURVIVES TEN DAYS NEXT TO HER MOTHER'S BODY ON SPORTS DRINK AND DRY NOODLES (*Daily Mail*, April 15 2004). Animals too can have miracle escapes, as in: DOWN BOY! PUP SURVIVES 120FT PLUNGE INTO THE SEA (*Daily Mirror*, March 7 2008). As David Helliwell explains: "Hard news is often bad news so we want to break up the court stuff, the police stuff, industry or whatever with something a little bit lighter – a bit more light and shade among the death and destruction."

MAGNITUDE: STORIES PERCEIVED AS SUFFICIENTLY SIGNIFICANT EITHER IN THE NUMBERS OF PEOPLE INVOLVED OR IN POTENTIAL IMPACT

Magnitude comes into play when a journalist rejects a potential story with the words "Not enough dead" (quoted in Harrison, 2000: 136). Martin Wainwright recalls how he decided to go to the scene of a rail accident at Selby:

> I heard about that on the news early in the morning and went out there when I knew that there were going to be more than just a couple of people killed. *It's got to be that level.*

But magnitude is relative, and other news values come into play, including relevance.

RELEVANCE: STORIES ABOUT ISSUES, GROUPS AND NATIONS PERCEIVED TO BE RELEVANT TO THE AUDIENCE

"News lives on a weird globe, distorted so that the local is magnified, and the distant compressed", observes Andrew Marr (2005: 61). "It's a question of the impact on people", says a BBC news editor, explaining why an accident in India did not make the news despite the fact that 60 people had drowned (quoted in Schlesinger, 1987: 117). In the gallows humour typical of newsrooms, this is sometimes referred to as McLurg's Law of public interest, after a (possibly apocryphal) editor who was said to rank events by how far away they occurred and/or the nationality of those involved, so that "one European is worth 28 Chinese, or perhaps two Welsh miners worth 1,000 Pakistanis" (Schlesinger, 1987: 117). It is not simply a question of prejudice or geographical distance. In the UK we get more stories about the USA than, say, Belgium because, although the latter is nearer to us and is a partner in the European Union, the UK shares arguably more linguistic and cultural reference points with the former. Away from international news, the concept of relevance affects selection about topics. That's why bulletins on BBC Radio One, aimed at young people, have so many news items about drugs or the entertainment industry; why the *Guardian*, which is traditionally read by many teachers (and students), has so many stories about education; and why the *Daily Mail*, aimed at middle-class and "aspirational" working-class readers, features so many stories about mortgages and property prices. Relevance works at a micro-level as well as the national and international level, so a local newspaper in a seaside town might have lots of stories about the menace of seagulls, whereas an equivalent publication in a rural area inland will be more concerned with the price of sheep, and a big city newspaper wouldn't touch either. Selecting news stories on the basis that they are likely to appeal to a certain type of audience, who in turn might appeal to a certain type of advertiser, is a form of commercial or **market-driven news**.

MARKET-DRIVEN NEWS

FOLLOW-UPS: STORIES ABOUT SUBJECTS ALREADY IN THE NEWS

"News is not news until someone else reports it", is how Phillip Knightley (1998: 197) sums up the attitude of too many editors. And so broadcast journalists scan newspapers and magazines for stories, print journalists monitor broadcast bulletins, and all of them constantly check news agency feeds, the websites of rivals, influential blogs, and Twitter. However, it is not normally enough to have the same as everyone else, so journalists remain concerned to "move the story on"; that is, to discover new information or introduce new angles. Follow-ups have a number of advantages for journalists, including the fact that background material is readily available, that contacts have already been identified, and that certain developments may be able to be predicted and therefore planned for.

MEDIA AGENDA: STORIES THAT SET OR FIT THE NEWS ORGANISATION'S OWN AGENDA

Sometimes news stories seem to be selected less for any intrinsic newsworthiness than because they fit the agenda of the news organisation, whether to promote certain commercial or political interests or to engender a sense of audience loyalty and identification. Examples of the former would include BBC-bashing stories in the Murdoch press, while examples of the latter range from local media encouraging people to carry organ donor cards to the *Sun*'s 2014 "Honour our VC heroes" campaign to restore and maintain the graves of British soldiers who had won Victoria Cross medals for gallantry.

SELECTION

All the various news values listed above interact with each other, and the more buttons pressed by a particular event the more likely it is to become news. But even events that satisfy several of the above criteria do not become news by themselves. First, they must be noticed, weighed up, selected and constructed. This role in selecting the news has led to journalists in general, and those working on newsdesks in particular, being described as **gatekeepers**. In this sense, the gatekeeper allows some events to pass through to become news while the gate is shut on other events. Since the emergence of the internet, and especially blogging, followed by Facebook and Twitter, it has frequently been claimed that journalists are no longer gatekeepers because more and more people have access to a wider range of information sources. Yet many of the major providers

> "One of the most potent weapons a newspaper has is to totally ignore an issue or a story."
> **David Yelland.**

of online news – and of stories shared via social media – were already big players in earlier forms of media (sometimes referred to condescendingly as "legacy media"). Websites such as that of the BBC or the *Guardian* may have been jazzed up with all manner of live-blogging, interactive features and user-generated content, but the primary news services they provide clearly still operate by selecting, filtering and processing information, or gatekeeping; arguably, that is precisely why they have proved so popular, because audiences trust the "brand".

Changes to the organisation, production and distribution of journalists' work, however, *can* impact upon the selection of news because, unlike traditional media, online news has no set deadline and therefore is never full or finished. Trevor Gibbons describes life as an online journalist for the BBC:

> There's more pressure to get something up immediately. Coming into a story a couple of hours after somebody else has done it is almost so late as to be no use. Writing for a newspaper, you pick one moment in time whereas we sometimes have an evolving story and we might go into a story four or five times in a day. And it's far easier to put background material *around* the story that you're doing. An internet site is never full and you never put it to bed. At any one time some bits are going out-of-date and need to be taken off.

But this is still recognisably a journalistic process, and Gibbons believes that selection remains key: "What makes a good story makes a good story online, in a newspaper or on the radio."

Which does not mean there are not different priorities. When I ask Carla Buzasi what makes a good story for the *Huffington Post*, she explains:

> I've just come out of our news meeting and for me it's one that makes me sit up and go, "Wow, I haven't heard that before". Or perhaps a new take on something, if it *is* something I've heard of before. Obviously we're all about starting conversations and kickstarting debates, so it doesn't have to be a story that's finished.

So does that mean that an unfolding story is actually better for online journalism than one with a neat ending?

bly, that's a good way of looking at it. If it's
g that can run and run then we like that.
find something that we believe in or that
rs are interested in then we'll cover it
obsessively, whereas what you see in the old media
is they'll cover that story once and then drop it. We
look at audience data and if we see something start
to gain traction we will continue to cover that story.

"TRY TO MAKE IT AS HUMAN AS POSSIBLE"

The digital age may have hugely increased the amount of audience data available to the media, and made it easier for people to access alternative sources of information, but for most people, most of the time, "the news" remains something that was at some stage selected and filtered by journalists (even if it has subsequently been forwarded or shared by a friend). Traditional skills live on alongside the new. From a newsdesk perspective, David Helliwell explains what he looks for when a reporter brings in a story:

> For a front page story you definitely need some sort of drama, some action or excitement, and you need something that's going to draw the reader in. Preferably you would be looking at something that is people-led. If you were looking at a robbery, for example, we would only consider it a good front-page robbery if we had some detail, some colour, so you got to know who was involved, who the victims might be. Not just a flat police statement that "two masked men sped off in a westerly direction with an undisclosed sum". Whatever it is – be it crime, industry, business, whatever – we would always try to make it as human as possible.

Take this typical regional newspaper splash about two 18-year-olds jailed for seven years for robbing an elderly woman – YOUNG THUGS CAGED: TERROR ATTACK ON PENSIONER (*Yorkshire Evening Post*, October 6 2001) – illustrated with mugshots of the two robbers. Helliwell says it was getting the photographs that helped elevate that story to page one:

Getting the pictures from the police, always a tricky business, definitely lifts it. People love to see who you're talking about. Even if we didn't have the pictures it would have been a strong page lead early on in the paper. It's the viciousness of what they did, the things they said to her, the judge's comments, and the seven years each, which are pretty heavy sentences. Even in this day and age these things are fairly rare.

Just as most crimes reported to the police are not covered by the media, most court cases also pass unreported. This is for logistical reasons as well as ideas of newsworthiness, because newspapers have cut back hugely on court reporters while broadcasting and online media cover only the most high-profile cases. Coverage of the courts often relies on a news agency reporter ducking and diving in and out of several cases looking for one with an interesting line or two, as Jane Merrick explains:

> A murder trial wasn't enough, it had to have two or three different angles. The agency was geared to the tabloids, because they were the ones who would buy most of our stuff, so it was very much human interest. One of the first court cases I did was a woman who had killed her lover's wife, but that wasn't enough to make a good story for the papers. I think she was in the chorus line and the victim was the lead singer in this amateur play, so that was the extra line.

However, with the right extra ingredients, even a relatively trivial offence has the potential to generate coverage, as in the must-read headline HOTEL GUEST HURLED ABUSE WITH HOSE UP HIS BOTTOM (*Metro*, November 13 2013). And a court case resulting from a dog-bites-man incident can still make the headlines, as in the tabloid tale that begins: "A judge stormed out of court yesterday screaming: 'It's a f****** travesty' after *she* was found guilty of failing to control her dog" (JUDGE'S *!@X RANT, *Sun*, December 15 2010). Yes, that was a swearing judge in the dock – you couldn't make it up. This being news, you don't have to make anything up, because people do newsworthy things every day.

SUMMARY

News can be seen as a selective version of world events, with a focus on that which is new and/or unusual. However, not all news is new; much of it is predictable, and some does not concern "events" at all. Journalists identify, select and produce news items according to occupational norms, including the concept of what will interest a particular target audience. Implicitly or explicitly, journalists measure potential news items against a range of criteria that have become known as news values. Academics have produced lists of such news values based on studies of journalistic output. Other theoretical models associated with the study of news include news as a social construct; journalists as gatekeepers admitting or excluding events; and news values being imbued with the dominant ideology of society. It has been claimed that the development of user-generated content and social media may be undermining the traditional role of the journalist as gatekeeper, blurring the boundary between producer and audience, and altering (to an extent) considerations of what is considered newsworthy.

QUESTIONS

Where do news values come from?
Have Twitter and Facebook changed what is considered news?
Is the news predictable?
If news is manufactured, does it mean it is not true?
Are there any gatekeepers now?

WHAT WOULD YOU DO?

You edit a news website and have two potential stories from which to select the lead item – that is, the one that will be presented most prominently on the site itself and promoted most heavily via social media. Both stories have been supplied by reliable and trustworthy reporters and include facts, opinions and quotes from a range of sources. One story concerns a woman who has advised her teenage daughter to have a baby and live on welfare benefits rather than try to find a job. The other story concerns a reported 160 per cent increase in the number of people using emergency food banks over the past year. Which story would you select as your lead item? What factors might influence your choice?

HOW MIGHT
YOU TACKLE
THIS ISSUE?

FURTHER READING

Ethical issues arising out of the way in which news is selected or excluded are discussed in *The Ethical Journalist* (Harcup, 2007) and *Understanding Journalism* (Sheridan Burns, 2013), while a critique of news values from the perspective of alternative journalists can be found in Whitaker (1981) and Harcup (2013). Both Randall (2011) and Hudson and Rowlands (2012) have useful chapters discussing the practicalities of finding and identifying news from the point of view of print and broadcast journalists respectively. Harrison (2000) includes a study of TV news values, while Harcup and O'Neill (2001) present the results of a content analysis of news values at work in the UK national press; also see O'Neill and Harcup (2009) for a wider treatment of the issue, and Palmer (2000) on news values as a system that transcends individual judgements. A somewhat dense but nonetheless useful overview of academic approaches to the study of news values can be found in a recent paper by Caple and Bednarek (2013). Phillips (2015) has a more reader-friendly chapter discussing academic definitions of news, Harrison's (2006) *News* is another readable explanation of academic analysis of the news process, and extracts from many studies – including Galtung and Ruge, Schlesinger, Shoemaker, and Gans – are reprinted and introduced in Tumber (1999). Stuart Hall's classic analysis of news values as ideology is also extracted in Tumber, but it is worth seeking out the full version from the original Chapters 3 and 4 of Hall et al (1978); happily, it has been made available again in a "35th anniversary edition" (Hall et al, 2013).

TOP THREE TO TURN TO

Johan Galtung and Mari Ruge (1965) 'The structure of foreign news…', *Journal of International Peace Research*
Tony Harcup and Deirdre O'Neill (2001) 'What is news? Galtung and Ruge revisited', *Journalism Studies*
Jackie Harrison (2006) *News*

SOURCES FOR SOUNDBITES

Tatum, quoted in Salas, 2007; Sheridan Burns, 2013: 54; MacEwen, quoted in Boorstin, 1963: 20; Waugh, 1943: 66; Wykes, 2001: 187; Yelland, 2013.

CHAPTER 4

WHERE DOES NEWS COME FROM?

The instant that the *Sky News* newsroom in London heard about an earthquake in Pakistan, Neal Mann on the foreign newsdesk immediately set about checking it out online. But it was what happened next that really brought home to him quite how social media has opened up new ways of sourcing stories:

> I took the United States Geological Survey information – it's freely available but I was one of the first people to get it – we ran it and immediately I put it on my Twitter feed. People in Pakistan came straight back to me within two to three minutes to say they were there and they'd felt the earthquake. They hadn't searched on Google to find out what was going on, they'd searched on Twitter and mine was one of the top tweets that surfaced, and also they saw that I was from a legitimate news outlet, which is key. Traditionally it would have taken quite a long time to find somebody involved in that situation but I had an immediate response from somebody and the thing is you can put in the checks to make sure they are in that location, but that's pretty easy once you've got their contact details. Traditionally we've always had to find our sources, and now, as journalists on social media, by engaging with the audience, people can find us.

TWEETING ABOUT PAKISTAN EARTHQUAKE

Not only did people who had experienced the earthquake find him, but they did so almost instantly – from several thousand miles away. Such direct contact may have been made possible by technology, but it still took Mann's journalistic *use* of the technology to make it happen. So the development of new ways of finding and sourcing stories needs to be seen as adding to the more traditional methods, not replacing them.

Journalists are surrounded by **sources** of potential stories, and Peter Lazenby, who worked for the

SOURCES

Sources are central to journalism. Sources are the people, places or organisations from whom potential news stories originate, and the people, places or organisations to whom journalists turn when checking potential stories. Allan Bell argues that "the ideal news source is also a news actor, someone whose own words make news" (Bell, 1991: 193–194). He lists the following news actors as major sources: political figures, officials, celebrities, sportspeople, professionals, criminals, human interest figures, and participants such as victims or witnesses (Bell, 1991: 194).

When assessing sources, a journalist's overriding consideration is *efficiency*, according to Herbert Gans: "Reporters who have only a short time to gather information must therefore attempt to obtain the most suitable news from the fewest number of sources as quickly and easily as possible" (Gans, 1980: 128). He has identified six interrelated "source considerations" used by journalists to evaluate sources of news. They may be summarised as follows:

Past suitability: sources whose information has led to stories in the past are likely to be chosen again and to become regular sources (although journalists or audiences might eventually tire of them).

Productivity: sources will be favoured if they are able to supply a lot of information with minimum effort by the journalist.

Reliability: journalists want reliable sources whose information requires the least amount of checking.

Trustworthiness: journalists evaluate sources' trustworthiness over time and look favourably on those they have found to be honest and who do not limit themselves to giving self-serving information.

Yorkshire Evening Post man and boy for 40 years until 2012, has long been one of the best at keeping his eyes and ears open for them. It was while shopping in a local supermarket one weekend that he spotted a card on the community noticeboard offering a reward of several hundred pounds for the return of a lost parrot. Thinking that it must have been "one hell of a parrot" to be worth so much, he called the number and discovered that it was indeed a rare breed. But it had not been lost. It turned out that it had been stolen by members of an international smuggling syndicate who were abducting exotic birds to order and delivering them in a private aeroplane to wealthy collectors. Not a bad story to bring home with the groceries on what was supposed to be a day off.

Cathy Newman agrees that stories can be found in the most random ways:

> There's no set routine for a story. My first ever scoop was when I was on the *North Devon Journal*. I was doing work experience, and somebody found blood on a clifftop path. The police launched a murder hunt. Actually, it turned out that a marksman had been hired by the council to go and shoot some of the wild goats. They hadn't told the public because they didn't want to upset the animal-lovers, so they'd done it under cover of darkness and they'd triggered this manhunt. So it was a great story, there were so many different angles to it, some people were angry about it, and there was a bit of a cover-up. And that was just from somebody being observant locally and wondering what the heck this blood was on the clifftop path.

> **"Have an eye open for what's going on in the world because you can find stories in the most random way."**
> *Cathy Newman.*

"Sources of news are everywhere", explains news agency editor Brian Whittle. Some sources will be routine points of contact for journalists while others may be one-offs. Some will be proactive, approaching journalists because they want **news access** for their views or information, while other sources may not even be aware that they *are* sources. A good journalist will look for leads from a range of sources and will certainly not rely on being spoon fed by the PR industry. Some of the most common sources of news are listed in *Box 4.1* and will be introduced later.

JOURNALIST-SOURCE POWER RELATIONSHIPS

Authoritativeness: everything else being equal, a journalist will prefer a source in an official position of authority.

Articulateness: sources capable of expressing themselves in articulate, concise and dramatic soundbites or quotes will be favoured when journalists need somebody to be interviewed. (Gans, 1980: 129–131)

For Gans, this process means that "journalists are repeatedly brought into contact with a limited number of the same types of sources" (Gans, 1980: 144). This apparent homogeneity of sources is reinforced by the fact that journalists use other journalists and other media as some of their main sources of ideas and validation. Pierre Bourdieu refers to this as the "circular circulation of information", arguing that journalists *consume* so much news because "to know what to say, you have to know what everyone else has said". This might be seen as journalists simply covering their own backs, but for Bourdieu (1998: 23–24) it results in "mental closure".

Are reporters' sources really drawn from as narrow a range as suggested by many scholars of news? If journalism *does* tend to privilege a narrow range of "resource-rich institutions" (Cottle, 2000: 433), then it does not *have to* do so. Studies of the alternative press suggest that it may not be the routines of news production themselves that determine the choice of sources but the ethos of the organisation, thus allowing for the alternative press to follow different routines allowing them to select "a different cast" of sources and voices (Cottle, 2000: 434–435; see also Whitaker, 1981; Harcup, 2013). Even within mainstream media and understaffed newsrooms, individual journalists retain some agency over which sources to approach, trust, return to and rely upon.

NEWS ACCESS

The question of who appears on or in the news is important to considerations of the public sphere, and journalists' tendency to rely on official sources is frequently said to benefit the powerful (Cottle, 2000: 427; McChesney, 2000: 49; McQuail, 2000: 288). Unequal access to the news has damaging social effects, argues Stuart Hall:

> Some things, people, events, relationships *always* get represented: always centre-stage, always in the position to define, to set the agenda, to establish the

YOUR CONTACTS

The sources listed in *Box 4.1* will form the backbone of any reporter's contacts. Your contacts' details will be kept in what we still tend to call a contacts book even if we just mean they are in our phone. Contacts books come in many shapes, sizes and technologies – and all ought to be backed-up in some way, just in case – but what they have in common is that they can be the difference between meeting the deadline and missing the boat. A contacts book will normally list organisations on an alphabetical basis, adding names, titles, main switchboard telephone numbers, direct lines, mobile numbers, Twitter handles, email addresses and home landline numbers where possible. Personal mobile and out-of-hours numbers are particularly important, as you may be working on stories early in the morning or late in the evening when most work numbers are useless. Cross-referencing is advised, to increase your chances of finding the right name and number in a hurry. And don't rely on being able to remember who somebody is and why you have their number in your book. Even Mr Memory would struggle to remember all the people a reporter will speak to in an average year, so add titles and a brief note to aid recall.

You will also need to build up a range of individual contacts, people associated with particular interests or issues, many of whom can be contacted via Facebook, LinkedIn and other social networking sites. Having such contacts categorised under their job, their hobby or their area of expertise can help you find that vital comment, that missing piece of information or that fresh angle much more quickly than if you have to start from scratch each time. People listed among your contacts will vary enormously depending on the type of organisation you are working for, the geographical or specialist patch you are covering, whether you work mainly on features or news, and how you develop your own particular niche of interest or expertise.

Useful people contacts are likely to include some of the following: academics; actors; administrators; agents; alternative health practitioners; anglers; architects; artists; astrologers; astronomers; athletes; authors; barristers; biographers; biologists; bloggers;

> "Sources of news are everywhere."
> *Brian Whittle.*

terms of the conversation. Some others sometimes get represented – but always at the margin, always responding to a question whose terms and conditions have been defined elsewhere: never "centred". Still others are always "represented" only by their eloquent absence, their silences: or refracted through the glance or the gaze of others. If you are white, male, a businessman or politician or a professional or a celebrity, your chances of getting represented will be very high. If you are black, or a woman without social status, or poor or working class or gay or powerless because you are marginal, you will always have to fight to get heard or seen. This does not mean that no one from the latter groups will ever find their way into the media. But it *does* mean that the structure of access to the media is systematically skewed in relation to certain social categories. (Hall, 1986: 9, emphasis in original)

Such media representations do not necessarily remain unchanged over time (Schudson, 1989: 280), and black and gay voices are now heard much more frequently than when Hall wrote the above words. However, notwithstanding that relationships between journalists and sources may be complex and subject to change over time – and that there will be occasions when the voices of the powerless do take centre stage – there remains a *tendency* for the powerful to enjoy "routine advantages" in news access (Manning, 2001: 139). For example, Gary Younge notes that black "community leaders" tend to be regarded as authoritative sources only when inner-city rioting breaks out: "While rarely summoned to the microphone in more peaceful times, they are in great demand when it comes to condemning wayward members of their community" (Younge, 2001). News access is discussed further in Chapter 5.

PASSIVITY

Journalists may like to say that sources are everywhere, but much of the time they use a narrow range of sources and are often accused of being too passive or even lazy – although perhaps the fault lies more with those employers who have cut staff numbers so much that reporters often do not have the time to be proactive. One study of the UK provincial press found that most stories appeared to be based on a single source and often amounted to little more than "free advertising and propaganda" for those builders; bureaucrats; business people; carers; cavers; celebrities; chefs; chemists; clairvoyants; climbers; collectors; comedians; community leaders; computer whizkids; councillors; counsellors; criminologists; cultural critics; dentists; designers; detectives; dietitians; disability campaigners; DJs; doctors; economists; engineers; environmentalists; estate agents; experts; explorers; farmers; feminists; film directors; film stars; financial experts; footballers; gardeners; gay activists; golfers; historians; hoteliers; imams; international experts; judges; lobbyists; magistrates; market traders; media tarts; midwives; millionaires; models; musicians; nurses; pet owners; pilots; police officers; political activists; priests; psychiatrists; psychologists; rabbis; ramblers; refugees; researchers; restaurateurs; sailors; scientists; shopkeepers; singers; social workers; sociologists; soldiers; solicitors; sports people; supporters; surgeons; teachers; translators; transport experts; trawler captains; TV stars; undertakers; union activists; vegetarians; vets; vicars; victims; writers; zoologists. Also, don't forget to list other journalists with whom you might be able to swap favours.

A contacts book is a living thing, so if you try to call somebody only to be told they are dead or retired, update your listings accordingly. You will also need to feed it by adding fresh contacts from stories on which you are working – even from stories on which you are not yet working, as consumer affairs reporter Kevin Peachey explains:

> I get loads of people ringing me up saying, "My tumble dryer has broken down and the bloke hasn't been round for three days to fix it". And there is an art to talking to these people. Some of the time they just want to talk to somebody about it, get it out of their system and have a good rant, and that's fine. But the bottom line is they are really useful, because if you log all your calls you realise there are trends there.
>
> One story I did as a result of that was when I got loads and loads of calls from people saying, "Something went wrong with my TV, phoneline, whatever, and it took me days to get through and complain to someone because all I got was a recorded message". So I wrote all these down, we then decided that we would test out 20 companies

> **"The source was really a chat with someone."**
> *Abul Taher.*

organisations with the resources to run slick PR operations (O'Neill and O'Connor, 2008: 498). Similarly, Bell points to a series of studies suggesting that, to a very large extent, "news is what an authoritative source tells a journalist"; alternative sources, including minorities and the socially disadvantaged, "tend to be ignored" (Bell, 1991: 191–192). A major study of UK national media found that a vast number of stories originated from some kind of public relations activity: "even in a sample based on the UK's most prestigious news outlets, journalists are heavily reliant on prepackaged information, either from the PR industry or other media", according to Lewis et al (2008a: 14). The consequence of this information subsidy is that "corporate and governmental voices speak loudly while public opinion is worryingly mute" (Lewis et al, 2008b: 30).

PRIMARY DEFINERS

For some cultural critics, notably Stuart Hall, the "skewing" of access to the media privileges the dominant forces in society by allowing them to establish the parameters of debate on social issues. Politicians, employers, the police and so-called experts become "primary definers" of events whose "primary definition sets the limit for all subsequent discussion by framing what the problem is" (Hall et al, 1978: 59). According to this analysis, journalists play the role of "secondary definers", circulating the interpretations of the powerful not because of any conspiracy but because "the hierarchy of credibility" reflects the social power structure (Manning, 2001: 138). The concept of primary and secondary definition has been criticised for neglecting the potential of media themselves to become primary definers (Critcher, 2002: 529) and for downplaying some of the complexities of journalist–source relationships (Schlesinger, 1990: 66–67; Manning, 2001: 15–17 and 137–139; Kuhn, 2002: 52–58).

POWER

The journalist–source relationship has been described as resembling both a dance and a tug-of-war (Gans, 1980: 116–117). McQuail says that the power of PR and spin means that "it has probably become harder for the media to make any independent assessment of their own of and find out how long it would be before we could talk to a human being. A lot of the companies we chose were based on the entries I had in my book. If 10 people ring me up about the same company then you know that's something you need to be looking at. In themselves there might not be much in it, but put them together and you can see trends.

I've literally just got a book, the same as my contacts book, and whoever they're complaining about, or the subject, I just stick in the number and a very small explanation if it's needed. Then you can always go back to them. Campaigns are another example. We don't just come up with these ideas off the tops of our heads, they're inspired by readers' letters or by reporters going out on to their patches and people saying, "What about this?".

Journalists have sometimes been accused of **passivity**, of relying on a small number of sources to come to them, but the best reporters are proactive. On a quiet news day you can simply go through your contacts book and call some of the people to whom you have not spoken for a while. You might pick up a story or two and, even if you don't, you have maintained relations with a contact.

> "Journalists are becoming more passive, often merely passing on information to the public that they have been given."
>
> *Deirdre O'Neill and Catherine O'Connor.*

Some journalists might be tempted to think that social networking and electronic communications have replaced the need to develop flesh-and-blood contacts. Not so, according to Neal Mann, who has personally met many of the people he engages with via social media:

I have 65,000 followers at the moment on Twitter, I've at least looked at each one of their profiles as they've followed me because if they're interesting I want to follow them back and engage with them. And what I want to do is take that engagement outside of the virtual world on Twitter into the real world – the ones that are interesting to me – because then as a result they become a potential source and I have a physical relationship with them rather than just a virtual one. That adds a whole other level of trust. They also know who you are as a person. That's something a lot of journalists need to understand about using social media: it's a way of getting to anybody around the world at any level, but

the value of information provided to them in such volume" (McQuail, 2000: 291). Larsake Larsson's study of relationships between reporters and local politicians found an interplay based on "the exchange of information for media exposure", in which sometimes the journalist would have the upper hand and at other times the politician (Larsson, 2002: 27). However, although journalists might highlight negative news, on a day-to-day level the agenda seemed to be set not by the journalists but by their sources:

> The local media obtain the bulk of their [municipal] news from matters addressed in municipal administrative and decision-making processes. Municipal news stemming from journalistic initiative is less common, since journalists' working conditions seldom permit independent inquiry and agenda building. They are forced, in a sense, to choose between the dishes offered on the municipal buffet table. Only rarely do they venture into the kitchen to see what the host may have hidden in the cupboard. . . . [The] media stay within the news selection frames determined by the organisations they report. (Larsson, 2002: 29)

This "framing" of media coverage may on occasions be achieved by those outside the power elite. For example, covering farmers' protests in Brittany prompted one journalist to express ethical concerns: "After ten days we wonder if we are not being manipulated. They called us out for a photo opportunity. We got the feeling of giving backing to demonstrators. Without us, they do not exist" (quoted in Neveu, 2002: 65). Yet it ought not to be forgotten that, within the context of the constraints discussed in Chapter 2, journalists themselves retain some power to *choose* between sources and to include or exclude certain perspectives. I remember covering a hospice visit by Princess Diana when Jimmy Savile turned up, uninvited, and the press photographers on the job unilaterally decided simply to ignore his attention-seeking presence. Fair play to them.

also it's a way that you can take it from the virtual to the physical, and ultimately get a lot of stories that way.

DOING THE CALLS

News agency boss Brian Whittle told me that his reporters' first job every day was to find out what had been happening on their patch:

> As far as newsgathering goes, we still do the old-fashioned things. So we get up early and do the calls. By the time I come into the office I've watched the telly, read at least a couple of national papers and a couple of locals. You're immediately tuned in to what's going on and you hit the floor running.

Whittle was talking before the ubiquity of social media, but that has not replaced the need to carry out the "old-fashioned" jobs, merely added to them. "The calls" – regular inquiries to a range of agencies – have long been a staple of newsgathering. Minimum calls will be the police, the fire brigade and the ambulance service, noting down anything of interest that has happened since the last time the calls were made, including updates to ongoing stories. In addition to some actual phonecalls, newsrooms will also be monitoring the emergency services' Twitter and other feeds. Weekly papers might do calls once a day; daily papers will make several rounds of calls a day; broadcast and online newsrooms, as well as news agencies, will usually do the calls hourly or even more frequently. Journalists covering coastal areas will find the coast-guard and lifeboat services included in their rounds of calls, while those covering areas popular with walkers or cavers may check with the mountain rescue service. A final round of calls will be made just before deadline. When I worked Saturday shifts for a Sunday paper I even had to ring the region's prisons asking if there had been any escapes or incidents, just in case.

Time was when calls used to involve journalists gathering at the local police station when a police officer would deliver a daily briefing on the latest crimes and misdemeanours by reading from the log of incidents. It might still happen like that in one or two places, but most calls these days are on the telephone, many to recorded voicebanks updated by press officers.

> "The good reporter is able to . . . find at least two good stories during a twopenny bus ride."
> *Frederick Mansfield.*

Even these are being phased out and replaced by online communication. Only a tiny proportion of incidents are made public by the police, as was demonstrated when freelance journalist Nigel Green (2008) used the Freedom of Information Act to find out how many incidents were dealt with by Northumbria police in a two-week period. The answer was 17,261, of which just 27 were publicised to journalists.

The system of routine calls is very much a one-way flow of information – self-evidently so in the case of voicebanks. Although journalists will occasionally find out about crimes from members of the public or personal observation, the vast majority of crime stories that make the news have been supplied by the police. It has been argued that this gives the police a privileged position as one of a number of **primary definers** able to influence how certain issues are reported and debated. This question of **power** relations between journalists and sources has been explored at length by academics, while journalists have been more concerned with the practicalities of getting the story. For journalists, making regular calls to the police and other emergency services – and following them on Twitter – is both a valid and a valuable way of generating copy. It provides a regular supply of stories, ranging from nibs (news in brief) to leads. What's more, such calls can usually be carried out routinely by any competent reporter even without any relevant personal knowledge or contacts, and they provide some insurance against the ignominy of missing something big happening on your patch. For these reasons, the calls will remain an important method of newsgathering alongside newer methods.

SOURCES OF NEWS

Organisations on the list of routine calls may be among the most reliable of journalists' sources but they are only a few of the places from which news comes. Common sources, listed in *Box 4.1*, are introduced below.

ACADEMIC JOURNALS

Research by academics, particularly scientists, published in peer-reviewed journals, is a frequent source of news stories. The journalist's job is twofold: to spot

BOX 4.1

COMMON SOURCES OF NEWS STORIES

Academic journals
Adverts
Airports
Alternative media
Ambulance service
Anniversaries
Archives
Armed forces
Arts groups
Blogs
Campaigns
Chambers of Commerce and/or
    Trade
Charities
Churches, Mosques, Synagogues,
    Temples
Colleagues
Community forums
Community groups
Companies
Consumer groups
Council departments
Council meetings
Council press officers
Councillors
Court hearings
Cuttings/diary
Email lists
Entertainment industry
Eyes and ears

Facebook
Fire brigade
Freedom of Information Act
Google alerts
Government departments
Health authorities
Heritage groups
Hospitals
Hyperlocal news sites
Inquests
Lateral thinking
Leaks
Letters
Libraries
Motoring organisations
MPs and MEPs
News agencies
News releases
Noticeboards
Official reports
Other media
Parish newsletters
People
Police
Political parties
Post offices
Posters
PR companies
Press conferences

Pressure groups
Professional bodies
Public inquiries
Pubs
Quangos
Readers/viewers/listeners/
    users
Reddit
Regeneration projects
Regulatory bodies
Residents' groups
Schools
Scouts, Cubs, Guides, Brownies,
    Woodcraft Folk
Social networking sites
Solicitors
Specialist online forums
Sports organisations
Support groups
Theatres
Trade associations
Trade press
Trades unions
Transport companies
Twitter
Universities
Websites
YouTube

---

a potential story among the qualifications and caveats beloved of academics, and to render the story intelligible and interesting to lay readers. There are almost daily examples, ranging from the quirky to matters of life and death.

ADVERTS

An advert for a high-powered job might alert you to the fact that the previous incumbent has left – maybe

they resigned or were sacked. And when a state school felt the need to appeal for money in *Private Eye*'s classified ads it prompted widespread coverage about the state of the education system.

AIRPORTS

As well as being arrival and departure points for celebs galore, airports can generate stories both positive (record journey times, new routes) and negative (accidents, noise, cancellation chaos, battles over runway extensions).

ALTERNATIVE MEDIA

Outsider journalism that can alert you to stories, sources or perspectives that might be overlooked by most mainstream media.

AMBULANCE SERVICE

A routine call to the ambulance service may provide early warning of accidents, explosions, and even the occasional birth on the way to hospital.

ANNIVERSARIES

Journalists love anniversaries, especially those with a five or, even better, a zero at the end. Births, marriages, deaths, inventions, disasters, and wars starting or ending are just some of the occasions given the anniversary treatment.

ARCHIVES

The release of official records (eg under the UK government's 30-year rule) can result in a fresh take on an old story.

ARMED FORCES

In peacetime the armed forces can generate stories through manoeuvres, recruitment campaigns and pictures of local boys or girls overseas, plus the occasional mysterious death or case of bullying that comes to light. During times of conflict, military briefings become events in their own right and military bases might become a magnet for anti-war protesters.

ARTS GROUPS

Apart from providing information about forthcoming events, arts groups can generate rows about funding or controversial subject matter.

BLOGS

Blogs can range from expert analysis on a particular topic to the amateurish jottings of people who really should get out more. Many are rubbish but others contain useful tips, insights and contacts that are ignored at your peril.

> "I've had stories where people have specifically come to me because of my social media profile to give me a story."
> *Neal Mann.*

CAMPAIGNS

Campaigners who want to influence public opinion on subjects ranging from animal rights to real ale are likely to come up with opinions or events that might generate news stories.

CHAMBERS OF COMMERCE AND/OR TRADE

As spokespeople for business, such organisations can be useful sources of stories or comments about anything from interest rates to Christmas shopping.

CHARITIES

Because charities need publicity to generate public donations, many are geared up to the needs of journalists, suggesting heartrending stories complete with photogenic victims, human or animal.

CHURCHES, MOSQUES, SYNAGOGUES, TEMPLES

Religious organisations may make the news by holding events, by having internal rows or by attacking the views of others. But if somebody tells you that a local authority is trying to ban Christmas, it is almost certainly not true.

COLLEAGUES

People you work with are likely to be parents, patients, residents, commuters and consumers, among other things. As such, they may come across events with the potential to become news – whether they recognise it or not.

COMMUNITY FORUMS

Local online discussion forums that, amid the questions about where to find an emergency plumber and so on, can alert you to events and controversies on your patch.

COMMUNITY GROUPS

A good source for rows and reactions, especially of the not-in-my-backyard variety.

COMPANIES

Behind the self-serving PR puffery, genuine business stories involve real products, real jobs, real profits or losses, and real people.

CONSUMER GROUPS

Consumer stories range from the mis-selling of pensions to the discovery of a mouse in a sandwich. When groups of consumers band together they can become a valuable source.

COUNCIL DEPARTMENTS

You will get some good exclusive stories if you manage to bypass the council press office to establish direct relationships with officers actually doing the work in departments such as housing or highways.

COUNCIL MEETINGS

Meetings tend not to be covered in the "parliamentary gallery" style of old, but they can still provide good copy as well as a chance to hang around and chat to councillors, officers and any members of the public who turn up to lobby on a particular issue. The lengthy documents accompanying most agendas (available online) may also have some gems buried deep within. Try to think of meetings and reports as a potential starting point for stories rather than an end.

COUNCIL PRESS OFFICERS

Sizeable local authorities employ teams of press officers, many recruited from the newsrooms of local newspapers. They *react* to journalists' queries, coming up with information, quotes and contacts while acting as a buffer between decision-makers and journalists. And they *proactively* distribute stories in the form of well-written news releases or well-timed telephone calls. David Helliwell says that council press officers with an eye for a good story should be able to get regular coverage in local and regional media because "they know what will turn us on". He adds: "Sometimes they knock out stories *before* the meeting, which is slightly disturbing."

COUNCILLORS

Local councillors often have something they want to get off their chest, especially in the run-up to an election.

COURT HEARINGS

"You ignore the courts at your peril," explains Brian Whittle, "because you get the best human interest stories from them." Court reporters dip in and out of several courtrooms looking for cases that fit the news values discussed in Chapter 3, hence the importance of good contacts with court staff, police, solicitors, and the Crown Prosecution Service. Some reporters, especially those working for agencies, will also go after background material on defendants and "after-match quotes" from victims and relatives.

CUTTINGS/DIARY

One story often leads to another, particularly if reminders are added to the newsdesk diary. Cuttings from previous articles are a major source of background information, but beware assuming that everything in a cutting is necessarily accurate. Certain myths seem to be recycled endlessly just because they were published once and other journalists have not bothered to check.

EMAIL LISTS

Adding your email address to specialist lists might generate some spam, but it might also generate some story leads.

ENTERTAINMENT INDUSTRY

This is an increasingly important source for today's media, as discussed in Chapters 3 and 7, although the line between puffery and journalism can be dangerously anorexic.

EYES AND EARS

Keep your eyes and ears open as you go about your life and you will be surprised at how many stories you can spot or overhear.

FACEBOOK

People setting up pages in support of quirky or grotesque campaigns can prompt stories in their own right, in addition to Facebook being a notice-board (and a means of sharing) of unprecedented proportions.

FIRE BRIGADE

One of the staple agencies for journalists' calls, checking with the fire brigade will provide early warning of house fires, motorway pile-ups and heroic rescues.

FORWARD PLANNING SERVICES

The Press Association is among the organisations that supply subscribers with details of forthcoming events, searchable by geographic area or specialist interest.

FREEDOM OF INFORMATION ACT

Obtaining figures from public authorities has become another staple of newsgathering in addition to being a key method used by investigative journalists (see Chapter 6).

GOOGLE ALERTS

Getting Google to let you know whenever it finds something on the web that uses a specific term (such as the name of your patch or a particular company or individual) helps you keep tabs on what people (including your rivals) are saying. But remember: even Google doesn't find everything.

GOVERNMENT DEPARTMENTS

As for council departments but on a national level.

HEALTH AUTHORITIES

Outbreaks of serious disease, funding crises, hospital closures and health promotion initiatives are all examples of news stories that may emanate from health authorities.

HERITAGE GROUPS

Campaigns to protect everything from historic woods to old gasworks can come up with some lively stories.

HOSPITALS

A hospital is not going to tell you about patients left overnight on trolleys, or given inappropriate treatment – those stories will come from other sources; but hospitals are a source of "good news" stories about cures, new treatments and general triumph-over-tragedy.

HYPERLOCAL NEWS SITES

Some non-commercial online media produced on a (very) local basis can provide early warning of stories that might have a wider interest.

INQUESTS

The coroner's court provides a regular supply of tragic stories for the local media with the most high-profile or unusual making it into the nationals. A major advantage for journalists is that most inquests are relatively brief encounters compared with criminal trials. Occasionally, a large number of similar cases might indicate a story bigger than just the immediate tragedy. (Incidentally, inquests and coroners do not exist in Scotland, where the sheriff's court may hold a fatal accident inquiry).

LATERAL THINKING

Lateral thinking involves making possible connections – between incidents, policies, decisions, statements, organisations, places and people – and having a good memory so that you can dredge up relevant information from the back of your mind. But lateral thinking is just the start: stories still need to be checked out, however good your memory.

LEAKS

Leaks of information, whether from close contacts or anonymous whistleblowers, can lead to exclusive stories. The protection of such sources is discussed in Chapter 2, while Chapter 6 examines some stories that originated from leaks.

LETTERS

Letters pages and online comment spaces should not be overlooked as sources of news. They contain opinions, questions, information and allegations that might repay further investigation. Sometimes a letter or email might become a news item in its own right.

LIBRARIES

Hard though it is for some people to believe, not everything is available online. Libraries retain a useful role in providing access to reference books, company reports, local history archives, indexes of local societies, community noticeboards and, by no means least, helpful librarians. Campaigns to save libraries from closure also make good stories.

MOTORING ORGANISATIONS

Organisations such as the RAC and the AA are always coming up with comments or surveys that make the news, and they are also good sources of reaction for anything to do with cars, roads or transport generally. However, given that people join for the recovery service rather than to have a mouthpiece, don't assume they speak for all motorists. The Environmental Transport Association (ETA) will provide a "greener" viewpoint.

MPS AND MEPS

MPs, Euro-MPs and members of regional and national assemblies need to maintain their profile with voters so they can usually be relied upon to make sure journalists know what they are up to. This means lots of dull statements and pseudo photo opportunities among the more genuinely newsworthy items. At a national level, political correspondents spend a lot of time talking to backbenchers, picking up gossip and gauging feeling; and don't forget that today's backbencher could be tomorrow's cabinet minister and the following day's prime minister.

NEWS AGENCIES

News agencies are the foot soldiers of journalism at a national and international level, allowing media organisations to cover stories in areas where they have few or no staff on the ground. "A lot of our work was actually finding people at the centre of the story," recalls Jane Merrick, "so, rather than just going along to a court case and reporting it, we would find the accused's husband and see if he wanted to talk. You have to do a lot of running around."

NEWS RELEASES

News releases, aka press releases, can be good, bad or indifferent. Some sections of the media are alarmingly full of scarcely rewritten news releases from councils, businesses, charities, universities and so on. Some news releases are pointers to genuine news, but many are a waste of everybody's time. Even the worthwhile ones should be treated more as a beginning than an end, and there may well be a better story if you read between the lines and think about what is *not* being said. Also, a simple phone call may avoid the embarrassment of reporting that something has happened just because a news release said it was going to happen, when it may have been cancelled at the last minute.

NOTICEBOARDS

Notices in shop windows, offices, libraries, colleges and elsewhere may tip you off about public meetings, petitions, planning applications or lost parrots.

OFFICIAL REPORTS

When confronted with an official report, don't simply rely on the executive summary. Newsworthy lines may be buried in the main text, demonstrating the value of cultivating friendly experts who will be able to help you understand such documents.

OTHER MEDIA

All news media monitor other media, all the time. Not that stories will simply be lifted. Not always, anyway. Different outlets require different treatments. To illustrate the point, Brian Whittle spreads on his desk a copy of one of the weekly papers on his patch, the *Knutsford Guardian*. He is excited by the potential of a story about some newts that have held up work on a traffic scheme:

> That's not the story at all. The real story is, this is one of the worst accident blackspots in the country, with a couple of people killed each year or even more, and they can't put this improvement scheme in because of a pond of great crested newts. The way we'll develop that is to go and see the wife of the latest victim, who will say to us, "Who is more important, my husband or a pond of bloody newts?" And, if you do the pictures properly, you've got a page lead in one of the nationals.

It happens at a political level too, with politicians' performances on the heavyweight broadcasting programmes being monitored for signs of splits or subtle changes of direction, as well as the latest comment on the controversy of the day. Jane Merrick explains:

> If they say something on TV you can use it. There are probably about four hours of political programmes on a Sunday, for example, and out of that there'll maybe be two quotes which will make a story. It's a daily cycle. If you're on the late shift you wait for the first editions of the newspapers to come in at about 10.30pm. Some newspaper will have been briefed about a story so you phone up the Home Office at 11 o'clock at night and they say yes it's all true, or no comment.

And so it goes on, with those newspapers influencing the next morning's *Today* programme (Radio Four) and the *Today* programming influencing TV news, the national press and online news sites – while all of them follow major sources (and each other) on Twitter.

PARISH NEWSLETTERS

There may be some spectacular rows lurking within their pages. Failing that, you might find stories ranging from an upcoming fête to a shortage of vicars. But you will have to put up with an awful lot of exclamation marks.

PEOPLE

Potential stories can be suggested by people you meet – or even just overhear – while at work, rest and play. This can range from somebody mentioning that they have just seen a police car parked in their street to rather more substantial fare. As a student journalist on work experience, Abul Taher was researching an education story about the influence of Islam on British campuses when he came across a stronger story:

> The leader of an Islamic extremist group made a passing remark that a lot of British Muslim students had gone to fight jihad in Bosnia, Afghanistan and Kashmir for the cause of Islam. I immediately latched on to that and he provided me with details of three

students from Queen Mary and Westfield College abandoning their studies to go to jihad. I checked with the college, and the story made it as an exclusive in the *Guardian* and generated a lot of response from other media. This was two years before September 11th. The source was really a chat with someone.

POLICE

Probably the single most important source for journalists, particularly in the local and regional media, is the police. Following the police on social media, making regular calls to police voicebanks and police stations, backed up where necessary with calls to the press office or preferably the investigating officer, between them result in an endless stream of stories about brutal killings, bungling burglars, callous thieves and have-a-go heroes. In addition to providing this rollcall of crimes, the police will sometimes tip-off the media about operations, allowing for dramatic pictures of dawn raids and drugs busts. Police may organise press conferences with victims' relatives. Experienced crime correspondents will develop their own networks of sources within the police, bypassing the press office where possible. However, there are now frequent complaints that police officers have become reluctant to communicate directly with journalists due to the chilling effect blamed on the phone-hacking scandal and Leveson inquiry.

POLITICAL PARTIES

Contacts within parties can be a fruitful source of stories about rows and splits, while party spokespeople will be more keen to let you know about the selection of candidates or the launch of policy initiatives.

POST OFFICES

A post office, particularly in a rural area, can be a focus for information and gossip on local people and events. Sadly, your chances of finding a village with its own post office seem to be diminishing each year. But a campaign to save or even reopen a post office can make a good story too.

POSTERS

Posters can be big news as I found out when my friend Jane once asked me: "Have you seen those awful Harvey Nichols posters?" I hadn't yet seen the adverts for the opening of a Harvey Nichols shop in Leeds, but she clearly found them offensive. The huge hoardings featured a woman wearing a dog-lead and collar, accompanied by the weak pun "Harvey Nichols Leeds (not follows)", and coincidentally had been placed alongside others promoting a local "zero tolerance" campaign to combat violence against women. "I don't know if you might be able to make it into a story", Jane added. The answer was yes, it could be a story if somebody complained, particularly because the existence of a formal complaint meant there was a row involving a high-profile, upmarket store popular with celebs, including the Princess of Wales. Having gathered some more outraged comments from locals and councillors, along with a dismissive response from the store's PR people, I filed copy to the national and local papers. Many gave it a good show the next day accompanied by pictures and obligatory puns such as: HOT UNDER THE COLLAR (*Daily Express*), HARVEY NICKS 'DOG GIRLS' UNLEASH A ROW (*Daily Mail*), TOP STORE IN THE DOGHOUSE AS 'RACIST AND SEXIST' POSTER UNLEASHES PROTESTS UP NORTH (*Guardian*) and STORE FAILS TO FIND FOLLOWING AMONG LEEDS LADIES WHO LUNCH (*Daily Telegraph*, all October 10 1996). The story was duly followed-up by broadcast media before finally becoming the property of columnists, who contributed their philosophical twopenceworth based on a pile of cuttings. Then it was forgotten, except by me. As every freelance knows, where there is a story there is a potential follow-up. Three months later, when the advertising watchdog declared the ads to be harmless fun, I dusted off the original story and bashed out fresh copy that was used in several papers – albeit in brief, because TOP STORE CLEARED was thought much less of a story than TOP STORE ACCUSED.

PR COMPANIES

Journalists and PR people love to hate – or at least poke gentle fun at – each other. But the fruits of the PR industry's labours are there for all to see in the media every day, so the reality is that PR *is* a major source for many journalists. The role of public relations as "information subsidy" to the media is discussed further in Chapter 2.

PRESS CONFERENCES

Away from the world of professional football clubs announcing new signings, far fewer press conferences take place these days because most journalists are simply too busy to go and collect information that can be sent by email. But police press conferences, for example during murder hunts, remain an important source of news. Press conferences are also likely to be held to announce the results of official inquiries or to unveil new appointments, and they give you a chance to question senior figures who may not otherwise be available. As with news releases, it is sometimes best to read between the lines and remember that the best angle might not even be mentioned from the platform. Try to get there early and hang around at the end, talking to other journalists as well as the participants, because you might pick up a useful tip. However, sometimes you might end up covering a televised press conference from your desk in the newsroom.

PRESSURE GROUPS

As with campaigns, except that pressure groups tend to be more long-term. Note how often the English Collective of Prostitutes is referred to in stories about sex workers, not because it necessarily represents the views of most women on the game, but because it is both quotable and easily accessible to journalists in a hurry.

PROFESSIONAL BODIES

Stories from professional bodies, such as those covering doctors or solicitors, may include disciplinary hearings or criticism of government policy. They are also seen as authoritative sources on anything to do with their profession.

PUBLIC INQUIRIES

Public inquiries can produce good copy, but remember to look beneath the surface. It was only by skim-reading hundreds of pages of official documents at a public inquiry into a major drought that reporter Peter Lazenby discovered that a serious suggestion to evacuate the entire city of Bradford had been tabled at a meeting between Yorkshire Water and the city's emergency planners because the water supply could not be guaranteed. It was just one line in a set of old minutes towards the bottom of a mountain of paper, but it made that night's headlines.

PUBS

Publicans and regulars can be mines of information about the community and, if you get chatting, they might tell you about anything from charity events to the death of a local character. Peter Lazenby delights in telling young journalists that more cracking news stories started out being scribbled on wet beermats than will ever be uncovered by reporters sitting at their desks. Not everyone has the personality to pick up a story in a pub, of course, and many of today's bars are not exactly conducive to chatting, but the point remains that off-diary stories come from *talking* and *listening* to people. As with post offices, pubs themselves can also be the subject of stories, from licensing rows to the decline of the traditional local.

QUANGOS

A quango is a "quasi-autonomous non-governmental organisation" operating at arm's length from ministers. Quangos can be sources of news by virtue of the work they do, how they spend public money, and by controversial appointments.

READERS/VIEWERS/LISTENERS/USERS

Journalism cannot exist without an audience and many members of the audience will suggest stories by emailing, texting, tweeting and telephoning – even occasionally by popping into the office (assuming your news organisation still has one) or by collaring a reporter at some public event. Some will tell you about personal gripes, some will describe impossibly complicated disputes, and some will tell you that government agents are using lamp-posts to beam poison rays into their bedroom at night. But others will come up with excellent stories. How you treat people will influence whether they come back to you next time. Readers' reactions to stories on social media can also

become the basis of follow-up stories. Engaging with the audience is discussed further in Chapter 14.

REDDIT

A social media site built on user-generated content that proclaims itself "the front page of the internet". It is often monitored by journalists for early warning of potential stories, but watch out for the occasional witch-hunt (as when Reddit users tried to identify the Boston marathon bombers in 2013 – with alarming results).

REDDIT ON
BOSTON BOMBING

REGENERATION PROJECTS

A huge amount of public money is spent on regenerating run-down areas or former industrial sites, and such projects can provide both "good news" stories and allegations of misspent funds and jobs-for-the-boys cronyism.

REGULATORY BODIES

Ofwat (water), Ofgem (energy) and all the rest are regular sources of stories about customer complaints, rising prices, excess profits and directors' pay. Broadcast regulator Ofcom can also be newsworthy as it adjudicates on complaints from the public on matters such as taste and decency.

RESIDENTS' GROUPS

See community groups.

SCHOOLS

Schools can provide good news stories about achievements such as productions, sporting feats and exam passes. They can also be the focus of tragic news, especially when trips go wrong, and of investigations into allegedly paedophile staff (often dating back many years).

SCOUTS, CUBS, GUIDES, BROWNIES, WOODCRAFT FOLK

As organisations dependent on attracting new members, youth groups are likely to let you know about events, exchange trips and so on. They also make the news because of changes in traditional activities, songs or uniforms.

SOCIAL NETWORKING SITES

Journalists now routinely check the social networking profiles of people who suddenly become part of the news.

SOLICITORS

"Solicitors are very good sources because they represent people who have been done down", says Paul Foot. It may be in their clients' interests to gain publicity for an appeal against a miscarriage of justice, a civil action for wrongful arrest, or a compensation claim for an industrial disease. Solicitors can become valuable long-term contacts, as Jane Merrick explains:

> There are three or four solicitors in Liverpool – and it's probably the same in most other cities – who tend to deal with the big cases. So it's a question of knowing them well enough, keeping them warm so they'll speak to you and contact you about cases. They like to see their names in the paper.

SPECIALIST ONLINE FORUMS

These might alert you to a potential story long before it is visible to more general and/or mainstream media.

SPORTS ORGANISATIONS

Apart from accounts of the winning, the losing and the taking part, you might also find stories about a lack of facilities, the sale of playing fields, or allegations of racism, sexism, homophobia or financial shenanigans. Every now and then certain news organisations or even individual journalists can find themselves banned by a professional football club that objects to critical reporting, as happened with Newcastle United in 2013.

SUPPORT GROUPS

Groups set up to support people with particular conditions or diseases can come up with fascinating human interest stories.

THEATRES

Events, celebrities, subject matter and funding are all ways in which a theatre may prompt a news story.

TRADE ASSOCIATIONS

The views of a particular industry might be newsworthy, particularly if it is calling for a change in government policy to prevent closures and job losses.

TRADE PRESS

As with academic journals, the trade and specialist press contain many stories of potential interest to the general reader, as long as you can identify and translate them. Journalists on specialist publications can also be interviewed as authoritative sources. For example, editors of railway or aviation magazines are often interviewed as experts after rail or air crashes.

TRADES UNIONS

Unions can be an excellent source of stories not just about industrial disputes, but about everything from pensions scandals to sexual harassment at work. The bigger unions have well-resourced research departments that are able to provide journalists with useful background material.

TUC MEDIA CENTRE

TRANSPORT COMPANIES

Cancellations, strikes, fares increases, punctuality figures, franchise bids, "journeys from hell" and crashes are all obvious news stories. Once in a blue moon you might even come across the occasional good news story from a transport company – an announcement of new investment, perhaps, or the opening of a new route.

TWITTER

Twitter has been described as – among many other things – acting like "the canary in the news coalmine" (Jarvis, 2008), providing early indications that something might be happening. Journalists of a certain vintage might lament the fact that somebody tweeting something is now considered news, but it can be – depending on who that someone is, what it is they are tweeting, and the context. It is certainly not all about celebrity gossip, as Neal Mann explains:

> Any journalist, particularly younger journalists, needs to understand that social media is a key part of their job, and if done correctly it's a place where they're

going to get a lot of stories and a lot of tips. I think one of the key things for a lot of journalists is that, traditionally, they may only be known on their patch, their beat, their area, but what Twitter in particular allows them to do is engage with anybody, worldwide in real time. That wasn't possible before. On social media you can have a conversation with somebody at any level of society, they may be a celebrity or a soldier in a war zone, you can engage with them, and a key part of using social media as a journalist is understanding that.

VERIFYING SOCIAL MEDIA CONTENT

Ways of engaging with people on Twitter will be discussed in more detail in Chapter 14.

UNIVERSITIES

Universities are a source of a huge range of stories, whether it is ground-breaking research, an unusual degree scheme or an ethical argument about accepting funding from a tobacco company. Student protests over fees or complaints about insufficient contact time can sometimes result in stories, as can the tendency for student unions to vote in favour of boycotting things, ranging from sexist songs to Israeli goods. Universities are also where you will find experts in everything from aeronautics to the zodiac.

WEBSITES

In addition to news from around the world there are countless potential stories lurking on the web in sites that are unusual, amusing, quirky, informative, provocative, dangerous, disgusting or just plain nasty.

YOUTUBE

The video-sharing website is now a major source of stories and user-generated videos as members of the public upload footage often shot on phones on occasions where no journalists are present, from atrocities filmed in conflict zones to a racist tirade (or even a drunken Christmas song) delivered to bewildered fellow-passengers on public transport. Some organisations or individuals now attempt to bypass journalists by posting announcements directly onto YouTube, as when the Olympic diver Tom Daley uploaded his "Something I want to say" video in December 2013 and told the world – in his own words – that he was gay.

"GET OUT MORE OFTEN"

The above list may not be exhaustive but it covers the major sources used by reporters to originate or check stories. How journalists obtain and evaluate information from sources is discussed further in Chapters 5 and 6. If you keep this list in mind as you watch the TV news, listen to a radio bulletin or read the news in print or online, you should be able to come up with a fairly good idea of where most stories are likely to have come from.

Some sources are less visible than others, however. There is evidence that the secret intelligence services MI5 and MI6 have attempted – and no doubt succeeded in some cases – to recruit and/or influence journalists (Keeble, 2001b: 117–119). And former Fleet Street journalist Simon Winchester recalls reporting "the troubles" in Northern Ireland and being given off-the-record briefings by military intelligence. Winchester would pass on the contents of the briefing to his audience, telling the nation that the young man shot dead by British soldiers the night before was a leading paramilitary. Only later did he realise that "most of what I gaily rebroadcast was, if not a pure figment of the imagination of some superheated British army intelligence officer, then to a very large degree, wishful thinking" (Winchester, 2001). This underlines the value to a journalist of maintaining a *questioning* attitude – a healthy scepticism, not to be confused with cynicism – no matter with whom you are dealing.

Putting non-attributable briefings with spooks to one side, the strongest news stories come from journalists *talking* to people – and getting people talking to you. Even a story that originates from a tweet or a news release will be improved by talking to people. Making an extra call or knocking on that extra door might make the difference between having the same story as everyone else or coming up with a different angle or a fresh piece of information. In the words of Andrew Marr (2005: 116): "Get out more often."

There is, then, no substitute for speaking to – and listening to – the people directly involved in a story. Getting hold of them may sometimes require you to be tough and single-minded. But it cannot excuse the behaviour witnessed by Edward Behr in an African conflict zone, as thousands of women and children waited to be airlifted to safety:

> Into the middle of this crowd strode an unmistakably British TV reporter, leading his cameraman and sundry technicians like a platoon commander through hostile territory. At intervals he paused and shouted, in a stentorian but genteel BBC voice, "Anyone here been raped and speaks English?". (Behr, 1992: 136)

Such insensitivity might get the story, but at what cost? As journalists we have a duty to ourselves, to our sources and to our fellow citizens to pause for reflection from time to time. Without some sense of humanity and empathy what is the point of our journalism? Lindsay Eastwood recalls one of the most satisfying stories of her career. It wasn't a big breaking news story produced in an adrenalin rush to deadline, but a television documentary about three women with post-natal depression, filmed over several months:

> I'm really proud of it. The women all wanted to do it because they thought that really serious post-natal depression, where you reject your baby, was swept under the carpet. They were really nervous about coming across as bad mothers or as fruitcakes, basically.
>
> I didn't want to over dramatise it so it was quite tricky and I was really, really anxious that they liked the end product. It went out on air and I was really, really nervous waiting to hear from these three women. They all rang and said, "That was just great, thank you so much." I wasn't bothered about what anybody else thought, it was just the women involved, it was really important that they all liked it.
>
> It's nice to get your teeth into something. You breeze in and out of people's lives on a daily basis and you ask them to do these things in front of camera, and do interviews and stuff, and they do it remarkably well. And you think, "I've only spent half an hour with you", so it was nice to get to know these people a bit more.

We might think of people as sources and of their lives in terms of potential stories, but a sense of humanity and a concern for ethics need not be in conflict with good journalism. Ethical considerations are discussed in more detail in Chapter 13.

SUMMARY

Journalists need sources to provide information that may be turned into news, and also to check information provided by other sources. Journalists tend to evaluate sources based on their previous experience of them, categorising some as reliable and others as less so. Journalists are surrounded by sources of potential news stories and will develop extensive lists of contacts. However, many academic studies have suggested that a high proportion of stories come from a relatively narrow range of sources, with some journalists being accused of being too passive. Some sources, such as the police, provide a steady supply of potential news stories. Although it has been suggested that some sources have the power to virtually guarantee access to the news and to frame debate on social issues, journalists are also sometimes accused of being *too* proactive and even manipulative in creating the news.

QUESTIONS

Why do journalists need sources?
Why do sources need journalists?
Why do some people or organisations get in the news more than others?
What is the effect of journalists using other media as a source?
Will journalists become irrelevant as more sources communicate directly with the public via social media?

HOW MIGHT
YOU TACKLE
THIS ISSUE?

WHAT WOULD YOU DO?

You are on a bus on the way to work (you are a reporter for a local radio station) when you over-hear a teenage passenger talking loudly into a mobile phone. You start paying attention when you hear the word "riot" mentioned, and it gradually sounds to you as if the phone conversation might be some kind of plan for a group of youths to gather in the town centre that evening in the hope of causing a disturbance on the streets. What would you do?

FURTHER READING

Randall (2011) offers a wealth of good advice on sourcing stories, and Keeble (2006), Frost (2010) and Sheridan Burns (2013) are all worth dipping into. Dick (2013) has a useful chapter on "devel-oping an online beat", and tips on sourcing stories via social media can also be found in Knight and Cook (2013). A starting point for ethical discussion about sources is Harcup (2007), which has one chapter introducing journalist–source relations and another discussing the ways in which victims' rela-tives are sometimes (mis)treated by journalists; the sourcing practices of alternative media are consid-ered in Harcup (2013) and Whitaker (1981). Manning (2001) is a good introduction to research and more theoretical frameworks on journalist–source relationships, while Tumber (1999) offers useful extracts and Hall et al (1978, 2013) is worth reading for the concept of primary definers. The results of detailed academic research into the sometimes limited range of sources in the news can be found in studies by Lewis et al (2008a and 2008b) and O'Neill and O'Connor (2008) that make uncomfortable reading for anyone who believes journalists should be the eyes and ears of the public.

TOP THREE TO TRY NEXT

Paul Manning (2001) *News and News Sources: A Critical Introduction*
Deirdre O'Neill and Catherine O'Connor (2008) 'The passive journalist: how sources dominate local news', *Journalism Practice*
David Randall (2011) 'Where do good stories come from?' (Chapter 4 of *The Universal Journalist*)

SOURCES FOR SOUNDBITES

Newman, interview with the author; Whittle, interview with the author; Taher, interview with the author; O'Neill and O'Connor, 2008: 498; Mansfield, 1936: 82; Mann, interview with the author.

CHAPTER 5

"THE BEST OBTAINABLE VERSION OF THE TRUTH": JOURNALISTS AS OBJECTIVE REPORTERS?

KEY TERMS

Accuracy; Agenda setting; Alternative journalism; Balance; Bias; Common sense; Emotionality; Facts; Hegemony; Impartiality; Journalism of attachment; Moral panic; Neutrality; Objectivity; Opinion; Oppositional reporting; Pragmatic objectivity; Primary definers; Strategic ritual; Subjectivity; Three-source rule; Truth; Verification

"Examine your words well," wrote George Eliot in the novel *Adam Bede*, "and you will find that even when you have no motive to be false, it is a very hard thing to say the exact truth" (Eliot, 1859: 151). Journalists have more reason than most to examine their words well, because they are in the **truth** business as well as the words business; yet the **accuracy** of Eliot's observation is demonstrated by the frequency with which journalists manage to get things wrong. How wrong? As wrong as when, some years back, the *Daily Mirror* proclaimed on its front page the exciting news of a new addition to the family of ex-Beatle Paul McCartney and the model Heather Mills: IT'S A BOY! EXCLUSIVE: MACCA BABY A MONTH EARLY (October 30 2003), only to follow it up the next day with: ER … IT'S A GIRL! AND SHE'S CALLED BEATRICE – NOT JOSEPH, accompanied by the tongue-in-cheek claim that "our baby scoop was half right" (*Daily Mirror*, October 31 2003).

Hmmm, perhaps. But, as former BBC director of news Richard Sambrook (2004) once put it, in a somewhat different context: "In journalism 'mainly right' is like being half pregnant – it's an unsustainable condition." Yet journalists frequently get things wrong and we are not the only ones. On the day that Jean Charles de Menezes was killed by police officers at Stockwell tube station in London – July 22 2005 – I watched the rolling news broadcasts on television. Witness after witness told what they had seen, which was essentially an Asian man in a bulky coat – maybe wearing a baseball cap, maybe carrying a rucksack – jump the ticket barrier, run like the wind, and be chased on to a tube train before being challenged and shot dead. There is no reason to believe they made any of this

> "Falsehood is so easy, truth so difficult."
> *George Eliot.*

TRUTH

Truth is slippery, and has arguably become increasingly so in recent decades as many of the apparent certainties of modernity have come under challenge. Yet for journalists the truth is still out there in the shape of "facts that are verified and explained" (Seib, 2002: 4); either you can get to this truth or you can't, and if you can't it's probably because somebody is trying to stop you. Such "general truth claims" have been replaced in much cultural analysis by a foregrounding of more subjective experience (Dovey, 2000: 25) or by a wider claim that the concept of there being *a* truth is merely a monologic *version* of truth produced from within a discourse that tends to be white, male and elitist (Allan, 1998: 124–126). Even reporters witnessing an event for themselves may be carrying all sorts of personal or cultural baggage that can impact on what they see as true and what they recognise as facts (Keeble, 1998: 182). Despite such claims, truth is not that difficult a concept to grasp, argues Matthew Kieran:

> In journalism, as distinct from fiction, there is a truth of the matter and this is what objectivity in journalism aims at. . . . Where reporting turns away from the goal of truth and journalists treat events as open to many interpretations, according to their prejudices, assumptions, news agenda or the commercial drive toward entertainment, the justification and self-confessed rationale of journalism threatens to disappear. (Kieran, 1998: 34–35)

Yet establishing the truth of something might require more than collecting an accurate set of facts, according to Thomas Patterson (2012), who points out that early media coverage of the US/UK invasion of Afghanistan "was often accurate in its particulars but off the mark in up and I am sure the journalists broadcasting such accounts did so in good faith, especially as this version of events seemed to match the initial impression being given by official sources. The next day's newspapers carried the same sort of material. The *Times*, for example, (mis)informed readers: "The suspect, described as being of Asian appearance and wearing a thick, bulky jacket, vaulted over a ticket barrier when challenged by police and ran down the escalator and along the platform of the Northern Line" (Fresco et al, 2005).

It emerged within days that he had not behaved in any such way (Honigsbaum, 2005). As the *Times* pointed out in a subsequent leader column:

> At the time of the shooting, Scotland Yard said that Mr de Menezes' clothing and his behaviour at the station were suspicious. This claim was buttressed by witnesses who claimed that he was wearing a bulky jacket on a hot day and that he leapt over the ticket barrier at Stockwell station. Now, it turns out that he was wearing only a light denim jacket at the time of his death: perfectly appropriate garb for the time of year. Nor was he carrying a bag or rucksack. There is apparently CCTV footage that shows him walking normally into the station, picking up a free newspaper and using his Oyster card to pass through the barrier. He allegedly began to run only when he saw a train pulling into the station, after which he boarded it and sat down in an ordinary fashion. (*Times*, 2005)

So, although the witnesses who spoke to journalists may have seen what they saw, they may not have seen what they subsequently *thought* they saw. It turns out that a man did vault the ticket barrier and run at high speed towards the train, for example; it was not Mr de Menezes, but a police officer.

OBJECTIVE REPORTING

It is entirely understandable that people who witness a traumatic event might put two and two together in a retrospective attempt to make sense of it, and that in the process they might make some assumptions that are wrong. As Eliot said, it can be very hard to say the exact truth. Yet the truth – sometimes referred

> "Reporting is not stenography. It is the best obtainable version of the truth."
> *Carl Bernstein.*

its assessments of Afghan society and the likely course of the war". And since then the advent of social media has fundamentally changed the relationship between journalism and the truth, argues Neal Mann of the *Wall Street Journal*:

> Traditionally, journalists only dealt in the truth. The thing with social media is that there's a lot out there that isn't true, but we have to understand that it's being published, and actually engage with that now. If everybody's talking about a news event, we've got to respect the fact that we know they're talking about it, and if they're not right then we have to engage with that. It's changed the way that we work with an audience. We don't just deal in truths any more, we actually knock things down. We're the ones who [sometimes have to] say: "That's not true." You gain even more respect if you do that.

So, whereas journalists may once have been able simply to ignore rumours they knew to be untrue, their job in the age of social media entails acknowledging such rumours and showing in what ways they are false – all without giving untruths even wider circulation. A slippery business indeed.

ACCURACY

Accuracy is frequently described as the single most important element of journalism because, without it, nothing else really matters very much. By accuracy is meant everything from the correct spelling of a name or attribution of opinion to evidence-based, in-depth coverage of complex or contentious issues. The pursuit of accuracy entails precision and double-checking, but even that is not always enough to prevent inaccurate reporting. A perfectly accurate account of a source's words (a politician's speech, for example), supported by a recording or a good shorthand note, may actually be factually inaccurate if the source is deliberately misleading journalists by exaggeration or omission, or even if the source is honestly mistaken. In 2002 many journalists and news organisations accurately reported claims by the Blair government that Iraq was stockpiling weapons of mass destruction, some of which could be ready for use within just 45 minutes;

to as the "objective truth" – is what journalists are aiming at; something that can be backed up with evidence, verified, and demonstrated to be the case.

Journalists strive to give not necessarily the absolute truth, but the most truthful version of events that can be obtained at the time. **Objectivity** for journalists has been defined as even-handedness, separating facts from opinion, and minimising the journalist's own views or prejudices (Boyer, 1981, cited in Watson, 1998: 98). Furthermore, broadcast journalists in the UK have a statutory requirement to be impartial. According to the BBC, **impartiality** entails "a mixture of accuracy, balance, context, distance, evenhandedness, fairness, objectivity, open-mindedness, rigour, self-awareness, transparency and truth". That's not all, because impartiality also requires "breadth of view and completeness" (BBC Trust, 2007a: 5–6). A survey of 2,000 people in the UK found 84 per cent of them agreeing – half of them "strongly" – with the statement "impartiality is difficult to achieve, but broadcasters must try very hard to do so"; only three per cent disagreed. However, this view is itself a partial one, because there was noticeably less support for impartiality among younger people, black people and working-class people (BBC Trust, 2007a: 19); perhaps some respondents felt that what is called impartiality is sometimes rather too partial to viewing the world through white, middle-aged and middle-class eyes.

THE NORM OF OBJECTIVITY

THE BBC ON IMPARTIALITY

> "The truth is rarely pure and never simple."
> *Oscar Wilde.*

Unlike broadcasting organisations, journalists working for newspapers, magazines or online have no statutory requirement to be impartial, whether between the commercial interests of competing proprietors or between rival political policies or parties. General elections would not be the same without blatant **agenda setting** headlines such as LABOUR'S TAX LIES EXPOSED (*Daily Express*, March 23 1992), A LABOUR GOVERNMENT WILL LEAD TO HIGHER MORTGAGE PAYMENTS (*Daily Mail*, April 7 1992) and OUR ONLY HOPE: IN CAMERON WE TRUST (*Sun*, May 6 2010). However, despite the fact that broadcasters are required by law to be impartial, TV and radio

when these weapons were neither fired nor found after the 2003 US/UK invasion, most experts concluded they did not exist. The worrying implication of this episode for journalists is that, simply by accurately reporting somebody's words, we might inadvertently end up amplifying an untruth, including on matters of life and death.

OBJECTIVITY

Objectivity is a "myth" that has been "thoroughly unpicked and discredited among the media theorists", according to Megan Knight and Clare Cook (2013: 106), who add that despite this it "remains firmly entrenched in the professional practice of journalism, and the more the profession comes under fire, the more objectivity is defended as a necessary part of the contribution that news organisations make to society as a whole". Myth or not, objectivity is certainly a concept with longevity. It hinges on separating independently verifiable facts from subjective values, and is associated with the Enlightenment project of rationality and the pursuit of scientific knowledge (Schudson, 1978: 293). Such grand thinking has been challenged, with some postmodernist theorists dismissing as naïve empiricism the idea that there is a truth that exists "out there" in the world, independent of discourse, just waiting to be discovered.

A commitment to objectivity in journalism can be defined as meaning that "a person's statements about the world can be trusted if they are submitted to established rules deemed legitimate by a professional community" (Schudson, 1978: 294). Michael Schudson further explains:

> The objectivity norm guides journalists to separate facts from values and to report only the facts. Objective reporting is supposed to be cool, rather than emotional, in tone. Objective reporting takes pains to represent fairly each leading side in a political controversy. According to the objectivity norm, the journalist's job consists of reporting something called "news" without commenting on it, slanting it, or shaping its formulation in any way. (Schudson, 2001: 150)

Journalism was not always expected to be that way, and the above norm was not central to 18th-century publications that helped establish the press as "a genuinely critical organ of a public engaged in critical political debate: as the journalists' election coverage can still be influenced by an aggressive press agenda focusing on certain issues (tax, immigration, crime, benefits, Europe) to the exclusion of others (homelessness, poverty, jobs, low wages, high rents, social exclusion). This process has been labelled "inter-media agenda setting" (McKnight, 2013: 70).

OBJECTIVITY IN WARTIME?

If objective reporting of elections is problematic – the country being divided – then what of objective reporting of warfare, when a country is supposedly united against a common enemy? That truth is the first casualty of war has become a truism, but objective reporting has repeatedly gone to the wall in the name of national unity. Research suggests that tabloid headlines such as GO GET HIM BOYS (*Daily Star*, January 16 1991) and the obsession of TV news with "smart bombs" and "star wars" technology painted a very partial picture of the 1991 Gulf war, rendering invisible some of the salient issues (including oil supplies), not to mention Iraqi civilian casualties (Philo and McLaughlin, 1993: 146–155). Reflecting shortly after that war, the BBC's John Simpson identified a gap in UK television's saturation coverage of the conflict: "As for the human casualties, tens of thousands of them, or the brutal effect the war had on millions of others . . . we didn't see so much of that" (quoted in Philo and McLaughlin, 1993: 155). Nor did we hear very much about the "undeclared war" waged against Iraq in the decade that followed. Figures released quietly by the Ministry of Defence in November 2000 showed that 84 tonnes of bombs had been dropped on southern Iraq by British aircraft over the previous two years (Norton-Taylor, 2000). This silent bombing campaign passed largely unnoticed by the UK media, which awoke only to cheer on occasional spectaculars with headlines such as WE BOMB BAGHDAD (*Sun*, February 17 2001). Note the use of "we" in the latter example – a tiny word with huge meanings.

"The way wars are reported in the western media follows a depressingly predictable pattern", wrote Phillip Knightley as US and UK forces were gearing up to invade Afghanistan in 2001, following the

> "The more one is aware of political bias, the more one can be independent of it and the more one claims to be impartial, the more one is biased."
>
> *George Orwell.*

fourth estate" (Habermas, 1992: 60). Early newspapers and periodicals were often expected to be partisan and "objectivity was not an issue" (Schudson, 1978: 291). The emergence of the US "penny press", with many papers being politically neutral or even indifferent as they sought mass readerships, brought a new range of news values privileging factual coverage of human interest stories over analysis or opinion (Allan, 1997: 304–305). The gradual adoption of objectivity as a normative standard of news reporting may have been encouraged by the development of wire services such as Associated Press (AP) from 1848. AP had a market imperative to concentrate on the bare facts, compressed into the intro, so that it could sell the same stories to newspapers with widely divergent politics. This strategy of unadorned reportage also helped AP staff overcome the unreliable nature of the new technology and placed a premium on brevity (Allan, 1997: 306).

But Schudson says the journalist's commitment to separating facts from values may have had more to do with the rising status of reporters in relation to their employers in the late 19th and early 20th centuries, and with a professional debate about objectivity in the years after the First World War. For him, "a self-conscious, articulate ideology of objectivity can be dated to the 1920s" (Schudson, 2001: 159–160). In the UK, as Chris Frost notes, the move towards a less partisan style of reporting gathered momentum only during the early part of the 20th century, culminating in the imposition of a statutory obligation to be impartial on the fledgling broadcasting industry (Frost, 2000: 159).

IMPARTIALITY

The words "impartiality" and "objectivity" are sometimes used interchangeably, but impartial reporting is generally defined as being neutral (up to a point), while objective reporting is taken to be the reporting of verifiable facts. Advocates of impartial reporting are often at pains to point out that it does not mean treating *every* argument as equally valid; if the evidence points overwhelmingly to two-plus-two equalling four, "due impartiality" would not require equal representation of anyone asserting that the answer is three or five. However, there are plenty

September 11 attacks in the USA: "Stage one, the crisis; stage two, the demonisation of the enemy's leader; stage three, the demonisation of the enemy as individuals; and stage four, . . . the atrocity story" (Knightley, 2001). Such coverage prepares the public for battle "by showing that the enemy is evil, mad and a danger to the civilised world" (Knightley, 2002).

What Paul Foot called "war fever" seemed to infect many UK newsrooms before and during the US-led invasion of Iraq in 2003 (with some exceptions, notably the *Mirror* and *Independent*). When the *Sun* reported the start of the Iraq war with the headline SHOW THEM NO PITY...THEY HAVE STAINS ON THEIR SOULS (*Sun*, March 20 2003), staff journalist Katy Weitz promptly resigned from the paper because, as she explained, "I want to be proud of the work I help to produce, not shudder in shame at its front-page blood lust" (Weitz, 2003). Just as Weitz was walking out of her job, some other journalists were becoming "embedded" with the military as one way of reporting from the front: living with the military, travelling with them, coming under their protection, and reporting under military restrictions. Unsurprisingly, perhaps, embedded reporters tended to adopt the perspective of their hosts and minders, as US journalist Gordon Dillow later admitted: "I found myself falling in love with my subject. I fell in love with 'my' Marines. . . . The point wasn't that I wasn't reporting the truth; the point was that I was reporting the Marine grunt truth . . . which had also become my truth" (quoted in Brandenburg, 2007: 957).

KATY WEITZ QUITS SUN

But it is not only those who move in military circles or who support their own government's war efforts who sometimes discard the cloak of objectivity. Reflecting on his own role in reporting conflicts around the world, including the Vietnam war, James Cameron wrote:

[O]bjectivity in some circumstances is both meaningless and impossible. I still do not see how a reporter attempting to define a situation involving some sort of ethical conflict can do it with sufficient demonstrable neutrality to fulfil some arbitrary concept of "objectivity". It never occurred to me, in such a situation, to be other

of grey areas and less clear-cut cases, and the BBC in particular subjects itself to frequent bouts of agonising over whether it is fulfilling its duty to be impartial.

According to McQuail, impartiality means "balance in the choice and use of sources, so as to reflect different points of view, and also neutrality in the presentation of news – separating facts from opinion, avoiding value judgements or emotive language or pictures" (McQuail, 2000: 321). For Frost, impartial reporting means that a journalist is *aiming* at the truth, whereas true objectivity would require giving the *whole* picture – a task as impossible for the journalist as it is (in an analogy borrowed from Hartley) for the cartographer (Frost, 2000: 38). That is because, like a map, a news report is still a selective, simplified and *mediated* representation of reality, rather than the reality itself.

Balance and neutrality have themselves been questioned (or problematised, in academic-speak) by some journalists who advocate their abandonment in situations where to be impartial would mean standing "neutrally between good and evil, right and wrong, the victim and the oppressor" (Bell, 1998: 16). This raises inevitable questions about *who* defines good and evil and whether journalists who *do* take sides automatically abandon any claims to be able to report events *objectively*. It could be argued, for example, that journalism unencumbered by neutrality might actually be *more* objective because the audience knows where the journalist is coming from. Viewed this way, *Socialist Worker* or *Indymedia* would be more objective than *BBC News* or *Sky News* because the political and cultural assumptions of the first two are made explicit – and can therefore be taken into account by audiences – whereas any political or cultural assumptions involved in the last two remain implicit or hidden.

AGENDA SETTING

The term "agenda setting" is associated with a study by Maxwell McCombs and Donald Shaw of media coverage and voter attitudes in the 1968 US presidential election campaign. They found that the media exerted a considerable impact on voters' judgements of what were the salient issues of the campaign (McCombs and Shaw, 1972: 323–324). On the basis of this and similar studies, it is argued that, although the media

> "Between elections, if you're relevant and intelligent and know how to popularise an issue, you can help set the agenda."
> *Rupert Murdoch.*

than subjective, and as obviously as I could manage to be. (Cameron, 1968: 72)

Cameron felt that **subjectivity** could be important and that a journalist's attitude should be upfront and, therefore, open to scrutiny or counter-argument. Similarly, George Orwell argued that readers could be freed of the influence of a journalist's "bias" only if readers were *made aware* of it (cited in Pilger, 1998: 525). Certainly there is no mistaking the attitude of John Pilger, writing in the *Daily Mirror* about the bombing of Afghanistan under the unambiguous headline THIS WAR OF LIES GOES ON:

> "To journalists, like social scientists, the term 'objectivity' stands as a bulwark between themselves and critics."
>
> *Gaye Tuchman.*

> There was, and still is, no "war on terrorism". Instead, we have watched a variation of the great imperial game of swapping "bad" terrorists for "good" terrorists, while untold numbers of innocent people have paid with their lives: most of one village, whole families, a hospital, as well as teenage conscripts suitably dehumanised by the word "Taliban". (Pilger, 2001)

Some journalists who reject Pilger's upfront campaigning style nonetheless question the professional commitment to objectivity when covering bloody conflicts. After ITN reporter Michael Nicholson adopted an orphaned girl he met while covering the Bosnian war, he said: "No, I don't believe in this so-called objectivity. You can still report the facts. You can still be as close to the truth as any person can be and still show a commitment, an emotional anguish. I don't see them to be contradictory" (quoted in McLaughlin, 2002b: 154).

Former BBC correspondent Martin Bell has called for what he labels "a **journalism of attachment**" when it comes to reporting some armed conflicts, in recognition of the fact that journalists have the power to *affect* the events on which they are reporting. He explains:

JOURNALISM OF ATTACHMENT

> I am no longer sure about the notion of objectivity, which seems to me now to be something of an illusion and a shibboleth. When I have reported from the war zones, or anywhere else, I have done so with all the fairness and impartiality I could muster, and a scrupulous attention to the facts, but using my eyes and ears and mind and accumulated experience, which are surely the very essence of the subjective. (Bell, 1998: 16)

might not be able to tell us what to *think*, they have an influence on what we think *about*. But agenda setting has since been dismissed as "at best a hackneyed half-truth" on the grounds that it downplays the existence of multiple agendas by media organisations and voters alike (Wilson, 1996: 30).

Media coverage can impact upon other media coverage in a process of "inter-media agenda setting", according to David McKnight, who has analysed the way in which the relentless pursuit of certain hobbyhorses by some journalists working for Rupert Murdoch's empire can influence the tone of debate in the wider public sphere:

> The high pitched nature of Murdoch's tabloid media, and its overtly conservative stance, has skewed the country's terms of debate much further to the right than would otherwise be the case. This process of setting an agenda for competing news media is one of the secrets behind Murdoch's ability to influence politics in the US, Britain and Australia. (McKnight, 2013: 70)w

However, McQuail argues that the direction of flow in the agenda-setting model could perhaps be reversed, raising the possibility that, rather than *setting* the agenda, the media merely *reflect* the attitudes of voters. For him, agenda setting remains a "plausible but unproven idea" (McQuail, 2000: 456). Much the same can perhaps be said about other theories of media effects and about the postmodern tendency to shift attention away from media production and on to media consumption, thereby privileging "the instability of meaning and the interpretative horizons of the audience" (Stevenson, 2002: 29).

SUBJECTIVITY

The foregrounding of subjective experience – it's all about *me* – may have become increasingly fashionable in parts of the mainstream media (Dovey, 2000) as well as on social media, but for the most part news journalism remains, defiantly, a bastion of the authoritative-sounding "objective" approach. This is a deeply undesirable state of affairs for cultural theorist John Fiske, who argues that journalists would better reflect the messiness of reality if they became more open, more like the writers of TV soaps, for example:

Christiane Amanpour of CNN has reflected along similar lines without necessarily rejecting the concept of objectivity itself as entirely illusory:

> I have come to believe that objectivity means giving all sides a fair hearing, but not treating all sides equally. Once you treat all sides the same in a case such as Bosnia, you are drawing a moral equivalence between victim and aggressor. And from there it is a short step toward being neutral. And from there it's an even shorter step to becoming an accessory to all manners of evil; in Bosnia's case, genocide. So objectivity must go hand in hand with morality. (Quoted in Seib, 2002: 53)

Taking such arguments a stage further are the few journalists who step aside from their reporting role and agree to appear as formal witnesses, for example at international war crimes tribunals. BBC correspondent Jacky Rowland was cross-examined by former Yugoslav president Slobodan Milosevic when she testified at The Hague in 2002 about events in Kosovo three years earlier. Afterwards, she explained why she felt prepared to defy colleagues' arguments that such an apparent compromise of journalistic independence might pose a threat to future war correspondents:

> "Comment is free, but facts are sacred."
> *CP Scott.*

> I believe that journalists are essentially witnesses to the events they report on. My testimony to the Hague tribunal was an extension of this. . . . When I met the witness who was due to take the stand after me – a woman who had lost eight members of her family in an alleged massacre by Serbian police – I felt that a journalist's arguments for not testifying looked rather weak. (Rowland, 2002)

As Rowland's case suggests, adhering to traditional journalistic objectivity while remaining true to a sense of moral responsibility can be a difficult ethical balancing act. It is not an issue faced only by those who report on conflicts in faraway places.

OBJECTIVITY AND "THE ENEMY WITHIN"

From enemies without to "the enemy within", which was how Prime Minister Margaret Thatcher and her

Objectivity is authority in disguise: "objective" facts always support particular points of view and their "objectivity" can exist only as part of the play of power. But, more important, objective facts cannot be challenged: objectivity discourages audience activity and participation. Rather than being "objective", therefore, TV news should present *multiple perspectives* that, like those of soap opera, have as unclear a hierarchy as possible. . . . [The] reporters should be less concerned about telling the final truth of what has happened, and should present, instead, *different ways of understanding* it and the different points of view inscribed in those different ways. So, too, they should not disguise their processes of selection and editing, but should open them up to reveal news as a production, not as transparent reportage. (Fiske, 1989: 194, my emphasis)

This argument that what is called objective journalism tends to support the status quo echoes the comment of the radical US journalist IF (Izzy) Stone, who regarded objectivity largely as simply going along with the majority view (Guttenplan, 2012: 473). His personal solution was to establish his own alternative media precisely to challenge the "common sense" that he felt was too uncritically reproduced in much mainstream journalism. The oppositional reporting of Stone and others typically rejects objectivity in favour of taking sides, but that should not necessarily be seen as abandoning the quest for the best available version of the truth.

JOURNALISM OF ATTACHMENT

Martin Bell's call for a "journalism of attachment" when covering certain armed conflicts has been criticised for naïvety in apparently being based on a belief that different sides in war zones can be divided into "goodies and baddies". However, Bell himself did not see it necessarily as promoting anybody as a goodie. He argued that it was more about having the freedom to report on situations where there was a clear aggressor without resorting to the formulaic balance of the "On the one hand this, on the other hand that" approach that so frustrated him when covering fighting in the former Yugoslavia in the 1990s. But will the public really be better informed if journalists have leeway to emote all over the

Fleet Street cheerleaders characterised the coalminers who staged a year-long strike against job losses in 1984–85. Much mainstream media coverage of the miners' strike was framed by a few key themes, with three phrases being repeated throughout the dispute: uneconomic pits, picket line violence, the drift back to work (Hollingsworth, 1986: 242–285; Philo, 1991: 37–42; Williams, 2009 and 2014b). In contrast, a decade later another group of workers found their battle largely ignored. More than 300 Liverpool dockers were sacked for refusing to cross a picket line in 1995, and for two years their campaign for reinstatement won support and considerable media coverage in other countries, but remarkably few headlines in their own country's media. At the time, one docker told me matter-of-factly that the UK government had imposed a "news blackout" on the story – it was the only explanation he could come up with for the dearth of coverage. But most editors do not need to be *told* to ignore "boring" industrial disputes in favour of sexy news or celebrity gossip, as Pilger notes:

> Because the myths of the "market" have become received wisdom throughout the media, with millions of trade unionists dismissed as "dinosaurs", the dockers' story has been seen as a flickering curiosity of a bygone era. That their struggle represented more than half of all working people caught up in the iniquities of casual or part-time labour, making Britain the sweatshop of Europe, was not considered *real news.* (Pilger, 1998: 354, my emphasis)

Objectivity, then, is not simply concerned with *how* a particular story is covered, but also with *what* is selected as a potential story – and what is ignored, whether consciously or because it has not even been noticed. It sometimes seems as if issues come from nowhere to dominate headlines for a few weeks before disappearing again; mugging, "devil dogs", flesh-eating bugs, video nasties, juvenile crime, single mothers, paedophiles, "happy slapping", obesity, video games, online trolls, "benefit tourists", "health tourists", asylum seekers and Roma gypsies are just some examples of people or phenomena that have suddenly become the subject of **moral panics**, during which those on the receiving end (and anyone with expert knowledge of the field) are often appalled by an apparent absence of objective reporting. There

place – "There you go again, bleeding all over your typewriter", as a Bosnian soldier friend once chided Bell (1998: 22) – or simply by journalists reporting the facts they have been able to ascertain, attributing information and opinion, and being honest about how much we don't know?

MORAL PANICS

A moral panic could be described as the periodic response of "right-thinking people" to someone or something perceived as "other". Stanley Cohen researched the Mods and Rockers youth subcultures of the 1960s, and summarised moral panics thus:

> A condition, episode, person or group of persons emerges to become defined as a threat to societal values and interests; its nature is presented in a stylised and stereotypical fashion by the mass media; the moral barricades are manned by editors, bishops, politicians and other right-thinking people; socially accredited experts pronounce their diagnoses and solutions; ways of coping are evolved or (more often) resorted to; the condition then disappears, submerges or deteriorates and becomes more visible. Sometimes the object of the panic is quite novel and at other times it is something which has been in existence long enough, but suddenly appears in the limelight. Sometimes the panic passes over and is forgotten, except in folklore and collective memory; at other times it has more serious and long-lasting repercussions and might produce such changes as those in legal and social policy or even in the way society conceives itself. (Cohen, 1972: 9)

In a classic study of social responses to mugging in the 1970s, Stuart Hall and colleagues concluded that a moral panic about what was then perceived as a race-specific crime was created by a mutually reinforcing circle between powerful "primary definers" (police, judges, politicians and so on) and the media to effect "an ideological closure of the topic" (Hall et al, 1978: 75). This shorthand equation of black youths with mugging in the 1970s was echoed three decades on in the media's readiness to associate Muslims with terrorism (Richardson, 2001: 229; Karim, 2002: 102; Seib, 2002: 114). However, as with agenda setting, it is possible that media coverage of a "moral panic" *reflects* rather than *creates* a public demonisation was a memorable example when, after more than a year of hostile press coverage claiming that asylum seekers had brought a crime wave to parts of Kent, the Association of Chief Police Officers (ACPO) felt the need to point out that:

> In Dover, continual interest from the media, locally and nationally, has been focused on the "apparent" *increase* in crime since asylum seekers have been in the town. In line with general trends in Kent, the local commander was able to report an actual *reduction* in all aspects of reported crime over a three year period. This generally resulted in the national media not reporting anything as this was not what they had been told by some locals and was *not what their editors wanted.* (ACPO, 2001, my emphasis)

Even a brief item about the publication of a new dictionary was once given the headline: NOW ASYLUM SEEKERS INVADE OUR DICTIONARY (*Daily Express*, September 26 2002). Similar themes are frequently to be found in the *Daily Mail*: ASYLUM: YES, BRITAIN IS A SOFT TOUCH! (February 1 2001) and QUEUE HERE TO WORK IN BRITAIN (November 2 2013) being just two of countless front-page splashes about the UK being overrun by foreigners. The *Mail* has long had an agenda of moral outrage and is often accused of abandoning notions of objectivity in favour of peddling a particular "Middle England" world view. Anyone with different opinions runs the risk of being portrayed as unhinged or, worse, anti-British, as with the newspaper's notorious attack on the late father of Labour party leader Ed Miliband as THE MAN WHO HATED BRITAIN (*Daily Mail*, September 28 2013). In the words of one of the title's former journalists: "You kind of know what the obsessions are, and you very much know you've got to do a story in a specific way" (quoted in Beckett, 2001).

OBJECTIVITY AS A "STRATEGIC RITUAL"

The above examples might suggest that objective reporting is honoured more in the breach than in the actuality. But this does not mean the concept of

of a particular social grouping at a particular time. Or is it a more circular process of mutual reinforcement of popular views – a form of "common sense"?

In the 21st-century UK, asylum seekers have joined "a long list of convenient scapegoats including the unemployed, those claiming benefits and those registered as disabled", according to a study by Philo, Briant and Donald (2013: 164–165), which traces how sometimes hysterical media coverage can have "a crucial impact in legitimising the hostility toward and bullying of the new arrivals". As with other targets of moral panics, asylum seekers are rarely given the opportunity of speaking for themselves, it seems. Researchers found that in 69 major media reports on asylum in 2011, there were a total of 146 people or organisations quoted, of whom just five were the people at the centre of the story: asylum seekers themselves (Philo et al, 2013: 94). Such findings prompted the conclusion that by effectively denying "the right of the stigmatised and excluded to be heard", much media coverage was encouraging the authorities to adopt a punative rather than a humane approach to refugees and other marginalised groups (Philo et al, 2013: 169).

> "Who you gonna believe, me or your own eyes?"
> *Chico Marx.*

STRATEGIC RITUAL

Tuchman's strategic ritual of objectivity is perhaps more concerned with ritual than with objectivity, given that the journalist retains the power to select who to quote and what evidence to include. Similarly, while writing this book, I have chosen who to interview, which publications to cite and what issues to address. But I have not acted in a vacuum and, just as journalists act under the influence of constraints discussed in Chapter 2, so I have made my editorial choices within a wider context that includes input from the book's publisher, feedback from members of the "audience" and an evaluation of the wants and needs of the "market" (that's you, dear reader).

In the Harvey Nichols story discussed in this book, it could be argued that I followed the strategic ritual and that the story was true. It could also be argued that the story had little independent objective existence because most of the opinions or actions that helped stand the story up were *solicited* by me after I received the initial tip-off. My fingerprints were all over the story that appeared in the next day's papers, even if they could not be detected with the naked eye.

objective reporting has no resonance for working journalists. In my experience, *most* journalists, *most* of the time, *do* attempt to be objective, even if they don't use that word much (in the UK, anyway) and even though their objectivity can be very different depending on the culture, market and ownership of the news organisation employing them.

According to Gaye Tuchman, objectivity can be seen as a **strategic ritual** that journalists use as a form of defence mechanism. She identified four routine procedures that allow journalists to claim objectivity for their work:

- The presentation of conflicting possibilities;
- The presentation of supporting evidence;
- The judicious use of quotation marks;
- The structuring of information in an appropriate sequence. (Tuchman, 1972: 299–301)

In this way journalists may regard themselves as fulfilling a professional commitment to objectivity by taking the following steps before publishing:

- looking at both sides of a story;
- assessing conflicting claims;
- assessing the credibility of sources;
- looking for evidence;
- not publishing anything believed to be untrue;
- in short, seeing if the story stands up.

In the light of the above formula, let's revisit the Harvey Nichols story discussed in Chapter 4. The initial source was known to me as someone reliable, so I immediately took her call seriously. My experience (or "nose for news" as old hands might call it) informed me it was a potentially newsworthy story because of the high-profile nature of the Harvey Nichols store at the time. After looking at the offending posters to confirm what I had been told, I suggested to my source that there might be a story if someone were to make a formal complaint. So, from her I obtained copies of several letters of complaint sent to the company and the Advertising Standards Agency. I also spoke to Harvey Nichols' PR people to get their side of the story and consulted

The formula of presenting conflicting versions in a story means that journalists – who are rarely themselves experts in a particular subject – do not normally have to decide between competing truth claims. As Keeble notes, reporters use sources to distance themselves from stories (Keeble, 2001a: 44). Sometimes journalists *do* privilege one source, or truth claim, over another. For example, in this chapter I have quoted ACPO as giving "the facts" about crime and asylum seekers. But is their account more objectively true than the lurid press headlines? Yes, in the sense that the ACPO version is based on crime statistics. But can such figures be regarded as objective when they are based only on *reported* rather than *actual* crime? By following the strategic ritual and stating from where information comes, and when it is disputed, journalists can absolve themselves from the responsibility of deciding who is right and who is wrong on such issues. As one journalist put it rather candidly, "We don't deal in facts but in attributed opinions" (quoted in Gans, 1980: 246).

Following Tuchman, the concept of the "strategic ritual" has subsequently been applied by academics as a way of helping to explain other facets of journalistic practice, including verification (Shapiro et al, 2013) (see below). There also exists a strategic ritual of "emotionality", according to Karin Wahl-Jorgensen (2013: 141), whereby emotional expression is allowed to appear in journalistic accounts but only within certain parameters, being largely "outsourced" and attributed to the protagonists within stories rather than the journalists themselves.

VERIFICATION

To establish the veracity (or otherwise) of a story, allegation or piece of information, journalists are expected to make a series of checks for accuracy. Such checks might include consulting official documents, seeking expert opinion, verifying the authenticity of a Twitter account, asking people if they have really made the comments they are said to have made and double-checking how to spell their name. However, according to research by Shapiro et al (2013), journalistic attempts at verification can be seen – rather like objectivity itself – as a form of "strategic ritual" in which journalists take certain steps to check certain facts more to deflect potential criticism than to achieve absolute truth. Their study concludes that the cuttings for background on the firm. I approached a senior elected member of the local council's women's committee to check whether or not she would be proposing that the council itself might lodge a complaint. She gave some strong quotes and said that she would indeed be proposing such a course of action. So I had some complainants, meaning the Advertising Standards Authority would have to investigate the issue; I had opinion from someone in a position of some authority; I had background information on the company involved; and I had a comment from the company, disputing claims that the posters were offensive. In other words, the story stood up.

If a story stands up, it will be written with the journalist taking care to give both sides. The journalist will make it clear when claims are disputed, will attribute information and opinion to external sources, and will not mix what appear to be facts with the journalist's own comments. At least, that is what *usually* happens. Things are not always quite that simple. For a start, aren't there often more than *two* sides to a story?

Even looking at "both sides" is not always strictly adhered to. One of my early assignments on one local paper was to report on residents' complaints about a group of Gypsies – the usual allegations of theft, defecation and general lowering of the value of property. Eyebrows were raised in the newsroom when I said I was going out to ask the Gypsies themselves for their version of events. It seemed that a comment from the police or local authority was thought sufficient to balance the story. But speaking to the people involved not only got a better story – the Gypsies threatening to move their caravans on to hallowed town-centre grassland if they continued to be hounded from pillar to post – but also revealed that many of them were more local than some of the "locals" who objected to them, having actually been born in the area (*Harrogate Advertiser*, September 23 1989). It was nothing special, it was just reporting. But, several decades on, it remains relatively unusual to see Gypsies (or asylum seekers, for that matter) quoted in response to allegations against them. There are exceptions, of course, but as a rule such communities tend to be rendered voiceless in mainstream media.

> **"Don't believe anyone, not even us."**
> *Radio B92 slogan.*

journalistic commitment to accuracy and verification is, in reality, a compromised professional norm whereby:

> A small, easily checkable, fact needs to be checked; a larger but greyer assertion, not so much – unless it is defamatory. Thus, verification for a journalist is a rather different animal from verification in scientific method, which would hold every piece of data subject to a consistent standard of observation and replication. (Shapiro et al, 2013: 668–669)

Despite such limitations, verification is central to the concept of objective reporting, as Carrie Figdor puts it:

> The ultimate aim of an objective news report is, of course, truth, but many statements in objective news reports may turn out to be false, despite our best efforts to verify. This is why it is not necessary for an objective news report to consist entirely of *true* statements. What is necessary is that it consist entirely of *objectively verified* statements. . . . It follows that the inclusion of a statement in an objective news report implies it is supported by sufficient objective evidence: it's not there because the reporter made a lucky guess or wishes it were true. (Figdor, 2010: 154, emphasis in original)

COMMON SENSE

Journalists use their common sense to assess whether something has the ring of truth about it. But common sense itself can be seen as socially, culturally and historically constructed, rendering it highly questionable as any sort of "objective" test. Useful here is the concept of hegemony, the way in which a dominant class is said not merely to rule a society but also to exert moral and intellectual leadership, albeit contested (Gramsci, 1971: 57). Hegemony goes beyond mere manipulation of opinion to saturate society and become regarded as "common sense" (Williams, 1980: 37–38). This does not mean that common sense contains *no* truths; rather, that common sense is "an ambiguous, contradictory and multiform concept, and *to refer to common sense as a confirmation of truth is a nonsense*" (Gramsci, 1971: 423, my emphasis).

PRAGMATIC OBJECTIVITY

For Stephen Ward (2010: 145), "traditional objectivity is a spent ethical force, doubted by journalist and academic".

Given widespread social prejudice against outsiders ("them"), is it not *more* rather than *less* important for journalists ("us") to get their side(s) of the story?

CHECKING THE FACTS

Reporters routinely assess conflicting claims, weigh the credibility of sources and check the facts by looking for evidence and seeking **verification**.

JOURNALISM FROM MULTIPLE PERSPECTIVES

But sources are not equal. If the police say that three people have been killed in a road accident, then journalists will report that "fact" without first feeling the need to drive to the scene, count the bodies and feel for a pulse. But if a motorist calls the newsroom with the same story, then a reporter will check it out – by calling the police – before reporting it. Checking the facts of a story begins with comparing what we have been told with what we "know" of the world; with our knowledge and experience; asking whether, at a **common sense** level, it has the ring of truth about it. If it doesn't, a potential story might be dropped at the outset as not being worth further effort.

If a potential story survives this first informal credibility test, we might check the facts further by looking at published sources, by observing matters at first hand, by talking to people involved and/or by consulting independent observers or experts. If the story involves an allegation, or even merely a hint of some kind of wrongdoing, it becomes even more important to seek independent verification. During their Watergate investigation in the 1970s, *Washington Post* reporters Carl Bernstein and Bob Woodward developed "an unwritten rule" whereby the newspaper would not publish an allegation of criminal activity unless two additional sources confirmed what they were told by their secret whistleblower, Deep Throat (Bernstein and Woodward, [1974] 2005: 79). Their rule-of-thumb has passed into journalistic terminology as the "three-source rule" (Brennan, 2003: 123).

Despite checking facts with one, two, three or even more sources, however, journalists surprisingly

In response, he has developed the concept of pragmatic objectivity by which, although acknowledging that a "perfect knowledge of reality" may not be possible, we can see the benefit of "imperfect journalists" being required to test information and justify their selection and interpretation (Ward, 2010: 149). In this sense, the task of pragmatic objectivity within journalism is:

> to develop methods for testing the story's selection of alleged facts, sources, and story angles. The goal of the objective newsroom is to produce well-grounded interpretations, tested through criteria appropriate to the evaluation of journalistic inquiry, that is, criteria that detect bias, challenge alleged facts and viewpoints, ask for evidence, and prevent reckless, uncritical reporting. (Ward, 2010: 147)

A form of reporting, in other words, that goes beyond the back-covering stance of the "strategic ritual", while recognising that it may still not be possible to ascertain the truth, the whole truth, and nothing but the truth. In articulating this as a new philosophical approach to objectivity, many journalists might feel that Ward is simply describing (in more academic language) what a good newsroom does anyway, every day.

frequently publish things that turn out to be untrue. Inaccuracies might appear because sources do not (yet) know the full story. Check out early coverage of one of the biggest news stories of the 21st century, the attack on the World Trade Centre on September 11 2001. Initial reports suggested that 10,000 people had been killed (*Sun*, September 12 2001; *Daily Mail*, September 13 2001). For weeks the news media were still reporting that up to 7,000 people had died, but by November that year New York police had put the death toll at 3,702 (Lipton, 2001). A year after the attack the official death toll had been reduced to 2,801 (Lipton, 2002) and in 2003 the tally was revised down further to 2,752 (BBC, 2003). By the fifth anniversary of the attack the official death toll was put at 2,749 and doubts were expressed about whether the precise number would ever be known for certain (Tutek, 2006). Yet that was a story on which countless journalists were working and about which the authorities were more than willing to speak to the media; how many more inaccuracies might creep into coverage if newsrooms are understaffed and/or if the authorities keep silent?

Inaccuracies might appear if a journalist has too little time (or inclination) to check an assumption, an old cutting or a press release. Inaccuracies might appear if a journalist misunderstands statistics or fails to spot that statistics have been misused by a source (Blastland and Dilnot, 2007). Inaccuracies might appear because a source has set out to deceive a journalist (Lagan, 2007; Morris, 2007). And inaccuracies might appear because a foreign correspondent, for example, might be under such time pressure to file for multiple outlets and platforms that they cannot go and see things for themselves, relying instead on regurgitating copy fed to them from thousands of miles away in London (Harcup, 1996).

> **"What they call 'objectivity' usually is seeing things the way everybody else sees them."**
> *Izzy Stone.*

VERIFICATION AND SOCIAL MEDIA

Sometimes people try to trick journalists by deliberately supplying false information, whether for reasons of propaganda, mischief or simply for the fun of it, and the media's increasing use of user-generated content has opened up new channels by which misinformation can enter the public sphere. Many journalists have been caught out by reproducing an erroneous "fact" that somebody has planted on Wikipedia, for example, and pictures from disaster movies are often sent to rolling TV news channels by viewers pretending to have witnessed a major breaking event. But when it comes to verifying such material, social media is a help as well as a hindrance, argues Neal Mann:

> People have always tried to fool news organisations and the prevalence of social media has really increased that, but we actually have more tools at our disposal to cross-reference and check if it's legitimate or not. You're looking for: is there any potential here for geolocation to find out a bit more information about where they are? Can you cross-reference any images they've posted with Google Earth or Google Street View? And simple things like what's the weather like and does the clothing fit?
>
> There is a danger of being fooled but with new media you can do more verification than you would traditionally have been able to do. And the great thing about Twitter over traditional sources is that you can see who they've engaged with over time. Who are the people they follow and who follow them? Are they people you trust? How long have they been on Twitter? What other social media platforms are they on? Are there links to them from legitimate places? There's a lot of simple checks that you can put in place and you can have those done in under a minute or two minutes.

Accuracy is more important than speed, according to Jemima Kiss, and that means verification:

> There's a bit of a fightback in response to the superficial viral web, whereby news organisations are realising that for real credibility they need to not try and compete with the gutter-scraping rewriting blog culture, which is very tired. They need to focus on proper original journalism, which includes

verifying information and skilfully explaining and summarising a breaking news event by writing and reporting their own stories.

Verifying information from user-generated content and social media is considered further in Chapters 6 and 14.

"SITUATIONS ARE ALWAYS COMPLICATED"

The Leveson inquiry heard evidence that inaccuracies sometimes appear in news stories because reporters have succumbed to pressure from on high to *make* a story stand up. I once came across a tabloid hack trying desperately to find non-existent irate white parents to condemn their local authority serving curry for school dinner, just because his editor had apparently already thought up a possible headline: WE'LL HAVE NAAN OF THAT! Mercifully, I don't think that particular story ever appeared; it had just been an editor's passing fancy at morning conference, later overtaken by the day's real events. Pure invention remains the exception in journalism, although Abul Taher warns: "A lot of people end up doctoring the truth for a good story. It's a job that is a daily ritual of moral and intellectual compromise."

A compromise it may be but, however imperfectly, most reporters seem to retain some sense of objectivity in their everyday routines. Jane Merrick gives a not untypical journalist's response when asked about objective reporting:

> When I sit down to write a story I never think, "Is this objective?" But I'm always aware of being fair and balanced and having both sides of a story. I'm not sure you *can* be objective. I've never really thought about it, to be honest.

Martin Wainwright *has* thought about it, and for him objectivity means approaching stories with an open mind, giving all sides their say, including as much contextual information as possible, and trying to show what underlies people's actions. This leads him to be critical of the more heart-on-sleeve style of journalism sometimes associated with the likes of James Cameron and John Pilger:

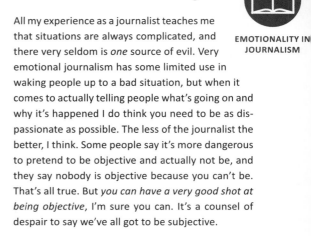

EMOTIONALITY IN JOURNALISM

> All my experience as a journalist teaches me that situations are always complicated, and there very seldom is *one* source of evil. Very emotional journalism has some limited use in waking people up to a bad situation, but when it comes to actually telling people what's going on and why it's happened I do think you need to be as dispassionate as possible. The less of the journalist the better, I think. Some people say it's more dangerous to pretend to be objective and actually not be, and they say nobody is objective because you can't be. That's all true. But *you can have a very good shot at being objective*, I'm sure you can. It's a counsel of despair to say we've all got to be subjective.

One solution to the conundrum, according to Stephen Ward (2010), may be to develop a more **pragmatic objectivity**, which puts philosophical debate about absolute truth to one side in favour of journalists developing working methods to test facts and, as far as is possible in the cut and thrust of the real world, to limit innacurate, harmful reporting. One of the best ways of guarding against inaccurate reporting is to acknowledge how easy it is to make errors, as Anna McKane (2006: 86) suggests: "Probably a general assumption that you have got it wrong, rather than a general assumption that you have got it right, would help. So develop the habit of checking everything three times." That is advice that would no doubt have appealed to George "examine your words well" Eliot, whose real name was Mary Ann Evans . . . until she changed the Mary Ann to Marian, apparently (Drabble and Stringer, 1990: 176). One of the very first things that journalists must learn is to get people's names right; the fact that one person might have several different names only emphasises how tricky even such a seemingly simple task can be. As US journalism professor Thomas Patterson (2012) puts it, "knowledge does not always yield precise answers" because our research might reveal how much we still don't know, meaning that "Sometimes, the effect of knowledge is to unearth new questions or uncertainties". Only sometimes?

SUMMARY

Objective reporting is commonly understood to involve separating verifiable facts from subjective feelings. Journalists' use of objectivity has been described as a "strategic ritual" to distance themselves from stories; a pre-emptive defence against the possibility of being accused of bias or lack of professionalism. This formula involves presenting conflicting possibilities and supporting evidence, with attributed opinion and information, in an appropriate sequence. The objectivity norm and the related concept of impartiality have been challenged for being impossible to achieve; for ignoring the existence of multiple perspectives; and even for being undesirable in conflicts between right and wrong. Nonetheless, while acknowledging that absolute objectivity may be as elusive as absolute truth, most journalists appear to retain some sense of objectivity when assessing whether or not a story stands up. The procedures established within newsrooms for such verification have been described as a form of "pragmatic objectivity" and are constantly being updated to take account of the latest technological tools available to audiences and journalists alike.

QUESTIONS

If objectivity is impossible, does it make any sense to aim for it?
Is biased journalism always inaccurate?
How would broadcast-style impartiality alter UK newspapers, magazines and online journalism?
How might reporting include multiple perspectives rather than just two sides?
Are objectivity and impartiality outdated concepts in the age of Twitter?

WHAT WOULD YOU DO?

You are a reporter and are sent by your news organisation to cover a speech by a senior politician; or, more likely, you are given the text of the speech and are asked to cover it from your desk. The bulk of the speech is concerned with technical or procedural issues of little or no interest to anyone not directly involved in the party political system. However, it includes a passage in which one section of the population (members of a particular religious or ethnic minority community, for example) is accused of being responsible for most anti-social behaviour in an area and of fuelling inter-communal tension and even violence. You happen to live in the area in question (and/or have family and friends who do) and you have reason to believe that the situation is far more complicated than is suggested in the speech on which you have been asked to report. What would you do?

HOW MIGHT YOU TACKLE THIS ISSUE?

FURTHER READING

Worth reading in their original forms are Bell (1998) on the journalism of attachment, Tuchman (1972) on the strategic ritual, Ward (2010) on pragmatic objectivity and Figdor (2010) on whether objective news is possible. Edited academic collections with readable and illuminating contributions covering objectivity include Kieran (1998), Bromley and O'Malley (1997) and Tumber (1999). McLaughlin (2002b) has an interesting discussion of objectivity, conflict and the "journalism of attachment", based in part on interviews with war correspondents. For a more theoretical perspective, Stevenson (2002) explores various Marxist explanations of the media – touching on objectivity, hegemony and moral panics – as well as the postmodernist challenge to the concept of the truth. Critcher (2002) subjects the concepts of moral panic and agenda setting to critical scrutiny within the context of the *News of the World*'s "name and shame" campaign on paedophilia. Frost (2010) provides a brief practical account of the basics of reporting and fact-checking. Handy hints on reporting accurately on – and questioning – anything to do with numbers, statistics and averages can be found in the entertaining book *The Tiger That Isn't* by Blastland and Dilnot (2007); Randall (2011) and McKane (2014) also have useful sections on the subject. John Pilger's (1998) eloquent if holier-than-thou critique of the world amounts to a sustained challenge to most of what passes for objective journalism in the mainstream media, and Nick Davies (2008) offers a similarly bleak view of how much of the fourth estate fails to get to the truth of many issues. BBC guidance on accuracy, impartiality and much, much more can be found on the BBC College of Journalism website (www.bbc.co.uk/academy/journalism/values). Finally, Dick (2013) offers pointers on verifying online sources.

TOP THREE TO TURN TO

Martin Bell (1998) 'The journalism of attachment', *Media Ethics*
Gaye Tuchman (1972) 'Objectivity as a strategic ritual…', *American Journal of Sociology*
Stephen Ward (2010) 'Inventing objectivity…', *Journalism Ethics: A Philosophical Approach*

SOURCES FOR SOUNDBITES

Eliot, 1859: 150; Bernstein, 1992: 24; Wilde, *Importance of Being Earnest*, Act 1; Orwell, quoted in Pilger, 1998: 525; Murdoch, in Channel 4, 1998; Tuchman, 1972: 297; Scott, quoted in O'Malley and Soley, 2000: 23; Marx, *Duck Soup*; B92, quoted in Seib, 2002: 99; Stone, quoted in Guttenplan, 2012: 473.

CHAPTER 6

"BE CURIOUS AND SCEPTICAL": JOURNALISTS AS INVESTIGATORS

Like many journalists, when the UK's freedom of information legislation eventually came into force in 2005, I was keen to have a go at seeing how effective it would prove in shining a bit of light into the darker corners of central and local government. While some targeted state secrets concerning wars and rumours of wars, and others went straight for the juicy scandal of politicians' expenses, I embarked on a more modest project. That was to find out how (and just how much of) the public's money is spent on corporate hospitality by the unelected people running one of the country's numerous quangos (quasi-autonomous non-government organisations). Quangoland is a place populated by the great and the good, who sit on each other's boards and spend an estimated £100 billion of taxpayers' money every year without the hindrance of elections or democratic accountability. So I used the Freedom of Information (FOI) Act to ask one such quango (a regional development agency called Yorkshire Forward, since disbanded) how much of our cash it was spending on corporate hospitality – wining, dining, hosting guests in boxes at big sporting events, that kind of thing – and for the names of the recipients of such generosity. In response to my initial FOI request, I was told that people's names were exempt information under data protection laws, and that even if it wasn't exempt, accessing such information would simply be too expensive, allowing the development agency to also refuse on cost grounds.

To cut a (very) long story short, I persevered with an internal appeal to Yorkshire Forward itself, followed by a referral to the Information Commissioner, and finally an appeal to the Information Tribunal. Three years later, after exchanges of correspondence and evidence amounting to well over 300 pages, I won a victory of sorts when the tribunal dismissed as "absurd" the argument of Yorkshire Forward and

INVESTIGATIVE JOURNALISM

Investigative journalism is placed at the "most active" extreme of the continuum of journalistic initiative by Denis McQuail (2013: 104), at the opposite end of the scale from churning out scarcely rewritten press releases or listing forthcoming events. Yet the very concept of investigative journalism is a problematic one, as Mark Hanna notes: "The term 'investigative journalist' smacks of pretension, and has few ardent adherents among practitioners. But it helps denote the self-motivation, the experience and knowledge, the methodology and the set of skills which sustain a journalist through a complex, lengthy assignment" (Hanna, in Franklin et al, 2005: 122–123). The term retains some currency among both practitioners and academics as denoting a particular type of journalistic inquiry, as defined by John Ullmann and Steve Honeyman:

> It is the reporting, through one's own work product and initiative, matters of importance which some persons or organisations wish to keep secret. The three basic elements are that the investigation be the work of the reporter, not a report of an investigation made by someone else; that the subject of the story involves something of reasonable importance to the reader or viewer; and that others are attempting to hide these matters from the public. (Quoted in Northmore, 2001: 188–189)

Such a definition is not without its own problems, particularly its reliance on the formulation "something of reasonable importance to the reader or viewer", which can be taken to mean anything from an obscure arms deal (for *Panorama* viewers, at least until it was forced to become a more populist programme) to the recreational drug-use of a Z-list celebrity (for redtop readers).

For Stephen Dorril, the methodology of investigative journalism "is characterised by in-depth and near-obsessional the Information Commissioner that individuals' names amounted to significant personal information that was exempt from release. But, although I won on the big principle, the tribunal also ruled that the information need not actually be released because collating it would cost the quango more than the £450 limit set by the Act. That wasn't the end of it, though. I put in a couple of fresh FOI requests: one, to get the names of those wined and dined over a shorter (and therefore cheaper) period of time; two, to discover how much the quango had spent on legal fees to help it resist my original request. This time I got the names I wanted within 20 working days and I also got the answer that Yorkshire Forward had given lawyers £19,641 of public money to argue that it would have cost too much public money to tell the public how our money was being spent.

Three years is not a realistic timescale for most journalistic inquiries, although the absurdity of the whole business allowed me to get a couple of stories out of it: QUANGO SPENDING IS A WELL-KEPT SECRET (*Guardian*, February 20 2008) and PUBLIC PRICED OUT OF GETTING THE FACTS (*Guardian*, March 5 2008). But not all requests take so long and, in any event, even old stories can sometimes become news, especially with a combination of lateral thinking and careful timing. For example, knowing that March 2014 would be 30 years since the start of the 1984–85 miners' strike, several months earlier I used FOI to discover internal BBC documents about controversial coverage of the dispute on TV news, allowing time for the material to be obtained, analysed, and written up for a book chapter (Harcup, 2014b) and a news story that were both hung on the peg of the 30th anniversary: DOCUMENTS REVEAL BBC CONCERN AT 'IMBALANCE' OVER COVERAGE OF MINERS' STRIKE 'BATTLE OF ORGREAVE' (*Press Gazette*, March 4 2014). The raw content of such material does not normally make a story on its own because it still needs to be contextualised, meaning that FOI has not so much replaced other forms of **investigative journalism** as become an additional method. Use of FOI has not done away with the need for human sources of information, nor does it mean there is no

> "Don't expose people who earn less than you do."
> *Paul Foot.*

research, dogged determination, accumulated knowledge, team-effort (though some of our best . . . have been loners), the crucial support of editors and the space to pursue stories not because of notions of the truth but because it might turn out to be interesting" (Dorril, 2000). The extent to which investigative skills are, in essence, the same as those used by "ordinary" journalists – but with added scepticism – varies according to which practitioner is consulted. However, it should also be considered that elements of investigation can come into otherwise simple reportage and that many journalists who conduct investigations also find themselves working on relatively straightforward news stories; investigative journalists and ordinary journalists not only inhabit the same universe, they may actually be the same people (as personified in this chapter by Deborah Wain).

CONSTRAINTS

For Stephen Dorril, investigative journalism enjoyed "a brief bloom in the sixties, flowered for a short period in the seventies, badly wilted in the eighties and is now effectively dead" (Dorril, 2000). Not dead but clearly in decline, according to Hanna, who blames structural changes within the media since the 1970s for "shrivelling" investigative journalism at its roots; changes such as relentless cost-cutting, under-staffing, speed-up and, on television, a ruthless drive for ratings (Hanna, 2000: 2–7). Working in such conditions effectively undermines the "relative autonomy" enjoyed by journalists (Manning, 2001: 105), an autonomy necessary if the time and space are to be made available for investigations. After all, investigative journalists might be seen as mavericks even by their colleagues, never mind their employers. As Tom Bowyer notes, investigations can frequently be unproductive, and "even the rarity of success earns the investigative reporter only the irksome epithet of being obsessional or dangerous" (quoted in Spark, 1999: 17). It has been claimed that today's recruits to journalism are "quickly schooled into understanding that investigative journalism is basically a myth and that their success is strongly related to their accuracy and skill in applying journalistic techniques and formulas" (Harrison, 2000: 113). Constraints, including the law, are discussed in more detail in Chapter 2.

need for friendly relations with a press officer; after all, if you are using the Act to uncover a scoop, you don't really want the requested material suddenly released to all your rivals at the same time as you get it, do you? So FOI is not a cure-all, but it is a useful tool that is available for all journalists (and other citizens) to use. Believe me, if I can use it, so can you.

"THERE'S SOMETHING IN THIS"

At a national, regional and local level FOI has been used to make public otherwise private information. This can range from how many police officers have been arrested for various offences (a favourite of the regional press, and always a worryingly large number each year) to the number of times a locksmith was called because MPs had locked themselves out of their parliamentary offices (since you ask, see MPs NEEDED LOCKSMITHS FOR PARLIAMENTARY OFFICES 382 TIMES IN A YEAR, *Huffington Post*, November 6 2013). Rather more serious use of official figures is made by "data journalism", which involves the collection and manipulation of data from existing or specially created databases or spreadsheets, looking for patterns, trends, mistakes or missing information that might make interesting items, and often using visualisation and/or interactive techniques to display the resulting stories. "They have been there all the time, sitting in the data", observes Mike Ward. "It's just needed a journalist to ask the right questions, run the right sequence of numbers" (Ward, 2002: 69). Getting hold of such information is easier thanks to FOI legislation, but it still requires time and skill in analysing it and, as with all journalism, it needs to be borne in mind that apparent connections may be as much coincidental as causal.

One journalist who used FOI to great effect, despite not being a specialist or working for a particularly investigative outfit, is Deborah Wain. During her time on the weekly *Doncaster Free Press* she revealed how one of the UK's biggest education projects had spent vast sums of public money on luxury travel, hospitality, consultants' bills, a huge

FOI AS INVESTIGATIVE JOURNALISM?

"All journalism should be investigative, from football to cookery."
John Pilger.

FOI AS LAZY JOURNALISM?

THE PUBLIC INTEREST

The UK government-appointed Nolan Committee on Standards in Public Life declared that "a free press using fair techniques of investigative journalism is an indispensable asset to our democracy", contributing to "the preservation of standards in public life" (quoted in Doig, 1997: 210). But, as we saw in Chapter 2, it can be difficult to decide what precisely is in the public interest, especially when the phrase is so freely bandied about by those on all sides of a supposed scandal. As McQuail notes:

> The underlying thinking is that freedom to publish, even where it harms individuals, can be justified only where a true public interest can be argued to exist, but not otherwise. In this context, public interest refers to such matters as increasing transparency, exposing wrong-doing, holding political and economic power to account, expressing public opinion and protecting the interests of citizens, etc. However, this line is a very difficult one to draw, especially where it concerns political figures, celebrities or others prominent in public life, whose entire private life can have implications for public conduct. (McQuail, 2013: 32)

It might be time, he suggests, to replace legalistic notions of the public interest with a broader conceptualisation of the "common good" informed by human rights thinking about the benefits of relatively open spaces for public expression and communication (McQuail, 2013: 33). The public interest and the public good are discussed further in Chapter 13.

FACTS

Investigative reporting typically abandons the journalistic convention of allegation-and-denial, or attributed opinions, in favour of an attempt "to establish facts which, if possible, decide the issue one way or the other" (Spark, 1999: 1). However, facts themselves are far from unproblematic. There does not exist some universally accepted supply of facts – just lying around waiting to be gathered – that will decide most issues. Individual facts might as well not even exist until a journalist "puts them into relation with other facts", according to Cockburn (1967: 147), who then goes even further: "In that sense all stories are written backwards – they are supposed to begin with the facts and develop from salary hike for the chief executive, and even a personalised number plate for a subsidised BMW X5 car – all in one of the poorest parts of the UK. "I don't think I really saw it as an investigation as such at the start, I saw it as a story and follow-ups", Wain says about her probe into Doncaster Education City, a £100 million partnership between a council and a further education college. Over an 18-month period she wrote between 20 and 30 stories, gradually uncovering the reality that lay behind the scheme's big budgets and grandiose promises, and eventually picking up one of the best awards that a journalist can win. We will come to that, but first, where did the story come from?

> We had an anonymous letter from an insider at the college, pages and pages of allegations. I was quite shocked by it. The temptation is to file it away in a desk somewhere, but I was also hearing snippets of information from other sources that made me think, "There's something in this". It was just a question of where to start.

> I got wind of the fact there was a report by the Learning and Skills Council into the deficit at the college, and that was the tangible thing I was looking for. So I used FOI to request that report, which confirmed that the college had gone from being very robust financially into being significantly in the red, and the purpose of the report was to look into financial problems.

Having got hold of official confirmation that questions were being asked about the project's finances, Wain's story was not just standing up – it was running. One thing led to another:

> The thing about the investigation is that there were so many different strands to it. After the initial couple of stories were published people came to me from the inside, again with lots of extreme allegations. You can't always use what your sources are giving you because the information is too specific and you might betray the source. But the same things kept coming up.

> FOI is the key; I probably put in half a dozen requests to the council, the college and the Learning and Skills Council. I managed to firm up most of the stuff from official sources through FOI, getting the facts and figures.

there, but in reality they begin from a journalist's point of view, a conception, and it is the point of view from which the facts are subsequently organised." Not all journalists would agree, but it is certainly true that the facts are sometimes disputed all the way to the libel courts and even the prison cell. Even when the existence of a specific fact is accepted, its relevance – or the interpretation placed upon it – may not be. Investigative journalists may therefore find themselves piling fact upon fact on what turn out to be shifting sands. Even so, the very pursuit of the facts, and the reporter's willingness sometimes to adopt the role of accuser, challenges the notions of formal balance and impartiality that are so important to much conventional reporting (Manning, 2001: 70). Facts and truth are discussed further in Chapter 5.

DEMOCRACY

For Hugo de Burgh, the investigative journalist plays a vital democratic role as "the tribune of the commoner, exerting on her or his behalf the right to know, to examine and to criticise" (de Burgh, 2000: 315). It is a tempting image, particularly for those of us who have tried our hands at such stories. But how democratic is it really? Quite apart from legal and economic constraints, there are other limitations on the democratic claims of investigative journalism. *Who* decides what is worthy of investigation, and on what basis? Some stories are undoubtedly seen as more sexy than others, and if there is the possibility of good pictures, film or audio material, then so much the better. Similarly, some people are seen as more deserving of sympathy – again it helps if they are photogenic – while others are easier to paint as villains.

Of course, investigative journalism can achieve results such as the jailing of corrupt politicians, but could that not be seen as perpetuating a myth that society is divided into a large number of fundamentally good people and a smaller number of fundamentally bad people? Where is the investigative journalism into *structural* forces in society? Largely notable for its absence. Instead, particularly on television, we are more likely to see personalised stories of goodies, baddies and heroic reporters. Hanna challenges us to consider whether, rather than exemplifying a democratic spirit, even the heyday of UK investigative

> "You have to be really tenacious and thorough, and just not give up."
> *Deborah Wain.*

Parallel with this, she was also speaking off-the-record to employees and on-the-record to their trade union officials, who were usually more willing to speak out publicly about staff unrest. That was not all:

> I also spent quite a lot of time going through the college board's papers in the college library. The papers are available but nobody ever goes. They had to hunt them out for me and I got a frosty reception. I had to sit in the basement, it was the middle of summer and I was sweltering, and at one point I thought I was going to be locked in overnight, I thought they might forget I was down there.

How did she manage to find the time, given that she was working in a small, understaffed newsroom within an empire (Johnston Press) not renowned for investing seriously in labour-intensive journalism over the past decade? What's more, at the time she was employed for just three days a week and had responsibility for the local health beat as well as being a general reporter. Wain explains the art of being a journalistic juggler in a matter-of-fact way:

> On Wednesday afternoons when the paper had been put to bed I would go and do my research. I'm quite used to multi-tasking and juggling numerous stories, and fitting in research as and when, really. I think as you get more experienced you can bash out quite a few stories on a day-to-day basis and create time for stuff that you are particularly interested in.

Working under a supportive news editor who had an interest in the mechanics of local government clearly helped, but Wain was also motivated by discovering a lack of public accountability as well as by her love of a good story:

> The thing that struck me was these huge sums of money. I think the college's spending was quite unaccounted for. There are people within the council and the college who have pooh-poohed the work that I've done because they don't get it. They don't get why people are asking questions, because they are so used to talking about these huge sums of money, £10 million here, £1 million there.

journalism in reality offered an "elitist and pompous" form of journalism (Hanna, 2000: 16). But perhaps more open forms of investigation can help challenge notions of elitism, as Paul Lewis argues:

> Investigative journalists traditionally work in the shadows, quietly squirrelling away information until they have garnered enough to stand-up their story. . . . But an alternative modus operandi is insurgent. . . . Investigating in the open means telling the people what you are looking for and asking them to help search. It means telling them what you have found, too, as you find it. It works because of the ease with which information can be shared via the internet, where social media is enabling collaborative enterprise between paid journalists and citizens who are experts in their realm. (Lewis, 2011: 31–32)

> "Remember, *All the President's Men* was so unusual they had to make a movie out of it."
> *Greg Palast.*

I like to come at a story from all angles. I found it really fascinating once I got into it, it became a challenge to try and peel back the layers. I think you have to be really tenacious and thorough, and just not give up. I enjoy storytelling so I really wanted to get to the story. I still do really, because I think there's still more to come.

There may indeed be more to come, but she had already done enough to be declared the joint winner of the 2007 Paul Foot Award for investigative journalism.

THE REALITIES OF INVESTIGATING

As a quietly spoken woman working part-time on a small local weekly rag, Deborah Wain fits none of the stereotypes of pushy investigative journalists as portrayed in movies such as *All the President's Men*, *Defence of the Realm* and *The Insider*, although she certainly has what Duncan Campbell (2011: 228) describes as investigative journalism's essential tools: "an inquiring mind, a lack of deference and great patience". As it happens, Paul Foot himself had watched *The Insider* the night before I turned up at his home to interview him for the first edition of this book. That film's portrayal of the intense relationship between journalist and source clearly struck a chord. "That's the key to all this, the source", he told me almost as soon as I walked through the door.

The Insider tells the true story of how journalist Lowell Bergman (played by Al Pacino) persuaded tobacco scientist Jeffrey Wigand (Russell Crowe) to defy a confidentiality agreement and blow the whistle on his former employers. As they battle against corporate lawyers and frightened TV executives, the pair go through all the emotions of trust, mistrust, and trust again before finally getting to tell the story. At one point the tormented Wigand tells the journalist: "I'm just a commodity to you, aren't I? I could be anything worth putting on between the commercials." Bergman promises not to leave his source "hanging out to dry" (Roth and Mann, 1999). It is a telling

JEFFREY WIGAND THE WHISTLEBLOWER

> "I tried to get my stuff from the horse's mouth – or the other end, at any rate."
>
> *Izzy Stone.*

exchange, raising ethical issues of motivation and responsibility.

Investigative journalists in movies are often shady characters who meet shadowy whistleblowers in dimly-lit carparks. They tend to be chain-smoking obsessives who won't take no for an answer; unorthodox loners who risk life and limb to establish the truth. The reality is often rather more mundane. Most investigative journalism would not make for dramatic footage – the meticulous cross-referencing of information strands, the days phoning people with similar names and trawling Facebook or the electoral roll to track somebody down, and the hours poring over obscure documents or computer databases until your eyes scream for mercy. It is true that, compared with other forms of reporting, investigative journalism may involve more time, more money and more risk (Palast, 2002: 9) and there is the occasional threat or even act of violence. But journalists in the UK are more likely to face legal or commercial **constraints** – not the least of which is understaffing – than to receive an invitation to sleep with the fishes.

Although investigative journalism remains an integral part of journalism's image and sense of self-worth and professional standing, in reality it is a minority pursuit. Whenever the topic of investigative journalism is discussed, somebody can be relied upon to say that *all* journalism is supposed to be investigative. But much journalism, as it is practised, is reportage. It is descriptive and/or based on attribution. Such everyday journalism proceeds on the basis of a reporter seeing or being told something and then passing that on to an audience in the form of a story, as Martin Wainwright explains:

> I'm not like a detective, I'm more of a describer. Somebody rang me up the other day and said he had a scandal which involved everybody from the Prime Minister downwards, and you think, "Oh God . . ." It's terribly difficult and you don't have very much time.

The head of news in one regional television newsroom described her brief as the production of human interest stories for ultra-busy people, adding: "Our role is not to be investigative" (quoted in Ursell, 2001: 191). To which one of the more polite responses would be, "What, never?".

ORIGINAL RESEARCH INTO WRONGDOING

What is commonly labelled investigative journalism goes beyond Wainwright's modest description of his role as that of a "describer". For David Randall, investigative reporting differs substantially from other reporting because it involves *original* research into *wrongdoing*, because someone is trying to keep the information *secret*, and because the *stakes* tend to be higher (Randall, 2000: 99–100). Although some investigations, including many in the Sunday redtop tabloids, expose nothing more than the personal predilections of a minor celeb, the very existence of whom many of us were previously and happily unaware, the credo of investigative journalism rests on its role in uncovering information that it is in the **public interest** for people to know.

Classic investigative journalism in the public interest is often said to be on the wane, following a high point in the 1970s (Doig, 1997: 189; Northmore, 2001: 183). As with all discussions about journalism, there is a long-established tendency to bestow "golden age" status on earlier periods, yet the sheer breadth of entries to the Paul Foot Award each year demonstrates that reports of the death of investigative journalism are greatly exaggerated. Before moving on to examine some more examples of investigative reporting, though, let's briefly consider a cautionary note sounded by Martin Wainwright, who believes that investigative journalists may sometimes be tempted to ignore shades of grey: "I'm always a bit suspicious of them, because often if you go into a story carefully you find there's another side to it, and it's not quite what it seems." That's a point worth keeping in mind: the need to retain a sense of scepticism even when consuming the work of journalists who have built their entire reputations on scepticism.

METHODS OF INVESTIGATION

When consumer affairs correspondent Kevin Peachey finds himself investigating dodgy companies and the like, how does he set about checking a story?

> First you look in the files, the archives, because the same issues crop up sometimes. Then the internet, to see if somebody else has written about them. Then it's contacts. Consumer stories are no different from any other specialism – if you've got good contacts that's half the battle. I've got enough people now who I can ring up and they can tell me whether there's something in it or not. I can see if there's a news angle in something, but as far as the law is concerned you need someone to explain it to you. So my most important contacts are in the trading standards service, in the same way as a crime reporter's best contacts are in the police.

It sounds simple. That is the point. There is no need for the mystique that too often surrounds the subject. Paul Foot insists there are dangers in treating investigative journalism as a separate genre carried out by "grand" journalists:

> It's a complete fraud, the idea that there is a race apart called investigative journalists. An ordinary reporter doing a perfectly ordinary story carries out these functions, the difference would be the enthusiasm and the scepticism with which you approach something.

Another difference might be the *time* you have available. Reporters required to churn out numerous stories every day will simply find life impossible if they question absolutely everything. On the other hand, journalists who invest their own time in working on their own stories can become known in the trade as "self-starters". If they are both lucky and skilled, they may be able to earn themselves the rare luxury of being given a specifically investigative brief. That was how Paul Foot was able to spend so much time at both the *Daily Mirror* and *Private Eye* "piling fact on fact to present a picture of cock-up or conspiracy" (Foot, 1999: 82).

Foot talks me through one of his most celebrated investigations, concerning the case of four men wrongly jailed for the murder of newspaper delivery boy Carl Bridgewater:

> I started writing about it in 1980. Ann Whelan, whose son was convicted, wrote to me at the *Mirror* a very moving letter. My initial feeling was, "What mother wouldn't say that her son was innocent?". So it was some time before I went up there. But

I went up to Birmingham and met her and her family. I wasn't convinced to begin with because it was a horrible murder and there was *some* evidence against them, there was a confession. It took quite a lot of time before I became in any way convinced, but I did become absolutely convinced, and as I did so I wrote with more and more certainty.

Ann found witnesses who said, "I told a pack of lies, I didn't realise how important it was". But mostly it was just going over the evidence that had been presented in court against them, reading depositions, the judge's summing up and so on, talking to everyone involved. There were things showing they were somewhere else at the time, that somebody else had done the murder, it just went on and on. I must have written at least 30 articles in the *Mirror*. Eventually the men were released in 1997.

> "Get off your asses and knock on doors."
> **LA Times *newsroom sign.***

Apart from his forensic skill and the willingness to immerse himself in countless legal documents, what is immediately apparent from Foot's account is the *repetition* of stories over a long period of time:

The *Mirror* subs would joke, "Here comes the man who supports the murder of newspaper boys", and occasionally the editor would say, "Oh Christ, you're not doing this again are you?" But the repetition is absolutely crucial because it encourages other sources to come forward.

"NOT ANOTHER FUCKING STORY ABOUT CHILD SEX GROOMING"

Repeating a story or, more accurately, persisting with an issue over a long period of time and producing a series of related stories, is often highlighted as a vital element in successful investigations. That was certainly the case with Andrew Norfolk's groundbreaking and harrowing investigation for the *Times* into the grooming of girls for sexual exploitation in Rochdale, Rotherham and elsewhere. As a story involving sexual abuse and violence against underage victims who did not all necessarily see themselves

as victims, with the girls overwhelmingly white and English and the men overwhelmingly from the Pakistani Muslim community, it was fraught with difficult ethical issues. Some of the ethical issues are discussed further in Chapter 13.

Norfolk admits holding back from looking into the issue at first because he knew it would be a "dream story" for racist organisations such as the British National Party. "That acted as a break when it shouldn't have done," he explains. "It was not knowing how to report that in a way that didn't pander to that racist picture of innocent white victims and evil Muslim perpetrators." The issue gnawed away at him for several years:

I had a growing sense of unease as from time to time a story would come through from an agency or a local newspaper about a court case, with a pattern that seemed to be girls of 12 to 15 where the first point of contact is in a public place. It wasn't online, it wasn't in the family, they weren't schoolteachers, but it was in a public place like a train station or a shopping mall. And the names were overwhelmingly Muslim men who had been convicted.

Eventually, on hearing a radio news bulletin mention that nine men had just been convicted of abusing a 14-year-old girl, he approached his home news editor and said: "Look, I've let this go far, far too long, will you give me some time to look at it?" Having been granted some time, he explains what happened next:

I thought the only way we're ever going to be able to write about this is on the basis of evidence and the first three months were trawling for information about convictions. Searches [on a database at the *Times*] for things like "crown court", words like "convicted", "girl", "sex offences", then narrow it down so it was not online, and there had to be at least two people convicted, so it wasn't a lone offender. We also looked at libraries, back issues of local newspapers, all that sort of thing. And we came up with, I think, 17 cases in 13 different towns and cities over a 13-year period, 1997 to 2010: 56 men had been convicted in those 17 cases, three of them were white, but there were less than half a dozen non-Muslim names. When I then looked into it I realised that the vast majority of the Muslims were from the Pakistani community as opposed to the Bangladeshi community or any other Muslim community.

Finding evidence of so many cases, Norfolk tried to do what any decent journalist would do in the circumstances: seek explanations from agencies and experts, in an effort to understand what's going on and why. So he approached police, the Home Office, other government departments, local authorities, and the children's charity Barnardo's, all to little avail:

> That's when we tried to talk to people and that's when I hit a brick wall like I've never hit a brick wall. They were terrified about what they knew and hadn't done anything about. I said, "On or off the record, I now know there's a specific problem here, I want to understand why", and they just point blank refused to speak.

But he stuck with it and eventually "two little doors opened" when an investigating police officer agreed to talk about a case and when a support group put him in contact with some victims' families. The result was a front page splash headlined REVEALED: CONSPIRACY OF SILENCE ON UK SEX GANGS (*Times*, January 5 2011) with four full pages inside. "There really was an extraordinary reaction," he recalls. "Within three days of our story the government had ordered a national scoping exercise to discover the scale of the problem, there was a parliamentary inquiry, and suddenly all the doors that had been shut started to open."

Job done, or so he thought. But *Times* editor James Harding (who later moved to the BBC) had other ideas, as Norfolk recalls:

> I genuinely thought, "That's it, done." It had been three months of research and another month of trying to speak to people and putting it together. And then James Harding called me down to London, I'd never had a one-to-one with him before, and he said: "You are going to carry on writing this story until every single colleague of yours on the *Times*

opens the paper and says, 'Oh my god, not another fucking story about child sex grooming', because that's the day we'll know we're making a difference. That is now your full-time job." I found him an inspirational editor. There were several points when I was at a really low ebb because it was all so horrible, and there were several points when I felt now we've done this, surely this is it – and I would walk into his office thinking, "Please, no more". And somehow in the space of 10 minutes he'd turn me around so that I wanted to carry on doing it. Now that's a real gift. He would send me emails saying, "Keep on keeping on".

Keep on keeping on is precisely what Andrew Norfolk did. Story followed story as the paper revealed the extent to which not only had extremely vulnerable girls been systematically groomed and abused by groups of men, but the victims had then been let down by the authorities that ignored their plight. As with Paul Foot's investigations (above), the publication of each story increased the chances of more sources coming forward as people who had not seen the original coverage gradually caught up. Not only official sources, who suddenly felt able to talk, but victims and their families too. Norfolk again:

> A victim in Rotherham, she hadn't really recognised what had happened to her until she read a story we did, she came to us. They didn't necessarily see themselves as victims at the start, and the guilt that they have that it's somehow their fault – they nearly all went back to their perpetrators because that's part of the grooming process.

The result of this victim coming forward was GROOMING SCANDAL OF CHILD SEX TOWN, which opened:

> A child in the care of social services was allowed extensive daily contact with a violent sexual offender who was suspected of grooming more than a dozen young teenagers to use and sell for sex, it is revealed today. (*Times*, August 23 2013)

On the front page and three inside pages Norfolk told the truly shocking story of the girl – who was twice made pregnant by the man while she was still a child – and of the authorities' even more shocking failure to protect her. She was quoted in the piece as saying, "I didn't think of myself as being groomed, but now I realise it was an abusive relationship". She also expressed the hope that other young women would read her story, reflect on their own experiences as teenagers, and find the courage to speak out (*Times*, August 23 2013).

"NOW I'M READY TO TALK"

Speaking out was what Cathy Newman's sources did for her *Channel 4 News* investigation into allegations made by women within the Liberal Democrats that they had been sexually harassed by a senior figure in the party – but they did not do it immediately. Newman explains that getting people to appear on camera is the big hurdle for TV investigations, but sometimes you have to be patient:

> I'd been in contact with her a few years before and she didn't want to speak about it at that point, and she then came to me out of the blue and said, "Now I'm ready to talk". We didn't rush them into making a decision about whether they wanted to appear on camera. Once we had one it became easier to persuade the others to speak. We just built a really trusting relationship with the women. You can't just go in there and stick a camera under their nose and expect them to speak. You've got to be very gentle. Also I think it is about track record as well, I've been nearly 20 years as a journalist now, they can see what I've done. I've protected my sources and I've protected people.

But allegations about the behaviour of the Liberal Democrats' election strategist Lord Rennard were only half of the story. The other half was that the women felt their complaints had not been taken seriously by the party hierarchy. Newman wanted to put that point on air to party leader Nick Clegg, but he declined to appear, so she took an unusual approach and telephoned an LBC radio phone-in show on which Clegg was appearing. "Cathy from Dulwich", as she was introduced to Clegg and listeners alike, defends the ambush:

To tell a story on TV you've got to have people on camera. Nick Clegg refused to do an interview with us for years. We got a bit fed up with this and decided to dial into his radio show and that was how we managed to get a response out of him, and that was quite engaging.

Some investigations still don't manage to make good television, though, either because they are just not very visual or because they would take too long to explain. *Channel 4 News* puts some of those online on its *Factcheck* blog. Newman explains the thinking:

> You weren't getting a straight answer from politicians, sometimes they were outright lying, so the idea was to pick on a particular statement that a politician had made and to say whether it was fact or fiction. Quite often it was fiction. Our most successful *Factcheck* probably was when Gordon Brown misled parliament on defence spending and he actually then had to own up to misleading parliament. That was particularly shocking because he made this claim more than once. David Cameron's done something similar on public sector jobs. But Gordon Brown had made this claim repeatedly, he wasn't backing down, so that was quite a moment really. It was the sort of thing that some journalists run a mile from but because of my background on the *FT* I'd been taught not to be scared of figures.

Factcheck is now more of a team effort and the results of its investigations can be seen at: http://blogs.channel4.com/factcheck/

"THROW NOTHING AWAY"

Another experienced investigator, TV reporter Christopher Hird, describes his own *modus operandi* as: first, check what is already in the public domain, then establish a chronology and look for connections, and then systematically look up anyone who might know anything (quoted in Spark, 1999: 53). Such activities will often overlap: checking the details of a company under investigation might give you some more names to contact; contacting those people might give you some more companies to check out; doing that might throw up other connections; and so on. That's why Randall advises "throw nothing away", because you never know when it might be useful (Randall, 2000: 108). During the Watergate investigation, Woodward and Bernstein filled several filing cabinets with all their notes, memos and early drafts of stories. Periodically they would review their files and make lists of previously unexplored angles (Bernstein and Woodward, [1974] 2005: 50 and 330). The careful filing and storage of potentially useful material is now more often in electronic form than on hard copy, although a combination of both is common. Backing-up files and saving emails and material from websites is also required. It is safer not to assume that something you have found on a website will still be there unchanged the next time you look, so save it somewhere if you might need it.

HARNESSING SOCIAL MEDIA

The spread of mobile phones and the growth of social media have both added to the toolkit available for journalists conducting investigations into certain topics. This is perhaps best exemplified by the way the *Guardian*'s Paul Lewis harnessed so-called user-generated content to debunk the official version of how newspaper seller Ian Tomlinson met his death in 2009. At the time the streets of central London were the scene of clashes between riot police and people protesting against the policies of the world's major economies (known as the G20), and it was amid such chaos that Tomlinson collapsed and died on his way home from working outside Monument tube station. Police told the media that he had simply suffered a heart attack, that no officers had encountered him before his collapse and that protesters had even hindered medics who attempted to save his life. This version of events was faithfully reported in much of the media, but Lewis smelled a rat and followed his suspicions that there might be more to the story.

He combined the old-fashioned "shoe leather" approach of tracking down and talking to anyone who might have been in the area with scouring social media including Twitter, Flickr and YouTube for relevant material and leads, all while asking questions and openly sharing information. Lewis explains the idea behind such online sharing and also the importance of taking steps to verify material:

> We became part of a virtual G20 crowd that had coalesced online to question the circumstances of his death. . . . It was incumbent on me, the journalist, to join the wider crowd on an equal playing-field, and share as much information as I was using as the investigation progressed. . . . Internet contact usually does not suffice for verification, and so I regularly met with sources. I asked the most important witnesses to meet me at the scene of Tomlinson's death, near the Bank of England, to walk and talk me through what they had seen. We only published images and video that we had retrieved directly from the source and later verified ... The break, though, as with most scoops, was partly the result of good luck, but not unrelated to the fact that our journalism had acquired credibility in the online crowd. (Lewis, 2011: 34–35)

> "We are trying to open a cupboard and shine a torch around – a feeble torch in a very large cupboard – and we don't know what's in the bits of the cupboard we can't see."
>
> *Andrew Gilligan.*

That scoop arrived when New York-based investment fund manager Chris La Jaunie sent the *Guardian* a video clip he had recorded on his compact digital camera on the day in question, when he happened to be in London for a business conference. His footage clearly showed Tomlinson shuffling along, hands in pockets, being struck from behind with a baton and pushed to the ground by a masked police officer. A visibly shocked Tomlinson then sits on the pavement as a protester comes to his aid while a group of police officers stand and watch. Together with photographs and witness accounts gathered by Lewis, this chance piece of user-generated content totally contradicted the official account of what happened, and the story culminated two years later when an inquest jury found that Tomlinson had been unlawfully killed.

It may have been fortuitous that a citizen had been filming in the right place at the right time, but it was no mere chance that he sent the result to the *Guardian*, as Lewis explains:

IAN TOMLINSON INVESTIGATION

> He knew the footage he had was potentially explosive. The options available to Mr La Jaunie were limited. Fearing a police cover-up, he did not trust

handing over the footage. An alternative would have been to release the video onto YouTube, where it would lack context, might go unnoticed for days and even then could not have been reliably verified. He said he chose to contact me after coming to the conclusion that ours was the news organisation which had most effectively interrogated the police version of events. (Lewis, 2011: 35–36)

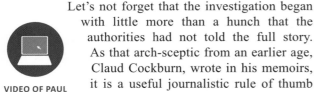

VIDEO OF PAUL LEWIS TALK

Let's not forget that the investigation began with little more than a hunch that the authorities had not told the full story. As that arch-sceptic from an earlier age, Claud Cockburn, wrote in his memoirs, it is a useful journalistic rule of thumb to "believe nothing until it has been officially denied" (Cockburn, 1967: 97).

GOING UNDERGROUND

If harnessing social media is a relatively new and very open form of investigation, the opposite is true of one of the longest-established forms of investigative journalism: when a reporter goes undercover and pretends to be somebody other than a journalist, with a view to discovering the truth behind a public facade. Kevin Peachey once went undercover – as a duck. He didn't have to dress up, he just bought products with a credit card and instead of signing his real name he signed it "Donald Duck", thereby illustrating how rarely card signatures were checked (this was in the days before cards had PIN numbers instead). He also exposed the trade in bogus qualifications by buying a fake degree on the internet. "You can have some fun with investigations," he says.

But going undercover can be a tricky, even dangerous thing to do. It can also be immensely satisfying when it comes off, especially when the story is then picked up by other media. Abul Taher recalls going undercover in France as one of his most rewarding assignments for the *Sunday Times*:

The story came from a simple idea that we should look at the migrant situation in Calais again, as there were reports that the situation was worsening. I went there posing as an illegal immigrant from Bangladesh, trying to get to the UK. It was a good exercise in information and intelligence gathering, which I did over a period of two weeks. I spoke to fellow illegal immigrants, charity workers and actual people smugglers – in the guise of an illegal immigrant – and managed to put together a good picture of the migrant problem in Calais, as well as giving a picture of the routes the migrants took from Asia to get to Calais.

The story line we got from it – that the French were building a new Sangatte refugee camp in Calais – caused a political uproar, with the Home Secretary making comments on it. Nicolas Sarkozy, by then president-elect of France, also condemned the plan. The story ran in the national papers for about a month.

The deception inherent within undercover journalism, which dates back to the 19th century at least, is typically justified by reference to the public interest. However, undercover journalists often find themselves accused of everything from entrapment to engaging in worthless stunts.

One of the pioneers of undercover reporting was Nellie Bly, whose lengthy list of exploits began in 1887 when she feigned mental illness and spent "ten days in a mad-house" for Joseph Pulitzer's *New York World*, emerging to expose the harsh reality of life for inmates in asylums – and to boost the newspaper's circulation. According to biographer Brooke Kroeger, Bly did not engage in "fishing expeditions" but "targeted specific situations or individuals in an effort to right wrongs, to explain the unexplored, to satisfy curiosity about the intriguing, to expose unfairness, or to catch a thief" (Kroeger, 1994: 206–207). However, her success sparked a "decade of girl reporter derring-do" involving ever more sensational "stunts", such as young female journalists standing in the street posing as flower-sellers in the hope of exposing any married men who propositioned them (Kroeger, 1994: 87–88 and 206). Well over a century later, BBC reporter Mark Daly initially found himself accused of stunt journalism when he went undercover to expose police racism; but when his shocking secret footage was broadcast the critics quickly changed their tune and praised his journalism as being in the public interest and therefore justifying his use of deception (Harcup, 2007: 38–39). Daly later reflected that he felt conflicted about "betraying" officers who thought he was one of them, and that he had "gone a bit native" while on the job, but that ultimately exposing their racist attitudes "was done in the public interest, and most importantly, was done ethically" (Daly, 2011: 95–96).

In addition to the methods already discussed in this chapter – from the straightforward and open to the controversial and clandestine – other investigative techniques used by some journalists have included:

- rummaging through targets' dustbins ("binology");

- the rather more sophisticated encryption of digital communication to prevent the state's security services knowing who you are talking to or what stories you are working on;

- setting up secure digital "drop boxes" to allow whistleblowers to supply information in confidence;

- using unregistered pay-as-you-go mobile phones ("burners") for talking to sensitive sources;

- paying cash-only for hotel rooms, meals and so on to avoid leaving trails that might lead back to a source;

- hiring private investigators to track people down;

- tricking organisations into handing over private information about individuals ("blagging"), which may involve a breach of data protection law;

- paying sources for information (which can also be illegal in some circumstances);

- and finally, the illegal hacking of voicemails, emails and computers (allegations of which now also have a tendency to result in an unwelcome appearance at the Old Bailey).

These and similar techniques are sometimes referred to as the "dark arts" of journalism (Davies, 2008). Quite apart from the legal and ethical considerations involved, it is in the interests of novice journalists to steer clear of the dark arts. The good news is that investigative journalism is still possible without resorting to them.

> "Listen to the loons."
> *Claud Cockburn.*

LEGWORK AND LATERAL THINKING

Targeted use of FOI and social media may have added to the investigator's armoury, but that does not mean there is no need to get out on the streets, as Paul Lewis's probe into the death of Ian Tomlinson demonstrates (above). And it was a combination of "legwork" and "lateral thinking" that allowed Brian Whittle's freelance agency to break a number of stories about the family doctor who turned out to be Britain's biggest serial killer, mostly of elderly women. After Dr Harold Shipman was convicted, the agency's reporters revisited the small town in which he had embarked on his murderous medical career a quarter-of-a-century previously. They investigated deaths for which Shipman had not even been charged, as Whittle explains:

> Before anybody else thought of it we obtained all the death certificates for the 22 people he'd signed while he was practising in Todmorden. Just looking at the death certificates told you that three people died in one day. We then went round all the addresses. A third of the houses no longer existed, and in another third the people had moved away and weren't contactable. But we did find relatives of the three people who died in one day, and we found relatives of the first male victim.
>
> This is old-fashioned reporting, it's knocking on doors, it's talking to people. If you turn up on the doorstep people will talk to you, if you ring them up it gives them the chance to put the phone down. If you want to find out about somebody you don't just knock on *their* door and the *next* door, you do the entire street. You do *both sides* of the street – two of you – and you do it again in the evening because people may be out in the daytime. Go to *every* address and ask, "What do you know about this person who lived here 25 years ago?"
>
> You don't know who you're going to find, maybe it's a son or whatever. Out of the 22, six or seven came out with absolutely key stuff. We were totally vindicated when the police started an investigation about a month later and sent various cases to the Crown Prosecution Service.

As well as uncovering new information about the man who was known as "Dr Death", the reporters' repeated visits also led them to a series of photographs showing Shipman partying with his wife – all smiles and silly hats. The pictures probably didn't add much to the sum of human knowledge but, thanks to an exclusive deal with the *Sunday Mirror*, they turned out to be lucrative for the agency as well as for the owner of the photos. This technique of hitting the doorsteps early and often will be familiar to anyone who has worked as an agency reporter on the frontline of domestic news; most would probably not call themselves investigative journalists, but that is (part of) what they are doing.

THE OTHER SIDE OF THE STORY

Despite the thrill of the chase – or perhaps precisely *because*, as a reporter, it's so easy to get caught up in the excitement of a pursuit – it is vital to question your *own* expectations and assumptions during any investigation. Then, once you have gathered your material from a range of sources, you must decide whether the story still has potential. If it does not stand up, either forget it or file it away for another day. But if it has substance, sooner or later you must confront your "target" with the allegations. "There are two sides to the story and everybody has a right of reply", explains Peachey:

> If they choose not to reply then that's fair enough, but we make every effort we can. In some cases we give them a 10 bullet-point letter through their door, if we know where they are, saying, "We're thinking of writing a story, these are some of the issues that have been raised, we want your reply". Give them sufficient time, a couple of days generally. Log your phone calls too, so that you know when you've left messages. A couple of times I've spoken to people who've given me some abuse down the phone – that always makes an interesting line in the story.

During her investigation in Doncaster, Deborah Wain repeatedly contacted the troubled college and its chief executive. "I gave him numerous opportunities to respond but he never did", she says. But the material she had gathered – official documents plus interviews

with other sources, written in shorthand notebooks, dated and filed just in case – was strong enough for publication. In larger newsrooms such stories would probably have been "legalled" by a lawyer beforehand, but Wain relied on her own knowledge of the legal system gained during her NCTJ training: "As a local paper, everything has got to be legally sound, you're not going to take the same risks as the nationals. Knowing the law, knowing what you can publish, is really key – and the stories were all strong enough."

WHAT HAS INVESTIGATIVE JOURNALISM EVER DONE FOR US?

What is achieved by journalists taking on this investigative role? For a start, journalists exposing miscarriages of justice, such as the Bridgewater Four, the Birmingham Six and the Guildford Four, all resulted in innocent people walking free from prison, eventually. Sometimes journalists are more concerned with sending guilty people *to* prison than getting innocent people *out*, and Michael Crick's determined pursuit of Jeffrey Archer helped ensure that his Lordship ended up behind bars rather than as Mayor of London (Tench, 2001).

Is that all it amounts to, though: springing the occasional innocent person and jailing the odd guilty one? Is investigative journalism really a force for **democracy** or merely a relatively minor subdivision of showbusiness (de Burgh, 2000: 315; Northmore, 2001: 185)? Paul Foot never doubted the social benefits of such work, explaining:

> Apart from getting people out of prison who shouldn't be there, there are things like the cancer drugs that were killing people quicker. The publication in *Private Eye* of four or five of those articles and the whole project was exposed. And Frank Wheeler, the busman up in Scotland who kept asking why the government had stolen the pensions surplus of the National Bus Company when it was privatised. That was £300 million. He says the whole thing changed when I went up there and spent a couple of days with him and his wife and wrote a piece for the *Guardian*, and then several things for the *Eye*. That

set of articles made a difference to those people in that they got their money back.

And Deborah Wain found that tens of millions of pounds of public money were being spent in Doncaster apparently without any effective accountability. The only public accountability was provided by the press reporting what was going on and informing its readers – the town's citizens and voters.

At the *Times*, Andrew Norfolk is in no doubt that his three-year grooming investigation was socially worthwhile because it placed a hitherto hidden scandal in the public domain:

Newspapers always like to pat themselves on the back but I definitely think we acted as the trigger for the debate starting, and then because we carried on producing new information about things that were going on in different parts of the country, it's not allowed it to go away. It has transformed the way the authorities approach it, from the terrible early examples – going to a house in the early hours of the morning when there was a 13-year-old-girl with a group of adult Pakistani males and they arrest the girl for being drunk and disorderly and leave the men alone – to now, when specialist training is being offered, every beat bobby is being told the warning signs to look out for, the number of investigations is just exploding. Another example would be the judges. We did a story about a girl who spent 15 days in the witness box, 12 of them under cross-examination from seven defence lawyers, being absolutely shredded and they were being allowed to explore areas that were nothing to do with the offence itself. Within weeks of that, suddenly they're announcing that only judges from a special panel will deal with such cases where there are multiple defendants.

So there has been so much that has changed for the good. We had a guy from the Ramadhan Foundation, he's from Rochdale himself, condemning what was going on, and there's been some brilliant work done by some Islamic scholars. And finally, two and a half years after we started writing about it, the Muslim Council of Great Britain held its first ever conference on child sexual exploitation, which was great. We have been doing for three years something that incontestably is public interest journalism. We probably haven't sold a single extra copy, trying to raise the plight of people who would never buy the *Times* in a million years, and effecting change for the better – it certainly wasn't to make money.

In 2014, after three years, Andrew Norfolk finally moved on to a fresh investigation, this time into child abuse at private boarding schools; it may be a different end of the social spectrum but it is a similar story of children being failed by some of those supposed to be caring for them.

IT'S ABOUT THE STORY, NOT THE JOURNALIST

As we have seen, then, investigative journalism is more about approach than it is about subject matter. It is more of an attitude than it is a genre. And just as journalists working on investigations will use many of the techniques they would use on "ordinary" stories – only more so – an inquiring and investigative approach can also inform otherwise mundane reporting. Increasingly, for example, journalists are putting in FOI requests to find information on all sorts of subjects. If a public authority is likely to hold information on something – from hygiene inspections of local takeaways to government files on reported UFO sightings – then an FOI request might be worth considering for any journalist working on virtually any story.

What are the main attributes necessary for a journalist to become an effective investigator? Paul Foot offers this summary:

> "Keep on keeping on."
> *James Harding.*

There are certain skills that you learn from experience, but the main point is to be curious and sceptical. You can't be an investigative journalist unless you are both curious and sceptical *all the time*. That, and the ability to ring people up and talk to them all the time, the ability to believe the most absurd things that people tell you – even when perhaps nine times out of 10 they're talking absolute bollocks.

David Hencke feels that journalists should guard against the trend prevalent in some television investigations of relying on secret filming and/or of presenting the reporter centre-stage, whereby "By the end, as with a John Wayne movie, we can safely go to our beds, knowing that all the villains have had their just deserts and that our hero has fought his way through, against the odds, and emerged victorious" (Hencke, 2001).

For Foot, the crucial thing remains the relationship between journalist and source: "The source is more important than the story. The whistleblowers who break cover and say, 'I'm not going to continue with this because I'm doing something wrong' – they are the goldmine. You do not sell them out." The source may be more important than the story, but both should be more important than the journalist, believes Wain. Referring to the above point from Hencke, as quoted in the first edition of this book, she tells me:

> You talk in your chapter about the notion of the investigative reporter as hero, and I have found that there has been a lot more media interest in the story of me getting that award – people *like* the story of the reporter on the *small* paper – than there ever was in the original story of what was going on in Doncaster with all that money. I think they should have been a bit more interested in that at the time.

SUMMARY

Investigative journalism goes beyond description and attributed opinion to uncover information, typically about powerful individuals or organisations. Many investigative skills will be used by "ordinary" journalists every day. Potential stories are typically investigated by combining information already in the public domain with material obtained through Freedom of Information laws, information leaked by whistleblowers and/or by talking to as many as possible of the people involved. There are frequent claims that investigative journalism has been in decline since its heyday in the 1970s, and that some investigations are stunts designed more for entertainment than for uncovering information that it is genuinely in the public interest to know. The digital age has seen the creation of new methods of revelation, including the huge quantity of secret information published by *WikiLeaks* and the crowdsourcing of user-generated content. Investigative reporting has been explained variously as an essential element of democracy, as favouring a simplistic narrative of "good versus evil" at the expense of questioning structural forces, as an esoteric form of journalism of little interest to most citizens, and as a tribune of the common people. It is probably all those things and more, and the concept remains a vital part of the self-identity even of journalists who themselves rarely conduct in-depth investigations.

QUESTIONS

Should all journalism really be investigative?
What are the main obstacles confronting journalists as investigators?
Is today the golden age of investigative journalism?
Why is investigative journalism said to be essential to democracy?
Do investigative reporters create a myth of good versus evil?

WHAT WOULD YOU DO?

You work for a news organisation that plans to increase the number of original investigations it conducts. Two suggestions for investigations have been suggested at editorial conference. One is to look into the economic and social factors that may help explain a reported 160 per cent increase in the number of people using emergency food banks over the past year. The other is to look into claims that the volunteers running certain charity food banks sometimes hand food parcels out to people who say they are needy without fully checking their "sob stories". Given that newsroom resources are tight, you are asked which of the two you think ought to be investigated. What factors might influence your choice?

HOW MIGHT YOU TACKLE THIS ISSUE?

FURTHER READING

Anybody interested in reading more about journalists as investigators should really start with *All the President's Men* by Bernstein and Woodward ([1974] 2005), which is at least as much about the journalistic process as it is about the scandals of the Nixon presidency. The film of the same name is worth seeing too, as is *The Insider*. For practical advice on using the UK's freedom of information legislation, see Heather Brooke's (2007) extremely helpful book *Your Right to Know*; to keep up to date with how FOI is being used by journalists and others see Matt Burgess' *FOI Directory* at http://foidirectory.co.uk/. As ever, Dodd and Hanna (2014) is essential to know where you stand in relation to the law. A personal account of investigative reporting is given in brief but typically entertaining fashion in Foot (1999), while Palast (2002) includes several of his own investigative reports as well as details of the processes involved. Spark (1999) offers an illuminating introduction to some of the main techniques, based on a series of interviews with practitioners; his account of the downfall of Jonathan Aitken is instructive, although the book contains little analysis. Lewis (2011) provides a blow-by-blow account of the investigation into the death of Ian Tomlinson, while Beckett and Ball (2012) explore the *WikiLeaks* phenomenon. Contributors to Mair and Keeble (2011) and de Burgh (2000, 2008) describe a range of investigations and also place investigative journalism within a wider social and academic context. The concept of the public interest is discussed in depth in Harcup (2007), which also includes an interview with the reporter who spent two months undercover in Buckingham Palace working as a footman to the Queen and with Andrew Gilligan on the case of Dr David Kelly.

TOP THREE TO TRY NEXT

Carl Bernstein and Bob Woodward ([1974] 2005) *All the President's Men*
Hugo de Burgh (2008) *Investigative Journalism*
John Mair and Richard Keeble (2011) *Investigative Journalism: Dead or Alive?*

SOURCES FOR SOUNDBITES

Foot, quoted in Knightley, 2011: 23; Pilger, quoted in C Adams, 2001; Wain, interviewed by the author; Palast, 2002: 8; Stone, quoted in Guttenplan, 2012: xiv; *LA Times*, quoted in Brennen, 2003: 126; Gilligan, quoted in Harcup, 2007: 17; Cockburn, quoted in Foot, 1999: 82; Harding, quoted in Norfolk interview with the author, 2014.

CHAPTER 7

"WE ARE IN THE ENTERTAINMENT BUSINESS": JOURNALISTS AS ENTERTAINERS

Anyone who has seen the film *Bridget Jones's Diary* is likely to remember the scene in which intrepid reporter Bridget concludes a piece-to-camera in a fire station by sliding down the pole with her backside descending directly on to the camera. Long-time regional television reporter Lindsay Eastwood recalled the scene when she was sent out to produce an "And finally ..." piece about the growth in popularity of pole dancing:

> Pole dancing is now regarded as a form of exercise rather than a seedy lap-dancing thing. There were all these very attractive women, and I'm not exactly the best example of a pole dancing babe, but I thought I'm going to have to be in this to make it funny, and to poke fun at myself. So I did a Bridget Jones style slide down the pole on to the lens of the camera, which did the trick really. It was just lucky that I had trousers on.

Such light and fluffy stories have long been a part of journalism. I recall working on a newspaper during a heatwave when some bright spark had the idea of testing the legend about it being "hot enough to fry an egg on the pavement". A posse was gathered and we rushed from the newsroom to put the theory to the test – but the egg steadfastly refused to fry. After half-an-hour we conceded defeat, scraped up the mess, and beat a retreat to the sound of jeers from drinkers who were enjoying the sun and the spectacle outside the pub next door.

It was not the best piece of investigative journalism I had ever been involved with. It was just a bit of fun – entertainment. Some stories are entertaining by virtue of their subject matter. Others can be rendered entertaining by being well written, by holding the attention of the audience, by the use of anecdotes or asides, or by injecting humour. One colleague used to speak of "sprinkling topspin and stardust" onto a news story, brightening it up with that extra bit of colour or drama

DUMBING DOWN

Debate about so-called "dumbing down" extends far beyond journalism to include education, the arts and society in general. Of direct relevance to journalism is the claim that news has been transformed into "newszak"; that is, "news as a product designed and 'processed' for a particular market and delivered in increasingly homogenous 'snippets' which make only modest demands on the audience" (Franklin, 1997: 5). Supporters of the dumbing-down thesis bemoan the fact that news is being "converted into entertainment" (Franklin, 1997: 5). Chris Frost writes that journalists are facing increasing pressure to become entertainers by "finding stories and features that will delight the audience rather than inform, titillate rather than educate" (Frost, 2002: 5). For Pierre Bourdieu, this results in journalists being so terrified of being seen as boring that they increasingly favour:

- confrontation rather than debate
- polemics or polarised views over rigorous argument
- promotion of conflict
- confrontation of individuals rather than their arguments
- discussion of political tactics rather than the substance of policies
- dehistoricised and fragmented versions of events. (Bourdieu, 1998: 3–7)

There is nothing new about the "perennial" complaint that "journalism just recently got worse", observes Samuel Winch. He argues that the boundary between news and entertainment is "socially constructed" and therefore to an extent arbitrary (Winch, 1997: 6 and 13). Back in the 1960s, the cultural theorist Stuart Hall observed – with to make it more entertaining. After all, we call news items stories because we adopt many of the conventions of the storyteller. Entertaining is not a new role for journalists, as this 19th-century verse demonstrates:

Tickle the public, make 'em grin,

The more you tickle, the more you'll win;

Teach the public, you'll never get rich,

You'll live like a beggar and die in a ditch. (Quoted in Engel, 1997: 17)

Even if we *do* want to teach the public, we won't get very far if nobody reads, watches or listens to our work because we have made the stories too dull. Without an audience there can be no journalism, and we are not likely to gather much of an audience if we do not seek, at least in part, to entertain as well as inform. Difficulties can arise when the distinction appears to be forgotten, as documentary maker Eddie Mirzoeff felt was the case when he asked for his name to be removed from a serious BBC2 series that had been "reversioned", with added music, to make it more zappy (Brown, 2003). As one of those responsible for commissioning television documentaries later explained: "The premium is to find brighter, more entertaining documentary programming. Documentaries can be seen as a rather painful dose of medicine, and I believe we are there to entertain people" (quoted in Brown, 2005).

As with documentaries, so with current affairs broadcasting, where there are recurrent complaints about the lines between journalism and entertainment being blurred and an unhealthy obsession with ratings-friendly subject matter such as sex, drugs, crime and anything-from-hell. Rather than well-informed talking heads given the time to discuss at length, there is a growing reliance on brief soundbites, fast cuts, odd camera angles, secret filming and often gratuitous reconstructions (usually, but not always, labelled as such). Dramatic mood music now accompanies much current affairs journalism on TV, including reconstructions of serious crime, and musical clips are becoming far more common in radio packages. Sometimes all this can make for gripping, engaging and informative journalism delivered in a style that is popular yet serious, innovative yet appropriate. Sometimes.

> "We are in the entertainment business."
> *Rupert Murdoch.*

little attempt at hiding his disdain – the apparent obsession of some UK newspapers with the private lives of celebrities:

> The marriages, engagements and divorces of celebrities *may* be of real public interest, and, in a general sense, they can help to give a very rough idea of how people other than those with whom most of us are acquainted live. But on the whole they contribute little to the kind of news we need to know to make sense of modern life: they become a species of "tittle-tattle", the instinct on the journalist's part for "getting the story" slipping away in the direction of gossip, scandal and irrelevant social-voyeurism. (Hall, 1967: 111, emphasis in original)

Not that entertainment and enlightenment need be seen as opposites. Journalism professor Mick Temple has gone so far as to argue that "dumbing down is good for you". According to his academic paper of that title, political news is no longer the preserve of a cultural elite:

> [T]he so called "dumbing down" of political coverage, referring largely to the simplification and sensationalism of "serious" news by journalists, is an essential part of the process of engaging people in debates about the distribution of resources in modern democratic societies. (Temple, 2006: 257)

In other words, many of the concerns of journalistic and academic critics voiced in this chapter can be seen as a form of elitism and/or nostalgia for a largely mythical golden age of journalism (Temple, 2006: 260).

AUTHORITY

Journalism and other media output increasingly emphasise – or foreground – the individual subjective experience at the expense of more general and authoritative "truth claims", argues Jon Dovey (2000: 25). As part of this process, it is claimed, the "we" of the bourgeois public sphere – which in any case was a rather narrow and male "we" – has now collapsed into "fragmented individualised subjectivities" (Dovey, 2000: 165). This can be translated into two contrasting ways of looking at media output (see *Box 7.1*). Such considerations form part of the cultural backdrop against which so many sections of the media now place

The emphasis that even serious current affairs programmes have to place on entertainment was highlighted in 2013 when *Newsnight* editor Ian Katz tweeted that one of the guests on the show was "boring snoring Rachel Reeves", a senior Labour MP. Perhaps Ms Reeves had thought she was taking part in a serious political discussion rather than an exercise in showbusiness. After Katz apologised for the tweet, the entertainment continued the following night when the hashtag "#fail" was put next to the editor's name on the programme's closing credits (Morse, 2013). As if that wasn't enough excitement for one year, *Newsnight* viewers were also treated to the on-off saga of Jeremy Paxman's beard, the Halloween-special scary dancing of fellow presenter Kirsty Wark, and a studio discussion about Cheryl Cole's bum tattoo (Herman, 2013). Was that the sort of entertainment Lord Reith had in mind when he laid down the founding principles of public service broadcasting as being to inform, educate and entertain? Probably not, but then his BBC did not have to compete with everything from *BuzzFeed* to the *Mail Online*'s "sidebar of shame".

> "Arguably, news has become more democratic, reflecting the concerns of a wider population rather than the views of a cultural elite."
>
> *Mick Temple.*

NEWSNIGHT AND ENTERTAINMENT

greater credence on user-generated content and audience comment than on authoritative pieces of journalism researched by specialist reporters. Media employers may celebrate user-generated content primarily because it is free, but many cultural theorists celebrate it more for the challenge to traditional hierarchies of authority that they believe it entails.

ELITISM

Critics of the dumbing-down thesis argue that it is an elitist concept, far too simplistic to do justice to the complexity of today's journalism – or journalisms. Paul Manning (2001: 7) suggests that there needs to be some entertainment value in journalism because "news audiences are unlikely to warm to a format that has the feel of a sociology seminar", while Denis McQuail (2013: 9) points out that:

> The much criticised news phenomenon of "infotainment" may fail to meet high standards of information quality and is related to "commercialisation", but it is not simply imposed from above on an unsuspecting and vulnerable public.

Rather, it could be seen as giving the public what they want as opposed to what an elite feel the public need.

BOX 7.1

TRADITIONAL AND POPULAR VIEWS OF MEDIA OUTPUT

(Dovey, 2000: 4)

TRADITIONAL	POPULAR
Authoritative	Reflexive
Film	Video
Public service	Reality TV
Observational documentary	Docu-soap
Investigation	Entertainment
Argument	Pleasure
TV news	TV chat
Working	Shopping
Elitist	Democratic
Boring	Fun

Since its launch in 2006, the website *BuzzFeed* has built a huge audience based in large part on the aggregation of viral online content – perhaps most notably pictures of kittens – and on producing entertaining listicles such as "52 things you never knew about Benedict Cumberbatch" and "12 incredibly ill-advised rejection letters" (both published April 11 2014). At the same time the *Daily Mail*'s spin-off *Mail Online* has turned itself into the world's most popular English-language newspaper website, largely on the basis of its (in)famous sidebar specialising in picture-led gossip items about the world of entertainment, many of which do not appear in the rather more prudish print edition. Although these two sites might be said to have taken the so-called "BuzzFeedification of news" to new levels, much of their content is reminiscent of the kind of entertaining material that has long been available in magazines.

"CRIME, CELEBRITY AND MIRACLE CURES"

Entertaining may not be an entirely new role for journalists, then, but in recent decades many have felt that the balance has tilted too far in that direction. One critic is former BBC war correspondent Martin Bell:

> I can think of no time in my life when we needed to be better informed about the world beyond our shores, and no time when we have, in fact, been worse informed. . . . The Palme d'Or for the **dumbing-down** of British television goes to ITN, which was once a proud name in journalism. . . . In hock to the advertisers, ITN set the trend by its decision, early in the 1990s, to promote an agenda of crime, celebrity and miracle cures – and to downgrade foreign news to a couple of slots a week on Tuesdays and Thursdays, unless anything more sellable happened closer to home. The judgements were not editorial, but commercial. (Bell, 2002)

STYLE OVER SUBSTANCE?

Research into changing trends in TV news in the last quarter of the 20th century found that there had indeed been a decline in the amount of political coverage and a

For Brian McNair, such blurring of boundaries between elite and popular culture means that journalism is less deferential towards the powerful than it was in the past (McNair, 2000: 59–60). He explains:

> [The] distinction between "serious" and "trivial" information is no longer one which can be taken as the basis for evaluating the public sphere. . . . An earlier form of detached, deferential, more or less verbatim political reportage has gone from the print media . . ., to be replaced by styles and agendas which, if they are occasionally entertaining, are at the same time more penetrating, more critical, more revealing and demystificatory of power than the polite, status-conscious journalisms of the past. And it is precisely the commercialising influence of the market which has allowed this to happen. (McNair, 2000: 60)

"The *Daily Star* is about making people smile."
Dawn Neesom.

Indeed, even daytime trash TV has been held up as an example of how a more populist approach can "capture and engage an audience who will fail to respond to more conventional coverage of social and 'political' issues" (Temple, 2006: 257). Kees Brants similarly argues that a mixture of "entertainment and consciousness raising" could help to "re-establish the popular in politics", taking in not only "the discursive and decision-making domain of politics but also the vast terrain of domestic life" (Brants, 1998: 332–333). For Gill Ursell, given the multiplicity of media outlets and experiences now available to potential audiences, it may well be that "exposure to *some* kind of news is arguably better than *no* exposure at all" (Ursell, 2001: 192, my emphasis).

shift towards a more tabloid domestic agenda, but that there was still "a healthy balance of serious, light and international coverage". However, the same researchers warned that increasing commercial pressures would pose a serious threat to this balanced approach in the 21st century (Barnett and Seymour, 2000).

Broadcast news may have taken on board elements of the tabloid agenda, but the redtops remain in a league of their own when it comes to the blurring of lines between news and entertainment through their coverage of sex, soaps and celebs. Consider a not untypical news page from the *Sun* in 2014. Of the four items on the page, the one that leaps out is AMY STEAMS UP THE TUB, featuring one huge photograph and two smaller pictures, all illustrating a story that begins: "TV beauty Amy Willerton flaunts her fabulous bikini body in this steamy photoshoot …" What is technically the page lead, KYLIE RATED, concerns "pop princess Kylie Minogue" apparently receiving "a bumper pay rise" for her role as a judge on a TV talent show. The two smaller stories on the page both also concern TV talent shows. Of course, there are more serious items elsewhere in the same day's paper, but most of these are also written and presented in entertaining fashion. That day's splash, revealing that Prince William had gone on a shooting trip just before he launched a campaign to save wildlife, is headlined BAD WILLS HUNTING on the front page, followed inside with THE ROYAL SOCIETY FOR THE PREVENTION OF CUDDLY ANIMALS. And a two-page news special on flooding in the south-west of England centres on a dramatic photograph of one house surrounded by water, headlined CANUTE: I'M STAYING PUT and a story about criticism of the head of the Environment Agency, given the personalised headline I'LL STICK THAT GIT'S HEAD IN LOO AND FLUSH IT (all from the *Sun*, February 8 2014).

Yet even the *Sun* can appear too po-faced for some, as *Daily Star* editor Dawn Neesom explains:

> The job of a newspaper has changed. Yes, it's important people get news but it's also important that they have fun, that they can open a newspaper and it makes them smile. I think the *Sun* is losing the plot.

> There is nothing to smile at in there. I don't want to read another campaign about paedophiles. I know they are out there and I know it's a problem but on a Monday morning I don't want to think, "Oh no, it's another week of more doom and gloom". (Quoted in Plunkett, 2003)

> "The focus is on those things which are apt to arouse curiosity but require no analysis."
> *Pierre Bourdieu.*

Such tabloid values have been crossing over into the self-styled "quality" press for many years now, according to academic commentators such as Bob Franklin (1997: 7–10). The *Times*, for example, has changed almost beyond recognition since it unleashed a highbrow classical music critic to review a Beatles record in the 1960s; the resulting article about the group's aeolian cadences and pan diatonic clusters baffled fans and Beatles alike. Serious newspapers now have a much "fluffier feel", in the words of one *Daily Telegraph* journalist (quoted in Ponsford, 2006), and have adopted many of the ideas and styles of magazine journalism. But engagement with popular culture, leisure, lifestyle and entertainment does not mean that newspapers necessarily *ignore* more traditionally weighty subject matter. Editors such as Alan Rusbridger, of the *Guardian*, argue that their papers and online offerings now have a much broader range of subject matter than in the past, incorporating the popular *alongside* the serious (Rusbridger, 2000). So he is unapologetic about the fact that his paper will now also report showbusiness stories about the aforementioned Ms Minogue – such as KYLIE LEAVES *THE VOICE* AFTER JUST ONE SERIES, accompanied with a photo displaying plenty of flesh (*Guardian*, April 12 2014) – in a way that would have been unthinkable at the time he became editor two decades earlier.

CELEBRITIES AS NEWS

Regional media are likewise part of the entertainment business as well as the information business, according to David Helliwell:

> First and foremost we're there to inform, but in this day and age you've got to do more than that because there's so much competition. There will always be pages in the paper where you are trying to be entertaining, to give people a read – features, the women's

supplement, travel pages, reporters trying the latest high street fad, that sort of stuff. It's a balance, but our two big sellers are still local news and local sport.

In fact, sports reporting has been moved much higher up the news agenda in recent years, with many stories about sports stars now given a prominence that would have bewildered earlier generations of editors. That's not because football is really more important than matters of life and death, as Bill Shankly used to say (he was joking, by the way). Sport is popular with a big chunk of the audience because it "is about fantasy and dreams, and these days at least half the population are having them" (Cole and Harcup, 2010: 114). And just as sport itself is a form of entertainment, so is sports journalism – even when it is also produced with a serious public interest purpose.

ENTERTAINMENT VALUES

As already noted in Chapter 3, editors tend to look favourably on stories with the capacity to entertain or amuse. One study of the UK national press found that many news stories seemed to have been included not because they contained serious information for the reader, but because of their entertainment value (Harcup and O'Neill, 2001: 274). Patricia Holland writes, in the context of the *Sun* but with wider resonance, that the concepts of news and entertainment have become more entwined:

> The relentless push towards entertainment values has meant that the definition of what makes "news" is itself constantly changing. The carefully established distinction between fact and opinion is now less easy to maintain. The need for accuracy has become dissolved into the excess of the headline, through a joke, an ironic exaggeration or an expression of outrage. (Holland, 1998: 31)

A number of components go together to form the entertainment package that influences news selection in erstwhile "serious" media as well as the more popular end of the market. These entertainment values include humour, showbiz, sex, animals, crime and pictures.

> "Dumbing down is a dumb term to describe something far more complex at work in society today."
> **Alan Rusbridger.**

HUMOUR

The news can often be a laughing matter and humorous stories are popular with newsdesks. When council workers took an unusually long time to mend a streetlamp it became national news not because of any particular significance, but because it echoed jokes about how many people it takes to change a lightbulb: FOUR MONTHS, 16 MEN AND £1,000 TO MEND LAMP (*Sun*, September 16 2002). Sometimes the opportunity for a headline pun is enough to warrant a story's inclusion, as when rock band the Red Hot Chili Peppers were accused of miming at a Super Bowl performance: THE RED *NOT* CHILI PEPPERS (*Daily Mirror*, February 6 2014).

SHOWBIZ

Stories about TV stars and other celebrities are rife in the tabloids, but all UK national media – normally with the exception of the *Financial Times* and one or two of the BBC's more austere outlets – now carry showbiz stories and/or compare people in real stories to fictional counterparts.

SEX

If there is a sex angle to a story it is regarded as more entertaining and is therefore more likely to be used, with the sex angle emphasised even if it is marginal to the events described (Harcup and O'Neill, 2001: 274). A sex story involving a celeb from showbiz or sport is even better, but ordinary civilians' sex lives are also covered at times. For example, court cases and employment tribunals with sex angles are more likely to be reported on, all other things being equal, than are those without.

ANIMALS

Animals feature in many entertaining stories about unusual behaviour. Igwig the iguana, for example, made the front page of the *Times* when he was involved in a court case because his owner threw him at a police officer after being ejected from a pub

(IGUANA IS CALLED TO THE BENCH, *Times*, February 26 2002).

CRIME

It is now nearly 70 years since George Orwell recorded the complaints of newspaper readers that "you never seem to get a good murder nowadays" (Orwell, 1946a: 10). But crime stories continue to fascinate journalists and audience alike, although the validity of crime news is compromised if journalists put entertaining their audience above reporting the facts or informed analysis, argues David J Krajicek, former crime reporter for the *New York Daily News*:

> [The] bulk of crime coverage amounts to drive-by journalism – a ton of anecdote and graphic detail about individual cases drawn from the police blotter but not an ounce of leavening context to help frame and explain crime. Too many of these reports begin and end with who did what to whom, embellished with the moans of a murder victim's mother or the sneer of an unrepentant killer in handcuffs. (Krajicek, 1998)

PICTURES

Many of the above stories provide opportunities to include entertaining, amusing, dramatic, tragic or titillating photographs and/or footage. *Sunday Express* editor John Junor once remarked that "a beautiful young woman lifts even the dreariest page" (quoted in McKay, 1999: 188), and his unreconstructed views live on in much of today's media, not least on broadsheet business pages when the cleavage count is frequently boosted by pics of lingerie models gratuitously illustrating stories about profits or losses at high street stores. Such selection decisions are no accident, as newspaper editor Sarah Sands explains:

> At the *Daily Telegraph* it takes a certain kind of English middle class beauty to melt the hearts of those elderly readers. In my time we made it a house rule to run at least one picture of Liz Hurley every day. Liz has passed on the baton. The new English rose is Samantha Cameron. (Sands, 2010)

Not forgetting Kate Middleton, aka the Duchess of Cambridge, who seemingly has the power to attract both tabloid and broadsheet press photographers to any and every "event" she attends. The power of pictures is discussed further in Chapter 11.

ENTERTAINMENT VERSUS ELITISM?

Finding entertaining ways of telling stories is part of the journalist's job, and it can be a very enjoyable part, as Lindsay Eastwood explains:

> I enjoy doing the "And finally ..." stories because you can be creative. I've done a giant mushroom story, and a dog that was allergic to grass so they made it these special little red wellies. That was sweet. I did a lollipop man who'd won a "best lollipop man" award and he did a rap, so we got him dancing with some kids. I did a baby boom in a Hull supermarket where everybody on the checkout had had a baby. We got them to do the Marge Simpson thing with the checkout going "ping" when the baby was scanned in. And they've even taken a shot of my cleavage for National Cleavage Day.
>
> You can have a lot of fun on TV. When you've been doing serious stories like the floods, it's nice to do the light stuff. The strangest thing I have covered recently was a live report from a naked bike ride in York by protesters trying to highlight environmental issues. On that occasion I think I had a really good excuse to defy the ITN remit of doing a reporter involvement piece-to-camera. It was a tricky job, since we are under strict guidelines not to show any genitals in our programme and yet the whole story was about naked people. I don't know how, but I managed to pull it off.

So how would she respond to anyone who said that such stories, or her Bridget Jones pole routine mentioned earlier, were too formulaic, in some way demeaning of the journalist's craft? "No, I don't think they're formulaic at all. I think news stories are formulaic. You know, you get the scene of the murder, you get eyewitnesses, you try and chase the family. That's formulaic. I think the 'And finally ...'s are a real challenge."

Whenever journalists address "popular" subjects, or report in ways intended to entertain, they run the risk of being accused of dumbing down or of lacking **authority**. And when critics accuse journalists of dumbing down, they in turn tend to be accused of cultural **elitism**.

Yet even the most serious news is reported in ways designed to be entertaining, to keep the audience engaged. That is why news is told in the form of stories that usually focus on individual people rather than abstract concepts; why news stories are written in language that is accessible, active and sometimes colourful; why news stories may be presented visually, creatively, or even in the form of a list.

A journalist's job is *both* to inform and to entertain. The trick – for journalist and audience alike – is to recognise the difference between the two and to understand that if it fails to inform then it ceases to be journalism. It is also worth remembering that sometimes the facts of a story, simply told, can be the most entertaining of all.

SUMMARY

Journalists have long sought to entertain as well as to inform, to attract and retain an audience. This takes the form of selecting entertaining subject matter (humour, showbiz, sex, animals, crime, pictures, sport) and of telling stories in entertaining ways. It has been claimed that the lines between information and entertainment – and between serious and popular media – have become blurred in recent years as part of the process known as "dumbing down". The dumbing-down thesis has in turn been criticised as elitist and dismissed as the harking back to a supposed golden age that probably never existed. As journalism entails entertaining as well as informing an audience, journalists and citizens both need to be able to recognise the distinction between the two.

QUESTIONS

Can journalism be both entertaining and informative at the same time?
Why do journalists tell news as stories?
Why is crime such big news?
Is the concept of an authoritative-sounding news bulletin inherently elitist?
Is *any* news better than *no* news?

WHAT WOULD YOU DO?

You are on work experience in the newsroom of a popular national newspaper when the picture desk comes up with an idea of how to cover the fact that a photograph of a member of the royal family naked has just been published overseas. The paper has agreed to a request from Buckingham Palace not to publish the original picture and you are asked if you would be willing to pose in the nude and take part in a humorous recreation of the scene in the controversial snap. The idea is to publish a mocked-up photograph of you (with no genitalia visible) alongside a caption telling readers that you decided to drop everything to recreate the royal pose for their benefit. You are told it is all a bit of harmless fun. What would you do?

FURTHER READING

For an entertaining historical account of the press as popular entertainment you can't do better than Matthew Engel's (1997) *Tickle the Public*. Anthony Delano's ([1975] 2008 and 2009) retelling of Fleet Street's finest in pursuit of Ronnie Biggs and Joyce McKinney, respectively, also help explain how to put the pop into popular journalism; as does *Tabloid Girl* by Sharon Marshall (2010), although she admits to adding a little "topspin" to her tales of redtop excess. For more academic perspectives, Franklin (1997) offers a cogent critique of the tabloidisation of the print and broadcast media in the UK, countered in part by McNair (2000), who argues that coverage of politics in particular has *not* been dumbed down, and Temple's (2006) provocatively titled paper, "Dumbing down is good for you"; also see Temple (2008). Dovey (2000) examines the "carnivalesque" excesses of so-called reality TV, raising questions of authority, authorship and the public sphere. Finally, Bourdieu's (1998) consideration of journalism concludes by sounding a warning note that journalism's increasing focus on human interest stories might have the effect of depoliticising citizens.

TOP THREE TO TRY NEXT

Anthony Delano (2009) *Joyce McKinney and the Case of the Manacled Mormon*
Matthew Engel (1997) *Tickle the Public: One Hundred Years of the Popular Press*
Mick Temple (2006) "Dumbing down is good for you", *British Politics*

SOURCES FOR SOUNDBITES

Murdoch, quoted in O'Neill, 1992: 30n; Temple, 2006: 262; Neesom, quoted in Plunkett, 2003; Bourdieu, 1998: 51; Rusbridger, quoted in Cole and Harcup, 2010: 124.

PART TWO

HOW TO DO JOURNALISM

In *Part One* we looked at what journalism is, at some of the many roles played by journalists and at the constraints under which journalists often have to work. The five chapters in *Part Two* go on to explain and explore the range of multimedia skills expected of journalists today as well as the basics that remain essential. The word "skills" may be frowned upon in some academic circles, as if the teaching of them is akin to training an animal to repeat an action of which it has no sophisticated understanding. But good journalism requires skills just as it requires a thinking, questioning approach; it is not unlike good scholarship, in that sense at least. Whether it be researching the strongest interview questions, writing an intro or editing a video, there are intellectual processes at work within journalism, as should become clear to anyone who reads the views of Cathy Newman and the other journalists featured in the chapters that follow. *Part Two* may be primarily concerned with explaining *how* to do journalism, but this cannot be done effectively without continuing to think about *why* we do journalism in the first place.

PART 2 VIDEO

CHAPTER 8
INTERVIEWING FOR JOURNALISM

The interview – the asking of questions and the recording of answers – is the basic ingredient of most news and features. The interview is "the chief tool of active journalism", argues Cedric Pulford, because "Without talking to people who can give us information or opinions, by phone or face to face, we can only print what others send us or recycle what has appeared somewhere else" (Pulford, 2001: 17). As a way of getting to the truth of a matter, the journalistic **interview** also has its detractors and has even been described as a manufactured encounter or **pseudo-event**. Yet interviewing remains *the* key tool at the disposal of reporters. It is also one of the most enjoyable parts of a journalist's job because it is an exercise in nosiness, allowing us to meet interesting people and ask them pretty much any question we like. As Lynette Sheridan Burns (2013: 91) points out: "You can ask questions of an interviewee you cannot ask a document."

INTERVIEWING SKILLS

> "O my body, make of me always a man who questions!"
> *Frantz Fanon.*

BE PREPARED

The interview may be a brief encounter over the phone, a lengthy affair over lunch, a setpiece live broadcast, a full kiss-and-tell buy-up or just a few questions answered via email or text. Whatever it is, you should have some idea *why* you are interviewing this particular person: for factual answers to one or two questions, opinions, quotes, emotions, description, scraps of colour, background, whatever. Many journalists stress the importance of meticulous planning to ensure they remain in control, working to set questions or even a "script" determined by the particular angle being pursued (Aitchison, 1988: 40–42). Planning anything that resembles a script may encourage a rather stiff and inflexible approach

INTERVIEW

The use of the interview as a tool in reporting is generally traced to 19th-century US journalism (Patterson, 2012); before then journalists tended to rely on observational reportage and/or commentary, sometimes augmented with discussion of evidence gleaned from documents. But from the second half of the 19th century onwards, interviewing gradually became a common practice in the press, first in the USA and then in the UK (Chalaby, 1998: 127). Interviews were not universally popular. They were seen by some at the time as invasions of privacy, with one editor dismissing interviewing as "the most perfect contrivance yet devised to make journalism an offence, a thing of ill savour in all decent nostrils" (Boorstin, 1963: 26). Today it is hard to imagine journalism without the interview, described by Thomas Patterson (2012) as probably "the handiest reporting tool ever devised". He continues:

> Interviewing relieves the journalist of having to undertake more demanding forms of investigation, and the interviewee's words can be treated as "fact" insofar as the words were actually said. Yet, the interview is not foolproof. Who is interviewed, what is asked, and even the time and place of the interview can affect the answers. Responses are subject to mistakes of memory or even a source's determination to mislead a reporter. (Patterson, 2012)

Whether or not interviewing and other forms of reportage do – or should – relieve journalists of any investigative burden is discussed further in Chapters 5 and 6.

PSEUDO-EVENT

The concept of the pseudo-event was introduced in Chapter 2. Daniel Boorstin (1963: 27) categorises the to an interview, but thinking of *some* questions in advance is certainly a good idea. Of course, an interview may take an unexpected turn – and that might be a route you want to follow – but along the way you should make sure you cover the ground you need to.

You will often have time to conduct background research before the interview. You might spend a couple of hours searching news archives and reading cuttings about the subject, looking for basic information and useful insights, and possibly thinking of an angle nobody has yet come up with. You might Google them, but remember to read beyond the first page of results and to not rely on Wikipedia as an infallible source; in fact, don't rely on *anything* as an infallible source. You might look in specialist magazines, consult reference books, and talk to colleagues or friends who know something about the subject – or who have something they would like to ask. When Simon Hattenstone told friends he was going to interview film director Woody Allen, for example, one suggested: "Ask him how somebody so ugly gets off with so many beautiful women?" It turned out to be good advice because it became clear it was the very question that Allen had "obsessed over for most of his adult life" (Hattenstone, 2007).

THE "WINNING GRACE" OF INTERVIEWING

There is plenty of often quite prescriptive advice available on interviewing techniques, but trial and error is the way most trainee journalists feel their way through their first interviews. Experiment with different styles and see what works for you in different circumstances. Remember that it is rarely a good idea to pretend to have a completely different personality from your own. Nor is it necessarily a good idea for every fledgling hack to try to be Jeremy Paxman, who is often said to have revealed that he approaches TV interviews by asking himself "Why is this lying bastard lying to me?". He didn't actually say that, he just quoted Louis Heren of the *Times* (Wells, 2005), who was in turn quoting some advice he

> "Listening is as important as asking the question."
> *Helen Boaden.*

media interview – alongside the press conference and the press release – as a form of pseudo-event; that is, not so much a way of *gathering* the news, more a way of *making* it. He explains:

> Nowadays a successful reporter must be the midwife – or more often the begetter – of his news. By the interview technique he incites a public figure to make statements which will sound like news. During the 20th century this technique has grown into a devious apparatus which in skilful hands can shape national policy. (Boorstin, 1963: 34)

Before interviewing became commonplace, notes Michael Schudson, US President Lincoln often spoke with reporters informally "but no reporter ever quoted him directly" (Schudson, 2001: 156). Schudson argues that the growth of interviewing on both sides of the Atlantic helped journalists establish themselves as a separate group, brandishing notebooks and practising something that came to be called objective reporting:

> In the late 19th century and into the 20th century, leading journalists counselled against note-taking and journalists were encouraged to rely upon their own memories. But by the 1920s journalism textbooks dared to recommend "the discriminate and intelligent use of notes". The growing acceptance of note-taking suggests the acceptance and naturalization of interviewing. This is not to say the interview was no longer controversial. . . . There was still a sense that an "interview" was a contrived event in which the journalist, in collusion with a person seeking publicity, invented rather than reported news. As late as 1926 the Associated Press prohibited its reporters from writing interviews. But generally, reporting in the United States by that time meant interviewing. . . . It [fitted] effortlessly into a journalism already fact-centred and news-centred rather than devoted primarily to political commentary or preoccupied with literary aspirations. (Schudson, 2001: 157)

Contrived pseudo-events, many interviews may be – but at least they are normally based on the asking of questions, both substantive and supplementary. With some had once received (Robinson, 2012: 219–220). But whoever coined the phrase, the "lying bastard" approach is definitely better suited to the interrogation of a slippery politician than it is to asking a nice old couple how they plan to celebrate their golden wedding anniversary.

Most journalists have to be comfortable speaking to all sorts of people, from millionaires to the homeless. This remains as true today as when Frederick Mansfield instructed trainees back in the 1930s:

> Personality counts for much. A reporter has to meet all classes of people, who are potential sources of news; to talk to Cabinet Ministers as well as costermongers, I am tempted to say on their own level, and to inspire in all the confidence essential to successful approach. The happy medium between the "inferiority complex" and cocksure audacity should be the aim – a reasonable self-assurance, born of a well-informed competence. The winning grace that will extract news equally from a Lord Lieutenant and a trade union secretary, is a great asset. A reporter touches life at all points and in his deportment should show respect for the feelings and opinions of others, no matter how much he may be out of sympathy with them. Journalism tends to breed cynicism and a hypercritical attitude, but good manners, and often diplomacy, forbid a display of contempt. (Mansfield, 1936: 87–88)

The impeccably-mannered Martin Wainwright believes that a journalist's main assets during interviews are being *curious* about people and allowing enough *time* to let them talk: "People can be diffident, so the interesting things sometimes come out only at the very end of an interview." Also, he adds, "people can open up more if you appear a bit naïve". Note the word *appear* in that sentence.

An example of somebody apparently opening up in this way came when the short-lived Conservative party leader Iain Duncan Smith hosted a lunch to get to know local journalists. A youthful reporter from the *Wanstead and Woodford Guardian* took the opportunity to ask him some friendly enough questions, in the course of which the Tory leader remarked that Tony

powerful people now preferring to speak in public only via Twitter, might future generations of journalists come to look back on the interview as a quaint relic from a bygone age?

CONTROL

The relationship between interviewer and interviewee has been described by feature writer Fiammetta Rocco (1999: 49) as an "ambivalent coupling", and John Sergeant's account of his own ambivalent encounter with Tony Benn hinges on the question of who should have the right to control an interview. Arguably things have become even more ambivalent. Although today's journalistic style may be less deferential than in some earlier times – as recently as 1951 Prime Minister Clement Attlee could get away with answering even the soft question, "Is there anything else you'd like to say about the coming election?" with a terse, "No", without being probed further (Katwala, 2010) – today's interviewees may be more media-literate and schooled in the arts of spin than were their predecessors.

> "You won't get anywhere without being a nosy sod."
> *Simon Hattenstone.*

It is not just senior politicians who have teams of spin doctors, minders, schmoozers and enforcers surrounding them. Many celebrities (or their people) also try to impose tight control on interviews by setting conditions in return for (limited) access, as Gary Susman explains:

> There's always an army of publicists hovering over our shoulders, some from the studios, some employed by the stars, all making sure we don't ask anything impolite or embarrassing or anything that strays too far from the movie. The threats are never spoken but always implicit – if you ask the star about his ex-wife, he'll walk out, and you'll have ruined the interview for yourself and your colleagues; or worse, you'll be blackballed from future junkets. (Susman, 2001)

This "increased PR interventionism" in interviews can result in "journalistic passivity and compliance in a sanitised promotional drive", argues Eamonn Forde (2001: 38). It can even lead to editors agreeing to give "copy approval" to PR companies acting on behalf of the most highly prized celebrities (Morgan, 2002b).

The relationship between journalist and source is explored in more detail in Chapters 4 and 6; control of the finished product is discussed in the section on quotes, below.

Blair's children had been used "ruthlessly" to promote the then Labour Prime Minister. The day after the local paper appeared, the interview was being quoted throughout the national media. Reporter Sara Dixon reflected on her scoop:

> A young Diet-Coke-drinking local reporter sitting opposite you in a Woodford restaurant is distinctly less threatening than a grilling on party policy under the glare of studio lights by Andrew Marr or Jonathan Dimbleby. But it is also a question of approach. . . . [Without] the roundabout questions of how have the past six months been treating you Mr Duncan Smith, the contentious statement would never have been uttered. The comment about Blair and his children is not a thing that is extracted in pugnacious interviews, rather it *emerges out of conversations*. (Dixon, 2002, my emphasis)

Conversation is the key to good interviewing. Even the briefest interview should involve the techniques of conversation, and that means *listening* as well as talking. Yet the listening part is too often overlooked, according to Carl Bernstein of Watergate fame: "One of the things I've observed having been interviewed so many times is that reporters tend to be terrible listeners. They have usually decided what the story is before they do the interview, and they will choose the one which will manufacture the most controversy" (quoted in Silver, 2007). So interviewers need to listen and engage with what is being said rather than just wait for a gap to fill with the next question on their list. In face-to-face interviews it is important to make eye contact, and in all interviews the interviewee needs to be reassured via sounds or gestures that the interviewer is still awake and, ideally, still interested.

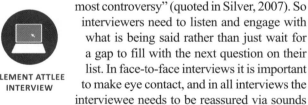

CLEMENT ATTLEE INTERVIEW

> "When a politician tells you something in confidence, always ask yourself *'Why is this lying bastard lying to me?'*
> Louis Heren.

ON THE TELEPHONE OR VIA SKYPE

You cannot make eye contact over the telephone, which is the way that most interviews are conducted. However, although there can be an impersonality about the phone, many journalists manage to develop chatty relationships with regular contacts whom they may never have met in the flesh.

VICTIM

The victim is a familiar character in journalism. Most information on victims comes from interviews with victims themselves if they are still alive, or from interviews with the bereaved. Thoughtful journalists may pause from time to time to consider why reporters and, presumably, readers are so fascinated with details of victims' lives. "Being the victim of crime is to lay oneself open to having one's privacy invaded", argues Chris Frost, who adds:

> Journalists need always to remember that victims of crime are not there by choice and rarely through any fault of their own. If the report will make things worse for the victim, then the journalist should think carefully about how the report should be handled. (Frost, 2000: 146)

And yet, do those critics who flinch from the very idea of "death knocks" not want to know about the person who was found dead in their neighbourhood last night? Where do they think such information comes from if not by interviewing distressed relatives, friends, neighbours and workmates? Sallyanne Duncan told fellow lecturers at an Association for Journalism Education seminar that journalism students should be encouraged to think positively about death knocks as one of the legitimate ways in which reporters can find things out and help those directly involved in events to have their say. Jackie Newton told the same event that journalists on death knocks should remember that the story on which they are working ultimately belongs not to the reporter or their editor but to the bereaved family – to whom it will always be more than just a story (Harcup, 2008).

The idea of the victim is considered in more detail in Chapter 9 and ethical issues are discussed further in Chapter 13.

QUOTES AND SOUNDBITES

A good quote or soundbite is highly prized. According to Allan Bell, direct quotation serves three key purposes in journalism:

> First, a quote is valued as a particularly incontrovertible fact because it is the newsmaker's own words. . . .
> A second function is to distance and disown, to

Tone of voice is obviously important, as is the manner in which you begin the call. When somebody answers the phone, you have no idea what they were in the middle of doing when you called – or whose call they might have been hoping for rather than yours – so it is not usually a good idea to launch into a fusillade of questions the second they come on the line. Speaking clearly, politely and not too fast, explain who you are and why you are ringing them. Ask for a few minutes of their time – be prepared to call back at a prearranged time if you are not on deadline – and try to sound bright, alert, friendly and non-threatening. It has been suggested that standing up while speaking on the phone exudes extra confidence, and that making facial and arm gestures can help inflect the voice with the appropriate tone (Keeble, 2001a: 63). I've also heard advertising reps being urged to "smile while you dial". That might be the sort of advice to make hardened hacks do the finger-down-the-throat routine, but it is endorsed by Sally Adams, who adds, "probably the most important thing is to *like* talking on the phone" (Adams with Hicks, 2001: 85, my emphasis).

Telephone interviews are almost always shorter than face-to-face ones, so you tend to get down to details pretty quickly. It is usually worth getting the interviewee talking by asking open questions such as "What happened to you?", "What did you see?" or "What did you think when . . .?". Their replies should prompt further questions. This is all well and good when you have called somebody and your research is fresh in your mind. But it's not so easy when *they* call *you* back hours or days later, by which time you may have forgotten why you wanted to talk to them in the first place. That's one reason why many journalists prefer to keep ringing somebody rather than rely on a return call that, if it comes at all, will probably be at the least convenient moment.

A halfway house between the telephone and face-to-face interview is one conducted via "voice over internet protocol" programs such as Skype or Facetime, using live video pictures as well as sound. Although interviewing somebody in this way clearly allows for more non-verbal communication than is possible over the phone, the result is often a rather

> **"As a journalist you spend most of your life rushing, but it's still worth spending as long as you can with people."**
> *Martin Wainwright.*

absolve journalist and news outlet from endorsement of what the source said. . . . The third function of direct quotation is to add to the story the flavour of the newsmaker's own words. (Bell, 1991: 207–209)

But most of what is said in most interviews will not be quoted directly; rather, the bulk of information gleaned from sources will be used as background or turned into reported speech. Bell argues that this power to edit "puts the journalist *in control* of focusing the story, able to combine information and wordings from scattered parts of an interview" (Bell, 1991: 209, my emphasis).

Ethical concerns are raised about this role of the journalist in selecting the parts of an interview to quote, the parts to paraphrase and the parts to discard, as Lynn Barber explains:

The journalist has *all* the power when it comes to writing the piece: she chooses which quotes to use and which to omit, which to highlight and which to minimise. I use a lot of quotes compared with most other interviewers, but they probably still only amount to at most two pages out of a twenty- or thirty-page transcript. So obviously with this degree of selection, one has almost limitless opportunities for "slanting" the interview, favourably or unfavourably. All I can say is that I don't aim to do that and I hope I don't. (Barber, 1999: 202, emphasis in original)

Similarly, the editing of video or audio interviews gives journalists the potential to mislead viewers and listeners. Any journalist tempted to flam-up a story by giving the impression that the interviewee said something they did not, should resist such temptation or cease to call themselves a journalist (Hudson and Rowlands, 2012: 294–295).

stiff and formal encounter unless the participants are already on friendly terms with each other. There is also the ever-present threat of the call suddenly ending due to technical problems, which does not make for a relaxed and free-flowing conversation.

A final word of warning on remote interviews conducted via the phone or on Skype. You need to be absolutely clear whether the interviewee is being serious or is joking. Given that you have few or no visual clues you may have to ask "Are you being serious?". Better to be thought of as lacking a sense of humour than to risk publishing a flippant or ironic remark as if it were a genuine opinion.

EMAIL AND TEXT

Telephone interviews may be impersonal, but trying to establish a rapport in written communication via email or texting can be even trickier. Traditionally, email or text interviews – like the faxed ones that briefly preceded them – have not been recommended except when they were the only way of getting through to somebody. That's mainly because they lack the instantaneous to-ing and fro-ing of spoken conversation, no matter how quick your fingers and thumbs are. Answers via text will usually tend to err on the side of brevity, whereas some email interviewees will write in rather stiff, formal language. Also, there is a limit to how many times questions and answers can be batted backwards and forwards before one side or the other gets fed up. Although email encounters tend to be more brisk and businesslike than do face-to-face or telephone conversations, it is possible to establish some kind of rapport so that the exchange becomes semi-conversational. Most of the interviews with journalists featured in this book were conducted face-to-face, but one or two were carried out over the phone and via email. Can you tell which?

Some people are happier to be interviewed by email because it means they can answer questions at their own convenience. Email may be the most convenient way of contacting a range of academic experts all over the world, for example, because your message will be waiting for them when they log on in their different time zones. Also, if you are

asking technical questions, email has the advantage that the interviewee will be putting the answers in writing for you, so your chances of misquoting the answer should be dramatically reduced.

Arguably, email has made it harder for people in positions of power to hide from journalists by resorting to the age-old device of never being available. When Paul Foot rang people from his desk at the *Daily Mirror* they tended to take his calls because of the kudos associated with that title, but when he switched to *Private Eye* such people often seemed to be "in meetings" whenever he telephoned. That can be a frustrating experience when investigating alleged wrongdoing, because you need to put allegations to those involved, as Foot explains:

> Getting information out of the people you're accusing is absolutely crucial to the whole operation. Just as email has changed our lives, the fax changed our lives. I got in the habit of faxing questions to people. Whereas if you rang them up they would never be available, once you've got the fax through, you're home. Because if you don't get an answer you can always say "well I faxed them with these questions". With the phone you might never get even to ask the question.

If you are going to contact an interviewee via email, it is safest to assume they would prefer to be addressed formally rather than informally, with a message that is spelled and punctuated correctly. And remember that you lose control of your email the moment you press *Send*, meaning that anything you have written may be forwarded to anyone to whom the recipient chooses to send it. It is always safer to assume that your emails or texts may one day be made public, possibly at a future Hutton- or Leveson-style inquiry or even in a trial at the Old Bailey – so think before you write or send anything.

> "The eye contact is really important."
> **Victoria Derbyshire.**

FACE-TO-FACE

When I interviewed the then Labour MP Tony Benn in his Chesterfield constituency office he brought out his own tape machine to record the conversation. He recorded all his interviews, partly to check later if he had been misquoted, but mostly to warn journalists not to stitch him up when writing their stories. Profile writer Lynn Barber expresses surprise that so few interview subjects make their own recordings to safeguard against being misquoted (Barber, 1999: 201). But Benn's refusal to accept that journalists should have total **control** of interviews managed to unsettle seasoned reporter John Sergeant, who recalls arriving at the MP's home to record an interview during the 1984–85 miners' strike:

> When he opened the door, I immediately noticed a small tape recorder, which he thrust forward, with its red light on, showing that it was recording. "Hello," he said; and I did not know whether to reply to him directly or speak into the tape recorder. I said hello to the machine. He then proceeded to give me a short lecture on the unfairness of the BBC's coverage of the miners' dispute. I took this in reasonably good heart, but *knowing that all my remarks were being recorded I said nothing which might be used against me.*
> (Sergeant, 2001: 236–237, my emphasis)

It was a rare case of the tables being turned, with the journalist rather than the interviewee having to think twice before saying anything. That particular interview ended with Benn erasing the BBC's tape with a demagnetising device, leaving the journalist in the unaccustomed position of being "struck dumb" (Sergeant, 2001: 238).

Happily, most encounters are less prickly affairs. Just as well because, unless you are accusing the interviewee of wrongdoing, you need to establish a *rapport* between the two of you. First impressions are important, so don't be late. Don't smell of booze or fags, unless you know that will help you fit in, and do dress appropriately – not as if you are going to a wedding or a funeral, but smartly enough so that your state of dress will not be an issue for the interviewee. Non-verbal communication is important, so show interest by making eye contact without staring, nodding but not nodding off. Give verbal reassurance that the interviewee is not speaking into a vacuum – laugh at their jokes, sympathise with their troubles, and use phrases such as "Really?", "Yes", "uhh-huhh" to demonstrate that you are engaged. But don't overdo it.

Learn to listen, interrupting their flow only if they are digressing too much and you are on deadline.

> "The only time I penetrated Tony Blair's defences over Iraq was by keeping eye contact while telling him he never seemed to be sorry."
>
> *Andrew Marr.*

Interrupting a dramatic narrative to check a minor detail – "How do you spell the name of the first boy eaten by the crocodile?" – can irritate the narrator. Make a note and check at the end. But don't be afraid to interrupt to clarify something you don't understand or to get some specific examples. Keep your eyes as well as your ears open because you might discover a visual clue to the interviewee's character (are they obsessively checking their phone, for example?) or a visual prompt for an unusual question. Clothes, hair, tattoos, piercings, pictures on the wall, books on the shelves, a pet, an unusual plant, a view from the window – all might spark off a question and lead to the discovery of a different angle.

Chat is more common at the end of an interview conducted in person than one conducted on the telephone, over Skype or via email, and sometimes this can result in further information or angles to follow up. Unless you don't mind risking any future relationship with the interviewee, you might think twice before quoting something said after a formal interview has finished without asking "Do you mind if I use that?". See the discussion later of "off-the-record" comments.

AUDIO AND TV INTERVIEWS

Much of this chapter deals with interviews for text-based journalism, whether in print or online. Increasingly, however, journalists who were once print-only are now also filing audio and video reports for online media (see also Chapter 11). Martin Wainwright quickly adopted a digital recorder for interviews, allowing him to upload audio files online after selecting the necessary information and quotes for his written news story or feature. "The thing I really like about it is that it allows people to speak for themselves", he says.

Interviews for audio and visual use – whether online or on radio or television – will rely on many of the same techniques as do interviews for magazines or newspapers. But there are also many differences, most notably the fact that you can use the speaker's *voice* as well as their words, and that there is a greater reliance on the open question to get them talking. Also, broadcast interviews often have more than an element of *performance* about them. Whereas the questioning is often invisible to the reader of a print interview, it is central to many broadcast interviews. None more so than when Jeremy Paxman asked Home Secretary Michael Howard the *same* question 12 times without getting an answer (Wells, 2005). However, aside from the setpiece studio slanging match or the doorstep challenge to an alleged rogue, the aggressive approach is not usually to be recommended. You will win few prizes by exhorting the organiser of a local charity jumble sale to "Come on, come on, answer the question!". So how does Cathy Newman approach TV interviews for *Channel 4 News*?

I'm not of the view that the interviewer or presenter should make themselves part of the story. I think you're there to get the very best answers out of the interviewee. Obviously you've got to be an engaging on-screen presence, but my questions can be quite short, whereas sometimes I think some presenters' longer questions can be self-indulgent. You're trying to get the best possible information out of the person you're interviewing. That's the key challenge. When we do pre-recorded interviews, in some ways it's easier because you can just meander a little bit and come back to an issue, but the problem with that is that it's all got to be cut down. It's very hard to edit it sometimes, to make sense. I think really carefully about the structure of an interview, what issue leads where, and depending on how somebody answers, you've then got to change tack, and it's all got to make sense for the viewer. That's the most important thing, taking the viewer with you.

> **"A journalist never knows what the interviewee thinks, only what the interviewee says."**
> *Lynette Sheridan Burns.*

However, actually listening to an interviewee's answers can sometimes be surprisingly difficult, as Newman explains:

I think that's the most important thing but in some ways it's the hardest thing because you've got people talking in your ear, there might be a problem with the next piece, so there's a crisis going on in the gallery and you're trying to concentrate on what someone is saying. My least favourite interviews are down the line, where there's a delay in the satellite and you can't really get a proper sort of interrogation because you can't really interrupt and that might mean if someone talks for a minute in an answer that's a third of your interview gone and you haven't had a chance to challenge them, so that's very frustrating. And you might not be able to hear them that well because the link might not be that good. So the most frustrating issues are when the technicalities detract from the journalism.

Not surprisingly, then, the interviews Newman enjoys the most are either with guests in the studio or out on location when there is plenty of time. One of her most memorable and moving interviews was with Tony Nicklinson, a paralysed man with "locked-in syndrome" who was campaigning for the legal right to die. She recalls the tearful encounter that took place over two-and-a-half hours in his home as her longest and saddest interview ever, yet one she feels privileged to have conducted:

I did the first interview with him and he blinked out every letter of every word via his wife [who held up an alphabet board], which was his means of communicating. So that was the most painstaking interview I've ever done, for him as much as for me. That was really memorable because he felt so passionately about what he wanted to get across in that interview. I think he helped change the culture around the law on right-to-die, he was a seminal figure in that debate.

Obviously in my job I've interviewed prime ministers, presidents, the Dali Lama, A-list Hollywood stars, but some of my most memorable pieces have been interviewing ordinary people in extraordinary situations, like Tony Nicklinson.

ASKING QUESTIONS

The precise nature of the questions you ask in any form of interview will be determined initially by its purpose and then by whatever research you have done in advance. But it is important that you listen attentively to people's answers and adjust your line of questioning if necessary. It is usually a good idea to get the interviewee talking in an open way at the beginning, even if you intend to end up by accusing them of some skulduggery. So, unless you specifically want a yes or no answer, try to avoid asking *closed* questions, such as "Did you see the accident?". To get them talking, opt for more *open* questions, such as "What could you see?". People often stop after a sentence or two, looking for reassurance that this is what you want. You might encourage them to continue by asking "And then?", or "What happened next?", but some interviewers prefer the trick of remaining quiet after the initial answer in the hope that the interviewee will go a bit deeper when filling the awkward silence.

> "'Why?' is the question I ask most often."
> **Fiammetta Rocco.**

Whatever the topic, you are likely to want to know the answers to the five Ws of journalism introduced in Chapter 1: Who? What? Where? When? Why? Plus, of course, How? You will often have to do some lateral thinking while listening. *Who* is that person? *What* is their relationship to so-and-so? *Where* did they meet? *When* did they arrive? *Why* did they go there? *How* did they travel? The answer to any one such question might end up providing you with the most newsworthy angle to a story. But you might never know if you don't ask. Clarify any vague answers such as "recently" or "about". Getting specific examples by asking "Such as?" can sometimes bring a dull interview to unexpected life. Do not be afraid to say: "Sorry, I'm not sure I've understood that. Could you please explain it again?"

Unless you are transmitting live, it is a good idea to ask towards the end: "Is there anything else you'd like to add?" It is polite, it stops the interviewee feeling annoyed that they didn't get the chance to talk about their pet subject, and they might just say something far more important and interesting than anything that has gone before. Then, make sure you have checked spellings, especially names, and exchanged contact details. And don't forget to thank people for their help and time. A little courtesy can go a long way.

OFF-THE-RECORD

An interviewee may tell a journalist that something is "off-the-record", meaning that you should not attribute the information to them. That does not mean that you cannot include the information in an unattributed form. Check exactly what information they are referring to.

They may have good reason – perhaps they might lose their job for criticising their employer in public – or they may be feeling paranoid with little justification. As the interview progresses they may begin to trust you more, so you could try suggesting that something said earlier off-the-record might be restored to on-the-record. But if you break your word, having agreed to something being off-the-record, then you will have betrayed a source. Confusion arises if somebody *assumes* that a journalist will treat something as off-the-record without making it explicit. And sometimes people just say things that, with hindsight, they wish they had kept to themselves. A journalist who combines a conversational tone with a keen news sense will sometimes be "lucky" enough to catch an interviewee in just such a mood. Jane Merrick recalls the time that, as a Press Association reporter, she made a routine telephone call to a petrol company press office at the beginning of a series of fuel protests that went on to paralyse the UK:

> It was during the protesters' first blockade of an oil refinery. In London the company's line was that petrol supplies won't be affected. When I called the PR guy in the North-West I got lucky because he was really annoyed and he said: "Don't these people realise we're going to run out of fuel by Sunday night?" I said, like, "Really?" And he said, "Yeah, and it's really peeing me off." I said, "OK, fine", put the phone down and ran the story, "Warning of fuel shortage by Sunday".

The warning became a national talking point and the panic buying of petrol increased as a result. Merrick continues:

> This guy got into so much trouble. He phoned me on the Monday and said: "It wasn't off-the-record because I didn't say it was off-the-record, but I shouldn't have said that to you because our line was that it was fine." When clearly it wasn't fine.

DOORSTEPS AND DEATH KNOCKS

Some interviews are fraught with difficulties, ranging from the boredom of hanging around for hours waiting for somebody to emerge through a doorway to the possibility of a punch in the face. The "doorstep" and the "death knock" bring out differing emotions in journalists and interviewees alike.

Doorstepping is a peculiarly British tradition, argues Matthew Engel. And a peculiarly ineffective one, it seems:

> Photographers and reporters descend on the home of a person touched by scandal or tragedy . . . and wait, in the hope of a picture of one of the actors in the drama or, far less probably, a comment. It is a tiresome and, for the reporters, almost always a pointless chore, unless they are actually paying to buy the story. (Engel, 1997: 279)

Not so, according to Nick Davies. He has no time for reporters who bully people, camp outside their homes and peer through their windows, but he argues that arriving unannounced on people's doorsteps remains an integral part of the journalist's armoury: "That's how you get good stories. It is the most exciting and most skilful part of our job" (quoted in Stevens, 2001).

When it comes to death knocks – calling on a bereaved family to ask for information, quotes and a picture – few journalists actually enjoy the task, although some adopt a macho pose and boast of their experiences. Codes of ethical conduct advise reporters to be cautious about intruding on people's grief, and families may be actively hostile to journalists' enquiries at such a difficult time. Some people genuinely welcome the chance to talk about the death of somebody close to them, even to a stranger with a notebook, while others may answer questions to avoid inaccuracies appearing in the media, or simply because they do not think of refusing. Deborah Wain is experienced at talking to victims' families after crimes, accidents or inquests. People usually seem to talk to her, so I asked her why:

> I try to be really straight with people when I interview them. I try to be polite and people respond really. I never give people the impression that I'm doing anything other than what I'm doing. On death knocks, be upfront. Don't try to be over-sympathetic, don't say "I'm sorry", because you obviously didn't know that person. It's a hard one to get right, a lot of it is play it by ear. Be straight about it, say this story will go in the paper and we want to give you, the family,

> "A lot of it is play it by ear."
> *Deborah Wain.*

the chance to say something about your son or whoever as a person. I've often rung people up and asked them if I can come and see them, rather than just turn up. Most people say yes. I'm a great believer that if people want to talk they will, or will ring you back. I know some people say don't do it over the phone or don't leave a message because they won't ring you back, but I don't think that's the case. If they want to say something they will get back in touch with you if you open that window of opportunity. I think women do better at death knocks. I know it's a bit of a cliché to send women out, but it's for good reason.

Reporter Sue White agrees on the importance of being polite and non-pushy, as she describes her own approach:

> Normally it would be quiet and I'd knock on the door. It would open a crack and someone would answer. . . . I'd say, "Hello, I'm Sue White from the *Birmingham Evening Mail*. We've heard from the police about the dreadful accident last night. Could I come in and have a word with you about it?" Almost everyone would say, "All right". . . . It's important to be very, very courteous and understanding. . . . I'd be taken in and sat in the lounge. It would be very quiet, they'd be stunned. I felt if I talked openly, in as friendly and sympathetic a way as possible – one person to another, making it clear I just wanted to confirm some facts – people would give me that information. I was usually right. (Quoted in Adams with Hicks, 2001: 142–143)

To the non-journalist the death knock might sound callous, even manipulative. But when we hear there has been a murder or a fatal accident, don't we *expect* the media to tell us about the **victim** – their name, how old they were, and something about their character and interests? This information does not appear in the media by osmosis, not everyone is yet on Facebook (nor is everything on it necessarily accurate), and full details are rarely supplied by the police or other third parties. Such details have traditionally been obtained by journalists knocking on the doors or ringing the telephones of relatives, neighbours, friends, schools and workplaces, and a recent study found that many bereaved families can find it a positive experience, if conducted sensitively – and preferable to finding that personal material has simply been lifted from social media:

> By believing in the value of interviewing the family the surveyed journalists enable the relatives to maintain a level of control over the story, something that is important to the bereaved, which may be denied to them when material is taken predominantly from the deceased's social networking sites, unless of course the journalist seeks consent from the family to reproduce quotes and pictures. (Newton and Duncan, 2012: 214)

Relatives don't have to be bereaved to be contacted by journalists at times of trauma. Jane Merrick was working for a regional news agency when news came through that the former Beatle George Harrison had been attacked, and that someone was being held by police in connection with the incident. She recalls:

> The name of the man arrested had got through the rumour mill so we contacted all the names in the [phone] book and I got to his mum first. I introduced myself as a journalist and she asked me what had happened. I said, "It's OK, I'll come out and speak to you." She said, "Tell me what's happened, is he OK?" I said, "He's absolutely fine but I need to come and see you in person". Then she got very defensive and said she would put the phone down if I didn't tell her what was going on. So I said, "There's been a bit of an incident that Michael has been involved in, but he's absolutely fine". She put two and two together and shouted to her husband, "Oh my God, Michael's stabbed a Beatle!" And then she put the phone down. In the end I had to go out there. Eventually she invited everyone in, but by then we weren't the only ones.

Reflecting on the experience, Merrick says:

> I felt terrible because you can't say straight out, "Your son has stabbed someone", and I was quite surprised that the police hadn't contacted her. It was a really difficult way to tell her, and I tried to soften it as much as possible, but you can't just be really mysterious and say, "I need to come and speak to you". With hindsight, I should just have established that she was the mother, and then turned up at the door to speak to her.

Brian Whittle favours the in-person approach rather than giving anyone the opportunity of putting the phone down on you. But people can still shut the door and tell a journalist to go away. The editors' code of practice instructs journalists that, except in cases in the public interest, they must not persist in questioning or telephoning people after they have been asked to stop. Harassment of unfortunate families does still go on, but nowhere near as much as it once did. As agency reporter Denis Cassidy says: "If you are told to leave, nowadays, then you leave" (quoted in Stevens, 2001).

THE DEATH KNOCK

QUOTING

As well as being a means of obtaining information, interviews provide journalists with direct quotes and their audio equivalents, soundbites. **Quotes and soundbites** are a vital ingredient of journalism, adding authority, drama and powerful or colloquial expression to an account. "The key to securing a good soundbite is to frame your question so the answer will sum up the respondent's position – their view, reaction or account of what they have witnessed", advise Hudson and Rowlands (2012: 107). Short video or audio clips containing soundbites can then be used for subsequent news bulletins in addition to the original report. But it is important not to misrepresent the interviewee in the editing of soundbites. If you don't wish to report somebody's views accurately, what is the point of interviewing them in the first place (Hudson and Rowlands, 2012: 295)?

Opinions differ a bit more on the editing of written quotes, although all agree that little purpose is served by including excessive repetition of phrases such as "like", "know what I mean?", or "urn" – unless you are doing it to make a point about the speaker. David Randall questions the use of quotation marks if what they contain is not "a word for word, syllable by syllable, accurate report of their actual words" (Randall, 2000: 187). But journalists frequently "tidy up" quotes. If they did not, it would be a remarkable coincidence that sources interviewed by tabloid journalists seem to speak in short, sharp sentences, while those quoted by broadsheet reporters speak in more complex sentence structures – even when they are the same people. Whittle defends the practice of editing quotes:

> I think you can put words in people's mouths in the sense that most people are not particularly literate. That's perfectly acceptable if you know what you're doing, but only experience can tell you that. We go over people's quotes. Don't misunderstand me on this, we're pretty careful about it.

Merrick found contrasting policies at work when she moved from another regional news agency to the Press Association: "At the agency we could paraphrase people almost and still put it in quotes because it would be neater, whereas at PA it's the *exact* words. Now I have two dictaphones as a back-up and tape everyone as well as take short-hand notes, to cover my own back really." Wynford Hicks and Tim Holmes urge a similar caution:

> [You] can always summarise quotes in indirect speech if tidying up causes difficulty – but you must never do the reverse: indirect speech can never be used as the raw material for a concocted quote. In subbing quotes . . . the key word is accuracy: the exact meaning of the original must be preserved. In condensing and clarifying a quote . . . you must never change the emphasis. So if somebody makes a statement that is qualified in some way, you remove the qualification at your peril. (Hicks and Holmes, 2002: 65)

The ethical line between tidying and changing can be a fine one. It can sometimes disappear entirely, especially if a reporter edits somebody's comments when making notes, then slightly strengthens them when writing up, before passing the story on to a sub who might tidy the quotes a bit more. The published result might end up being wholly unrecognisable to the interviewee, not just in words but in meaning. The golden rule when selecting or shortening quotes, and pruning out repetitions or irrelevancies, is to retain not just the interviewee's *voice* but the speaker's *sense*. Otherwise, why bother quoting at all?

SUMMARY

Journalists interview sources – on the telephone, over Skype, in person, by email or text – to obtain information, facts, opinions, analysis, description, emotion, colour, background, direct quotes and soundbites. The interview has been described as an ambivalent encounter in which the interviewee controls what information they disclose but, with the exception of live broadcasts, the interviewer retains control of which bits of the interview are passed on to the audience. Interviews can themselves create news and in this sense can be seen as pseudo-events. Ethical issues associated with interviewing include questions of intrusion into grief, copy approval, selection of material and editing.

QUESTIONS

Why do journalists interview people?
Why do people agree to be interviewed by journalists?
How can journalists prepare for interviews?
Who's in charge, the interviewer or interviewee?
Is it ever right to edit people's quotes or soundbites?

WHAT WOULD YOU DO?

You are sent to interview a newly elected Mayor face to face to write a profile for your local news organisation. As you get up to leave, the Mayor relaxes, begins to joke, chats about their student days 20 years ago, boasts about how much alcohol they consumed back then, and hints at a youthful history of sexual promiscuity and occasional use of cannabis – before adding, "Of course, that was all off-the-record" and bidding you goodbye. What would you do? And would it make any difference if the Mayor were Labour or Tory, male or female, gay or straight?

HOW MIGHT YOU TACKLE THIS ISSUE?

FURTHER READING

Despite the sometimes prescriptive tone, there are many good tips and instructive anecdotes to be found in Adams with Hicks (2009), while Hudson and Rowlands (2012) offer guidance on broadcast interviews and Beaman (2011) deals with radio interviewing specifically. Randall (2011), Sheridan Burns (2013), Sissons (2006) and Pape and Featherstone (2005), among others, all have useful general sections on interviewing, while McKay (2006) includes two chapters specifically on magazine interviews. For a different perspective on the death knock, Harcup (2007) includes a chapter on crime reporting that features an interview with a victim's relative as well as a crime reporter. Finally, if you can track down a copy, Silvester (1994) is a mammoth collection of historical interviews.

TOP THREE TO TRY NEXT

Sally Adams with Wynford Hicks (2009) *Interviewing for Journalists* (second edition)
Gary Hudson and Sarah Rowlands (2012) 'The interview', Chapter 4 of *The Broadcast Journalism Handbook* (second edition)
Christopher Silvester (ed) (1994) *The Penguin Book of Interviews*

SOURCES FOR SOUNDBITES

Fanon, 1967 [1970]: 165; Boaden, quoted in Hudson and Rowlands, 2012: 90; Hattenstone, 2007; Heren, quoted in Robinson, 2012: 220; Wainwright, interview with the author; Derbyshire, quoted in Hudson and Rowlands, 2012: 85; Marr, quoted in Barnicoat, 2007; Sheridan Burns, 2013: 92; Rocco, 1999: 50; Wain, interview with the author.

CHAPTER 9

WRITING NEWS

"Can an algorithm write a better news story than a human reporter?" asked *Wired* magazine in 2012, to which any journalist worth their salt would answer: "Of course not." But perhaps it's not a question of writing *better* copy, but a greater *quantity* of (cheap) copy. The *Wired* story, written by a human as it happens, reported a claim that "the universe of newswriting will expand dramatically, as computers mine vast troves of data to produce ultracheap, totally readable accounts of events, trends, and developments that no journalist is currently covering" (Levy, 2012). Far-fetched? Well, by the following year media boss David Montgomery was telling anyone who would listen that his Local World chain – the third biggest provincial newspaper company in the UK – intended to "harvest content and publish it without human interface" (Hollander, 2013).

NEWS WRITING BY ALGORITHM

Such talk is pretty depressing for journalists to hear, but the idea of using robots to replace flesh-and-blood hacks has obvious attractions for proprietors: no attitude problems, no ethical qualms, no maternity leave. It's not even an original thought. Michael Frayn invented just such a news machine half a century ago in his novel *The Tin Men*, in which a computer "could be programmed to produce a perfectly satisfactory daily newspaper with all the variety and news sense of the old hand-made article" (Frayn, [1965] 1995: 37). We saw in Chapter 3 that in some ways news can be predictable and repetitive. This is partly because little happens that hasn't happened somewhere before. But it is also because some news is indeed written, or constructed, in the predictable and formulaic way satirised by Frayn. Some, but not all; and even that which is rather formulaic is still the result of human intervention. Yet reporters can still sometimes be heard to say about a particular story that "it writes

> "In all cases, abolish the abstract and use the particular."
> *David Randall.*

STORIES

Journalists do not so much write articles as *stories*, argues Allan Bell: "Journalists are professional storytellers of our age. The fairytale starts: 'Once upon a time.' The news story begins: 'Fifteen people were injured today when a bus plunged . . .'" (Bell, 1991: 147). According to Dan Berkowitz, journalists develop "a mental catalogue of news story themes, including how the 'plot' will actually unravel and who the key actors are likely to be" (quoted in Cottle, 2000: 438). Traditional stories start at the beginning and continue to some sort of resolution at the end. But news stories often start with the end – or at the moment when the main action occurs. As Bell notes, the central action of news stories is told in a non-chronological order, "with result presented first followed by a complex recycling through various time zones" (Bell, 1991: 155). So a typical news story "moves backwards and for-wards in time" (Bell, 1991: 153).

Then, rather than being resolved neatly, news stories often finish in "mid-air" (Bell, 1991: 154). This is not simply because news values and journalists' training dictate that the least important material be left to the end, but also because many stories are ongoing. The version of events given in the newspaper has always been merely a snapshot taken at deadline time; the advent of online news and 24-hour broadcasting without fixed deadlines allows stories to be constantly updated, but no update is ever guaranteed to be the final word.

MYTHS

Simon Cottle argues that storytelling has long been used by society to "tell and re-tell its basic myths to itself", thereby reaffirming society as (after Anderson) an "imagined community". Viewed in this way, "news becomes a symbolic system in which the informational itself". That is, it is such a good story that, having established the intro or the top line, the rest flows almost effortlessly from the notebook or phone to the finished product. An experienced reporter will be able to rush from a courtroom or a news conference and, seconds later, be filing a perfectly constructed news story. It looks like magic to the beginner who has to pore over every word, but it can be learned with practice and it is made possible by the fact that journalists already have potential **stories** in their heads. It has even been said that many news stories are rewrites of ancient **myths** in contemporary settings.

THE LANGUAGE OF NEWS

> **"If you can read your intro in one breath, your reader can probably absorb it very easily in one reading."**
> *Anna McKane.*

There are some obvious differences in the writing styles of different types of media, including differences over the amount of colour, and the number of adjectives, allowed into news copy. For example, when Jane Merrick worked for a regional agency selling mostly to the redtop tabloids, her copy would be sprinkled with words such as "brave", "pretty" and "tragic". When she switched to the Press Association she quickly learned that PA's style was to remove all such adjectives. But, although journalists working for different outlets may differ in their news values and their stylistic flourishes, they mostly share a common language – a basic grammar of journalism. Study the language of news stories in newspapers or their websites and you will find that most news is written in the past tense, reporting on something that has happened or been said. This contrasts with broadcast and some online news – and tweets – in which the present tense is more common, although the past and even future tenses also make appearances. You will find that reporters' sentences are mostly active rather than passive, with somebody *doing* something rather than having something done *to* them. And you will find that concise writing is the norm – journalists never circumambulate the domiciles when they could simply go round the houses.

HOW TO WRITE

So news sentences are made up of active and concise language. They also tend to be short. They generally have a subject and a verb, although the subject may be implied. Paragraphs (pars), too, are

content of particular 'stories' becomes less important than the rehearsal of mythic 'truths' embodied within the story form itself" (Cottle, 2000: 438).

Jack Lule argues that journalists repeatedly write the news in terms of myth; that is, stories that draw on archetypal figures and forms to offer exemplary models for human life" (Lule, 2001: 15). Not *every* news story is written in such terms, but many are. Why? Because, for Lule, stories already exist before they are written:

> Journalists approach events with stories already in mind. They employ common understandings. They borrow from shared narratives. They draw upon familiar story forms. They come to the news story *with* stories. Sometimes the story changes as the journalist gathers more information. But the story doesn't change into something completely new and never before seen. The story changes into . . . another story. (Lule, 2001: 29, emphasis and ellipsis in original)

He identifies seven enduring myths that are told and retold by journalists through supposedly fresh news stories. They are:

- the victim – transforming death into sacrifice;

- the scapegoat – what happens to those who challenge or ignore social beliefs;

- the hero – the humble birth, the quest, the triumph and the return;

- the good mother – models of goodness;

- the trickster – crude, stupid, governed by animal instincts;

- the other world – the contrast between "our" way of life and the "other";

- the flood – the humbling power of nature (Lule, 2001: 22–25).

Consider the crime stories that make up such a large proportion of our news, particularly at a local and regional level. As we have seen in Chapter 4, most crime news is supplied by the police. Journalists can predict that there will be a reasonably steady supply of crime news and how many of the various types of crime are likely to occur much shorter than in other forms of writing, often just one sentence long, sometimes two or three. Journalists are taught to use short pars because when stories are set in newspaper columns long pars look like indigestible and off-putting chunks of text; stories on web "pages" may not be in such narrow columns but they still require paragraph breaks to make them appear easier to digest. Shorter pars are also thought more likely to keep the attention of readers, although some variety in longer stories is probably a good idea. Wynford Hicks (1998: 43) offers the following advice: "In news a par that goes beyond three sentences . . . is likely to be too long; never quote two people in the same par: always start a new one for the second quote; never tack a new subject on to the end of a par." When you are a beginner you won't go far wrong if, when in doubt, you start a new par.

BBC JOURNALISTS ON WRITING

STRUCTURE: KISS AND TELL

Most news stories follow the "KISS and tell" formula – KISS standing either for "keep it short and simple", or "keep it simple, stupid". I have heard journalists on a local freesheet being told to imagine they were "writing for your granny". Complexity, abstract notions, ambiguity and unanswered questions tend to be frowned upon and subbed out of news copy, along with anything that seems to be the reporter's personal opinion.

News stories should answer the Five Ws that, along with an H, are the starting point of most journalism: Who? What? Where? When? Why? And: How? Like this: "Lady Godiva [WHO] rode [WHAT] naked [HOW] through the streets of Coventry [WHERE] yesterday [WHEN] in a bid to cut taxes [WHY]" (Hicks et al, 1999: 15). News should be specific, not general; clear, not vague. Telling the Five Ws is one way of achieving this. In most cases you shouldn't try to answer *all* those questions in the intro – it would be too wordy and clumsy – but news intros are likely to give us the answers to two or three of the Five Ws. The others should normally follow fairly quickly afterwards.

> "Names and places change but the story remains essentially the same."
> *Jack Lule.*

on their patch. A murder will be a shock in a rural village but almost expected to occur in an inner-city area (though it may still come as a shock to those who live in nearby streets). It does not take long for recruits to journalism to absorb how particular crimes tend to be covered. Murder victims, for example, might be innocent (wouldn't hurt a fly), heroic (have-a-go-hero) or tainted (gunned down in a drugs turf war), and this approach helps determine how much effort is expended on painting a sympathetic picture of their lives by means of comments from family, friends and neighbours, duly illustrated by snaps from the family album or lifted from Facebook.

Angela Phillips has reduced Lule's list of myths to five basic narratives that influence news stories "by selection and exclusion" and which "can overwhelm, or completely change the emphasis and interpretation of the information". Her list of familiar narratives is:

- Overcoming evil.

- Transformation.

- Tragedy.

- Romance.

- Coming of age, aka rags to riches (Phillips, 2007: 13–20).

also know as

For Lule, the telling of news stories as myth usually helps to "manufacture consent" towards the existing social order. However, such ideological power is not predetermined because news is "messy and complicated" and is "a site of personal, social, and political struggle from its conception by a reporter to its understanding by a reader". Therefore, mythic stories might potentially be used to offer alternative perspectives on society (Lule, 2001: 192). Phillips agrees:

> Myth and metaphor are not, by definition, conservative and uncritical. They can also be used to challenge the status quo and to break down conventions. Transgressive stories are often more arresting than those that operate within conventional normative boundaries. When we read sympathetic stories about people who have, conventionally, been treated as pariahs, they challenge our assumptions. . . . The challenge is to understand the power of myth, to know how to use it, but also how to subvert it. (Phillips, 2007: 23–24)

A good news story will be important and/or be of potential interest to the audience; it will be based on evidence, with sources of information and opinion clearly attributed; and it will be written in clear, precise and active language. But how will it be structured? Traditionally, trainee journalists have been taught to think of the structure of a news story as a triangle, a pyramid or, more commonly, an **inverted pyramid**. However it is visualised, the idea is that the most important information should be at the top, followed by elaboration and detail, ending up with the least important information at the bottom (Hicks et al, 1999: 16). If space is short, the material at the bottom can be removed, and what's left should stand alone and still make sense. So a 500-word article could swiftly be transformed into a nib (news in brief), a four-par story for a website or, with a bit of tweaking, even a tweet. Combined with the Five Ws, the pyramid – or inverted pyramid – is a good way of starting to think about constructing relatively simple news stories. The most striking or important information goes at the top – usually several of the Who? What? Where? When? Why? How? – and the rest follows in diminishing order of importance.

THE INTRO

The intro is crucial because it sets the tone for what follows. A poorly written intro might confuse, mislead or simply bore the reader; a well-written intro will encourage the reader to stay with you on the strength of the information and angle you have provided. A good hard news intro generally conveys a maximum of impact with a minimum of punctuation. Like this:

TIPS ON WRITING NEWS

> "Lots of facts, plainly stated and grouped with drama and maybe a dash of sentiment –
> no more. That's the journalistic cocktail."
> **James Milne.**

> A boy of 15 was being quizzed last night after allegedly stabbing to death his teacher in class. (MURDER IN CLASS, Paul Sims, *Sun*, April 29 2014)

That sentence contains just 18 words and a full stop but it tells a dramatic story in miniature, with the details to come in subsequent pars. OK, so "quizzed" is a bit of journalese, but everyone knows what it means in this context. Reducing punctuation to a minimum is not a hard-and-fast rule, though,

INVERTED PYRAMID

Although the image of the inverted pyramid is commonly used in journalism training, it also has its critics. Don Fry of the US-based Poynter Institute, for example, argues that readers will not be able to fully comprehend a news story written according to the inverted pyramid model because "the background goes at the bottom, somewhere between 'boring' and 'dull'. Without background, readers cannot understand the story, and simply give up before they get to the information they need". He prefers the idea of a "stack of blocks" consisting of a beginning, a middle and an end, in which "The beginning predicts the middle in form and content, and the ending cements the main points into the readers' memories" (Fry, 2004). The concept of the inverted pyramid and the order in which more or less important information is placed also raises the question of who decides what is more or less important, and on what basis. This is where the writing of news depends on an understanding of the news values discussed in Chapter 3, so the order in which a story is told will largely be determined by the news values that operate in a particular newsroom at a particular time (Smith and Higgins, 2013: 77).

But the inverted pyramid model is not simply a technical method to follow or a neutral means of storytelling, according to Daniel Hallin. He argues that where information appears in a story, and how it is inflected, can have an ideological effect by emphasising some views or voices and by marginalising others. To illustrate the point, he suggests that reporting of the Vietnam war saw a "reverse inverted pyramid" in operation, whereby the nearer the information was to the truth, the further down the news story it would be placed (cited in Schudson, 1991: 148–149). Then again, as we have seen, the truth itself is not always a simple matter.

ATTRIBUTION

One of the primary questions of journalism is "Who says?", argues Bell, who suggests that, as a lot of news is based on *somebody saying something*, a pertinent question for journalists and readers is to ask what credentials the source has:

> Attribution serves an important function in the telling of news stories. It reminds the audience that this is

and sometimes commas can be used for effect as in this equally dramatic intro:

> Two *Times* journalists escaped over the Syrian border yesterday after being double-crossed, kidnapped, beaten and shot by a rebel gang in the north of the country. (*TIMES* JOURNALIST SHOT IN SYRIA BY KIDNAP GANG, Foreign Staff, *Times*, May 15 2014)

That's still only 26 words (if we count the hyphenated "double-crossed" as one), but the addition of two commas helps convey the impression of the victim's ordeal being one thing after another. And it's one hell of a story. As is this example of the insertion of a well-placed dash into a 21-word intro:

> Giant waves driven by 91mph hurricane-force winds swept away sea defences yesterday – and left a vital railway line dangling in mid-air. (91mph STORMS WASH AWAY RAILWAY TRACK, Piers Eady and Richard Smith, *Daily Mirror*, February 6 2014)

The three intros above are quite different from each other but all are based on a journalistic decision about what is the most important and/or most dramatic element of the story. Note that none includes the names of the people involved or precise locations. That's because, as Lynette Sheridan Bums explains, the news intro is akin to somebody who is in a hurry blurting out the main point of a story:

> News writing always starts with the most important fact. When you report on a football game, you do not start with the kick-off, you begin with the final score. So it is with news. If someone were to blow up the building across the street from where you work today, when you got home you would not start the story by saying, "Today seemed like an ordinary sort of day, little did I know how it would turn out." You would say, "Someone blew up the building across the street!" In other forms of journalism it is fine for your story to have a beginning, a middle and an end. News stories, in contrast, blurt out something and then explain themselves . . . (Sheridan Burns, 2002: 112)

Study news intros on any given day and you will see a variety of techniques at work. In the literature of journalism training, these are often

an account which originated with certain persons and organisations. It is not an unchallengeable gospel, but one fruit of human perception and production among other conceivably alternative accounts. In theory a news story should be regarded as embedded under a stack of attributions, each consisting of source, time and place. (Bell, 1991: 190)

Attribution of sources is important to the notion of journalistic balance, writes Keeble:

> Reporters use sources to distance themselves from the issues explored. Rather than express their views on a subject, reporters use sources to present a range of views over which they can appear to remain objective and neutral. The title or descriptive phrase accompanying the quoted person clarifies the bias. But this is the bias of the source, not the reporter. (Keeble, 2001a: 44)

> "Who the hell's gonna read the *second* paragraph?" The Front Page.

Good attribution is necessary but insufficient to produce good journalism, writes Nick Davies in his critical examination of the news industry, *Flat Earth News*. He quotes a Press Association editor explaining: "What we do is report what people say accurately. Our role is attributable journalism – what someone has got to say. What is important is in quote marks." For Davies (2008: 83), this approach renders such journalists incapable of discovering the truth because: "Whether what is said is itself a truthful account of the world is simply not their business." . . . If the Prime Minister says there are chemical weapons in Iraq, that is what the good news agency will report" – even if the truth turns out to be somewhat different. This is where the so-called "strategic ritual" of objective reporting comes in, as discussed further in Chapter 5.

drawback

TEXT

Many words have been written in recent decades analysing media output from a perspective that says a text is not simply a collection of words and/or images, but "the meaningful outcome of the *encounter* between content and reader" (McQuail, 2000: 349, my emphasis). In other words, the work of the journalist only becomes a *text* when it is read by somebody. And, given that as members of an audience we bring our own knowledge, experience, expectations and prejudices into play whenever we read a news report, the same item may be capable of multiple meanings given fancy names, such as the "delayed drop". Here's an example of the delayed drop:

> It is the world's most isolated country, a place where the weekly television highlight is *It's So Funny*, a long-running comedy show in which two uniformed soldiers perform slapstick sketches in between lectures about the greatness of Supreme Leader Kim Jong-un.
>
> Now, however, hope – or at least variety – is at hand for the people of North Korea. After months of negotiations with the British government, the totalitarian dictatorship has finally selected three BBC programmes that the state is willing to consider showing its people: *Dr Who*, *Top Gear* and *Teletubbies*. (NORTH KOREA WANTS OUR *TOP GEAR*, Zander Swinburne, *Independent on Sunday*, April 6 2014)

Such a delayed drop, in which the point is not immediately apparent, is often used for light or faintly amusing stories such as the one above, but on occasions it can also work for more grim subject matter.

As with so much in journalism, there is no strict rule saying that a particular kind of story should have a particular kind of intro. The familiar question "What works?" is best answered through observation and trying it out.

Let's look at some more intros, this time all concerning the same event:

> A murder investigation has been launched after a shopkeeper died following an attack, said to have been carried out with a machete, which left another man seriously injured. (MAN ARRESTED AFTER ROTHERHAM SHOPKEEPER DIES IN 'MACHETE ATTACK', *Independent*, October 16 2013)

With all due respect to the *Independent*, that's rather an underwhelming and very passive intro, the first six words of which could apply to several stories most weeks. Also somewhat staid is this version from another quality newspaper, which leads on a slightly different angle:

> A man of 27 has been arrested on suspicion of murder after a shopkeeper was killed and a man badly hurt in Rotherham. (SHOPKEEPER KILLED, *Times*, October 16 2013)

(this tends to be known in academic circles as *polysemy*). Of interest here is the work of Mikhail Bakhtin, who spoke of language as *dialogic*, that is, everything we say or write is in some sense both *responding* to things that have already been said and *anticipating* future responses: "The living utterance, having taken meaning and shape at a particular historical moment in a socially specific environment, cannot fail to brush up against thousands of living dialogic threads" (Bakhtin, 1935: 76).

But where does the journalist figure in all of this? Critical analysis of texts sometimes gives the impression that the work of the journalist is irrelevant to the production of meaning by the audience. Just because a text is *capable* of being interpreted in many ways does not mean it necessarily *will* be, though, and "many media genres are understood by most of their receivers most of the time in predictable ways" (McQuail, 2000: 485). According to Colin Sparks:

> To acknowledge that any text is polysemic is not the same thing as to say that it is capable of *any* interpretation whatsoever. Put more concretely, the sense which people can make of newspapers depends at least in part in *what the journalists have actually written in them in the first place.* (Sparks, 1992: 37, my emphasis)

As McQuail (2000: 485) notes, there is "a power of the text that it is foolish to ignore"; journalists will presumably be relieved to be told that their work is not always rendered redundant by the role of active audiences.

Media texts are sometimes subjected to what is described by academics as "critical discourse analysis", a method of textual, linguistic analysis that aims "to reveal what kinds of social relations of power are present in texts both explicitly and implicitly" (Machin and Niblock, 2008: 246). However, although such analysis may tell us what can be read into a text, it may be more limited in explaining how and why a particular piece of work came to be the way it is. As David Machin and Sarah Niblock point out, a discourse analyst may believe that a photograph has been selected to convey a particular ideological message, yet it may turn out that the picture was chosen primarily because it was cheap (or free) and handy. "Simply, we cannot understand a text in isolation from its production" (Machin and Niblock, 2008: 246–247).

> "Always, always, tell the news through people."
> *Arthur Christiansen.*

Contrast those with this:

> A man wielding a machete carried out a terrifying attack which left one man dead and another seriously injured in a butcher's shop in Rotherham. (MAN KILLED IN BUTCHER'S SHOP MACHETE ATTACK, Helen Pidd, *Guardian,* October 16 2013)

Which intro has the most impact? Helen Pidd's version I would suggest, although some might quibble with the word "terrifying". As my colleague David Holmes put it in one of the *#NCTJreporting* tweets he sends each year to help journalism students improve their news writing: "Avoid adjectives. You report. Readers can decide what to think."

Tabloid newspapers are rarely afraid of using adjectives to describe situations or people, as in this intro about the same incident:

> A shopkeeper was hacked to death yesterday by a crazed attacker wielding a machete. (MACHETE ATTACKER KILLS BUTCHER IN HIS SHOP, *Daily Mail,* October 16 2013)

Do we need to tell readers that the attacker was "crazed"? Opinion among journalists will differ on that; but, let's face it, this did not appear to be an everyday act of violence. It even prompted use of the word "maniac" in the following version, which included additional information about the incident itself:

> A machete-wielding maniac killed a butcher before going on a mile-long rampage smashing up shop fronts and car windows yesterday afternoon. (MURDER MILE, Stephen White, *Daily Mirror,* October 16 2013)

A further angle made it into this intro:

> A butcher was hacked to death in his shop yesterday by a machete-wielding ex-employee. (MANIAC KILLS BUTCHER IN MACHETE RAMPAGE, Paul Sims, *Sun,* October 16 2013)

That was how the nationals covered the story, but how about those closer to the scene? The region's broadsheet newspaper adopted a sober approach:

> A shopkeeper was killed in his store and another man seriously injured in a suspected machete attack in South

Yorkshire. (STREET TERROR AFTER 'FAMILY MAN' KILLED IN FOOD STORE, Rob Parsons, *Yorkshire Post*, October 16 2013)

In contrast, the local daily newspaper perhaps got closer to conveying the drama of the incident, and the fear felt by those who witnessed it, with this very active intro:

> A killer knifed a butcher to death and left a shopworker fighting for his life before wielding a machete on a terrifying rampage through the streets of Rotherham. (COMMUNITY LEFT TO MOURN LOSS OF 'TRUE FAMILY MAN', Nik Brear and Richard Blackledge, *Sheffield Star*, October 16 2013)

Then, when the even more local weekly published this intro online the following day, it seemed to reflect the fact that by that stage the drama was over and it had become a time for investigation and mourning:

> Investigations are continuing into the death of a "popular" community butcher who was fatally injured in an attack at his shop. (TRIBUTES PAID TO POPULAR SHOPKEEPER AFTER EASTWOOD ATTACK, Tom Sharpe, *Rotherham Advertiser*, October 17 2013)

So there we have one newsworthy event, multiple potential angles and nine variations on the intro. They range from 14 words to 28 words, have just two commas between them (both of which are in the first example) and not one was written by an algorithm. All the intros have different strengths and weaknesses and all are worthy of study by anyone learning to write news.

The above intros focus on the incident itself, but sometimes it might be something about the subject's *life* rather than the manner of their *death* that provides the angle, as in:

> A ten-pin bowling champion who dedicated her life to helping youngsters, has died suddenly. (BOWLING CHAMP DIES, *Yorkshire Evening Post*, October 24 2002)

Or the focus might be on the bereaved:

> A grief-stricken mother today told of her shock when her teenage son suddenly collapsed and died after

> **"Words are facts. Check them (spelling and meaning) as you would any other."**
> *Keith Waterhouse.*

complaining of a swollen throat. (MOTHER'S GRIEF OVER DEATH OF SCOTT, 19, Kim McRae, *Bradford Telegraph and Argus*, November 27 2001)

Some intros manage to combine the victim with grieving loved ones and the act of discovery, as in this example:

A property tycoon and his wife found the body of their "sweet and gentle oddball" son lying in a pool of blood at his home. (PROPERTY TYCOON FINDS "GENTLE" SON KILLED AT HOME, Laura Peak, *Times*, October 25 2002)

The above intros, and countless other variations, tend to focus on one or two elements. They give us what the journalist has decided is the best news line, and they do it quickly and clearly. Occasionally you will find an intro that breaks with such conventions of news writing. Here is an example of delaying the most important information even in the most serious of news stories, about police realising they might be dealing with a serial killer. It seems to work, maybe because the story was so big that most readers could be assumed to have heard the basic facts by the time they read the following day's front page.

> "Find yourself writing 'it is believed'? Don't. Explain who thinks what, and why."
>
> **David Holmes (@spikefodder).**

The man walking along Old Felixstowe Road, near the village of Levington, could not be sure at first. In the failing light he stepped off the road and approached the darkened form. Only then was he sure. She was naked, lying in the wet scrubland where she had been dumped. It was 3.05pm.

Forty minutes later a police helicopter hovered over the open ground south of Ipswich as detectives sealed off the area and covered the body with tarpaulin. The glare of the helicopter's searchlight lit up the wasteland below and there, 100 metres away from the bustle of police activity, the pilot saw the second body. (SNATCHED, KILLED AND DISCARDED, Sandra Laville, *Guardian*, December 13 2007)

Although the style is not conventionally newsy, even the above intro begins its narrative not at the beginning of a journey but at the moment just before the bodies were discovered. The writing conveys an atmosphere and paints a scene, in addition to conveying information.

Sometimes, however, a journalist will delay an obvious news angle simply because they have thought of a more interesting approach, as in this example about a community campaign for a zebra crossing:

Woe betide anyone who crosses Jade Hudspith when she grows up. For the Bramley schoolgirl has already shown her mettle at the tender age of nine by collecting no less than 100 names on her petition for a zebra crossing outside Sandford Primary in busy Broad Lane. (JADE ON WARPATH FOR ZEBRA CROSSING, Sophie Hazan, *Yorkshire Evening Post*, October 30 2002)

Despite the use of the word "less" (shouldn't it be "fewer"?), it shows that an imaginative intro can lift even a relatively straightforward story.

However, something such as the delayed drop that might work in print does not necessarily work so well online, as Carla Buzasi explains:

You've got a lot less time to hook people into a story, so you probably give away more than you would in a traditional news writing sense in that first sentence. So, "This is what happened and now let me explain to you," rather than luring them in and leading them up to the big reveal.

That's just one of the reasons why so-called "shovelware" – the uploading of the text of newspaper or magazine articles straight to the web – tends to be frowned upon even on newspaper-driven websites. Online news stories tend to have more straightforwardly informative intros featuring terms that are most likely to be used in online searches, and are more likely to use the present rather than past tense to reflect the immediacy of the medium.

THE REST OF THE STORY

After the intro, what comes next? If the pyramid is a basic starting point for thinking about intros and simple news stories, it can come to seem inadequate for more complex and/or lengthy stories, particularly those based on many different sources. David Randall talks of constructing such stories through "building blocks" which should be linked logically to each other (Randall, 2000: 175). Richard Keeble prefers the concept of stories having a *series* of inverted pyramids:

> News stories, whether of five or thirty-five pars, are formed through the linking of thematic sections. The reader progresses through them in order of importance, except on those few occasions when the punch line is delayed for dramatic reasons. The journalist's news sense comes into operation not only for the intro but throughout the story. Who is the most important person to quote? Who is the next most important person? What details should be highlighted and which left to the end or eliminated? How much background information is required and where is it best included? All these questions are answered according to a set of news values held by the reporter. (Keeble, 2001a: 108)

Let's take two examples from the stories introduced earlier. The full *Daily Mirror* story about the 91mph winds consists of 407 words in 20 sentences, giving an average sentence length of around 20 words. There are 16 paragraphs, 12 of which consist of a single sentence and four of which contain two sentences apiece. After the intro we have details of the numbers of families evacuated from certain locations and some specific examples of damage caused, enlivened by this quote from somebody living in Dawlish, the worst-hit town:

> Resident Robert Parker, 62, sobbed: "I'm shell-shocked – I feel like I've been in a battle zone. I've lived here 14 years and never seen anything like this." (91mph STORMS WASH AWAY RAILWAY TRACK, Piers Eady and Richard Smith, *Daily Mirror*, February 6 2014)

The story ends with the latest weather prediction followed by details of government reaction to the storms and a promise that an extra £100 million would be spent on tackling flooding.

The *Times* story about the property tycoon's "oddball" son is longer and more complex, but is still written in a concise news style. It consists of 602 words in 34 sentences and 19 paragraphs, giving an average sentence length of around 18 words – actually slightly shorter than the average in the tabloid story above. After the intro we

are quickly given names, time, location and the information that somebody is being questioned by police. The basic story having been told, we are then given detail, colour, context, attribution and quotes. There are descriptions of the victim based on interviews with neighbours, background on the location, the results of the post-mortem examination, and quotes from the police. The continuing police presence at the house is then linked to the fact that the bereaved parents are being comforted by police family liaison officers, which leads in turn to quotes from a statement issued by the family. The story ends with some extra biographical details about the father.

This device of blurting out the basic story, and then telling it in more detail, is common in news. In most cases, chronology goes out the window when it comes to writing news. But it is important that, in a desire to include all the most important information, you do not end up writing a story that reads like a *list of points*. Ideas, sentences, paragraphs should be linked and follow on in some kind of logical sequence, or series of sequences. Facts, description, context, reported speech and direct quotes must all be *woven* into the text, to achieve a whole. Study the structure of news stories and you will see how neat are the links, how smooth are the transitions, and how additional information is slipped in without disrupting the flow.

Note too the use of quotes and **attribution**. Direct quotes can add authority, drama, immediacy or emotion to an account as well as giving the reader a sense of the quoted person's voice and personality. Direct quotes will normally be outnumbered by reported speech and/or the attribution of facts and opinions to sources. Together, they tell the reader "who says so". Keeble says that clear attribution is particularly important when covering allegations and counter-allegations (Keeble, 2001a: 103). Yet some journalists fail to give adequate attribution in stories for fear of what Randall terms "a certain loss of journalistic virility". He argues: "The reader should never have to ask 'How does the paper know this?'" (Randall, 2000: 179). As a reporter with the Press Association, Merrick observed this differing attitude at first hand:

There is always attribution in our intros, to prove to our customers that it's properly sourced. We have to say "police said today …" or "an inquest heard today …" Newspapers then get rid of the attribution in their intros.

But good journalism retains the attribution somewhere in the story.

When writing a story for any news organisation you should always retain the idea that your **text** is to be read – and understood – by others. As Keith Waterhouse notes, we rarely hear people at bus-stops using words such as "bid" or "probe", or phrases such as "love-tug mum" or "blaze superstore". Nor do we hear them saying things like "Did I tell you about young Fred being rapped after he slammed his boss? He thinks he's going to be axed". He warns:

> Words that have never managed to get into the mainstream of the language are suspect as a means of popular communication. They are, and remain, labels. They do not convey precise meanings. The reader looks at the label, opens the tin – and finds a tin of labels. (Waterhouse, [1993] 2010: 230)

Labels have their uses, but precise meanings are what we should be aiming for.

HEADLINE NEWS

Finally there is the headline. I say finally because ethical journalism means writing the story, and particularly the headline, only *after* doing the research. Thinking up the headline first and then going out to find a story to fit is a dubious although not unknown practice. Ideally the headline placed above an item will accurately reflect the gist of the story without replicating the precise wording of the intro. Online headlines tend to be self-explanatory, using key words to increase the prominence of the story when people search the internet for information on particular topics; this is what is known in the trade as search engine optimisation or SEO. It means avoiding a word such as "local", for example, because people interested in news about a particular place will search for that place by name.

In contrast, a good print headline can be more cryptic, as long as it does the job of enticing readers to sample the fare beneath. To do that properly needs human input, not algorithms or robots, as is demonstrated each time (surprisingly often) an understaffed and template-driven newspaper sends a story to press beneath HEADLINE GOES HERE or, my particular favourite: HEADY HEADY HEADY. So, can an algorithm write a better news headline, intro or story than a human reporter? Of course not.

SUMMARY

News is written in active and concise language with an emphasis on short sentences and short paragraphs. News is structured with the most newsworthy information first. News is told in the form of stories, but these stories are not normally recounted in a chronological order. Journalists may have storylines already in mind when approaching events and this may affect how those stories are constructed. It has been suggested by some scholars that many news stories are the retelling of ancient myths in contemporary settings. Although readers may interpret news stories in different ways, their interpretations will be based, at least in part, on what the journalist has written.

QUESTIONS

Why are news reports called stories?
Can a story ever really "write itself"?
Is it true that the news is populated by familiar characters?

Why is attribution so important when writing news?

What's wrong with thinking of a headline in advance?

WHAT WOULD YOU DO?

HOW MIGHT YOU TACKLE THIS ISSUE?

You hear from the police that a local 10-year-old girl (Jane Doe) has been reported missing, having last been seen around 16.00 hours yesterday in the vicinity of the school that she attends, Green Grange Junior. Jane is described as white, slim and about 4ft 3in tall, with blue eyes, freckles and shoulder-length, blonde hair. She wears spectacles with silver coloured frames. She was wearing a black jumper with a school logo on it, a white cotton T-shirt, black trousers and a black, waist-length coat. Police say she did not return home after school and has not been seen since. The family home was searched overnight but there was no sign of her. Jane has a mobile phone but does not take it to school with her. It was in her bedroom and police officers have taken it away for examination. Her parents and their friends and neighbours joined police in searching for her over-night and the search is continuing today. Police say they are becoming increasingly concerned for the girl's welfare. How would you write an intro of between 14 and 28 words for a news story based on the above scenario. Which angle(s) would you emphasise and why?

FURTHER READING

The books by Randall (2011) and McKane (2014) both contain a wealth of good advice on writing news, and also well worth checking out are Sheridan Burns (2013), Phillips (2007), Pape and Featherstone (2005), Sissons (2006) and Keeble (2006). It may not come in book form, but David Holmes' (and others') tweets using the hashtag *#NCTJreporting* are no less valuable. Hudson and Rowlands (2012) and Bradshaw and Rohumaa (2011) have useful chapters on writing for broadcast and online journalism respectively. Reah (1998) offers an introduction to the textual study of news stories, while Smith and Higgins (2013), Bell (1991) and Richardson (2006) all subject the language of news to detailed linguistic analysis. Lule's (2001) thought-provoking work on news as myth provides an alternative perspective to both practitioner and linguistic accounts of news construction. And don't forget to read, watch and listen to a wide range of news stories from a wide range of media.

TOP THREE TO TRY NEXT

David Holmes' tweets (@spikefodder) *#NCTJreporting*

Anna McKane (2014) *News Writing* (second edition)

David Randall (2011) 'Writing for newspapers', Chapter 13 of *The Universal Journalist* (fourth edition)

SOURCES FOR SOUNDBITES

Randall, 2011: 169; McKane, 2014: 31; Lule, 2001: 54; Milne, quoted in Mansfield, 1936: 221; *The Front Page*, from Hecht and MacArthur, 1974; Christiansen, quoted in Williams, 1959: 191; Waterhouse, [1993] 2010: 249; Holmes, tweet by @spikefodder, May 16 2014 .

CHAPTER 10

WRITING FEATURES

KEY TERMS

Analysis; Anecdotes; Backgrounders; Columnists; Commentariat; Confessional journalism; Description; Facts; Feature writing; IHTM; Intro; Linking words; Long-form journalism; Opinion; Payoff; Profiles; Quotes; Reflexivity; Subjective experience; TOT

It begins like this. A short sentence followed by another. Maybe even another. Nothing is explained, not even what "it" might be, let alone what "this" is. In this case it is an example of the way in which a feature article might start. But it could start in an entirely different way. Because, unlike hard news stories, a feature intro might make a diversion up what appears to be a dead end, it might beat about the bush, and it might take a leisurely, scenic route to its destination. Just make sure there *is* a destination and that you allow the reader to come along for the ride too.

The word **features** typically covers all editorial content apart from news, sports news, reports of sporting fixtures, letters, users' comments and blogs, although blogs are sometimes counted as features too (especially guest ones). Features tend to take longer to read than news items and, as a result, their days are sometimes said to be numbered in an age of short attention spans and fast-moving online and social media. More specifically, serious in-depth features and long-form journalism are thought to be at risk, not least from a perceived shift towards lighter and more list-based feature material, or "it happened to me" (IHTM) horror stories. But in-depth and long-form journalism "is undergoing something of a revival", believes Jemima Kiss, precisely because "the snatchy web has reinforced how important reflection, research and a considered article should be".

LONG-FORM JOURNALISM

The online-only *Huffington Post* tends not to distinguish between news and features when it comes to style or subject matter, says Carla Buzasi, but "where there might be a division is when we post that content". She explains:

> So for weekends when people have got a bit more time we might save something we've been working on and post it at the weekend because it's a longer

FEATURES

The distinction between news and features is widely accepted. However, a different perspective is offered by David Randall, who argues that too many journalists "see the reporter as an earnest collector of 'facts' and the feature *writer* as someone who wanders around thinking of fine phrases which save them the trouble of doing much research" (Randall, 2000: 193, emphasis in original). He continues:

> The truth is that trying to make distinctions between news and features does not get us very far. In fact, it is positively dangerous. It produces narrow thinking which can restrict coverage of news to conventional subjects and puts writing it into the unimaginative straitjacket of a formula. With features, it encourages the insidious idea that normal standards of precision and thorough research don't apply and that they can be a kind of low-fact product.) . . . The opposite, of course, is the case. Most news pages could benefit from a greater sense of adventure and a more flexible approach to stories. Similarly, most features sections cry out for sharper research and less indulgent writing. There is no great divide between news and features. *Best to think of it all as reporting.* (Randall, 2000: 193–194, my emphasis)

Taking issue with those who emphasise the importance of relying *only* on facts, Angela Phillips points out that features can show how there is more to life than that:

> I agree that journalism must be based on evidence, but that evidence can also be drawn from our own memories and observations of our own emotions, as well as from the experiences, emotions and memories of others. It should be animated by the

read. And if you've got a major interview you might do a short news story to go out today and a longer read to go out tomorrow, and we'll tease one with the other.

"I WROTE ABOUT HOW THE REST OF US FELT"

The traditional difference between news and features has been described by Nell McCafferty in the following terms, based on her own experience on the ground (literally):

> It is the modest ambition of every journalist to write a front-page story – the big one at the top left-hand side, with large headlines, that tells the world the main event of the day. The front-page story tells what happened, where, when, and gives the explanation usually of the person in charge. If you want to know how the rest of us feel about it, you turn to the inside pages. I discovered, early on, that I'd never be able to write a front-page story. I'd be inclined to argue with the person in charge, and feel obliged to give the other version in brackets. I discovered this particularly on Bloody Sunday in Derry when I was lying on the street while people around me got shot dead. I saw everything while the other reporter was at the back. He, rightly, wrote the front-page story, because somebody had to establish the name of the officer in charge, interview him, and provide all the deadly details. Had it been up to me to phone the officer, the row would still be going on and the story would never have been written. My version appeared on the inside pages. I wrote about how the rest of us felt, lying on the ground. (McCafferty, 1984: 14)

That's a feature. But such a personal account is just one form of feature. Organisationally, a news organisation's features desk usually takes responsibility for reviews, horoscopes, TV listings, advice columns, gardening tips and so on, as well as news backgrounders, analytical articles, thinkpieces, picture spreads, profiles and celebrity interviews. A magazine's features are what define it as a "brand",

> "These days so much of what ends up on the front page is a feature. Even when you are covering a war, you want to experience it, the feel of it."
> *Mary Hadar.*

quest for truth, but tempered by an understanding of how difficult that quest can be. (Phillips, 2007: 4)

The quest for the truth is considered further in Chapter 5.

COLUMNISTS

Reporting may be central to journalism, yet the media marketplace often appears to value celebrity columnists more highly than it does the reporters who get their hands dirty actually finding things out. Francis Wheen laments this state of affairs:

> [The] getting and giving of information now seem to be a minor function of the press, as newspapers become "lifestyle packages" stuffed with It girls and solipsists who witter on profitably about their love lives or their shopping habits. . . . [The] status of the reporter – as against the lifestyle gusher, or the sad sap who rewrites PR handouts about minor pop stars for a showbiz column – has been dangerously downgraded. (Wheen, 2002: xii–xiii)

Not all columnists are "lifestyle gushers", of course; many concentrate on more social and political issues and some base their columns on extensive research. The most high-profile of such columnists and commentators, ranging from Polly Toynbee of the *Guardian* to Trevor Kavanagh of the *Sun*, have been described as constituting a "commentariat" that is "taken seriously by most of those who constitute the political class" (Hobsbawm and Lloyd, 2008).

SUBJECT

Why is it that features can be about virtually any subject, when news tends to be more restricted? Features need not necessarily conform to the notions of "newsworthiness" discussed in Chapter 3, but how much *agency* do journalists have in choosing subjects and style? Certain subjects will be either *in* or *out* at certain titles or at certain times, and journalists quickly absorb expectations of what is required of them, sharing a set of "formulas, practices, normative values and journalistic mythology passed down to successive generations" (Harrison, 2000: 108).

even though many mags also have news sections. And in broadcasting, as Andrew Boyd notes, the term "feature" often means a human interest or "soft news" story:

> The hard news formula calls for the meat of the story in the first line. . . . The feature style, which leads the audience into the story rather than presenting them with the facts in the first line, is used more freely wherever greater emphasis is placed on entertainment and a lighter touch than on straightforward and sometimes impersonal, hard news. (Boyd, 2001: 73)

Features should not be thought of as synonymous with entertainment, though. Features also deal with serious topical issues at greater length, and in greater depth, than is possible in simple news reports (Boyd, 2001: 127).

Another form of feature is the opinion column. **Columnists** have proliferated as newspapers and magazines have conceded much of their traditional breaking news role to broadcast, online and social media, and as publishers seek to distinguish one brand from another. Some columnists are engaged for their knowledge and insight and others because they can turn out an entertaining sentence or two. It is usually their task to be controversial – to get the publication talked and tweeted about – but *safely* controversial, within the limits of what the target readership will find acceptable. A columnist who steps over this shifting, invisible line might find themselves the target of a twitterstorm and, if the publication's own readers or advertisers join in, looking for a new job.

Whether they represent strong opinion, expert analysis, an individual profile or a piece of descriptive writing, good features require both content *and* style. They have a beginning, a middle and an end – usually in that order – not to be confused with Philip Larkin's phrase about a beginning, a *muddle* and an end (cited in Adams, 1999: 50). Features should also have a theme, an idea, something to say. However, many features are rather formulaic affairs, as Brian Whittle points out:

> "There is no one correct way to write a feature."
> *Sharon Wheeler.*

Some subjects are selected for feature treatment "solely to attract certain advertisers" (Randall, 2000: 21). This is particularly the case in magazines and magazine-influenced newspaper supplements – covering subjects as diverse as fashion, finance, education, gadgets, gardening, cars, travel and food – where editorial features act as bait to attract readers to the advertisements that provide the sections with their economic *raison d'être*. For Bob Franklin, formerly serious publications are increasingly producing advertiser-friendly feature copy and relying on opinion over fact, often about subjects he dismisses as "cripplingly banal" (Franklin, 1997: 7–10). Writing in a US context, Hanno Hardt argues that such business-friendly journalism is anti-democratic in its effects because it speaks to people as consumers rather than as participants or citizens (Hardt, 2000: 218–219).

THE PRESENCE OF THE JOURNALIST

The personal pronoun "I" is absent from "normal printed texts", according to Roger Fowler (1991: 64). Yet it appears in many features. Jon Dovey notes that "confessional modes of expression" have proliferated in journalism and beyond since the 1990s (Dovey, 2000: 1). Letting the journalist appear as an *actor* in the drama may be driven by a desire to tell stories in more interesting ways, but for Dovey it also reflects a changing cultural climate:

> [We] are witnessing the evolution of a new "regime of truth" based upon the foregrounding of individual subjective experience at the expense of more general truth claims. . . . Subjectivity, the personal, the intimate, becomes the only remaining response to a chaotic, senseless, out of control world in which the kind of objectivity demanded by grand narratives is no longer possible (Dovey, 2000: 25–26)

But how new is this foregrounding of the journalist? Not very, according to Lynn Barber:

> [This] supposedly new postmodern development of the picaresque interview actually has very long antecedents. Rudyard Kipling's 1889 interview with Mark Twain starts with a good ten paragraphs about the difficulty of finding Mark Twain's house, complete

If you look at women's mags, the stories have got to be TOT – triumph over tragedy. There's got to be a happy ending, otherwise they won't run them. It's unbelievable, they're so formulaic, they're homogenised. They are the Mills and Boons of today.

But that is only part of the story. There are also features that illuminate, features that have the power to make us laugh out loud or cry into our cornflakes, features that impart information or question our assumptions, that make us look at things in different ways or shine a torch into some darkened corner. And features that are simply good writing. The best way to learn about features is to *read*, *write* and *rewrite* lots of features. Also, get other people to read your features because it helps remind you that, like all journalism, features are produced for the *reader* not the *writer*.

with the statutory cab-driver who doesn't know the way. (Barber, 1999: 199)

The personal voice of the journalist has always been there, agrees Rosalind Coward (2013), although she adds that it may indeed be becoming louder. If features *have* shifted towards reflexivity in recent years, will this eventually challenge the "regime of truth" represented by the classic "impersonal" method of telling the news? Such questions are discussed further in Chapter 5.

THAT MARK TWAIN FEATURE

ANECDOTE

Behr's argument that an anecdote can illustrate a "general truth" raises the question of what exactly *is* a general truth? In any event, couldn't an anecdote just as easily illustrate a generally held falsehood?

WHERE DO FEATURES COME FROM?

Virtually anything can be the **subject** of a feature, and sources for feature ideas are similar to the news sources discussed in Chapter 4. With features, however, there is a tendency for more ideas to come from personal experience. For example, Leah Wild wrote a double-page feature about her battle with bureaucracy to get a toilet seat suitable for her daughter, to which a sub added the rather unimaginative headline: THE STORY OF MY DISABLED DAUGHTER'S TOILET SEAT (*Guardian*, March 7 2002). If a lot of your 20-something mates are still hanging around the parental home, you might think of writing a feature on the choices and problems confronting this generation. You might abandon the car and start cycling to work, prompting a feature on how lorry drivers seem to be out to kill you. You might be on a postgraduate journalism training course, so you could think of submitting an account of your experiences to the media or education pages of one of the national papers or to a trade website such as *Press Gazette*. If you have a horror story to tell, or a story with a TOT twist, even better.

> "Our feature pages should be sprinkled with star dust or whatever it is that women wear that catches the light at first nights."
>
> *Arthur Christiansen.*

Just as news feeds on itself, features are often prompted by other features and by news. A common cycle is that one news story is followed up with more news stories, then background features, and by the third or fourth day it becomes a peg for columnists to hang their personal opinions on; then, when lots of high-profile columnists (the so-called "commentariat") get their teeth into a subject, it can in turn influence the news agenda. Sometimes the topic will be rounded off with a "why oh why?" piece in one of the Sunday papers. It can reach farcical proportions, as when film star Kate Winslet mentioned in an interview with *Radio Times* that she wanted to lose some weight after giving birth. This prompted a feeding frenzy by tabloids and broadsheets alike, who ran feature after feature on obesity, dieting, Hollywood waifs, eating disorders and working out in the gym, topped off with a columnist complaining that it was about time Kate Winslet stopped going on about her weight. As *Private Eye* commented at the time, it was "a perfect example of the reverse-alchemy whereby one nugget of news can be transformed into several tons of base metal" (*Private Eye*, 2001).

> "Most British newspapers now have more columns than the Acropolis."
>
> **Ian Jack.**

Let's suppose you've got a better idea than that. And that you've done your research along the lines suggested in Chapters 4, 5 and 6. Before you lay a finger on your keyboard, Sally Adams suggests that you consider the results of your research and ask yourself: What's

- the most startling fact you've discovered?
- the best anecdote unearthed?
- the most astonishing quote?
- the most surprising event?
- the item with the greatest "Hey did you know that . . .?" factor? (Adams, 1999: 74)

When you've done that, you should have a fair idea of the angle you want to take, so it's time to start writing.

BEGINNING

The feature intro, sometimes known as the lead, is hard to pin down because there are so many different styles. The main purpose of the intro is to make the reader want to read on, so the key question is: What works? It might focus on a specific place at a specific time, maybe on just one person even if many others are involved, as in this example:

As night fell over Page Hall in Sheffield on Thursday evening, Barrie Rees started layering up. Thinsulate hat, gloves, a warm jacket, sturdy trainers, his two walking sticks. He hooked an electronic cigarette on a cord around his neck, and hoped someone else would bring a pen and paper to note down observations. The 64-year-old was ready to go out on patrol.

Rees limped his way lightly down the tightly packed terraced streets of his north Sheffield neighbourhood to the Pakistani Advice Centre on Page Hall Road, where he was meeting other members of the recently formed Page Hall Residents Association.

"They called us vigilantes," said Rees. "What a joke! Look at me and my sticks. Usually there's another on a mobility scooter. In summer we had a pregnant lady with us. Vigilantes! Couldn't be anything further from the truth. We're just a group of ordinary local people who don't like being intimidated in our own neighbourhood, trying to make the newcomers understand how life works here." (Helen Pidd, *Guardian*, November 16 2013)

HELEN PIDD'S FEATURE ONLINE

Only after having set the scene and introduced readers to one of her main characters does Pidd go on to explain the context of the events of that Thursday evening: that the local MP had warned of dangerous tensions between locals and Roma and Slovakian migrants. It was not just any local MP but a former Home Secretary, David Blunkett, and his comments had been picked up by sections of the national media, excited by talk of riots and vigilante action. Pidd's feature allowed some of those involved to speak for themselves in more measured tones, and we will return to it later.

A different way of opening a feature is with a general statement, as in this exploration of the case of a Texan woman who killed her five children:

Mental illness has never been much of a mitigating factor in the great retributive machine that is the US criminal justice system. (Andrew Gumbel, *Independent*, March 14 2002)

Gumbel goes on to detail two other cases before getting around to asking, "Why would anyone imagine that the heartbreaking case of Andrea Pia Yates would be any different?". It seems like he is taking a long time to give us the "meat" of the story, but we do not read these opening sentences in isolation. They are put in context by the "page furniture" so important to features: in this case the stark headline IN GOD'S NAME superimposed on a picture of the mother, accompanied by the explanatory standfirst:

> Andrea Yates was a respectable wife and mother, raising a God-fearing family. Then, one fine morning last summer, she drowned her five children. Why? Only now can the full, dreadful story be told. (Andrew Gumbel, *Independent*, March 14 2002)

Presentation is important to the ways in which journalism is consumed, and features depend more than hard news on being sold to the reader "by means of a complex of headlines, pictures, blurb, standfirst . . . caption and significant quotation" drawing out "the mood and underlying substance" of the feature (Hodgson, 1993: 247–248).

A famous photograph is central to a tabloid profile of a South African woman: a photograph of the body of her teenage son being carried away from a protest in Soweto 37 years earlier. Not only did the paper display the picture itself on a full page accompanying the feature, but it was the peg on which the intro and the entire piece were hung:

> She is the woman Nelson Mandela called his hero – the mother of the dead child being carried from a demo in this iconic news photo.
>
> In his Robben Island cell, Mandela was shocked to hear of the appalling killing of 13-year-old Hector Pieterson, Dorothy Molefi's only son.
>
> The forgiveness and dignity shown by this amazing woman in the face of shocking apartheid brutality

was a shining example for Mandela. (Andy Lines, *Daily Mirror*, December 9 2013)

An awful lot of adjectives there, and "iconic" is a horribly overused word, although in the above instance it is probably justified. Do a Google image search for "Hector Pieterson 1976" and judge for yourself.

Whereas news writing tends to concentrate on giving answers rather than asking questions, features are usually more open to the unresolved question. Occasionally you might even begin a feature with a question:

> What on earth is going on at the National Theatre? We certainly know what is not going on. Previously announced productions of *Alice and Wonderland* and *The Playboy of the Western World* have been postponed indefinitely . . . (Michael Billington, *Guardian*, October 10 2000)

Note the double meaning of the phrase "going on". Billington's intro gives us a pretty clear steer that the feature is going to discuss recent events at the National Theatre, and if we want to find out what's been going on then we will read on.

At other times an intro is designed to draw in the reader with a piece of descriptive writing, as in this stark example:

> Drissa takes off his T-shirt. His numerous wounds are deep and open – down to the bone. If it weren't for the maggots that have nested in his skin, he would surely have succumbed to gangrene.
>
> Drissa was a slave on an Ivory Coast cocoa plantation. Forced to work for 18 hours a day on little or no food, and locked in a small room with his fellow captives at night, he was regularly, systematically, brutally beaten. It is scarcely credible that such cruelty and disregard for human life should be employed in the production of a chocolate bar. (Fiona Morrow, *Independent*, September 27 2000)

It is possible to imagine the material in the Drissa intro being rewritten as a news story along the lines of: "Slaves on a cocoa plantation are systematically

> "Read over your compositions, and where ever you meet with a passage which you think is particularly fine, strike it out."
>
> *Dr Samuel Johnson.*

beaten and denied food, according to . . ." But the feature intro is effective because of its focus on the individual, because of the rhythm of the writing (". . . regularly, systematically, brutally beaten . . ."), and because of the delayed contrast between the horrors described and the realisation that the purpose of this brutality is the production of a mere chocolate bar.

A frequently used device is to include **the presence of the writer** in the story itself, as in this example:

> It was a simple assignment: go and interview the editor of *Who's Who*. I duly bunged in a request to Messrs A & C Black, the publishers. "I'm afraid not," the firm's spokeswoman, Charlotte Burrows, informed me sternly. "All the editors have to remain anonymous, to protect them." Protect them from what? "From people wanting to be in *Who's Who*." (Francis Wheen, *Sunday Telegraph*, March 17 1996)

This interface between journalist and subject is a popular one with feature writers, not just to attract the reader but also to set the tone for what follows. From the above paragraph, for example, we are left in little doubt that Wheen feels the publishers need to be brought down a peg or two.

Sometimes a little *dramatic licence* is employed, as in this example from a profile of a crime writer:

> Harry Patterson, aka thriller writer Jack Higgins, is a man of cast iron habits. I find him sitting at his usual table in his favourite Italian restaurant, his perennial glass of champagne in hand. On the table in front of him lie the tinted glasses of unvarying design that make him look like a hit man. (Cassandra Jardine, *Daily Telegraph*, February 25 2000)

Or this intriguing opening with the echo of a thousand westerns:

> A silence descended on the little grassy racing track behind the car park of the Jolly Friar pub in the former pit village of Blidworth, on the border between Nottingham and South Yorkshire, when Mark Pettitt appeared. It was an uncomfortable silence, the kind you get in cowboy films when the gunman walks into the small town. For Mark Pettitt is currently the most unpopular man

in whippet racing. (Paul Vallely, *Independent*, August 11 2000)

Unlike the who, what, where, when and why of the hard news story, the feature intro sometimes leaves the reader with little clue as to the subject about to be addressed. Consider this anecdotal and colloquial intro:

> Standing in a night club in Banja Luka in the Republic of Serbska, I'm starting to feel a wee bit nervous. We've bunked out of Nato's vast metal factory base with five pissed squaddies for a Friday night on the town, and the locals have got wise to the fact that we're Brits, mainly because the squaddies are wearing Sheffield United shirts. Three terrifying Serb boneheads are gathering nearby, getting just that bit too close for comfort. No one is talking to us. We stand out like sore thumbs. (Stephen Armstrong, *Guardian*, September 25 2000)

STEPHEN ARMSTRONG'S FEATURE ONLINE

It turns out to be a feature about a music radio station in former Yugoslavia, run by the British Army to win the "hearts and minds" of young locals.

Some idea of a target audience can inform the way a feature begins. See, for example, the use of detail, description and cultural references in the following intro that was perfect for the now-defunct *Word* magazine but which may not have been deemed appropriate by other less self-consciously "in the know" publications:

> The office where Will Self writes gives you the astonishing feeling that you're sitting inside the writer's brain. Situated right at the top of his house, there are dictionaries and cigars and pipes and ashtrays. There are spindly steel chairs and a bike. There's a window with a view of Stockwell. And then there are the Post-It notes. Hundreds of them. They cover each wall in perfect yellow ranks like erudite rising damp, each one bearing a mnemonic phrase in Self's intense, italic handwriting: "GUIDE TO NON-EXISTENT COUNTRIES" or "CRACK WHORES" or "THE PASSION OF BENNY HILL." Frankly, Will Self's office feels very much like the obsessive loony's inner sanctum in the climactic scenes of a *Seven* or a *Silence Of the Lambs*. (Andrew Harrison, *Word*, May 2008)

Freed from the constraints of hard news, feature writers sometimes make use of a more poetic style. Take this extended *metaphor* that, combined with description, anecdote and the presence of the journalist, introduces an analysis of Coca-Cola:

> There is a slight problem with the front door at Coca-Cola's European headquarters. It is gleaming and wide, like a movable wall of glass, with the outline of a row of giant Coke bottles gleaming across, but it will not open properly. The lock seems to be broken; visitors must knock to gain the attention of reception. The glass, though, is very thick, and the headquarters is in the middle of a noisy shopping centre, in the middle of perhaps the busiest roundabout in west London. The receptionists take quite a while to look up, clack across the lobby, and unfasten the door. There is time to take in the lobby's blaze of logos and bright red walls, as if the building were a vast Coca-Cola vending machine, with a malfunction. (Andy Beckett, *Guardian*, October 2 2000)

ANDY BECKETT'S FEATURE ONLINE

The key phrase comes in the last three words, and the feature goes on to explore whether Coca-Cola is indeed malfunctioning as a global corporation.

A slightly less elaborate example of imagery at work comes from a local newspaper feature about inner-city areas in a so-called boom city:

> On a clear day people in parts of Beeston and Holbeck can see the cranes towering over Leeds city centre at yet another multi-million pound development.
>
> For many in the communities north of the Aire, the cranes helping to build the latest upmarket apartments or plush offices are symbols of hope and opportunity.
>
> But for some in poverty-stricken Beeston and Holbeck, they are a depressing reminder of a successful local economy that is largely passing them by. (David Marsh, *Yorkshire Evening Post*, March 20 2002)

Rhythmic writing and use of contrast to paint a picture can be as effective on a page as when spoken, as this transcript of the intro from a radio dispatch by Alan Johnston demonstrates:

> Gaza is battered, poverty-stricken and overcrowded. It's short of money, short of space, short of hope and many other things. But it's not short of guns. There are about a dozen different, official security forces. Alongside the police and the army, there's the Presidential Guard, there's the Preventive Security Unit and so on. There are more security men here per head of population than almost anywhere on earth, but sadly they deliver very little in the way of security. (Alan Johnston, *From Our Own Correspondent*, BBC Radio Four, October 7 2006)

The above passage works partly because of the quality of the writing, and partly because we know that it has not been composed in a London newsroom far from the action but from "here", in Gaza itself. It is based on good reporting as much as a good prose style.

Feature intros, as we have seen, often focus on something quite specific, something human, some tiny detail – painting the little rather than the big picture. Of course, it can all go horribly wrong. Back in the day when journalists dictated their words of wisdom down the phone, they would often be asked by a deeply unimpressed copytaker: "Is there much more of this?" It was a useful reminder that we do not write for ourselves.

MIDDLE

If the beginning is the single most important element in feature *writing* – because it doesn't matter how good the rest is if readers never venture beyond a dull intro – then the middle is usually the *point* of it all. Even the best intro in the world can't salvage a feature with nothing to say, with no substance.

The content and structure of a feature will vary depending on the subject matter, the style of the publication, the perceived interests of the readers, the intentions of the writer, and on the time and energy available for research. Features rarely "write themselves"; they must be worked at so they do not come across as a series of unrelated points or as a meandering but aimless stroll around a topic. That means there must be some thought – even some logic – to the order in which subjects are introduced, shifts of emphasis are made, and the tone of writing is altered.) It is an internal logic rather than a formula and will differ from feature to feature, publication to publication and journalist to journalist.

A feature will utilise some or all of the following, often overlapping with each other:

- facts
- quotes
- description
- anecdotes
- opinions
- analysis.

FACTS

All features need facts. Apart from straightforward opinion pieces and the most personalised "lifestyle" columns, that means research. (The process of gathering facts for features is essentially the same as for news – interviewing people, consulting databases, reading reports, witnessing events, searching social media and so on) – with the main difference being that features tend to be (written over a longer period of time and tend to contain more words) They may *tend* to be written over a longer period of time but that is not always the case, and much valued is the hack who can turn out a 1,500-word piece in an hour or two without making it read as if it has been cobbled together at the last minute.

Ideally there will be the time to (consult a wide range of sources and the space to include a lot of the information gathered during your research) Andy Beckett's feature on Coca-Cola, for example, is full of facts gleaned from a variety of sources, including cuttings, websites and books, as well as a range of interviews with actors and "experts" alike; dates, prices, percentages and ingredients are all introduced to support the analysis, description and anecdote that structure the feature. (When you have a lot of facts to include, you may wish to make your feature more digestible by including the facts at appropriate points in the text rather than in off-putting chunks; alternatively, you can separate some facts into a "factbox" for a sidebar)

QUOTES

As with news stories (direct quotes can add authority, drama and powerful expression to an account.) Helen Pidd's piece about Sheffield residents on patrol is peppered with quotes from all sorts of people that give it a real sense of real people talking. In contrast, in the Texas mother feature discussed earlier, the first direct quote is a long time coming, after the writer has already given us a lot of the story in his own words. When it arrives it is worth the wait, being a controversial opinion simply expressed by a credible source:

> "It seems we are still back in the days of the Salem witch trials," one of Yates's lawyers, George Parnham, commented after the verdict was returned on Tuesday afternoon. (Andrew Gumbel, *Independent*, March 14 2002)

More direct speech will normally be included in profiles of individuals, because (the subject's voice, their use of language) can be as important to the story as what they are saying. This is often where the quietly spoken can be allowed to speak in their understated way, as in the first time we hear directly from Dorothy Molefi, telling the story of the day her son was killed:

> Dorothy, now 70, recalls June 16, 1976, as if it was yesterday.
>
> Speaking exclusively to the *Daily Mirror* in the front room of her Soweto home she said: "I remember it very well. It was a cold day and in the morning Hector asked me if he could wear long trousers to school.
>
> "I said he couldn't and off he went. The next thing I knew, he had been shot dead. You can see him wearing his short trousers in the photo." (Andy Lines, *Daily Mirror*, December 9 2013)

DESCRIPTION

There's an old journalistic maxim: "Show, don't tell." In other words, use description to express what you see, and let readers make up their own minds what to think about it. We have already seen many examples of description in the intros quoted above. David Randall offers the following guidance:

Description brings the story alive, takes readers to where you have been and evokes atmosphere. . . . So long as you remember that description goes into a story to aid readers' understanding and not provide you with an opportunity to display your latest vocabulary, it will be an aid to clarity and not an obstacle to it. . . . Avoid vague, judgmental adjectives and descriptions. To say that an office is "imposing" tells you something, but not very much. Far better to say that it is so big that you could park two cars in there, that it has plush red carpet, a new black desk with brass fittings and that the windows command a view of the capital. That gives a far better idea. Apply this thinking to people, too. . . . Descriptive writing is about finding ways of *bringing something to life*, not the random sprinkling of adjectives through a piece.
(Randall, 2000: 182–183, my emphasis)

ANECDOTES

Anecdotes play a far greater role in features than in news stories, where they are often squeezed out by tight word limits and an emphasis on the facts. As well as sometimes being funny or moving, anecdotes can help explain how the actors in a story felt or reacted, tell us something about the human condition, and create a big picture by painting small pictures in sufficient detail. Foreign correspondent Edward Behr says that even the most "trivial, nonsensical **anecdote** can be made to illustrate a general truth" and may reveal more than the "careful marshalling of facts" (Behr, 1992: x). While interviewing schools careers' advisers for a background feature on a strike, I took a note of the sort of incident that wouldn't have made it into a hard news story but which helped bring a worthy but potentially dull feature to life:

> Staff first realised something was brewing in the summer, when their leased yucca plants were unceremoniously removed and office supplies of pens and paper suddenly dried up. "One of our managers was telling us there was no financial crisis just as a yucca was wheeled out behind her," recalls Lisa Cooper.
> (Tony Harcup, *Guardian*, October 10 1995)

In a stroke of journalistic genius, a sub came up with the headline FIRST THEY CAME FOR THE YUCCAS, a reference to Pastor Niemoller's famous lament: "First they came for the Jews ...".

OPINIONS

Some features make the opinions of the writer clear, others do not – it depends on the style, the subject, the publication, and on whether the writer *has* an opinion. But there is usually more opinion in features than in news, from a greater variety of sources. Rather than the traditional "both sides of a story" adopted in much news, features often allow room for more subtle or nuanced differences of opinion to emerge. And it is not unknown for the stated opinion of the writer to have changed by the time the feature ends.

> "Nothing wrong with opinions. . . . But they need some sort of anchorage in fact."
> *Francis Wheen.*

ANALYSIS

Again, not all features are analytical, but they have more scope for analysis than do tightly written news stories with a more immediate focus. Beckett's Coca-Cola feature includes a range of analyses of the company's performance, based on its historical position, on its product diversification, and on its brand image. Apart from the writer's own analysis of what is going on, he invites Coke's UK chief and a range of independent experts to put forward their own explanations. In the Texas mother feature, the case is analysed by reference to how a similar case would have been handled in the UK, with a British lawyer explaining that Yates would probably have been cleared on the grounds of temporary insanity, if she had been tried at all. More likely, she would have been sent to a psychiatric hospital until she was declared fit enough to be discharged. The purpose of such analysis in features is to take journalism beyond reportage and description; not just to tell us what is going on but to help us *understand* it a little more.

THE END

As with the intro, the feature ending – known as the "payoff" because it rewards the reader for sticking with you – can come in all shapes and sizes. Whereas news stories often end on the least important information, allowing them to be cut from the bottom upwards, features tend to have a more rounded ending. This might mean a summary of what has gone before, a return to the scene of the intro, or a new twist to leave the reader pondering.

Lines' profile of the grieving mother ends in plaintive, heart-breaking fashion:

> Dorothy has borne her loss stoically saying: "It was God's will."

> But then she adds sadly: "I used to visit the graveyard a lot – I don't go quite so much now. He was my only son you know." (Andy Lines, *Daily Mirror*, December 9 2013)

Pidd's account of tensions on the streets also ends on a quote, this one <u>looking forward</u> rather than back:

> Ten-year-old Christian Kandrak had only been in Sheffield since February but had already picked up a South Yorkshire twang as he explained he had dreams of becoming a paid interpreter: "I like to be in England. I want to learn English so that I can get a good job, to make money. That's why Slovakians come here." (Helen Pidd, *Guardian*, November 16 2013)

Gumbel's story of the mother who drowned her children ends by referring to the unrepentant state prosecutor, leading to the <u>payoff:</u>

> Her conviction is clearly another feather in his cap. Whether it advances the cause of civilisation, however, is another matter. (Andrew Gumbel, *Independent*, March 14 2002)

So the subject of that feature turns out not to have been the woman who killed her children, but the US justice system itself.

Another form of payoff is the return to the opening scene but with a twist, as in Armstrong's feature about the British Army running a radio station as part of Nato's Stabilization Force (SFOR) force in Bosnia:

> Back in the club, you could believe there is some hope. The squaddies have split and they're all in the middle of the dance floor, hands in the air as the DJ builds a storming set. There are Croats and Serbs and Bosnians here and people may be slagging off SFOR but they're buying the squaddies rounds of Amstel. The guy on the podium with the lurid green glo-sticks steps down and chats to me about music, always music, and doesn't want to know when I get on to politics, so that just for one, naïve, 1988 Summer Of Love moment you actually do think that music could make a difference. Or maybe that's just the beer talking. (Stephen Armstrong, *Guardian*, September 25 2000)

We are back in the opening scene but everyone is more relaxed, and we have heard an upbeat story about music promoting peace, love and understanding. Then the final sentence arrives to raise a question mark about the meaning of everything we have just read. Similarly, Beckett's lengthy piece on Coke's problems in Europe is put into perspective by the payoff quote from an analyst:

> If Coca-Cola get people in China and India to drink one more a year, they needn't give a toss about people like us. (Andy Beckett, *Guardian*, October 2 2000)

Better informed we might be, but let's not kid ourselves that we know everything.

PUTTING IT ALL TOGETHER

Whereas news stories for print are normally written in the past tense, features are often written in the present tense. The only hard-and-fast rule on the tense of a feature is to be consistent throughout, and even that rule can occasionally be broken if there is a good reason. Variety is important when it comes to the length of sentences, though, because too many long sentences can become a stodgy read and too many short ones can have a jerky effect.

In a good feature the transition between different sections and different ideas should be smooth and easy, with the reader not having to break sweat to find out what you are getting at. <u>Linking words and phrases</u> are therefore essential in good writing. Do not simply give the reader a succession of points apparently unrelated to each other, and do not leave your quotes flapping in the breeze. Strive to link one idea with the next, one paragraph with the previous one.

Linking words and phrases can be as simple as *and* or *but*. Again, variety is important. This chapter, for example, has so far included the following linking words and phrases, among others: (in this case … but … because … more specifically … that's … and … though … also … another … however … there are also … for example … although … only having … a different way … goes on to … whereas … note … at other times…this … or … consider this … it turns out that … take this … a slightly less … the above … that means … rather than … in contrast … this is often … again … so … another … then)

It is a useful exercise to take a feature from a newspaper or a magazine and go through it highlighting the linking words or phrases.

SUMMARY

(A feature may give background information and analysis on a topical issue; may profile a person, place or organisation; may convey controversial opinion; and may be entertaining in style and/or content) Virtually anything can be the subject for a feature, although subject matter will be selected according to the perceived interests of readers and advertisers. Features tend to be longer than news stories and tend to use more sources. There are many styles of feature writing and features do not conform to the "inverted pyramid" formula of most news reporting. Journalists working on features sometimes have (greater freedom to experiment with style) and the journalist may be included in the story. The "confessional" mode of feature writing has been increasingly prevalent in recent years, and it is argued that this reflects wider social changes that challenge "general truth claims" in society.

QUESTIONS

Are some subjects more suited to features than news?
Why do star columnists tend to be paid more than reporters?
Why do we see "I" in features but not in news?
Is there a blurring between features and news?
Is long-form journalism self-indulgent in the digital age?

WHAT WOULD YOU DO?

Remember the scenario from Chapter 9? You hear from the police that a local 10-year-old girl (Jane Doe) has been reported missing, having last been seen around 16.00 hours yesterday in the vicinity of her school, Green Grange Junior. Police say she did not return home after school and has not been seen since. The family home was searched overnight but there was no sign of her. Jane has a mobile phone but did not take it to school with her. It was in her bedroom and police officers have taken it away for examination. Her parents and their friends and neighbours joined police in searching for her overnight and the search is continuing today. Police say they are becoming increasingly concerned for Jane Doe's welfare. Let's suppose somebody else is handling the immediate news story and that you are asked to work on a feature about the efforts to find Jane. How would you go about it and what sort of feature intro might you be able to write?

HOW MIGHT
YOU TACKLE
THIS ISSUE?

FURTHER READING

Perhaps the best place to start is Angela Phillips' (2007) excellent *Good Writing for Journalists*, which reproduces and analyses a range of interesting features; in the process it provides numerous pointers to better writing. Also worth checking out are Wheeler (2009), Pape and Featherstone (2006), Keeble (2006) and Adams (2008), among others, while McKay (2006) includes a useful chapter specifically on magazine features. For an introduction to the process of writing reviews, see Gilbert (2008). Randall (2011) is critical of the strict division between news and features, but his emphasis on reporting is welcome and his writing tips are invaluable. Coward (2013) deals specifically with confessional journalism and the so-called "featurisation" and "feminisation" of contemporary journalism, while Dovey (2000) offers an academic analysis of reflexivity within journalism (and beyond). Don't just rely on books, though, however good they are. Make sure that you read a wide range of features from a wide range of media.

TOP THREE TO TRY NEXT

Sally Adams (2008) 'Writing features', Chapter 3 of Hicks et al's *Writing for Journalists* (second edition)
Angela Phillips (2007) *Good Writing for Journalists*
Sharon Wheeler (2009) *Feature Writing for Journalists*

SOURCES FOR SOUNDBITES

Hadar, quoted in Phillips, 2007: 1; Wheeler, 2009: 3; Christiansen, quoted in Williams, 1959: 190; Jack, 2006; Johnson, quoted in Hicks et al, 1999: 124; Wheen, 2002: xiii.

CHAPTER 11

TELLING IT IN SOUND AND VISION

Cathy Newman freely admits that, when she switched from print to **broadcast journalism**, it took a while for her to grasp the centrality of visuals to television news. "When I first started in TV I think a lot of my stories were pretty much newspaper stories on TV, I didn't really think much about the pictures", she says. As most of her early stories for *Channel 4 News* were about Westminster politics, the available pictures tended to be pretty dull anyway: lots of green benches in parliament punctuated with familiar set-ups of men in suits getting out of cars or walking down stairs. She certainly thinks about the pictures now:

> "To tell a story on TV you've got to have people on camera."
> *Cathy Newman.*

> It's all journalism at the end of the day, but you've got to turn it into TV. You've got to try to find a way to make it visually interesting. So a lot of what I do, once I've got a story and nailed it down, is then getting interesting voices to talk about it and bring that story to life, and then find an interesting way of illustrating it.

That's still easier with some stories than with others. Newman's investigation into allegations made by a number of women members of the Liberal Democrats – discussed in Chapter 6 – is an example of the latter, as she explains:

> It was quite a challenge visually because we had two on-camera interviews, and one anonymous interviewee initially, and just quite a lot of walking down the street, set-up shots, and quite a few shots of Lord Rennard in his ermine, which is not the most telegenic of stories.

Happily, finding a way of illustrating a story is not always as arduous:

> For some of the stories I've done the pictures are a gift really. For example, when I went out to the Congo

BROADCAST JOURNALISM

Journalism on radio and television shares with print journalism the basic techniques of news gathering and storytelling, although the importance of sound and pictures for broadcast journalism can affect both *which* stories are selected and *how* stories are covered. Paul Chantler and Sim Harris argue that radio is "the best medium to stimulate the imagination" because "pictures on radio are not limited by the size of the screen; they are any size you wish" (Chantler and Harris, 1997: 5). Just as pictures (in the head) are important for radio, so sound is also vital for television, especially the sound of people's own voices (Holland, 2000: 79). Therefore, stories with the potential for good pictures and/or audio stand a far higher chance of being covered by broadcast journalists than those without either; and reporters covering important but dull stories without good sound or vision may try out imaginative ways of *creating* them through stunts, extended metaphors, or imaginative pieces to camera.

Broadcast journalism tends to have a more immediate *feel* than does print journalism, reporting things that are happening now rather than things that happened earlier (even when this is an illusion). According to a classic study of the television industry, broadcast journalism is far from the "random reaction to random events" that it sometimes appears:

> On the contrary, it is a highly regulated and routine process of manufacturing a cultural product on an electronic production line. In stages of planning, gathering, selection and production broadcast news is moulded by the demands of composing order and organisation within a daily cycle. The news is made, and like

with Angelina Jolie and William Hague. To have this odd couple – the celebrity and the politician – going around a refugee camp, and this amazing African light, that was great in terms of pictures. Obviously there were some really harrowing stories, and lots of children for whom that refugee camp was home, so that was a story with very difficult subject matter. But because of where I was and who I was with it was really easy to turn that into engaging television.

BROADCAST REPORTING

It could also be turned into poor television by somebody who does not know what they are doing, so it is worth pointing out that picture-led stories do not really tell themselves any more than text-based stories ever really write themselves. Even the most promising material requires journalistic skill and judgement to create the finished product.

"IT'S PICTURES YOU'RE LOOKING FOR ALL THE TIME"

This central importance of **pictures** to television also struck Lindsay Eastwood when she left newspapers for broadcasting, in her case on regional TV news. "It's pictures that you're looking for all the time", she says. Other obvious differences included the difficulty of persuading people to appear on screen (as opposed to chatting with someone while making a few notes), the fact that her own clothes and hair assumed new importance, and the "frustrating" amount of time it suddenly took to get anything done. As somebody who had covered parish council meetings for her local newspaper as a 16-year-old on work experience, she also noticed that an awful lot of regional TV news involved following up stories that had already appeared in the local press or elsewhere.

> "Fires and destruction make good TV."
> *Lindsay Eastwood.*

Frustrating is a word Eastwood uses frequently when discussing the differences between print and television. But that is only one side of the story. She recognises that there are other stories on which broadcasting really comes into its own:

any other product it carries the marks of the technical and organisational structure from which it emerges. (Golding and Elliott, quoted in Manning, 2001: 51)

Notwithstanding the powerful image of an "electronic production line", individual journalists can still affect content to some extent through their own contacts, skills and attitudes (Manning, 2001: 53). Reading the words of TV journalists Cathy Newman and Lindsay Eastwood throughout this book, for example, it is clear that although they operate within constraints laid down by employers and broadcast regulators, both still have room to develop their own contacts, stories and creativity as journalists.

Yet there is now so much material being pumped into newsrooms electronically that there are fears that some broadcast journalists may forget where news actually comes from in the first place:

> We must guard against one of the biggest dangers of all, especially with the increasing use of new technology. There could be a tendency to think of news as that which simply appears on the screen or the printer. Never forget that real news is what you go out and find through your own efforts. (Chantler and Harris, 1997: 64)

For Jackie Harrison, a shift towards a "faster, racier style of news presentation" raises further questions about the quality of information and interpretation provided to citizens: "[What] appears to be a tinkering with production techniques and format style by news organisations eventually has an effect on news content and the amount of information available, and ultimately on the relationship of terrestrial television news to the public sphere" (Harrison, 2000: 29 and 42). Not that there is anything wrong with "fancy video effects" in themselves:

> [A]s long as the viewer can tell they are fancy video effects (layered shots, graphics or electronic wipes, for example) rather than a use of the technology to cheat the viewer, that's acceptable. Re-enactments of events by actors should be clearly labelled as such, and you should only show details of which you are absolutely certain. There is no place in journalism for making pictures up, any more than you can make up the facts of a story. (Hudson and Rowlands, 2012: 295)

Where we obviously excel is breaking news, because you're there when it happens. You get it on first whereas a newspaper is the day after. That's where you get your kicks. That's the main thing to be proud of if you're working for TV, and radio is even more immediate. Television is good at showing things as they are, like fires, devastation. Also, you can show how people talk. In a newspaper you have a quote but you don't get the personality of the person. I love doing voxpops because you get a range of people and you can see and hear what they're like.

The Bradford riots in the summer of 2001 still count as one of her most satisfying stories because all the above criteria were met. The riots were breaking news, and few things are more visually dramatic than petrol bombs being hurled through the air by masked youths. Being on the spot meant that broadcast journalists could report events as they happened and use the authentic voices of people on the streets.

> "It is a standing joke in the BBC that any award-winning news package should have helicopters in it, no matter the story."
> *Andrew Marr.*

> The riots stick in my mind because I was out there filming in the thick of it. That was an unbelievable experience really. Very scary. We ended up in a car behind the rioters. We thought they were people going to watch but they were people going to join the riot. So we were driving in the same direction as them and we gradually realised we were getting into a situation where it would be impossible to turn around and get away. We spotted these guys with scarves over their faces, carrying hammers and a crowbar and we thought, "We'd better get out of here". We were trying to cover up our equipment and we managed to drive off and got behind police lines. There were bricks coming over. We were trying to find a spot to film because obviously behind police lines you can't see the rioters in front, so we were trying to get on high places on either side of the road. But we were also trying to watch our backs. Then there were rowdy people coming round the side of us. I interviewed some. You want to be interviewing the young folk that are involved, saying, "Why are you doing it?" I did feel a bit of hostility a couple of times, but nothing too in-your-face. There were

As with everything in journalism there is a fundamental ethical dimension to the editing of sound and pictures, as Hudson and Rowlands (2012: 294) insist: "As soon as you misrepresent the truth or distort the facts as you understand them, what you are engaged in is not journalism. It is trickery or fraud, and completely unethical."

PICTURES

The centrality of pictures to television can result in disproportionate coverage of telegenic stories and less coverage of socially important but visually dull issues. This is not a complaint heard only in academic circles. Journalist Andrew Marr makes a similar point when he writes that TV news is biased towards anything that can be illustrated with striking, exciting or unusual footage:

> Television news has been good at covering the controversy over whether fox-hunting should be banned. This has something to do with the visual appeal of foxes, hounds, horses, red coats and picturesque lanes, not to mention colourful urban demonstrations. Television news has been less good at covering the struggle over the European constitution, or the fight for better long-term care for the elderly. Television news likes plane crashes and train crashes because of how they look. It is mostly bored rigid by car crashes, which kill many more people, but not all at once. Similarly, television news looks overseas and it likes boy soldiers and tanks rather than peacemaking and reconciliation. (Marr, 2005: 291)

This stress on pictures also affects story selection in print and online media, but it is felt at its keenest on TV where the level of editorial interest in an item "is often determined by the pictures available" (Hudson and Rowlands, 2012: 29).

The news value of pictures is discussed further in Chapters 3 and 7.

INFOGRAPHICS

Presenting information in the form of a graphic is at least as old as the pie chart, but it has come into its own in the digital age in which data can be displayed and compared in a vast range of ways and where the element of interactivity a lot of university students involved so they were quite articulate about why they were doing it.

A television reporter needs to be prepared for almost anything for the sake of telling a story with pictures, such as when Eastwood put on a pair of waders to stand waist deep in water while reporting from inside a house during serious flooding:

> That's another difference from reporting it for a newspaper. The photographers were going out in the boats with their wellies on, but the [print] reporters were nowhere to be seen, they were in the community centres where everybody had been evacuated to, getting the human story. But we have to be in there in the houses that are waist deep, which is fun. You do get the smell and the sense of absolute devastation, the shoes and the photos floating around in the house and everything is ruined, which you wouldn't experience as a newspaper reporter. But you've still got to try to get the human side as well, of course. It's not quite as glamorous as it's made out to be, but it gets the old adrenalin going.
>
> Also, on the first day of the floods all the technology kept packing in because it was raining so hard, the cameras were getting wet and stopping working – we were drying a camera with a hairdryer. Give me a notepad! My top tip is: pencils rather than pens, when it's raining.

Eastwood was on the case again when the Prime Minister eventually visited the flood-hit areas:

> We worked our socks off all day tearing around the region trying to keep up with his schedule of visits. He obviously had a police escort, and me and the cameraman were constantly playing catch-up. We had a really tight turnaround time to make the programme but managed to get a really good item on air by the skin of our teeth. A couple of residents affected by floods were quite angry and vocal and we managed to barge through the media scrum and get close enough to get some good "actuality" sound of them having a go at him. One woman in Hull told him to "Get your finger out".

allows website users to click on those elements they wish to explore further. There are numerous ways of visualising stories and data, ranging from simple word clouds to complex mashups incorporating video and audio, and an increasing number of tools and apps available for journalists to use. Imagination and experimentation in such a rapidly developing field is no bad thing, but it is important to remember that it ought to serve a journalistic purpose rather than simply show-off technical wizardry. "When visualising data it is important to ensure that any comparisons are meaningful", warn Bradshaw and Rohumaa (2011: 61): "Visualisation should also be used only when it adds something to a story."

> "[Television] can teach, it can illuminate; yes, and it can even inspire. But it can do so only to the extent that humans are determined to use it to those ends. Otherwise it is merely wires and lights in a box."
>
> *Ed Murrow.*

We also managed to get quite close to him as he was heading for his car to leave Toll Bar near Doncaster. I shouted a question at him and was amazed when he turned back and came over and gave us a really good reply; the press liaison people had said he wouldn't be doing any interviews. That was satisfying. It just proves it's always worth pushing the boundaries in these situations to see what you can get. Nothing ventured, nothing gained.

On occasions, instead of "tearing around" after breaking news, she has had the luxury of making a documentary film, such as the one about post-natal depression discussed in Chapter 4. Getting the right pictures to tell such a story at length can be both a challenge and an opportunity to be more creative than there is usually time for in the more hectic world of news reporting. Filming for the post-natal documentary took place off and on over several months:

> **"Never speak unless you can add to the picture showing on the screen at the moment."**
> *John Arlott.*

> We followed three women and I managed to keep the same cameraman, which helps. He was a fantastic cameraman, and the editor was superb as well, and I felt that I'd got to a stage where I could be a bit more artistic. We tried to be quite creative. The women were in mental torment and thinking horrible thoughts about their babies, but how do you illustrate that in pictures? We did blurry kind of shots and treated the shots. One of the women said she used to walk around her village in a daze and she would just find herself somewhere, so rather than having her walking we did the cameraman walking through the village, filming it from her point of view. So there are techniques you can use without it looking too reconstructed.

REWRITING THE RULES ONLINE

Innovative ways of telling stories are not restricted to television; nor are moving pictures. Video journalism is now well established, not just on standalone websites such as the *Huffington Post*, but also as part of the online offering of what we used to call newspapers. The possibilities are both endless and endlessly exciting, believes Neal Mann:

The rules are being completely rewritten. This is like the great rock'n'roll revolution in music happening to journalism and we don't have to play by the rules that we used to have to play by. We don't have to make a TV package in the way we usually make it. I recently worked with another guy at the *Wall Street Journal* to produce a piece [about healthcare in the USA] that was shot exclusively through head-cam that allowed people to experience effectively different people's lives and allowed people to go deeper using interactive video. I could never have done that as a TV journalist. I would have had to do a traditional news report but I didn't, I ripped up the rulebook and did something new. That, for young journalists, is incredibly exciting. They need to understand that they're not going into a broadcast world or a print world.

The *Wall Street Journal*'s aforementioned interactive "personalized tour of Obamacare" incorporates audio interviews, **infographics**, links to the text of relevant news stories, expert pieces to camera, plus a searchable map to identify what state is doing what, all introduced via a point-of-view narrative shot on head-cameras. The result is a viewer-friendly way of introducing quite complex material. Website users can decide which bits to click on and in which order, and you can experience it for yourself here: http://graphicsweb.wsj.com/documents/prescribed/?mg=inert-wsj

INTERACTIVE ONLINE REPORTING

Clickable maps, as featured by the *Wall Street Journal*, have added a new dimension to many stories online. Sarah Hartley recalls the first one that appeared on the website of the *Manchester Evening News*, displaying the locations of gun killings in the Greater Manchester area. When you clicked on a specific location, up popped a photograph and biography of the victim combined with a link to online articles about the case. Things then moved on, as Hartley explains:

> The one on gun crime wasn't truly interactive, because it just pinpointed places. But we have since done an interactive map of traffic blackspots across the region, and people can come and add their own

traffic information to it. You just click on it and add your problem and we've had hundreds of people taking part. People plot their own experiences – it's the principle of crowdsourcing.

From being a novel innovation just a few years ago, interactive maps are now an everyday element of news output, with examples from just one day in the summer of 2014 ranging from a CNN map detailing Iraqi oil fields to a *Liverpool Echo* map helping readers find out where to park for the Open golf championship.

PICTURES TOO GOOD NOT TO SHARE

Video may be increasingly important but that does not mean the end of the still photograph. An innovative approach to photographs succeeded in taking a fresh look at an old story in the run-up to the 70th anniversary of the 1944 D-day landings that had been the beginning of the end of the Second World War. Reuters photographer Chris Helgren (2014) visited Normandy, and photographed holidaymakers enjoying themselves on the same beaches and in the same coastal towns that seven decades earlier had been the scene of around 3,000 deaths in one day as Allied forces landed in France.

> "If your photographs aren't good enough, you're not close enough."
> *Robert Capa.*

Displayed alongside grim black-and-white pictures of soldiers and military hardware at exactly the same locations in 1944, Helgren's colour pictures for the 2014 anniversary provided a striking contrast that got a good show in many outlets. But the pictures took on a further life when the old and new ones were merged to create a series of haunting images in which infantrymen and tourists spookily inhabited the same space. As Carla Buzasi recalls, when the merged photographs appeared on the *Huffington Post* the item became a must-share one for many people. "That's gone nuts", she says: "When I saw the pictures I knew it would do well because if I have that emotional reaction to it then I know other people will too. The content was so good that people wanted to share it." And share it they did, more than half a million times on Facebook within days. It is probably a safe bet that not only were hardly any of the people sharing those pictures on social media

alive when D-day happened, but nor were the parents of most of them; yet the images struck a chord. See them for yourself at: http://huff.to/1jZjICw

Despite this enduring power of the still photograph, press photographers are often among the first to be sacrificed when publishing companies cut costs. In particular, the regional press in the UK often seems to be run by people who think readers will be satisfied with blurry snaps taken by reporters, PR pick-up pics, or something lifted from social media or submitted by a reader. Yet the ability to display photographs in online slideshows, with or without accompanying audio, has opened up new possibilities at the same time as others appear to be closed off.

Over the past decade or so, the availability of photographs and videos shot by non-journalists has transformed the ways in which some events are reported, with digital communication meaning that material can be transmitted around the world within minutes, even seconds. The Asian tsunami of Boxing Day 2004, the London tube and bus bombings of July 2005, the Burma pro-democracy protests of 2007 and the Chinese earthquake of 2008 were four of the earliest and biggest examples of images captured by "amateurs" being used by journalists to help tell dramatic stories. Then in 2009 a member of the public happened to be in the right place at the right time to photograph a stricken plane that had safely splashed-down on New York's Hudson River, and he tweeted the picture to the world even before the major news networks had got to the crash scene. The so-called "Arab Spring" of 2010–12 took what is sometimes described as "citizen journalism" to new levels. From the most serious of life-and-death stories such as these, to the most frivolous items – Fenton the runaway dog, anyone? – the use of footage from non-journalists is now a fact of life for virtually all sections of the media.

TELEVISION'S "POOR INFANTRY"

Such "user-generated content" can prove useful even to journalists working at a local or regional level, as Lindsay Eastwood explains:

Especially on a weekend when we are limited with cameras and people, you do get lots of footage emailed in. People generally don't want anything for their footage, I think they get quite a thrill. Some of it's ropey but some of it's really good, so that's a real help now. Sometimes there's stuff that's a real Brucey Bonus.

It's not just members of the public out with their smartphones, tablets and digital video cameras these days. Traditional TV reporters on assignment are also likely to bump into other journalists videoing the event for some website or other. Eastwood again:

> If you go out on a story now you see your usual suspects from other TV channels and you also see these other people with little video cameras, and you think, where are they from, are they students? And they're from the *Yorkshire Post* or the *Hull Daily Mail* or wherever. The thing is, not to be disparaging, but they kind of sometimes get in the way. There's a limit to what people will do for the cameras; if you're asked too many times, eventually the last person to ask is going to get a "No". But, although we're "proper TV", they've got as much right to do it as we have.

And even "proper TV" isn't quite what it was in the heyday of fully staffed newsrooms and documentary strands, even on commercial channels in the regions. "Television has become a low-wage industry with a few on-screen stars being paid silly money and with management eating up a lion's share", according to ITV's former health and science editor Lawrence McGinty (2014): "There's not much left for the poor infantry."

Cathy Newman recognises that "there's a terrible hierarchy of resources" within TV, adding: "I'm really lucky, once you get to a certain level you have the luxury of those resources behind you." She explains her worries about pressures to turn reporters into one-person bands:

> I came [into TV] in the last generation of people who had the luxury of a producer and picture editor – the lighting and soundman had gone by the time I got in. I can see the logic behind the

reporter doing everything – shooting, cutting – but my worry is for investigative journalism, and that takes time, and you need to have the time go off for a few days. Also, if you're running a story and you're trying to get a different take on it, or trying to get an exclusive interview, if you're having to shoot it and cut it I'm not sure you have the time to make those contacts or earn their trust. . . . I feel for them. It's a whole different ballgame.

Lindsay Eastwood is one who went through those changes and she can see some pros as well as some cons:

> They had this massive swathe of redundancies here and taught us all how to edit, so now you're drawn back here [to the studio] quite a lot because the technology is here. The deadline's a bit tighter because you think, "I've got to come back and edit this".
>
> I'm completely non-technically minded, but I find basic editing quite all right. When you've got time, if you've shot a story the day before and then you've got the next day to edit it, it's fantastic. Being a control freak, I do quite like being in control and I can choose the shots. Before, when you were sitting with an editor, after a certain number of times trying a certain thing, you'd feel a bit like you were doing their heads in and you'd stop; whereas now, if you're doing it yourself, you can try and try and try and try and try to see if there's a better clip a bit further along. *If* you've got the time. When it becomes stressful is if you've had quite a hard day out on the road, you're up against it when you come back here and the pressure's on, and something goes wrong with the machine. It all gets a bit fraught.
>
> The other thing that's happened is we've lost all the soundmen and the two-man crews. In certain situations it was really good to have another person there, say if it was a rowdy situation, to watch your back. But it can hinder. On a breaking story it's sometimes a lot quicker for you to be holding the microphone while running around with a cameraman, you're much more portable, really.

A RICH MIX OF STORYTELLING TECHNIQUES

Different branches of journalism do not exist in isolation and journalists now have to think across traditional divides and delivery mechanisms. When I interviewed Martin Wainwright for the first edition of this book, he told me:

> There's a feeling that people get their immediate news from radio, television and internet, so the *Guardian* [newspaper], rather to my sadness, has become a bit stodgy with very long analytical articles. One good way out of that is we have the website. We have audio, which is just like radio, so at the Great Heck rail crash I did a couple of audio reports, saying, "I'm standing here in front of the train". I love doing stuff for them.

When re-interviewing him a few years later I reminded him of those words and asked if he still felt the same way. He did, only more so:

SKIDDAW AUDIO-VISUAL REPORT

> Oh, I was very far sighted. That was in the early days of using mobile phones for the audio. . . . I really enjoy working online, there's the sheer quantity of stuff you can get out of one story now. I had to go up Skiddaw [a mountain in the Lake District] the other day to report on a three-course meal that was cooked up there. It wasn't a very big story in the paper – as usual my wonderful words were cut by about two-thirds and there was one picture – but we had a longer story online, we had a picture gallery online, I had to do two blogs about it, and we also had audio in the newsdesk podcast.

Another plus of telling stories in sound and vision is that, although it can mean more work, it can't usually be done by a journalist sitting at a desk. "In order to do audio and video, you've actually got to be there", says Wainwright. "So there is hope."

Editorial conferences today typically look at how stories can be run across platforms, as Sarah Hartley explains:

> Some things lend themselves to video because they are just so visual. We do some separate audio too. We encourage the print reporters to record

interviews with people, so we do get some quite nice little podcasts with celebrities we're interviewing. Sometimes we can use an audio package from the radio with a series of pictures and make a slideshow package.

At the *Huffington Post*, which has only ever existed online, this is not thought of as multimedia or converged journalism: it's just journalism. Carla Buzasi explains:

> We try to make everything look as interesting as possible. An ideal story would have video, it would have photographs, it would have great text, and it would have something interactive on there as well, whether that's a poll, a quiz, a chance to comment, links to a blog on the same topic. It needs to look interesting. We want to surprise readers and keep them on that page for as long as possible. Everything comes back to if the content is brilliant, and if it's not you can't dress that up. It could mean it's a great picture, it could mean a good quote, or it could mean a hilarious video.

That means thinking of audio-visual material not as an after-thought but as integral to the story. Buzasi again:

> Where are you going to put the pictures on the page? You might want one at the top. Graphic pictures we tend to put below the fold to give people the option not to scroll if they don't want to see them. You've got to think about everything as you craft the words.

This also means thinking in terms of search and of sharing, as she explains:

> We know that unless you've got about 250 words on a page you're not going to perform well in search rankings. So, with a great picture we'll still try to create 250 words around it. We don't always do that because we might think that's not the sort of thing that's going to perform well in search anyway, and that we're better off with just a great headline that will get people clicking via social. But something with search potential, say a red carpet event, people might well be searching for that the next day. Quite possibly the video or the picture will speak for itself but we will create more words around it to make quite sure that our version of that shows up.

The result of all this can be a rich mix of story-telling techniques, with more ingredients – wikis, podcasts, live interactive chat, animated graphics, things we haven't yet thought of – being added to the mix all the time. All this can be shared and discussed on social media, which can in turn be fed back into further coverage. However, no amount of technological bells and whistles should deflect journalists from an understanding that it is the quality of reporting that remains the most important thing in journalism. And sometimes, as many a radio journalist will tell you, the best pictures are the ones that exist only inside your head when you listen to a good piece of audio.

AN "ALMOST IRRATIONAL MEDIUM"?

And finally, as they say, with all this talk of digital technology and convergence it is easy to overlook the continued existence of "the true outsiders of journalism", which is how Martin Rowson categorises himself and fellow press cartoonists. He argues that topical cartoons are not mere illustrations but are serious journalism:

> Despite a 300 year long tradition – from Hogarth onwards – of using funny pictures to make deadly serious moral, political and social points, cartoons – and, naturally, cartoonists – aren't taken too seriously. In addition they're often seen as semi-detached from the proper business of journalism because of their existence in such a different, unquantifiable, almost irrational medium. In a strange way cartoonists are journalistic chimeras: how they think, what they express and its effect on the readers makes them much more like columnists than illustrators, and personally I see myself as a visual journalist rather than as any kind of "artist". (Rowson, 2001)

CARTOONS AS JOURNALISM

The periodic outbreaks of controversy over cartoons, including the occasional death threat, suggest that at least some readers also take them very seriously indeed.

SUMMARY

Journalists are increasingly working across different media sectors and platforms in a process that used to be referred to as integration or convergence, but which now tends to be thought of simply as journalism. Broadcast and online journalism may differ in style and detail but they also share certain core processes with each other and with print journalism: the identification of news, the collection of information, the verification of evidence, the selection of material and the presentation of stories. Although pictures have long been important for newspaper and magazine journalism, they are central for all television and some online journalism (including the websites and social media output of radio stations). Much video footage and many still photographs are now supplied by the audience (user-generated content) or by journalists who are expected to be all-rounders.

QUESTIONS

How does the availability of pictures affect which stories are covered?
Whose voices do we hear the most and least in audio items?
Why do staff photographers seem to be an endangered species?
Is there still a role for "proper TV"?
Are cartoons really journalism?

HOW MIGHT YOU TACKLE THIS ISSUE?

WHAT WOULD YOU DO?

Let's return to the scenario featured in Chapters 9 and 10. That is, you hear from the police that a local 10-year-old girl (Jane Doe) has been reported missing, having last been seen around 16.00 hours yesterday in the vicinity of her school. Police say she has not been seen since. The family home was searched overnight but there was no sign of her. Jane has a mobile phone but did not take it to school with her. It was in her bedroom and police officers have taken it away for examination. Her parents and their friends and neighbours joined police in searching for her overnight and the search is continuing today. Police say they are becoming increasingly concerned for the girl's welfare. If you work for a multimedia news organisation, what ideas do you bring to the first editorial conference of the day for telling the story in sound and vision?

FURTHER READING

For detailed guidance and discussion of the practicalities of telling stories in sound and vision on TV, radio and online, the best place to start is the excellent *Broadcast Journalism Handbook* by Gary Hudson and Sarah Rowlands (2012). *The Online Journalism Handbook* by Paul Bradshaw and Liisa Rohumaa (2011) includes chapters covering audio slideshows, podcasts and online video journalism. Dodd and Hanna (2014) will guide you on the legal position both about copyright and about filming or recording on the streets and elsewhere. The website of the BBC College of Journalism includes a wealth of practical guidance on skills such as filming, editing, presenting and multimedia storytelling: www.bbc.co.uk/academy/journalism/skills.

On the topic of the BBC, for an unwieldy but fascinating collection of contributions on the corporation "in crisis" – when isn't the BBC in crisis? – see Mair et al (2014). For discussion of academic analysis of broadcast journalism, try Chapman and Kinsey (2009), Cushion (2012), Harrison (2000), Bromley (2001) or Barnett (2012); for radio specifically, see Starkey and Crisell (2009). And as a reminder of the power of the still photograph in newspapers and magazines, and as a discussion of the role of the image within journalism, you probably still can't beat Harold Evans' ([1978] 1997) *Pictures on a Page*. You will have to hunt around in libraries or secondhand bookshops, but it will be worth it.

TOP THREE TO TRY NEXT

BBC College of Journalism website (www.bbc.co.uk/academy/journalism)
Jane Chapman and Marie Kinsey (2009) *Broadcast Journalism: A Critical Introduction*
Gary Hudson and Sarah Rowlands (2012) *The Broadcast Journalism Handbook* (second edition)

SOURCES FOR SOUNDBITES

Newman, interview with the author; Eastwood, interview with the author; Marr, 2005: 291; Murrow, 1958: 38; Arlott, quoted in Kelner, 2013: 102; Capa, quoted in Epstein, 2014.

CHAPTER 12
STYLE FOR JOURNALISTS

KEY TERMS

Brand image; Consistency; Copy; Grammar; House style; Ideology; Imagined audience; Language; Orwell's six rules of writing; Plain style; Political correctness; Punctuation; Spelling; Style guide; Voice

The name may not mean much to younger readers, but Elizabeth Taylor was once one of the most famous – and glamorous – women in the world. According to journalistic folklore, when she was asked how she was feeling during a visit to London towards the end of the 1950s, she duly replied with a quotable quote: "I'm feeling like a million dollars." Her remark was faithfully reported in most of the following day's newspapers, but only in the *Daily Telegraph* did it become: "I'm feeling like a million dollars (£357,000)." Only that newspaper's style guide stipulated that any amount given in a foreign currency must always be followed with a conversion into sterling. As *Telegraph* historian Duff Hart-Davis (1990: 9) put it, the absurd Liz Taylor quote was an example of the paper's "slavish devotion to its house rules".

All news organisations have a concept of house **style**, that is, the **language** in which stories should be written. Why? Because, arguably, consistency in such matters of detail "encourages readers to concentrate on *what* its writers are saying" (Hicks and Holmes, 2002: 19, emphasis in original). A publication's strictures on style can say as much about what the publication is *not* as what it *is*, as this entry from a more recent *Telegraph* (2008) style book indicates: "*Brave* is an acceptable adjective to apply to somebody who has perpetrated a courageous act. Its usage to describe the demeanour of somebody suffering from a serious illness is tabloid." Rarely can the word "tabloid" have been used with such disdain.

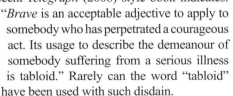

ANALYSIS OF STYLE GUIDES

Many newsrooms have their own style books and/or have searchable electronic guides, while some rely on new recruits picking up unwritten rules from more experienced colleagues. Such guides contain stipulations, reminders and points of clarification, and the details will change over time:

STYLE

> **"Never use a long word where a short one will do."**
> *George Orwell.*

Like all such style guides, the one presented in this chapter contains a mixture of common practice, pointers towards correct use of English, points of clarification and attempts at attaining consistency. The aim is to "eliminate undesired idiosyncrasies" in copy (Bell, 1991: 83). However, it no doubt contains its fair share of "personal idiosyncrasy and whimsy" (Cameron, 1996: 323). The underlying ethos of most such guides, as of Chapter 9 on writing news, is the plain, terse style of writing advocated by the journalist, novelist and essayist, George Orwell:

> A scrupulous writer, in every sentence that he writes, will ask himself at least four questions, thus: What am I trying to say? What words will express it? What image or idiom will make it clearer? Is this image fresh enough to have an effect? And he will probably ask himself two more: Could I put it more shortly? Have I said anything that is unavoidably ugly? (Orwell, 1946b: 151–152)

Orwell went on to list six rules of writing, to be relied upon "when instinct fails":

- Never use a metaphor, simile or other figure of speech which you are used to seeing in print.
- Never use a long word where a short one will do.
- If it is possible to cut out a word, always cut it out.
- Never use the passive where you can use the active.
- Never use a foreign phrase, a scientific word or a jargon word if you can think of an everyday English equivalent.
- Break any of these rules sooner than say anything outright barbarous. (Orwell, 1946b: 156)

There are unmistakable trends in house style: in grammar, loose, colloquial usage is more accepted than it was; there is less punctuation, ie there are fewer capital letters, full stops for abbreviations, apostrophes, accents etc; in spelling, shorter forms are increasingly common and the . . . -ize ending has lost ground to -ise . . . (Hicks and Holmes, 2002: 21)

Speaking of trends, given that online journalism may now be read by audiences in different countries, to what extent do journalists need to be aware of this new, more international readership? "A lot", says Jemima Kiss of the *Guardian*, where the online readership is now roughly one third in the UK, one third in the USA and one third in the rest of the world. Kiss continues:

You could say that the UK is our minority audience. That said, I would think readers value our Brit take on the world, hence coming to us in the first place. So it is important to keep the personality and tone of our voice, for example the humour.

Ah yes, the humour. As in this unimprovable entry from the *Guardian* style guide:

Goths (uc) Germanic tribe that invaded the Roman empire

goths (lc) Sisters of Mercy fans who invaded the Shepherd's Bush Empire (*Guardian* style guide; Marsh, 2007)

GUARDIAN STYLE GUIDE

The number of opinions about style seems to be matched only by the vehemence with which each one tends to be expressed. But, amid the rules and regulations, style guides can indeed be repositories of humour, as here:

Lazy journalists are always at home in *oil-rich* country A, ruled by *ailing* President B, the *long-serving strongman*, who is, according to the *chattering classes*, a *wily political operator* – hence the present *uneasy peace* – but, after his recent *watershed* (or *landmark* or *sea-change*) decision to arrest his prime minister (the *honeymoon is over*), will soon face a *bloody uprising* in the *breakaway* south. . . . Towards the end, after an admission that the author has no

Although they are described as rules, implicit within them is that the writer *thinks* about words rather than using them automatically. But too much questioning might not go down well with colleagues, as is suggested in the Adrian Mitchell poem *Early Shift on the Evening Standard Newsdesk*. When writing a story about heavy fog, one journalist in the poem suggests replacing the traditional "thick blanket" with "sodden yellow eiderdown", only to be asked: "Are you insane?" The lesson of this, according to Jean Aitchison (2007: 195), is that the conservative language used in particular news outlets can provide audiences with "a comforting sense of security and continuity".

While aiming to eliminate insanity and inconsistency *within* a title, a style guide also identifies those "minor style choices by which one news outlet's finished product is *different from another's*" (Bell, 1991: 82, my emphasis). As Deborah Cameron points out, style guides produce distinctive voices for different titles by subsuming the voices of individual journalists (big name columnists usually excepted) under "corporate norms". Such rules help differentiate one news organisation from another and, by reflecting the usage or aspirations of a target audience, contribute towards what might be termed a "brand image" (Cameron, 1996: 320–324). This may go some way towards explaining why the *Daily Telegraph*, for example, issues its journalists with a list of banned words that include "toilet" and offers advice such as: "Christmas lunch is what most of our readers would eat, not Christmas dinner" (*Telegraph*, 2008). Jenny McKay (2006: 62) points out that magazines such as *Rolling Stone* and the *Spectator* avoid the "corporate monotone" of a restrictive house style by allowing "more scope for the individual voice of the writer to be heard". However, this very absence of house style can itself be seen as part of the brand image of those particular titles.

It has been argued that the issue of house style goes beyond simple choices over presentation to have an ideological effect. Paul Manning argues that the journalist's concern to meet restrictive stylistic requirements can result in "less discursive news treatments and fewer opportunities for a wider range of news sources to inject critical or oppositional voices" (Manning, 2001: 60). Thus the mode of address of the *Sun* newspaper, for example, has been categorised as "heterosexual, male, white,

> **"We misspelled the word misspelled twice, as mispelled, in the Corrections and Clarifications column."**
> *Guardian correction.*

idea what is going on, there is always room for *One thing is certain*, before rounding off the article with *As one wag put it . . .* (*Economist* style guide, 2008)

And here:

amok: no Daily Telegraph style book would be complete without the observation that only Malays can run amok. See also berserk . . .

berserk: no Daily Telegraph style book would be complete without the observation that only Icelanders can go berserk. See also amok. (*Telegraph* style book, 2008)

> **"Every word must be understood by the ordinary reader, every sentence must be clear at one glance, and every story must say something about people."**
> *Harold Evans.*

conservative, capitalist, nationalist" (Pursehouse, cited in Stevenson, 2002: 101). So style guides themselves can be seen as ideological, irrespective of whether their authors see them as such:

> Though they are framed as purely functional or aesthetic judgements, and the commonest criteria offered are "apolitical" ones such as clarity, brevity, consistency, liveliness and vigour, as well as linguistic "correctness" and (occasionally) "purity", on examination it turns out that these stylistic values are not timeless and neutral, but have a history and a politics. They play a role in constructing a relationship with a specific imagined audience, and also in sustaining a particular ideology of news reporting. (Cameron, 1996: 316)

A SAMPLE STYLE GUIDE

What follows in this chapter is an example of a style guide. That means it is likely to contain a fair number of prejudices, pet hates and arbitrary preferences as well as what some would no doubt dismiss as **political correctness** gone mad. Many of the house rules below will be almost universal among journalists within the UK, but many will not. Student journalists should study the styles of different organisations and be aware that, even if it is not codified in a written guide, some form of house style will certainly exist. Anyone entering a newsroom on work experience or as a new recruit will quickly need to get to grips with that particular organisation's preferences on a range of stylistic issues – whether to abbreviate Councillor to Coun or Cllr, whether to cap up Prime Minister, whether to end words with –ise or –ize, whether the editor still prefers women who chair organisations to be labelled "chairman", whether to use single or double quotation marks, and so on – and to apply such rules consistently. When you change jobs you will have to do it all over again. Eventually, of course, you might be in a position to break or even change the rules – but first you need to know what they are. The following guide will give you an indication of current style within some UK newsrooms and will highlight some issues worth

Yet journalists can on occasion break with consensus, both in terms of style and in terms of ideology. When Nell McCafferty covered the Dublin criminal courts for the *Irish Times* she abandoned the conventional rules of court reporting and journalistic style, as she explained in the introduction to a collection of her descriptive and often plaintive articles:

> Because these people have suffered more than enough by appearing in court in the first place, I never used their real names and addresses. I have named the Justices who decided their fate. Hopefully, this collection of articles will put them in the dock for a change. (McCafferty, 1981: 2)

And organisations representing marginalised communities – even marginalised groups of journalists – sometimes produce their own suggested style guides in an effort to raise the consciousness of mainstream journalists about issues such as gender, race, sexuality, health and poverty.

LANGUAGE

Language is "never altogether neutral", argue Smith and Higgins (2013: 5), and it can be used "to empower as well as disempower." Journalists themselves may often be dismissive of academics' close textual analysis, but choices over language are inseparable from issues of truth and "what really happened", argue linguists Robert Hodge and Gunther Kress:

thinking about. At the same time, it just might help you to write better copy.

THE STYLE GUIDE

A

a or an before h? If the h is silent, as in hour, use an; otherwise use a, as in *a* hero.

abbreviations Abbreviations such as *can't* or *that's* are increasingly common in today's media but some still frown on them unless they are in direct quotes. Shortened versions of words such as doctor (Dr) or Labour (Lab) do not need full stops, nor do initials such as GP, BBC or MP (which should be upper case with no spaces). Explain all but the most famous abbreviations either by spelling out: National Union of Students (NUS); or by description: the transport union RMT. If the initials are commonly spoken as a word (such as Nato) they form an *acronym*.

accommodation Double cc and double mm. If in doubt, think double room.

acronyms A word formed by using the initial letters of other words, as in Nato (North Atlantic Treaty Organisation). Explain all but the most famous like this: train drivers' union Aslef; or Acas, the arbitration service.

Act Upper case in the full name of an act, as in the Official Secrets Act.

addresses Most addresses in news articles give the street, not the number. But if giving the full address for contact details, write it as follows: 999 Letsby Avenue, Sheffield SI 3NJ.

adrenalin Prefer to adrenaline.

advice, advise Advice (noun) is what you ask for or give. Advise (verb) is the act of giving it.

adviser Prefer to advisor.

> "A piece of writing can drone or it can splutter or it can mumble or it can sing. Aim for the singing kind – writing that has life, rhythm, harmony, style – and you will never lose your reader."
>
> *Keith Waterhouse.*

It is common for linguistically-oriented critics to attend too much to language, and to overvalue the importance of what is contained in words, especially words in written texts; but the opposite can also be the case. All the major ideological struggles will necessarily be waged in words, through texts that circulate in various ways by virtue of various technologies, in forms of language that bear the traces of these struggles in innumerable ways. (Hodge and Kress, 1993: 161)

For Cameron, even the plain language celebrated by Orwell – and more or less embraced by most UK news media to this day – also has ideological implications:

The plain and transparent style recommended by Orwell is particularly well suited to the prevailing ideology of modern news reporting as simply "holding up a mirror to the world", and it is not coincidental that this style is most strictly adhered to in news rather than feature items. The use of a plain, terse, concrete language in news items – a language that deliberately aims not to draw attention to itself as language – is a code, not unlike the code of realism in fiction, and what it conventionally signifies is unmediated access to the objective facts of a story. It implicitly conveys to us, in a way a less self-effacing kind of language could not hope to do, that what we are reading is not really a representation at all: it is the simple truth. . . . [It] is the linguistic analogue of the camera never lies, and should be treated with similar suspicion. (Cameron, 1996: 327)

POLITICAL CORRECTNESS

What is often referred to as political correctness is largely a matter of simple courtesy, argues Jenny McKay, but that does not mean it has no political significance:

In the early days of the struggle by ethnic minority groups and women for social equality many journalists dismissed the idea that choice of words

affect Not to be confused with *effect*. To affect is to change. Such a change may have effects.

ageing Not aging.

ages Andy Carroll, 26; or 26-year-old Andy Carroll; or Carroll is 26 years old.

Aids Prefer to AIDS.

A-levels Hyphen and lower case l.

all right Two words unless you are quoting a title such as *The Kids Are Alright.*

Alzheimer's disease Upper case A, lower case d, and note the apostrophe.

among Prefer to amongst.

ampersand (&) Use in company names when the company does: Marks & Spencer. Otherwise avoid.

and You may begin sentences with the word *and*. But not every sentence, please.

apostrophes Use an apostrophe to show that something has been left out of a word (eg *don't*, short for *do not*) and to mark the possessive (eg *John's foot*). Plural nouns such as children and people take a singular apostrophe (eg *children's games*, *people's princess).*

armed forces Lower case.

Army Upper case A if referring to *the* (ie British) Army. Army ranks can be abbreviated as follows: Lieutenant General (Lt Gen); Major General (Maj Gen); Brigadier (Brig); Colonel (Col); Lieutenant Colonel (Lt Col); Major (Maj); Captain (Capt); Lieutenant (Lt); 2nd Lieutenant (2nd Lt); Regimental Sergeant Major (RSM); Warrant Officer (WO); Company Sergeant Major (CSM); Sergeant (Sgt); Corporal (Cpl); Lance Corporal (L Cpl); Private (Pte). Do not abbreviate Field Marshall or General.

asylum seeker Two words, no hyphen. And try to remember that there is no such thing as an "illegal asylum seeker", whatever the internet warriors or that bloke down the pub would have you believe.

made any difference. (This was perhaps surprising since they had staked their lives and livelihoods on the fact that words did matter.) Now, however, many of the bigger publishing houses have recognised that there is something excluding about, for example, writing which uses the male pronoun, he, all the time when the people who are being described are in fact a mixture of he and she. . . . [T]he phrase "politically correct" is often used to denigrate worthwhile attempts to think about the full significance of a writer's choice of words. Of course, the prescriptive aspect of this can be taken too far but the underlying motive is, in many cases, less sinister than polite. (McKay, 2006: 72)

> "Plain English is always the democrat's best defence."
> *Andrew Marr.*

A dismissive attitude towards what is often seen as a politically correct approach to issues such as racism, sexism and disability can limit the extent of ethical debate among journalists who work within mainstream media (Keeble, 2001b: 1–2). Yet journalist Gary Younge (2006) argues that the widespread abandonment of once common words, such as "darkie" and "spastic", should not be seen as political correctness at all; rather, such changes occurred as a result of social progress, "not imposed by liberal diktat, but established by civic consensus". Incidentally, the passage about "mentally handicapped" children featured in the *What would you do?* section of this chapter is based on a fairly unremarkable feature published in a Fleet Street title in the 1980s.

B

backbenches One word, as in backbencher.

bail, bale Somebody might be on police *bail*, and a cricket player will be familiar with *bails*. But a boat could be *baled* out, and a pilot could *bale out* of an aeroplane.

Bank of England Upper case B and E. Subsequently the Bank.

bank holiday Lower case.

banknote One word.

barbecue Not Bar-B-Q, BBQ or barbie, please.

Barclays Bank Upper case Bs, no apostrophe.

bare, bear Often confused. *Bare* means unclothed, unadorned, just sufficient, and to reveal; *bear* means to carry, to produce or give birth, and a furry animal.

begs the question Probably best avoided because even the experts seem to disagree about what it means.

biannual Means twice a year. Often confused with *biennial* (every two years) so probably best avoided.

Bible Upper case. But biblical is lower case.

billion One thousand millions. Write the word in full (£1.4 billion) except in headlines (£1.4bn).

birthplace One word.

boffins This word lives on as journalese for scientists and other researchers, but it really shouldn't, should it?

Boxing day Upper case B, lower case d.

breach Means to break through or to break a promise or rule. Not to be confused with *breech*, which is either part of a gun or something to do with short trousers.

breastfeeding One word.

brownfield One word.

brussels sprouts Lower case, no apostrophe.

> "Formats are never neutral in their ideological implications."
> *Paul Manning.*

BSE Bovine spongiform encephalopathy, but not normally any need to spell out. You may refer to it additionally as "mad cow disease".

Budget Upper case B if this is *the* Budget set by the Chancellor of the Exchequer, otherwise lower case.

but You may begin sentences with the word *but*. But not too many.

byelection Prefer one word.

bylaw Prefer one word.

bypass Prefer one word.

C

cabinet, shadow cabinet Lower case

caesarean section Lower case.

canvas, canvass Tents are made of *canvas*, whereas politicians may *canvass* for support.

capitals UK media now use upper case letters far more sparingly than they did even just a few years ago. Clarity and consistency can sometimes be at odds with each other, in which case clarity should be allowed to win.

cappuccino Lower case with a double p and double c. If in doubt, think double shot.

Caribbean One r and two bbs.

cashmere A fabric, not to be confused with *Kashmir* in the Indian subcontinent.

cemetery Not cemetry or cemetary.

censor Means to suppress and should not be confused with *censure*, meaning to criticise harshly.

centre Not center.

century Lower case, with numbers, as in 9th century or 21st century.

chairman, chairwoman Prefer chairman if it's a man, chairwoman if it's a woman, and chair if it is simply a position (eg The committee's first job will be to elect a chair). Lower case.

Chancellor of the Exchequer Upper case C and E. Subsequent mentions: the Chancellor.

Channel tunnel Upper case C, lower case t.

cheddar, cheshire cheese Lower case.

Chief Constable Upper case Cs for a particular Chief Constable, lower case for a meeting of chief constables.

Christian Upper case C, though unchristian is lower case.

Christmas day Upper case C, lower case d.

churches Full name, upper case, eg Sacred Heart Roman Catholic Church; then Sacred Heart, or just the church if it is the only one mentioned in the story.

citizens advice bureau Lower case, no hyphen or apostrophe.

city centre Two words, no hyphen.

CJD Creutzfeldt-Jakob disease, but not normally any need to spell out. You may refer to it additionally as "the human form of BSE".

> "All the major ideological struggles will necessarily be waged in words."
> *Robert Hodge and Gunther Kress.*

clichés Some say "avoid clichés like the plague", but opinions vary. Keeble (2001a: 117), for example, advises reporters to avoid saying that so-and-so is "fighting for her life" when a hospital reports her condition as "critical", on the grounds that it is a cliché. Maybe it is, but isn't critical also a cliché? At least fighting for her life gets a bit closer to the drama of the situation. Clichés are hard to avoid completely, they change over time, and they do sometimes convey just the right meaning in a minimum of words. As a rule of thumb (cliché alert!), whenever you are tempted to use a cliché in your copy, stop and ask yourself if it really is the best way of expressing precisely what it is you want to say. Some particularly tired words and phrases are listed in *Box 12.1*, but you've probably got your own pet hates (is that also a cliché?).

TWEETS ABOUT 'JOURNALESE'

company names Use spellings, upper or lower case letters, and apostrophes as the companies do themselves, even if they are ungrammatical or annoying.

conman, conwoman Both one word.

connection Not connexion.

BOX 12.1

NAMED AND SHAMED: A CLICHÉ TOO FAR

- a big ask
- a bridge too far
- acid test
- after the Lord Mayor's show
- as so-and-so looks on (in picture captions)
- at the end of the day
- baby-faced assassin

- back to square one
- baptism of fire
- between a rock and a hard place
- bitter end
- blaze of glory
- bombshell
- brutal murder

- bubbly character
- budding (in stories about young people)
- bull in a china shop
- burning issue
- chickens coming home to roost
- closure (as prerequisite for moving on)

(Continued)

(Continued)

clutch defeat (or victory) from the jaws of victory (or defeat)

cold comfort

crack troops

cyberspace

drop-dead gorgeous

early doors

elephant in the room

end of

enigmatic

enormity

fairytale ending

fairytale romance

fears are growing

first the good news . . .

fit for purpose

flash in the pan

flushed with success (in stories about toilets)

genuine six-pointer

go figure

gobsmacked

goes without saying

hardworking families

high-level summit

high-speed chase

his/her indecision was final

hit the ground running

hopes were dashed

horns of a dilemma

I have to say

iconic

in our DNA

interesting to note

ironically

is the new black

is the new rock'n'roll

it has to be said

it remains to be seen

jaw-dropping

kept himself to himself

kick-start

last but not least

leave no stone unturned

legend

level playing field

LOL

mass exodus

mega

meteoric rise

morning after the night before

move on (following closure)

must-win

named and shamed

national treasure

OMG

only time will tell

personal demons

pillar of the community

purrfect (in stories about cats)

pushing the envelope

quiet confidence

raced to the scene

revellers

rich tapestry

rich vein of form

ripe old age of

sea change

simple as

speculation was rife

stakeholders

step change

step up to the plate

storm in a D-cup (in stories about bras or breasts)

strut their stuff

sweet smell of success

SW19 (in tennis stories)

take the bull by the horns

taken its toll

the devil is in the detail

the last taboo

the silent killer

the small matter of

thinking outside the box

to be fair

to die for

too close to call

top-level summit

torrid time

tragic mum (or tot, or whoever)

tsunami (except when it actually is one)

tucking into festive fare (in picture captions)

unfriend

untimely death

up in arms

veritable feast

wake up and smell the coffee

wake-up call

war of words

wardrobe malfunction

who knew?

Conservative party Upper case C, lower case p. *Conservatives* and *Tories* are also acceptable. The Conservative party is singular; Conservatives are plural.

Continent Upper case C only if you are referring to *the* Continent, ie mainland Europe.

convince You convince someone *of* the fact; you do not convince someone to do something, you *persuade* them.

co-operate, co-operative, co-op With a hyphen because that's how it's pronounced. Lower case unless it's *the* Co-op.

Coroner's Court Bradford Coroner's Court, with upper case and apostrophe. But lower case if general, eg "The cause of death will be decided in a coroner's court".

council leader Lower case.

councillors Lower case for councillors in general, but upper case for titles of individual councillors. Some newsrooms prefer Coun, others prefer Cllr.

councils Upper case on first use – Sheffield City Council – then just the council if it is the only one referred to in the story. The council *is* rather than the council *are*. Cabinets, panels and boards can all be in lower case.

couple Plural, so the couple *are* planning a holiday, not *is*.

Crown Prosecution Service Upper case first letters. May subsequently be abbreviated to CPS.

curate's egg Does not mean a bit good and a bit bad, because an egg that is good in parts is still rotten. But why are you even thinking of using this phrase at all?

D

dashes Two dashes may be used – as in this example – to mark a parenthesis. One dash may also be used to introduce an explanation, add emphasis or mark a surprise. But avoid littering your copy with too many dashes.

dates Most UK publications go for March 21, or March 21 2016. Not March 21st; nor 21 March; nor March 21, 2016.

day-to-day Hyphenated.

D-day Just the one upper case D, plus a hyphen.

decades 1980s, 1990s, 2000s, 2010s with no apostrophe. Swinging 60s is acceptable only if used ironically (and sparingly). Some prefer noughties for the 2000s; others ban it.

decimate Means to kill or remove a tenth of the population – not to defeat utterly or to have a big win over your opponents. However, even some pedants have now admitted defeat on this one.

defuse Means to render harmless or to reduce tension. Often confused with *diffuse*, meaning spread about.

disabled people Not the disabled or the handicapped, please.

discreet Means circumspect and should not be confused with *discrete*, meaning separate.

disinterested Means impartial, but is often confused with *uninterested*, meaning bored or not interested. Even a disinterested journalist ought to be very interested.

Doctor Abbreviate to Dr without a full stop.

dots Use three dots (ellipsis) to indicate that something has been omitted when quoting a document; also if you want to indicate that more could be said on the subject, eg "But that's another story . . .".

double-decker bus Not double-deck.

drink driving Not drunk driving. Court reports should include the actual measurements and a comparison with relevant legal limits, which in most of the UK are: 80 milligrams of alcohol in 100 millilitres of blood; 35 micrograms of alcohol in 100 millilitres of breath; or 107 milligrams of alcohol in 100 millilitres of urine.

E

earring No hyphen.

Earth This planet's name takes an upper case E.

east Lower case e if it is a description (east Leeds) or a direction (head east), but upper case E if it is the name of a region or a county (the North-East).

Ebola Many news organisations use an upper case E but some do not, so check.

E.coli Upper case E, lower case c, with a full stop and no space.

e-commerce Hyphenated, lower case. But doesn't most commerce involve e-commerce now?

ecstasy Lower case. Write Es only if you are quoting somebody.

Edinburgh Not borough. *See also Middlesbrough* and *Scarborough.*

eg Means for example. Lower case, no full stops.

email No hyphen.

enclose Not inclose.

euro Lower case for the currency. For the plural, some prefer euro and some prefer euros, so check and be consistent.

exclamation marks Known in the trade as "screamers", these are found by the dozen in the work of amateur journalists and editors of parish newsletters. They should generally be avoided except in titles, when quoting somebody shouting at the top of their voice, or when someone genuinely exclaims ("Ouch!"). They should certainly not be used to signal that something is supposed to be funny! Ha ha ha!!!

exhaustive Means comprehensive, but is often confused with *exhausted*, meaning tired.

expense Not expence.

eyewitness One word, but what's wrong with witness?

F

fairytale One word, but make sure you really are talking about a fairytale.

fast food Two words, no hyphen.

fewer Means smaller in number so you can count 'em, eg fewer hours of sunshine, fewer people. Should not be (but often is) confused with *less*, which means to a smaller degree, eg less sunshine, less money.

firefighter Prefer to fireman.

first, second Not firstly, secondly.

first aid Lower case.

flaunt Means to show off or display something, but is often confused with *flout*, meaning to disobey contemptuously.

focused Prefer to focussed.

foot and mouth disease Lower case, no hyphens.

fulsome Means excessive or insincere, so *fulsome praise* means excessive praise rather than generous praise. Often misused and/or misunderstood, so ask yourself if it really is the best word to convey your precise meaning.

G

GCSE, GCSEs Upper case, no full stops, and the plural takes a lower case s.

general election Lower case.

gentlemen's agreement Not gentleman's agreement. But *verbal agreement* might be less sexist, unless you are referring specifically to gentlemen.

getaway One word (as in getaway car).

God Upper case if you are using it as a name, lower case for gods in general.

government Lower case.

government departments Prefer upper case for formal names, like this: Department for Environment, Food and Rural Affairs; Ministry of Justice. Use lower case for descriptions, as in environment department or justice ministry.

graffiti Two ffs, one t.

green belt Two words, lower case, no hyphen.

green paper Lower case.

greenfield Prefer one word.

Greens Upper case for the Green party, lower case for the wider green movement and for the food that you should eat up.

gunman One word.

Gypsy Upper case. Prefer to Gipsy.

H

half Prefer half-a-dozen, half-past, half-price, halfway, two-and-a-half.

hardcore One word.

headteacher Prefer one word.

heaven/hell Both lower case.

height We may be well into the 21st century, but most UK newsrooms still give people's heights in feet and inches (6ft 1 in). Other heights (eg buildings) are more likely to be given in metres (12.25m) or centimetres (25cm).

hello Not hallo or hullo.

heyday Not hayday or heydey.

hiccup Not hiccough.

high street Lower case if referring to general shopping but upper case if it is the name of an actual street.

hijack One word.

his, hers No apostrophe.

hi-tech Hyphenated. Possibly a bit of a cliché by now.

hitman One word.

housewife Unless you are reporting on somebody who has married a house, find a better description.

humour Not humor.

hyphens Many words begin life as two words, become hyphenated, and eventually become one word – but rushing in too soon can create confusion. Check individual entries and in other cases be guided by current media practice, by pronunciation, and by the need for clarity.

I

ie Means that is to say. Lower case, no full stops.

in order to An over-used phrase that can often be removed from copy without affecting meaning.

income support, income tax Lower case.

infinitives Avoid split infinitives when they may confuse, when they may sound inelegant, or when working for a boss who will fire you on the spot for using one. But as Raymond Chandler boldly told one of his editors: "When I split an infinitive, God damn it, I split it so it will stay split" (Chandler, 1984: 77).

inner-city Normally hyphenated.

inquests A coroner *records* a verdict. A coroner's jury *returns* a verdict.

inquiry, inquiries Prefer to enquiry, enquiries.

internet Lower case. But if you mean the more specific (and more recent) web, say so.

ise Prefer to ize, eg organise.

its, it's There is no apostrophe in the phrase *its death*, meaning the dog's death, just as there is no apostrophe in the phrase *her death*. The apostrophe is introduced when *it's* is short for *it is*. It's that simple.

J

jack russell Lower case for the dog (but upper case for the former wicketkeeper).

jail Prefer to gaol.

jibe Not gibe.

jihad, jihadi, jihadist All lower case and no need for italics. But do use with care.

jobcentre, jobseeker's allowance Lower case.

judges Full name and title for the first mention, eg *Judge Roger Scott*; then *Judge Scott* or *the judge*. High Court judges are known as Justice, as in *Mr Justice Henriques*; then *the judge* or the full version – not Judge Henriques. Recorders (part-time judges) are known as *the recorder Mrs Mary Smith*. Full-time magistrates who used to be known as stipendiary magistrates are now district judges (magistrates courts).

Junior Abbreviate to Jr without a full stop.

K

kick-off Normally hyphenated.

kilogram, kilometre, kilowatt Abbreviate as kg, km, kw.

knockout Prefer one word.

Koran Upper case.

L

Labour party Upper case L, lower case p. Subsequent mentions: Labour. Both are singular.

labour Not labor.

lamp-post Hyphenated.

landmine One word.

lay, lie He was *laying* the table while she was *lying* on the bed.

layby One word.

lead, led Leeds Rhinos *lead* the table now, but Huddersfield Giants *led* at the start of the season.

less Means to a smaller degree, eg less sunshine, less money. Should not be confused with *fewer*, which means smaller in number, eg fewer hours of sunshine, fewer people.

liaison Not liason.

Liberal Democrats Upper case L and D. She is a Liberal Democrat (singular). She is a member of the Liberal Democrats (plural). May also be abbreviated to Lib Dems.

licence You need to buy a TV licence (noun). You will then be *licensed* (verb) to own a TV.

linchpin Prefer to lynchpin.

lists Introduce a list with a colon: separate elements with semicolons; end with a full stop.

literally I'll literally explode if I see another example of this word being used inappropriately. Er, no I won't. But here's an idea: only use the word "literally" to convey its literal (exact, basic) meaning.

Lloyds Bank No apostrophe although there is one in the Lloyd's of London insurance market.

loathe A verb meaning to hate, not to be confused with loth, meaning reluctant.

Lord's Note the apostrophe in the name of the cricket ground (but not in the House of Lords).

lottery Lower case.

M

McDonald's Upper case M and D, plus an apostrophe.

mankind Use only if you intend to exclude females, otherwise use humankind, humanity, or people.

Marks & Spencer Subsequently M&S.

Mayor Upper case when referring to a particular person (eg "London Mayor Boris Johnson"), but lower case when referring to the job of mayor in general.

measurements For long distances, use miles; for people's heights, use feet and inches; for people's weights, use stones and pounds; for drinks, use pints; otherwise, use metric measurements. In time we will no doubt switch fully to metric measurements as advocated in an informative guide produced by the UK Metric Association (2002), but that time does not seem to have arrived quite yet.

media Plural (the media *are*), not singular.

medieval Prefer to mediaeval.

memento Not momento.

mentally handicapped Do not use. Prefer person "with learning difficulties".

mentally ill Refer to "mentally ill people" or someone "with mental illness" rather than to "the mentally ill".

mic Abbreviation for microphone. Prefer to mike.

midday One word, no hyphen.

Middlesbrough Not borough. *See also Edinburgh* and *Scarborough*.

midweek One word.

mileage Not milage.

million One thousand thousands. Write in full (£1.4 million) except in headlines (£1.4m).

miniskirt One word. Or short skirt, two words.

minuscule Not miniscule.

misuse One word, no hyphen.

Morrisons Not Morrison's.

Mosques Full name, upper case, eg Drummond Road Mosque. Then: the mosque.

mph Lower case, no full stops, as in 20mph.

MPs No apostrophe.

Miss, Mr, Mrs, Ms Courtesy titles are now usually used only for subsequent mentions in news reports, so John Smith becomes Mr Smith after the first time. The exception is court reporting, for which many organisations refer to defendants by their surname alone (Smith) while others reserve that discourtesy only for those who have been found (or have pleaded) guilty.

Muslim Prefer to Moslem.

N

names Always check the spelling and use both first and family name on first mention. Do not use initials except in those rare circumstances where somebody famous is known by their initials (eg OJ Simpson), in which case there are no full stops.

national lottery Lower case.

nationwide One word.

Nazism Not Naziism.

nearby One word.

nightclub One word. But does anybody still call them that?

no one Two words, no hyphen.

north Lower case n if it is a description (north Leeds) or a direction (head north), but upper case N if it is the name of a county or a region (North Yorkshire, the North-East).

north–south divide Lower case, connected by a dash (en-rule).

numbers One to nine inclusive should be spelled out; 10 to 999,999 should be given in numbers, with commas to mark thousands; then 2 million, 4.5 billion. Exceptions: speeds will be expressed in numbers, eg 5mph; temperatures take numbers, eg 30C (85F); sports scores will have numbers, eg 2-1; but numbers at the beginning of a sentence will normally be spelled out, eg "Seventeen England fans were arrested last night…"

O

off-licence Hyphenated.

Ofsted, Ofcom Just an upper case O.

oh! Not O!

OK If OK is OK then okay is not.

O-levels Note the lower case l and the hyphen.

online One word.

P

parliament Lower case.

passerby One word. Plural: passersby.

pensioner Not OAP.

per Prefer *£20,000 a year* to *per year* or *per annum*.

per cent Some prefer %, percent or even pc, but be consistent.

persuade *See convince.*

phone No apostrophe.

place names Use an official website, an atlas, a gazetteer or an A–Z to check spellings. Never guess or assume.

play-off Prefer two words, hyphenated.

plc Lower case.

police South Yorkshire Police, then the police. Also lower case for the police in general. Note that police are plural, while police force (or service) is singular, so "police *are* investigating . . ." but "the South Yorkshire force *is* short of money". Police ranks can be abbreviated as follows: Chief Superintendent (Chief Supt); Superintendent (Supt); Chief Inspector (Chief Insp); Inspector (Insp); Detective Inspector (Det Insp); Detective Sergeant (Det Sgt); Sergeant (Sgt); Detective Constable (DC); Constable (PC). Do not use WPC. Do not abbreviate Chief Constable, Deputy Chief Constable or Assistant Chief Constable – write it in full at first, then Mr or Ms.

postgraduate One word.

postmodern One word, lower case.

post mortem Lower case, two words, no hyphen; and you should always refer to a *post mortem examination.*

Prime Minister Upper case P and M.

principal The first in rank or importance, who may or may not believe in certain *principles.*

prodigal Means recklessly wasteful, not simply someone who returns.

programme Not program, unless it is a computer program.

prostitutes Not vice-girls, please. Some media prefer the term sex workers.

protester Prefer to protestor.

Q

queuing Not queueing.

quotes As a guideline, use double quote marks unless there is a quote within a quote, which should have single quote marks; but note that many magazines in particular do the opposite. If a quote runs over more than one paragraph, open each paragraph with quote marks but close them only once, at the end of the full quote. Punctuation marks such as commas and full stops normally come inside quote marks when a full sentence is quoted but outside if just a phrase or partial sentence is quoted.

R

refute Means to disprove, not to deny.

reported speech Should be reported in the past tense.

restaurateur Not restauranteur.

reviews Always give full details of title, venue, when the run ends and so on, including certificates for films.

ring-road Prefer lower case, hyphenated. Also: inner ring-road and outer ring-road.

robbery Means theft using force or the threat of force, and should not be confused with theft in other circumstances or with burglary.

rock'n'roll One word with two apostrophes.

Rolls-Royce Upper case, hyphenated.

Royal Air Force Prefer upper case, then the RAF. RAF ranks may be abbreviated as follows: Group Captain (Group Capt); Wing Commander (Wing Cmdr); Squadron Leader (Sqn Ldr); Flight Lieutenant (Flight Lt); Warrant Officer (WO); Flight Sergeant (Flight Sgt); Sergeant (Sgt); Corporal (Cpl); Leading Aircraftman (LAC). Do not abbreviate Marshal of the Royal Air Force, Air Chief Marshal, Air Vice Marshal, Flying Officer, or Pilot Officer.

Royal Navy Prefer upper case, then the Navy. Naval ranks may be abbreviated as follows: Lieutenant Commander (Lt Cmdr); Lieutenant (Lt); Sub Lieutenant (Sub Lt); Commissioned Warrant Officer (CWO); Warrant Officer (WO); Chief Petty Officer (CPO); Petty Officer (PO); Leading Seaman (LS);

Able Seaman (AS); Ordinary Seaman (OS). Do not abbreviate Admiral, Vice Admiral, Rear Admiral, Commodore, Captain, Commander or Midshipman.

rugby Always distinguish between rugby league and rugby union. Use of the term *rugger* for either code should probably be a sacking offence.

S

Safeway Not Safeway's.

Sainsbury's Not Sainsbury.

Scarborough *See also Edinburgh* and *Middlesbrough.*

schizophrenia This is a complicated illness so do not insult sufferers by using the term lazily to mean somebody who appears either undecided or inconsistent.

school names As in Bracken Edge primary school.

scrapheap One word.

seasons As in autumn, winter and so on, lower case.

Secretaries of State Prefer upper case titles, as in *Education Secretary Nicky Morgan*, but the trend is for the caps to go.

Senior Abbreviate to Sr without a full stop.

September 11 Preferred to 11th or 9/11.

shear, sheer It will be *sheer* luck if you manage to *shear* the wool off that sheep.

Siamese twins The preferred term is now conjoined twins.

sit, sat He was *sitting* on the left until the teacher *sat* him in the middle. You may write that he sat on the left; do not write that he *was* sat on the left, unless he was placed there by a third party.

soccer This term should be banned because, in the UK at least, it is hated by most people with an interest in it. Say *football* instead.

south Lower case s if it is a description (south Leeds) or a direction (head south), but upper case S if it is

the name of a region or a county (the South-West or South Yorkshire).

spokesman, spokeswoman The former if it is a man, the latter if it is a woman, and spokesperson if it is neither (eg an emailed statement).

standing, stood She was *standing* at the back until the photographer *stood* her at the front. You may write that she stood at the back; do not write that she *was* stood at the back, unless by a third party.

stationary, stationery With an *a* it means not moving, with an *e* it means writing materials (think "e for envelope").

streetwise One word.

swearwords Swearwords can offend many people for little purpose, especially outside direct quotes. Stop and think before using, and be aware that different publications can have *very* different attitudes, with tabloid newspapers being among the most prudish. Incidentally, if arranging a live audio interview, be careful about inviting a representative of the West Kent Hunt or a Culture Secretary named Jeremy Hunt, as BBC journalists Nicky Campbell and James Naughtie can testify.

T

targeted Not targetted.

taskforce One word.

temperatures Prefer celsius with fahrenheit in brackets: 7C (45F).

Tesco Not Tesco's.

that or which? That defines, which informs. This is the style guide *that* is included in this book. This book, *which* is published by Sage, includes a style guide.

theirs No apostrophe.

times Use am and pm, not hundred hours. Some editors will not allow 12 noon or 12 midnight because what other noon or midnight are there? Just noon and midnight will normally suffice.

tonne Prefer to ton unless instructed otherwise, but be aware that they are different. A tonne (1t) is 1,000kg or 2,204.62lb; a ton is 2,240lb.

trademarks™ Take great care with these, and use an alternative unless you mean the specific product in question. So, if you mean ballpoint pen, don't write Biro.

trillion A thousand billion; that is, a million million.

tsar Not czar.

T-shirt Prefer to tee-shirt.

U

under way That *under way* should be written as two words was drummed into journalists of a certain vintage, which means that many of us get irrationally annoyed when we see it reduced to one word. I have no idea why to be honest, but there you go: you have been warned.

unique Something is either unique or it is not. It cannot be very unique.

universities Like this: Sheffield Hallam University or the University of Sheffield. Then just the university.

V

Valentine's day Prefer upper case V, lower case d, and note the apostrophe.

VAT Upper case, no need to spell out any more.

versus Prefer a lower case v for Warrington Wolves v Saint Helens. Not vs.

W

Wall's Note the apostrophe.

Wal-Mart Note the hyphen.

wander, wonder You may *wander* from place to place while others *wonder* why you don't settle down.

war Prefer lower case, eg Iraq war, apart from the First World War and Second World War.

web, website, world wide web All lower case. But if you mean the wider internet, say so.

weights A common rule is to still give people's weights in stones and pounds (12st 3lb) even if other weights are in tonnes (17t), kilograms (36kg), grams (75g) or milligrams (12mg).

welfare state Lower case.

west Lower case w if it is a description (west Leeds) or a direction (head west), but upper case W if it is the name of a region or a county (the North-West, West Yorkshire).

whatsoever One word.

wheelchair-bound Few people are strapped into a wheelchair for 24 hours a day, so this should be banned in favour of saying someone has to *use a wheelchair*, is a *wheelchair user*, or was *in a wheelchair* at the time in question.

whereabouts Are plural.

while Not whilst.

whiskey, whisky *Whiskey* is for Irish and *whisky* for Scotch.

withhold Not withold.

workmen Use only for describing a specific group of workers who are indeed all men, otherwise prefer workers.

World Trade Centre Not Center.

wrongdoing One word.

X

x-ray Lower case, hyphenated.

Y

yo-yo Lower case, hyphenated.

yorkshire pudding, yorkshire terrier Lower case.

yours No apostrophe.

Z

zero Plural zeros, not zeroes.

zigzag One word, no hyphen.

SUMMARY

All news organisations have rules governing style, whether or not such rules are codified in written guides. Their purpose goes beyond minimising mistakes in spelling, grammar and vocabulary to ensuring consistency *within* outlets and differentiation *between* brands. The most common style in UK journalism is based on the plain style advocated by George Orwell. It has been claimed that style is not neutral and that stylistic choices and presentational formats can have ideological implications by reducing openings for critical voices. The plain style of news reporting draws attention away from itself as language, leading to suggestions that it purports to be unmediated truth rather than a representation. In turn, the rejection of conventional journalistic style may be seen as stylistically and ideologically challenging or transgressive.

QUESTIONS

What is the point of house style?
Does style change over time?
Can words ever be neutral?
Is there a blurring between the language used in tweets and in formal journalism?
Has political correctness gone mad?

WHAT WOULD YOU DO?

You have to sub-edit a human interest feature about a young woman who runs a community dance class in her spare time. It begins like this:

> The leggy dancer is putting the youngsters through their paces. They throw themselves into the dance work-out just like thousands of others who attend similar classes across the country. But there is one big difference. These children are mentally handicapped. Their tubby little bodies, often a symptom of down's syndrome or mongolism, strain to kick to the music's driving beat. Minds that will never achieve maturity strive to please the pretty teenager who makes no allowance for their physical and mental shortcomings...

What changes, if any, would you make to the piece of copy above?

HOW MIGHT YOU TACKLE THIS ISSUE?

FURTHER READING

The classic text on journalistic style probably remains Harold Evans' (2000) *Essential English for Journalists, Editors and Writers.* Although dated even in its revised edition – but not as prehistoric as its original title of *Newsman's English* – it remains full of good advice on essentials such as active writing and wasteful words. Hicks (2013), Hicks et al (2008), McKane (2014) and Fryer (1998) all offer good general advice and Waterhouse ([1993] 2010 also 1994) is always worth reading on the subject of writing. House style is discussed further in Hicks and Holmes (2002), which also includes a brief style guide containing some interesting differences from and similarities to the one used in this chapter. HW Fowler's (1983) *Dictionary of Modern English Usage* is a handy companion for any journalist, along with a decent online and/or printed dictionary and possibly an occasional visit to the website of the Plain English Campaign (with its free guides and its "gobbledygook generator") at: www.plainenglish.co.uk

Style guides themselves can increasingly be found online. See the BBC News version at www.bbc.co.uk/academy/journalism/news-style-guide

Others worth checking out include:

The *Telegraph* at: www.telegraph.co.uk/topics/about-us/style-book/
The *Economist* at: www.economist.com/styleguide/introduction
The *Guardian* and *Observer* at: www.guardian.co.uk/styleguide

And the *Guardian*'s style guide and production editor David Marsh (2013) has produced a book on grammar that is more entertaining than that sounds; you can also follow @guardianstyle on Twitter. Bloomberg journalist Robert Hutton (2013) has also done his bit to make the world a much brighter place with *Romps, Tots and Boffins*, a witty and wise guide to "journalese", much of which was crowdsourced via Twitter.

For more academic critical reflection on – and study of – the language of journalism, the best place to start is Smith and Higgins (2013); also see Fowler (1991), Bell (1991) and Richardson (2006). See also a special issue of *Journalism Studies* (Vol. 9, No. 2, April 2008) on language and journalism guest edited by John Richardson (2008). Deborah Cameron's research paper, "Style policy and style politics", remains a rare example of journalists' internal style guides being subjected to the kind of academic scrutiny usually reserved for journalists' published output (Cameron, 1996), while Jean Aitchison's (2007) *Word Weavers* is also worth a look. Incidentally, Cameron and Aitchison have both held the eyebrow-raising title of "Rupert Murdoch Professor of Language and Communication" at the University of Oxford.

TOP THREE TO TRY NEXT

Harold Evans (2000) *Essential English for Journalists, Editors and Writers*
George Orwell (1946b) 'Politics and the English language', in *Inside the Whale and Other Essays* (1962)
Keith Waterhouse ([1993] 2010) *Waterhouse on Newspaper Style*

SOURCES FOR SOUNDBITES

Orwell, 1946b: 156; *Guardian*, September 28 2007; Evans, 2000: 15; Waterhouse, 1994: 143; Marr, www.plainenglish.co.uk; Manning, 2001: 60; Hodge and Kress, 1993: 161.

PART THREE

WHAT NOW FOR JOURNALISM?

An ethical approach to journalism underpins the entire book but is most explicit within *Part Three*, which also considers some of the ways journalism has changed and some of the ways it hasn't. The recent growth in use of social media to gather and spread news has been striking, but it has not entirely eroded distinctions between journalist and audience; at this time of flux, it is worth taking a step back from the latest piece of technological wizardry to remind ourselves what journalism is for as well as what it could become. If we value journalism primarily as a means of informing society about itself, of asking awkward questions, then it seems to be a pretty good bet that there will still be people producing journalism in one form or another in the future even if we cannot yet know how (or even *if*) it will be paid for or on what platforms or media it will be delivered. No matter how the journalism "industry" develops in the years ahead, journalism as a practice is likely to remain an activity that *can* be socially worthwhile and ethical at the same time as being fun (as the journalists featured in the three closing chapters will tell you). If the future is unwritten, as someone else once said (Joe Strummer, I believe), then readers of this book will be among those writing the future of journalism.

PART 3 VIDEO

CHAPTER 13

AN ETHICAL APPROACH TO JOURNALISM

It was a court case unlike any other. Not only did journalists pack the press bench and an overspill room at London's Old Bailey on July 4 2014, but there were journalists in the dock too, flanked by security guards. Chief among those in the dock was Andy Coulson, the man who had edited the biggest-selling newspaper in the UK before going on to work in 10 Downing Street as spin doctor to David Cameron. Coulson was sentenced to 18 months in prison for conspiring to hack phones during his time as deputy editor and then editor of the *News of the World*. He had denied it, but a jury found him guilty after a trial lasting eight months. Sentenced alongside him for phone-hacking offences were three former news editors of the paper and a private investigator, all of whom had pleaded guilty before the trial began. Their sentences ranged from four months in prison suspended for a year (plus 200 hours of unpaid community work) up to six months in prison. It was not **ethical journalism**'s finest hour.

The court was told that for several years during the first decade of the 21st century, the top-selling Sunday newspaper that campaigned for tougher action against criminals had itself functioned as a "thoroughly criminal enterprise", in the words of prosecutor Andrew Edis. Mr Justice Saunders said during sentencing:

> The true reason for the phone-hacking was to sell newspapers. In an increasingly competitive market, the editor wanted to make sure that it was his paper that got the stories which would create the biggest headlines and sell the most newspapers and he, and others at the newspaper, were prepared to use illegal means to do that. No doubt Mr Coulson was under considerable pressure to maintain, if not increase, market share. He had been appointed as editor at a very young age. He was ambitious and it was important

> "Every journalist who is not too stupid or too full of himself to notice what is going on knows that what he does is morally indefensible."
>
> *Janet Malcolm.*

ETHICAL JOURNALISM

Ethical journalism may be regarded by some as an oxymoron. However, despite such cynicism, ethical journalism has resonance as a term used to describe journalism conducted in line with both the letter and the spirit of relevant ethical guidelines and codes of conduct; journalism that is informed more by a commitment to the public interest than to concerns about financial gain. This concept of ethical journalism can be seen as a beacon to help illuminate the tricky path through conflicting demands, loyalties and the sorts of constraints discussed in Chapter 2. However, notions of what is and isn't ethical journalism may change over time as well as varying between different countries and workplaces. An empirical study of journalists' beliefs about ethical journalism in 18 countries (including Australia, China, Spain and the USA) found that "ideological, cultural and societal factors" within the different countries played a "critical and sometimes dominant" role in how journalists approach ethical dilemmas (Plaisance et al, 2012: 654). Journalism in different countries is the product of different systems, and this can impact on what is regarded as ethical journalism, as Angela Phillips points out:

> While the professionalised "liberal" model of journalism is often held up as a norm, it is in fact a minority trend in a world where politically aligned journalism is arguably more common than neutral "objective" journalism and journalists are as likely to see themselves as commentators as they are to see themselves as neutral information gatherers. . . . One of the very few things that seem to unite journalists globally, at least as an ideal worth fighting for, is autonomy from state control. (Phillips, 2015: 60)

for him to succeed. He, amongst others, passed that pressure down to their subordinates. There was great competition between the various desks. The evidence in the case is that there was considerable pressure on desk heads to get good headline-grabbing stories every week and there was little concern for how they got them. (Saunders, 2014)

The judge went on to use the phrase "cover up" to describe the way the public, parliament and the Press Complaints Commission (PCC) were misled for years by the Murdoch empire, which maintained that just a single rogue reporter had been responsible for the hacking. In fact, the court was told, many other journalists were involved and thousands of phone-hacks were carried out in the hope of finding potential stories. People whose private communications were intercepted included crime victims, royals, celebrities and their agents, politicians, sports stars, friends and family of the aforementioned, and even random people with vaguely similar names. The judge noted that "as nobody knew how the *News of the World* had got the stories, an undercurrent of distrust developed between friends and family who suspected each other of selling the information" (Saunders, 2014).

Individual journalists react differently to mention of the whole so-called **hackgate** saga. Many are quick to point out that they personally have never hacked a phone, would never have dreamed of ever doing so, adding that the behaviour of Coulson and co has tarnished the good name of most ordinary, decent journalists. Others wonder if the tactics deployed at the *News of the World* were not just an intensified version of what is almost bound to go on at the more competitive, redtop end of the journalistic spectrum; and that if every journalist who has ever done anything a bit dodgy is going to end up in the dock at the Old Bailey then the prisons are going to be even more overcrowded than they are already. Many get nervous or uncomfortable at the sight of journalists being arrested and tried, even if they have no particular sympathy for the individuals involved. Some argue that what a number of *News of the World* employees got up to was reprehensible but that the law has caught up with the perpetrators, so what's the problem? Others point out that many of those responsible got away with it for years, with the police only investigating

> **"Most of the time, the public interest defence was trumped-up nonsense."**
> *Piers Morgan.*

Another constant is that journalists are in reality engaged with ethics even when they (or critics) don't realise it, as Plaisance et al (2012: 641) argue: "Whether they are explicit in doing so or not, journalists are in constant engagement with ethics theory as they move through the continuous cascade of decisions that comprise the messy, complicated and often compromising production of news."

HACKGATE

Hackgate is the inelegant label for the phone-hacking scandal that led to the closure of Rupert Murdoch's *News of the World* in 2011, the establishment of the Leveson inquiry into press ethics, the demise of the Press Complaints Commission (PCC) to be replaced as self-regulator by the Independent Press Standards Organisation (Ipso), and the arrests of numerous journalists on suspicion of a variety of alleged offences ranging from bribing police officers to conspiring to pervert the course of justice. It began with the arrests in 2006 of the *News of the World*'s royal editor and a private investigator for hacking into the mobile phone messages of several individuals, including members of the royal family. When the pair were jailed the following year, publishers News International (now News UK) blamed it all on a single bad apple or rogue reporter, an explanation that seemed to be accepted by police, the PCC and those senior politicians who were keen to remain friends with the Murdochs. But investigative journalism (primarily by Nick Davies of the *Guardian*) gradually revealed that illegal phone-hacking had taken place for several years on an industrial scale; allegations of hacking eventually extended beyond the *News of the World* and the Murdoch empire. An official investigation into the culture, practices and ethics of the UK press was established by Prime Minister David Cameron and presided over by Sir Brian Leveson, who wearily pointed out that it was the seventh time in less than 70 years that the government had felt the need to commission a report into the state of the press. During almost nine months of public hearings (streamed live on the inquiry website), evidence was given by hundreds of witnesses, including proprietors, editors, ex-editors, reporters, victims of press intrusion, politicians, police officers, academics and representatives of the by then largely-discredited PCC.

The 92 recommendations of the subsequent Leveson Report (Leveson, 2012) included a proposal for a new, properly after the dogged investigative journalism of Nick Davies at the *Guardian* had shamed the authorities into finally taking the issue seriously.

Under the law in the UK there is no **public interest defence** to justify phone-hacking, but many journalists and others might still have been more supportive of the alleged hackers if the stories they were investigating were truly in the public interest and if information could not have been obtained in any other way. After all, ethical journalism can sometimes be in conflict with the law, as in the protection of sources cases considered in Chapter 2. But when stories are largely concerned with celebrity gossip, where is the public interest that might justify (ethically even if not legally) such intrusion into people's private lives? Given the numbers of journalists around the world who are imprisoned or worse simply for trying to report on the activities of governments or big business, is it not a trifle embarrassing for journalists to get themselves imprisoned for reporting about love-rat legovers?

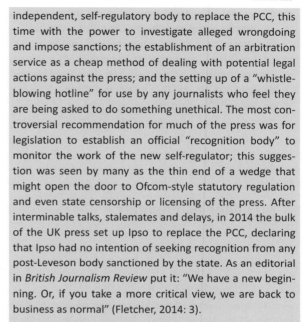

THINKING ABOUT WHAT YOU ARE DOING

The phone-hacking scandal has brought into the public domain discussion of issues around press freedom, privacy, statutory regulation, self-regulation, concentration of media ownership, bullying and the commercial pressures under which many journalists work. But it would be wrong to think of ethics as being concerned only with big stories and major scandals.

Ethical issues have cropped up throughout this book – sometimes labelled as such, sometimes not – just as they crop up throughout the life of a journalist. Journalists can help prepare themselves by being aware of what is laid down in industry guidelines and of codes of ethical practice, such as the National Union of Journalists (NUJ) code in *Box 13.1*. Journalists can also forewarn themselves by learning about relevant cases and by thinking (and talking) about

> "Invading privacy for the public good expresses the truth that justice sometimes requires a private good to be subordinated to a public one."
> *Karen Sanders.*

independent, self-regulatory body to replace the PCC, this time with the power to investigate alleged wrongdoing and impose sanctions; the establishment of an arbitration service as a cheap method of dealing with potential legal actions against the press; and the setting up of a "whistle-blowing hotline" for use by any journalists who feel they are being asked to do something unethical. The most controversial recommendation for much of the press was for legislation to establish an official "recognition body" to monitor the work of the new self-regulator; this suggestion was seen by many as the thin end of a wedge that might open the door to Ofcom-style statutory regulation and even state censorship or licensing of the press. After interminable talks, stalemates and delays, in 2014 the bulk of the UK press set up Ipso to replace the PCC, declaring that Ipso had no intention of seeking recognition from any post-Leveson body sanctioned by the state. As an editorial in *British Journalism Review* put it: "We have a new beginning. Or, if you take a more critical view, we are back to business as usual" (Fletcher, 2014: 3).

PUBLIC INTEREST DEFENCE

We have heard a lot about the public interest throughout this book but particularly in Chapters 2 and 6. That is because the concept implicitly underpins much of what journalists do every day, but it is also used explicitly to justify activities that would be regarded as unethical without such a public interest defence. The editors' code of practice allows some of its strictures to be set aside where it can be demonstrated that it would be in the public interest to do so. This public interest exception covers clauses on privacy, harassment, children, hospitals, crime, clandestine devices and subterfuge, and payments to criminals. It does *not* apply to the clauses relating to accuracy, opportunity to reply, intrusion into grief or shock, victims of sexual assault, discrimination, financial journalism, confidential sources, or payment to witnesses in criminal trials, for which there are no public interest exceptions in the editors' code. The Ofcom broadcasting code and the BBC editorial guidelines also allow for certain forms of journalism to be broadcast only if there is an overriding public interest and for the issue of the public interest in freedom of expression to be balanced against people's expectations of privacy (see Dodd and Hanna, 2014, for details). Examples of whether what they are doing (or being asked to do) is fair, honest and genuinely in the public interest.

Contrary to popular imagination, many journalists do think very carefully about what they are doing, while they are doing it; do normally try to be sensitive to ethical issues and nuances; and, much though it might irk certain editors, do have a conception that **human rights** ought to be taken

the public interest defence being deployed would include the *Telegraph*'s use of leaked (some might say stolen) information to expose the fiddling of expenses by politicians, and the use of deception by a BBC journalist to reveal racism within the police (see Chapter 6).

However, "the division between private and public is rarely absolute" (Cooper and Whittle, 2009: 97–98), leading

---

BOX 13.1

NUJ CODE OF CONDUCT

A journalist:

1 At all times upholds and defends the principle of media freedom, the right of freedom of expression and the right of the public to be informed.

2 Strives to ensure that information disseminated is honestly conveyed, accurate and fair.

3 Does her/his utmost to correct harmful inaccuracies.

4 Differentiates between fact and opinion.

5 Obtains material by honest, straightforward and open means, with the exception of investigations that are both overwhelmingly in the public interest and which involve evidence that cannot be obtained by straightforward means.

6 Does nothing to intrude into anybody's private life, grief or distress unless justified by overriding consideration of the public interest.

7 Protects the identity of sources who supply information in confidence and material gathered in the course of her/his work.

8 Resists threats or any other inducements to influence, distort or suppress information and takes no unfair personal advantage of information gained in the course of her/his duties before the information is public knowledge.

9 Produces no material likely to lead to hatred or discrimination on the grounds of a person's age, gender, race, colour, creed, legal status, disability, marital status, or sexual orientation.

10 Does not by way of statement, voice or appearance endorse by advertisement any commercial product or service save for the promotion of her/his own work or of the medium by which she/he is employed.

11 A journalist shall normally seek the consent of an appropriate adult when interviewing or photographing a child for a story about her/his welfare.

12 Avoids plagiarism.

The National Union of Journalists believes a journalist has the right to refuse an assignment or be identified as the author of editorial that would break the letter or spirit of the NUJ code of conduct. The NUJ will fully support any journalist disciplined for asserting her/his right to act according to the code.

(The code was last amended in 2011; check for updates at www.nuj.org.uk)

into consideration when weighing up the pros and cons of certain types of coverage.

Take Andrew Norfolk and the child grooming investigation discussed in Chapter 6, a story that was extremely delicate and fraught with ethical considerations from the start. Given that it involved sexual assault, race, religion, vulnerable children and community tensions, it would have made Norfolk's life much easier if he had simply ignored the story altogether. Instead, he found a way of tackling it, despite knowing that far-right racists might exploit it and that anti-racists might accuse his newspaper of fuelling prejudice. He admits that the investigation caused him lots of "anguish", especially in the first year, and not just because the details of the assaults themselves were so distressing:

> "Read a piece that just quotes a 'source', and nine times out of 10 it will have been simply made up by a hack on deadline who's desperate to get to the pub."
> *Sharon Marshall.*

> It's been horrible to write a story about a town and then the EDL [English Defence League] turn up and march through that town. We tried very hard, and would usually put somewhere in each article that most child sexual abuse is carried out by white men acting on their own. But those models [of offending] were known about and this one wasn't.

For some critics, labelling those convicted as "Muslim" might be seen as irrelevant or even dangerous, but Norfolk points out that members of the Asian Hindu and Sikh communities would complain when that was *not* done because they did not wish to be implicated in such cases in the public eye. Instead, when reporting the convictions of groups of Muslim men, the *Times* went out of its way to also give space to different Muslim voices who were speaking out against the attitudes that seemed to lie behind the offences. In addition to race, religion and gender, there is perhaps also a class dimension to this particular saga, as Norfolk explains:

> For many years in white liberal society, in which I include myself in this mea culpa, there was a complete distortion between life as it seemed to be and the reality of life being lived on the ground in some of those white working class estates in the north. And into that void step the jackboots of the BNP [British National Party], and there was fertile ground for them to sow their seed because there

to frequent arguments about what it is – and what it is not – in the public interest for us to know about. Perhaps part of the problem lies in the language used to express the concept, argues Karen Sanders:

> Undoubtedly the notion of public interest serves a useful normative role: it is the yardstick by which editors, publishers and broadcasters determine the boundaries of ethical behaviour. However, it is also unclear and abstract. . . . The notion would repay closer scrutiny and perhaps recasting in the form of public or common good rather than that of "interest" which smacks of economism. Invading privacy for the *public good* expresses the truth that justice sometimes requires a private good to be subordinated to a public one. . . . The careless invasion of privacy . . . simply undermines journalists' claims to be truly serving the people. (Sanders, 2003: 90–91, my emphasis)

But who is to define the public good? And isn't there more than one public?

HUMAN RIGHTS

The idea that the world's citizens have certain inalienable rights is expressed in the Universal Declaration of Human Rights. Article 19 of the declaration, which was agreed by the United Nations General Assembly in Paris in 1948 in the wake of the Holocaust and Second World War, asserts specifically that everyone has the right to freedom of opinion and expression, and the right to seek, receive and impart information and ideas through the media. This has been used as a rallying cry by journalists and groups around the world campaigning against censorship and for freedom of information. The Human Rights Act 1998 incorporated the European Convention on Human Rights into UK law, allowing the courts to weigh up the right to freedom of expression (Article 10) against the right to privacy (Article 8). This has resulted in media organisations sometimes using the law themselves, for example to challenge the idea that certain terrorism-related trials might be held in secret, and sometimes having the law used against them, as when an injunction is sought to prevent publication (Dodd and Hanna, 2014). Like so much in ethics, human rights often come down to weighing up competing arguments and interests.

were people who thought that nobody else was helping them.

In truth, then, the grooming, violence and sexual abuse of the girls was only part of the story. The other part was how the girls and their families had repeatedly been failed by authorities, from social services up to the judiciary, who tended to see them simply as white working class girls making poor life choices. All of which meant the survivors and their families had no particular reason to trust a Fleet Street journalist suddenly wishing to report their plight, so Norfolk had to tread very carefully there as well and did not approach victims directly because of their vulnerability and young ages. Instead he made contact with family support groups and gradually built up sufficient trust to allow one-to-one meetings and interviews to take place.

WHO IS REPRESENTING WHOM?

Tricky and upsetting as it was, Norfolk's investigation was a million miles away from the demonising anti-Muslim headlines that often appear in some UK newspapers. His painstaking and evidence-based reporting ought not to be confused with the sort of caricatured coverage of Islam that, as the Leveson inquiry was told, led to reporter Richard Peppiatt walking out of the *Daily Star* because he felt much of what he was writing had ceased to be recognisable as journalism (Peppiatt, 2012). But it is not only in the redtops that the headlines sometimes seem to be at odds with the reality lived by some sections of society; nor is it only in relation to race, faith and class. A recent study by the industry group Women in Journalism found that – notwithstanding the high proportion of journalists (and journalism students) who are female – men continue to dominate front page news in the UK national press, as reporters, sources and subjects of stories:

> "The press must take care not to publish inaccurate, misleading or distorted information, including pictures."
>
> *Editors' code of practice.*

> We found that 78% of all front page bylines were male; 22% were female. . . . Of all those quoted or mentioned by name in the lead stories, 84% were men, and just 16% women. . . . We also found significant differences in the roles that named men and women play in news stories, for example, three-quarters

REPRESENTATION OF WOMEN

of "experts" were men; and 79% of "victims" were women. (Bawdon, 2012: 8–9)

Another study carried out the same year found, among other things, "a lack of context in reporting leading to inaccurate, incomplete or misrepresentative and misleading impressions of women" in the press. The authors also found:

> a repeated celebration of young, "attractive" women, but often in a way that infantilised them and focused on their looks and private lives rather than on their achievements; common mocking of the appearance of older women if they were seen at all; general clear exhortations on how women should look and behave; and an almost visceral undermining of women in power, or those who seek publicity for their views. (Eaves et al, 2012: 8)

How people are represented (or not) in the media, and by whom, is as much an ethical issue as are the more obvious ones such as privacy or intrusion into grief, and such issues cannot be wished away by pretending they don't exist.

ETHICAL RESPONSIBILITY

In the process of looking at journalists at work, we have considered a range of influences that impact on their practice. However, influences do not necessarily have to be thought of negatively, simply as constraints. Some influences may be interpreted as positive, even liberating. For example, although codes of conduct (see *Box 13.1*) can certainly be seen as constraining the behaviour of journalists in some ways, they may also help journalists to *resist* what they see as unethical behaviour and to *defend* journalistic integrity (Harcup, 2002a, 2002b and 2007). As the novelist and journalist HG Wells put it in a message to his fellow NUJ members way back in 1922:

> We affect opinion and public and private life profoundly, and we need to cherish any scrap of independence we possess and can secure. We are not mere hirelings; our work is creative and responsible work. The activities of rich adventurers in buying, and directing the policy of, groups of newspapers is a grave public danger. A free-spirited,

well-paid, and well-organised profession of journalism is our only protection against the danger. (Quoted in Mansfield, 1943: 518)

If journalists are not to be the "mere hirelings" of the wealthy, as Wells put it, then surely we must take seriously our commitment to independent-minded observation, investigation, verification, scrutiny, accuracy and fairness in addition to honing an ability to communicate clearly and entertainingly. Jake Lynch argues that the challenge facing journalists is to take seriously the "ethic of responsibility" that goes with the job, particularly in the era of instantaneous mass communication. He believes that an emphasis on entertainment-driven "news-lite" can have damaging consequences both for our work and for the world on which we report:

THE ETHICAL JOURNALISM INITIATIVE

> "Broadcasters must avoid unjust or unfair treatment of individuals or organisations in programmes."
> *Ofcom broadcasting code.*

In this information age, journalists are not disconnected observers but *actual participants* in the way communities and societies understand each other and the way parties wage conflict. . . . We live in a media-savvy world. . . . Every time facts get reported, it adds to the collective understanding of how similar facts will likely be reported in future. That understanding then informs people's behaviour. This is the feedback loop. *It means every journalist bears some unknowable share of the responsibility for what happens next.* (Lynch, 2002, my emphasis)

And so we return to the point made in Chapter 1 and throughout this book: journalism is not simply an interesting job; journalism *matters* because it informs discussion in the public sphere. This social role in informing citizens means that a good journalist will be a reflective practitioner and will be aware that he or she is not simply an entertainer or a teller of stories. Reflection is required because skills alone "are not enough" (de Burgh, 2003: 110). The actions of journalists, individually and collectively, can make a difference to journalistic outputs and thereby, as both HG Wells and Jake Lynch argue, can make a difference to people's lives. Journalists make choices every day: what stories to cover, which sources to consult, whose door to knock on, what questions to ask, who to believe, what angles to take, whom to quote, what quotes to use, how much context to include, what words to use, what pictures to use, what to leave out, and so on. They may not be entirely free choices, they are not taken in a vacuum, and sometimes there will be orders from on high, but for the most part a journalist's work still involves *choices*; and the journalist whose choices are not anchored in some sense of ethical responsibility may simply be blown this way and that by prevailing commercial and political winds. As Lynette Sheridan Burns writes:

> Professional integrity is not something you have when you are feeling a bit down at the end of a long week. It is a state of mindfulness that you bring to everything you write, no matter how humble the topic. . . . Put simply, given the power that you have to do good or harm by virtue of the decisions you make, under pressure each day, the least you can do is think about it. (Sheridan Burns, 2002: 11)

Not just *think* about it but also *talk* about it and even occasionally *do something* about it (Harcup, 2002a, 2002b and 2007).

ETHICS AROUND THE WORLD

SUMMARY

An ethical approach to journalism takes account of issues raised in the industry's various codes of conduct, whether voluntary, self-regulatory or statutory. Such an approach demands accurate reporting and justifies intrusion into people's private lives only when there is evidence that such intrusion is warranted by a wider public interest or public good; but critics say the system of self-regulation has allowed sections of the UK press in particular to flout such guidelines. Ideas about ethical journalism may change over time, may differ between different media platforms or sectors, and may also be different in different countries; there might be occasions when what is regarded (by journalists and other citizens) as ethical behaviour might differ from what is lawful. Journalists tend to guard their independence both from the state and (up to a point) from their employers. Although some employers seem to believe that ethics are whatever a proprietor or editor says they are, it has been argued that *all* journalists need a sense of ethical responsibility and to think about the consequences of their work, because journalism can have an impact on individuals and on wider society. The Leveson inquiry and phone-hacking trials are seen as marking a low point for ethical journalism, but it should be remembered that ultimately it was journalists and not the police who revealed the extent of the hackgate scandal and cover up.

QUESTIONS

Why should any journalist below the rank of editor bother with ethics?
Don't people only need privacy if they are up to no good?
When might it be unethical to report something that is true?
What have human rights got to do with journalism?
Do journalists really need a whistleblowing hotline?

**HOW MIGHT
YOU TACKLE
THIS ISSUE?**

WHAT WOULD YOU DO?

We are back with the scenario introduced earlier in the book, about the search for 10-year-old Jane Doe. Police have found a body that has not yet been identified and your news editor asks you to visit the family home to seek an immediate interview with the parents, adding that if nobody is at home you should wait outside and spend the time using your phone to see what family members and others might be posting on Facebook or other social media. What ethical considerations might arise from this assignment?

FURTHER READING

The *Leveson Report* itself and the evidence presented to the inquiry are all worth reading, or at least dipping into, and can be found online at:
http://webarchive.nationalarchives.gov.uk/20140122145147/http:/www.levesoninquiry.org.uk/ (Leveson, 2012).

For details of how we got there, the best places to begin are *Dial M for Murdoch* by Watson and Hickman (2012) and *Hack Attack* by Nick Davies (2014), while James Hanning's (2014) *The News Machine* tells the story from the point of view of private investigator Glenn Mulcaire. For more on the fall-out from the whole business, see Keeble and Mair (2012) and Mair (2013). For wider discussions of ethics and journalism see Harcup (2007), Frost (2011), Meyers (2010), Sanders (2003) and Wyatt (2014) for starters. For discussion of the ethics of listening (not of the phone-hacking kind), see Wasserman (2013), and for an illuminating series of case studies of journalists dealing with difficult ethical decisions, see *When Reporters Cross the Line* by Purvis and Hulbert (2013). After all those, Sharon Marshall's (2010) *Tabloid Girl* might provide a little light relief.

TOP THREE TO TRY NEXT

Chris Frost (2011) *Journalism Ethics and Regulation* (third edition)
Tony Harcup (2007) *The Ethical Journalist*
Christopher Meyers (2010) *Journalism Ethics: A Philosophical Approach*

SOURCES FOR SOUNDBITES

Malcolm, 2004: 3; Morgan, quoted in Hattenstone, 2005; Sanders, 2003: 90; Marshall, 2010: 230; Editors' code, in PCC, 2012; Ofcom, 2013.

CHAPTER 14

ENGAGING WITH THE AUDIENCE AND SOCIAL MEDIA

"I like tweeting while I'm on air", says Cathy Newman of television's *Channel 4 News*, adding: "There's a sense of immediacy about it, a sense of urgency, when you're live on air." And so, between her share of presentation and interviewing duties, she uses **Twitter** to flag up what's coming later in the live show, to explain "reverse-ferrets" about planned items that have been postponed or cancelled at the last minute, or to engage in real-time conversation with members of the audience about pieces that have just been aired. Not just the stories themselves, either. "Last night there were many more comments about the new top I had on than about the story we had done on Iraq", says Newman. Such is life on television in the age of social media, for women especially.

The *Guardian*'s Jemima Kiss was quoted in the second edition of this book as saying: "Much more could be done with messaging services like Twitter." That was in 2009 and back then it tended to be mostly just the more tech-savvy journalists who used Twitter. Over the following couple of years it found its way into the toolkit of virtually every newsroom, although some embraced it with more enthusiasm than others. And today? "It's completely part of the furniture now", says Kiss. She continues:

> I think organisations are a lot more sophisticated in how they use Twitter and are confident enough to let individual journalists do what they want to do in their own voice – Twitter is made for individuals to communicate, not organisations – but have also invested in specialist staff. We have a very established community team which pushes and promotes all our content across Twitter, Facebook and other networks. I think there's an understanding that different content

> "There's no such thing as a personal Twitter feed as a journalist."
> *Neal Mann*
> *(@fieldproducer)*

JOURNALISTS' USE OF TWITTER

TWITTER

When Emily Bell declared that, "Twitter is already a far more effective tool for reporting, discovery, dissemination and collaboration than anything the BBC will ever produce" (Bell, 2013), it was merely one of a long line of bold pronouncements about the transformational power of digital and social media in general and of Twitter in particular. "As with most media technologies, there is a degree of hyperbole about the potential of Twitter", observes Alfred Hermida (2010), who nonetheless argues that it can indeed undermine journalists' traditional role as gatekeepers of information. For Hermida, Twitter should be seen as an example of a digital "awareness system" – a form of "ambient journalism" – that creates "new kinds of interactions around the news, . . . enabling citizens to maintain a mental model of news and events around them" (Hermida, 2010). Similarly, Jones and Salter (2012: 171) note that the "polyvocal, fragmented, two-way discourses" found on Twitter can offer an alternative to "traditional journalistic narratives".

Can, but don't necessarily, according to a study of social media use in eight countries (including the UK and USA) which found that although "social media are clearly important to the news habits of a significant minority", they are still a minority. The authors rejected the technological determinism that accompanies much discussion of Twitter et al on the grounds that "technology alone does not drive developments in how many people use social media for publicly oriented purposes", and concluded: "One should never assume that access equals use or that potential equals practice" (Nielsen and Schroder, 2014).

There is evidence (Hedman and Djerf-Pierre, 2013) that journalists are more frequent users of social media suits different platforms: Twitter for breaking news, Facebook for more discursive things and Pinterest or Instagram for visual things.

For Kiss, then, having a personal voice in social and online media is vital even when working for a large news organisation:

> I think it's quite good that journalists can have a personality, at least if they are covering an area where that is appropriate. Online I think it is hugely important to be forthcoming about who is saying what and why. As soon as you have a personality, a name, and even a byline pic, the level of engagement, the quality of discussion, is much more civilised.

If Jemima Kiss was an early adopter, joining Twitter just a few months after its launch in 2006, Cathy Newman was still earlyish compared to most journalists, signing up in 2009. Newman sees her use of Twitter entirely in journalistic terms:

> **"We're all about starting conversations and kickstarting debates."**
> *Carla Buzasi*
> *(@carlabuzasi)*

> I think it's got to be a professional tool because if you start blurring the professional and the personal then you get into trouble. I came off Facebook because it's too time-consuming and I saw it more as a personal tool than a professional tool. But Twitter is almost like an unofficial news service or wire, and you can follow people you respect and get their take on stories, and I think it's also a shop window for journalists like me. I can tweet about what story I'm doing, I can ask people what questions they think we should be covering in an interview. You get the odd gem, so that's good, but it is pretty much a shop window. I'm quite focused about it. I know a lot of people tweet a lot more than I do, but I have quite a rigid divide between personal and professional life. I can't really live my life by Twitter. I probably am at my most active on Twitter during the show because I try to drum up interest in what's coming up next or get comments on what's just been, and I think that's a really useful way of engaging with people.

JOURNALISM AND NEW TECHNOLOGIES

Such interaction between journalists and their **active audience** has become the new

than are members of the general population, which may result in some journalists – not to mention some academics – having a skewed idea of quite how central online news is or isn't in most people's lives. It might also result in some journalists orientating themselves so much towards Twitter in particular, where lots of other media types also hang out, that they fail to notice how on many local newspaper websites in the UK it is actually Facebook that tends to be a bigger driver of traffic among ordinary people (ie non-media types).

Research suggests that, as with earlier new technologies, use of Twitter has undergone a process of "normalisation" whereby journalists now routinely use it to gather, source and drive traffic to news reports, which will then be subject to comment and interpretation by other users. The fact that the journalist is only one voice among many in this process prompts Hermida to ponder if people's use of Twitter to share and contest the news has the potential to create new forms of journalism:

> Emerging research suggests new paradigms of collaborative and collective newsgathering, production and management at play, facilitated by the sociotechnical dynamics of Twitter. The result may be journalism but not as we know it, breaking with classic narrative structures and deviating from long-held and fiercely defended norms. (Hermida, 2013)

That may be the result. Or maybe it won't. If it wasn't on the list of banned clichés, I'd be tempted to write: only time will tell.

ACTIVE AUDIENCE

The audience has long been said to be active in the sense that people bring their own interpretations to all media output, but since the arrival of online journalism and social media the term has also been used to show that journalism is no longer as one-way or linear as it was in pre-digital days. However, whether or not it is text-based or includes a selection of tweets, videos, still pictures, interactive maps, audio, links to original documentation, or other ways of telling a story, such as slideshows or animation, journalism on the internet is still journalism and is still informed by the "core journalistic principles and processes" of identifying normal and it marks something of a shift of emphasis as well as a change of tone.

JOURNALISM AS CONVERSATION

Audience input used to mean the letters page and it then expanded to include phone-ins on radio and occasionally on TV too. But it was the emergence of the web followed by blogging, "citizen journalism", users' comments and then social media that really began throwing up different answers to the communication question posed in Chapter 1 of this book: *Who says what to whom, through what channel and with what effect?* Blogging, for example, was said to have "reshaped globalised communications and in doing so has demanded that journalists re-evaluate and reform their practices" (Knight, 2008: 118). The result of all this interactive technology and social media is, for Megan Knight and Clare Cook (2013), a form of collaborative networked journalism that is creating a media landscape in which distinctions between journalist and audience are fast disappearing, "and the crowd – not journalists – are in control" (Knight and Cook, 2013: 3–4). Other commentators are more guarded about what many regard as the hype around the transformational impact of social and digital media on relations between journalist and audience (Hedman and Djerf-Pierre, 2013; Nielsen and Schroder, 2014). But whether or not the crowd really are in control, more of them seem to be joining in the conversation, often at the invitation of journalists.

Sarah Hartley writes two blogs, for example: one about food and one about journalism itself. For her, "What you're trying to do with a blog is to conduct a conversation". Meaning?

> **"People don't like just to be shouted at, they want to take part."**
> *Sarah Hartley (@foodiesarah)*

ENGAGING VIA SOCIAL MEDIA

Sometimes a blog will be the start of a conversation about finding something out, asking people to join in, asking people to give you information. The best blogs should be like that, really. What you're first putting out there isn't the definitive and isn't the history, it's the start of a *process*. It's all the revisions and the feedback, and the things that come along after, that are probably more important than what you first started

potential stories, gathering information, selection and presentation (Ward, 2002: 6 and 30). Where online journalists tend to differ from other journalists is in the way they relate to their respective audiences, according to a study in the Netherlands:

> [The] bottom-up concept of "the public" suggests that this group of journalists is much more aware of an active role for the people they serve than their offline colleagues. This is an interesting result, as it ties in with the discourse of new-media technologies in which they are perceived to empower people and further democratise the relationships between consumers and producers of content (be it news or information). It also connects to online media logic as a concept which includes the notions of *the audience as an active agent* in redefining the workings of journalism. (Deuze and Dimoudi, 2002: 97, my emphasis)

In this context of redefinition, journalists are said to need – and to be undertaking – a serious rethink about what their function might be in the future:

> News is now entrenched in social media spaces and the observations of non-journalists are increasing their circulation and these voices require the services of curators, weeders and archivists. Journalists are responding by rethinking their professional role so they might find ways to add value in the facilitation of social dialogue as gatherers and sharers of information. (Jones and Salter, 2012: 171–172)

Gathering information, adding value and sharing it – isn't that what journalists have always done anyway?

USER-GENERATED CONTENT

The phrase "user-generated content", or UGC, may be recent, but the phenomenon itself is not new. A reader's letter published in a newspaper or a magazine is an example of it at work in traditional media, and other examples would be the historical photographs sent in by readers, the reports of flower shows and sporting events contributed by non-journalists, radio phone-ins, and the seemingly endless scribblings of amateur community or village correspondents that are still carried in some local and regional newspapers.

with. A good online journalist now will be able to bring that right round, because it is a never-ending story. You've got no deadline, you've got no bedtime, you just keep on forever. And things can stay online forever. On my food blog, two years ago I wrote about Marmite and I'm still getting feedback and responses to that two years later because some people are only reading it today, so it's a new story to them and they've got something to add to it. It really doesn't end.

As someone who began in newspapers before moving online, Hartley has seen at first hand this move towards journalism as conversation, adding: "People don't like just to be shouted at, they want to take part, so that shift has happened."

Hartley, like Jemima Kiss, was interviewed for the second edition of this book. But, unlike Hartley, Kiss has spent her entire career as a journalist online. She told me back then that, if the purpose of journalism is "to inform and educate, to hold people in authority to account, to document and interpret development and change", then blogging should be seen as just one more way of making such material available:

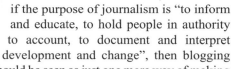

THE AUDIENCE AS
PARTICIPANTS

> "There is enormous potential in collaborative journalism between news sites and readers."
>
> *Jemima Kiss (@jemimakiss)*

I get very tired of the discussion about the definitions of what a blogger is, what a journalist is and what a blogging journalist is. Blogging is primarily just a publishing system – it was born of the web and suits it perfectly – easy to browse, in reverse chronological order and easily indexed and linkable. Blogs work just as well for news as they do for opinion. In terms of how blog culture has developed, blogging demands a strong individual voice, but using a personality works well to counter the impersonal nature of the internet. . . . I think that communication is now also more central to news and opinion than it has ever been, because platforms are now more easily two-way. I have faith in most people to be able to discern wheat from chaff so I think the role of writers and editors will remain important, but I do think that once the industry eventually gets over its historical snobbery of involving the public, there is enormous potential in collaborative journalism between news sites and readers.

And let's not forget bystander Abraham Zapruder's home movie of the President Kennedy assassination as far back as 1963. However, digital communication has transformed the volume and speed of user-generated content so much that dealing with it is now a major part of the thinking of most journalistic operations. "What is critical about this public behavioural shift towards an explosion of UGC is that mainstream media are making space for this production within newsrooms . . . and within news items", observes Rena Kim Bivens (2008: 116–117). "On some occasions, the flood of UGC linked to a breaking news item has actually reversed the traditional flow of news."

THE DIGITAL ECONOMY

The people running online businesses, including digital media, sometimes portray themselves as if their workplaces are some kind of caring, sharing post-hippy idyll. But they are still businesses. Des Freedman (2014) takes issue with academic commentators and media gurus who argue that the digital and online economy is a fundamentally new, citizen-friendly form of business activity. In reality, he argues, "the structure of the digital economy looks a lot like the structure of the analogue economy and is marked by dominant players in all its main sectors" (Freedman, 2014: 100). According to Robert McChesney (cited in Freedman, 2014: 101):

> The best way to imagine the internet is as a planet where Google, Facebook, Apple, Amazon, Microsoft, and the ISP cartel members each occupy a continent that represents their monopoly base camp. . . . The goal of each empire is to conquer the world and prevent getting conquered by someone else.

What's that got to do with journalism? Quite a lot, argues Granville Williams:

> [T]he oft-repeated neo-liberal argument [is] that the internet will set us free by giving us more news to consume, more diversity, more of everything. The contention is that the internet will disrupt power structures and neutralise traditional gatekeepers, but the reality is very different. The most-visited news websites in Europe, Britain, the US and Australia are the websites of the dominant national

Half a decade on, does she feel that blogging is being replaced by Facebook and Twitter? It's not quite that, she says, although the advent of social media has contributed to things speeding up:

> Certainly in the tech news space there's a real fatigue about blog content – nobody has time to read it and certainly we don't have time to write it. Blogging seems to have shifted away from something an individual would do to being a very polarised platform, either for high-end, authoritative and expert writers who use *Medium*, for example, to low-end trashy celebrity viral sites like *BuzzFeed* and *Upworthy*. I'm not sure how much appetite there is for the public to blog at length anymore – it's less that Facebook etc have taken over and more that there just isn't enough time for normal people to do all this stuff, let alone have a real life.

Time has always been an issue for journalists but the demands have multiplied in recent years. In addition to her tweeting, TV journalist Cathy Newman, for example, now also writes three blog articles every week which she says has "massively" increased her workload. Writing the original blog post might just be the start, because there is now an expectation in many quarters that readers' comments should often receive a response. Whether to respond to comments, and how often, is often down to the individual journalist or blogger, and Newman says she rarely reads below-the-line comments on her blogs because of the unpleasant sexism that so often lurks there. But at the *Huffington Post*, in contrast, it is company policy to read and respond, just as it is always to use social media to push content and promote the brand. Carla Buzasi explains:

> We're all about starting conversations and kickstarting debates. We do respond to comments, that's the policy. When you respond they realise there's actually a human involved. Our journalists push stories out every way they can, they're mini-marketeers of their own content. It's not enough just to write that story. The journey of that story is a lot longer and they should be looking at it during the day, is it

news organisations. News aggregation sites on social media are simply reproducing the news stories from these sources and, far from creating different, more diverse sources of news, reinforce the mainstream news agenda. (Williams, 2014a: 19–20)

CITIZEN JOURNALISM?

Blogging, tweeting about the news, posting readers' comments online or contributing UGC to mainstream media are all sometimes referred to as forms of "citizen journalism". Such citizen journalism tends to be seen as part of the more general blurring of boundaries between journalist and audience – sender and receiver – that has been facilitated by digital technology. Although it can be difficult to discern quite what practices such as sending in weather pictures taken on mobile phones or creating some of the more self-obsessed blogs have to do with either citizenship or journalism, some bloggers do clearly concern themselves with traditional journalistic attributes such as reporting and verification. Andrew Sullivan describes blogging as "peer-to-peer journalism", more like a 24-hour broadcast than "a fixed piece of written journalism". When readers of his blog began responding not merely with opinions but also with fresh information, he saw that the blog's advantage over traditional one-way journalism was that it could "marshal the knowledge and resources of thousands, rather than the few" (Sullivan, 2002). This potential passing of control from journalists to users holds out the promise – or threat – that journalists will lose their role as gatekeeper (Hall, 2001: 53; Knight and Cook, 2013: 4).

Much theorising on the subject of the internet proceeds from an assumption that everything has changed, while others counter that nothing *fundamental* has changed. For Jackie Harrison, "[T]he availability of greater sources of news does not guarantee an engaged or enlightened citizenry (any more than anything else does), and earlier claims to this effect about the internet and the digital citizen now seem exaggerated" (Harrison, 2006: 206). And, as Natalie Fenton (2012: 142) argues in relation to networking and communication via social media: "Networks are not inherently liberatory; network openness does not lead us directly to democracy. The

> "Increasingly the online audience doesn't just want to be told the story, it wants to be part of the story."
>
> *Trevor Gibbons (@trevorgi)*

performing well, do we need to give it another push, can we get a different angle on it? It's about taking responsibility for that too.

Buzasi says that trolling, whereby users post abusive comments and/or threats, is less of a problem at the *Huffington Post* than it is in some other online media because it took a policy not to publish comments from those wearing cloaks of invisibility:

> We've done everything we can to stamp out trolling, so people can't leave anonymous comments on the site. People have to have a Facebook account to log in. There's a nasty side to the web and we do everything we can to be responsible about that and to protect our journalists.

If journalism *is* becoming more of a conversation, then perhaps the participants need to remember their manners a bit more often. Martin Wainwright is a web and Twitter enthusiast, but he is not a fan of abusive and anonymous comments:

> "The idea that one person at a digital news operation is its social media editor is laughable."
> *Danny Shea (@danielshea)*

> Interaction is very good, and it's much easier now to be picked up for making mistakes. Mistakes are built in to daily journalism, and all that matters is that you correct them. But the tone of the comments – some of them you think, "I really would not want to meet these people". They dominate, and I can't understand why they are allowed to be anonymous. You get some blogs that have 300 comments, but when you look it's mainly two people going on and on at each other.

However, research at two local newspaper websites in the UK suggests that journalists' common perceptions about comments' threads – about the level of abuse and the domination by a tiny number of users – might be unfounded or exaggerated (Canter, 2013). Then again, even one or two drops of venom can still poison a conversation.

I ask Jemima Kiss if the sort of things she reads posted online ever makes her despair of the audience, and what can be done about it. "No," she says, adding:

> Commenters are not really typical of the wider audience, thankfully. Just have a brutally efficient

practices of new media *may* be liberating for the user but not necessarily democratising for society." So, on the one hand we have the "communicative possibilities that are suggested by horizontally rather than vertically organised information structures"; on the other hand, it is argued that new technologies are part of "the accumulation of capital, commodification and the disappearance of public space" (Stevenson, 2002: 184). In other words, the most important issue is not technology itself but the uses to which it is put, and such uses are unlikely to be uniform. While the internet *can* be used to facilitate a more active citizenship, and online journalism *can* play a role in that, many people seem content to use online technologies just for shopping, entertainment or social networking. Members of the audience do not necessarily always want to be active, it seems; or maybe they *are* being active, just not in ways predicted or desired by some of the more enthusiastic commentators.

If Williams (2014a: 20) is right that online news and social media *tend* to reproduce a mainstream agenda, it is not the full picture. Some "communes of resistance" to dominant discourse remain in existence and new ones spring up, both online and offline (Castells, 1997: 358). And, arguably at least, the label "citizen journalism" might be more appropriately applied to dissident or alternative media (Harcup, 2013) than to people posting videos of kittens on YouTube or tweeting about what a TV presenter is wearing on screen.

and highly vigilant moderation team, flag up potentially contentious pieces to them *before* they are published, for example Israel/Palestine, make it very clear to abusive commenters that they will be blocked and barred. And have a good transparent system for doing so.

Her point about the people who post comments not necessarily being typical of the wider audience is reflected in Jakob Nielsen's *90-9-1 rule* which states that, as a rough rule of thumb, "In most online communities, 90% of users are lurkers who never contribute, 9% of users contribute a little, and 1% of users account for almost all the action" (Nielsen, 2006). It also tallies with Cathy Newman's experience of the difference between the online world and real life:

> It's quite funny because when I walk down the street people are universally lovely, they say how great I am, lovely stuff, you know, "What a role model for women," and so on. And that's really nice. Even if it's not true, I like it. But on Twitter it seems to me, because of the anonymity, that people will say the most vile things that I'm sure they wouldn't dream of saying to your face. There is a lot of misogyny. I very rarely read the comments below a blog for that reason, whereas if it's in a tweet to you, if they're really vile, I can block them.

Putting yourself in the public eye has its downsides. Although much trolling is aimed at women, it can also be targeted at men, as Neal Mann of the *Wall Street Journal* points out. He urges those with substantial followings on social media to be aware of potential dangers:

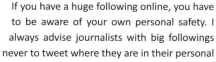

JOURNALISTS' 'BRANDS' ON TWITTER

> If you have a huge following online, you have to be aware of your own personal safety. I always advise journalists with big followings never to tweet where they are in their personal life, for example. You need to be aware of what you're publishing and your location, which traditionally wouldn't have been an issue unless you were covering very, very volatile subjects. But people can have an obsession with individuals that publish daily and regularly. That shouldn't scare journalists off but it should be something that they're aware of.

"THAT'S WHERE THEY ARE, THAT'S WHERE YOU SHOULD BE"

If prolific users of social media are not exactly representative of the wider population, and if a few of them are nasty pieces of work, is there any point engaging directly with the audience at all? Mann is in no doubt that there is and that social media is now a key part of a journalist's job:

> Journalists have to be where the audience is and also where the sources are. If that meant in the past that the sources were in a particular pub, or outside a factory where you think there might be a story, you'd go there. Social media usage is just increasing exponentially so it makes no sense as a journalist not to be where the audience is and where the potential sources are. That's where they are, that's where you should be. If you look at the data and the shift towards social consumption, we have to go and get them, we have to go and engage with the audience rather than arrogantly expecting them to come to us.

For many journalists that means treading a tricky line between representing yourself as an individual and representing the news organisation for which you are working. Mann again:

> Journalists traditionally would have just broadcast in the voice of their organisation. That doesn't work on social media because everybody else is using their own voice and people don't want to just hear from a robot. As a result, journalists need to put personality into what they do. The key thing to understand is that you are working for a news organisation, and as a result you need to uphold their standards and remember that you are publishing on behalf of the news organisation. There's no such thing as a personal Twitter feed as a journalist, you are a publisher, but the thing that's really key is getting across some personality and working out what your brand is. I, for example, have done breaking news for a long time, but I've shifted my brand now into digital strategy – but [on Twitter] I also weave in music and surfing, which is a huge part of my life. Nobody questions my objectivity

because I like particular areas of music, the same with surfing. People engage with that and they see you as a human being and that increases their trust in you.

If we reflect on the fact that print journalism has developed over hundreds of years, and broadcast journalism over the best part of a century, then we may remind ourselves that we are still at an incredibly early stage even of online journalism, never mind **user-generated content** and journalistic use of social media. As different formats and techniques emerge – including tweeting direct from court cases and curating multimedia coverage of major events via Storify or similar – nobody really knows which ones will stand the test of time. The emergence of the live-blog, which brings together a range of sources and opinions around a particular event in real-time, is an example of an online innovation hailed by some as the future of reporting, while most of the potential audience are probably still unaware that live-blogs even exist let alone spend all day engaging with one. But for big events such as elections or major speeches they do add something new that is informative and interactive at the same time, as prolific live-blogger Andrew Sparrow explains:

> Blogs are not the same as conventional news reports. Conventional, objective, third-person news reporting is a form of storytelling that evolved with newsprint. Blogging is a different form of storytelling, which evolved with the web. You could write a blog like an old-fashioned news report, but that would be like having the ability to broadcast a TV news bulletin and just using it to show someone reading out a radio news script (which is what TV did in the early days, before they worked out how to use the medium properly). The key point about the web is that it is interactive; readers can contact you in real time, and they expect you to reply. As a result, all the best blogs have an authorial voice. . . . Readers also accept this because the author's subjective voice is just one of many in the blog. Blogs like mine use a lot of aggregation, and that means that if someone like David Cameron gives a speech, I may well include dozens of different voices, in the form of tweets, quotes and blogposts, from journalists, commentators or politicians expressing

an opinion about what Cameron said. In this respect, in being open to multiple viewpoints, blogging is an inherently liberal medium. (Sparrow, 2014)

So his blog incorporates opinion and input from social media but it remains a form of reporting. And that means taking care to be accurate, not just speedy, opinionated or entertaining.

LIVE-BLOGGING IN PRACTICE

If journalists are to survive within **the digital economy** and stand out in an era of social media and so-called **citizen journalism**, then it will probably be because journalists are seen as the ones most likely to be passing on accurate information. Speed may be vital in today's journalism, says Mann, but even speed is not as crucial as accuracy:

> Fast is unbelievably important on Twitter as a journalist, but you have to be fast and be right. You will lose trust immediately if you aren't right. You need to engage with a conversation in a 24-hour news world that's going at an incredible speed, and be one of the main voices in it, and to do that you have to be quick – but you have to be accurate.

Jemima Kiss also puts accuracy at the top of her list of the core requirements of a journalist working in any form of media, online or offline: "Accuracy, research, respecting sources, clarity, understanding an audience, knowing which questions to ask, using your initiative and being extremely persistent."

THE RISE AND FALL OF THE SOCIAL MEDIA EDITOR

Just a few years ago there was no such job within news organisations as the social media editor. Then, around 2010, the more tech-savvy newsrooms began seeing the appointment of social media editors: that is, a journalist with specific responsibility for utilising social media technologies such as Facebook, Twitter and YouTube, and for engaging with audiences via such technologies. However, even as many newsrooms were only just catching up with this trend, others were already moving on;

as early as 2013 the social media editor was declared redundant on the grounds that *all* journalists ought now to be undertaking such duties (Fishman, 2013).

Neal Mann served his time as social media editor before becoming a multimedia innovations editor (another job that didn't exist five minutes earlier and that might not exist in five minutes' time). Does he agree that the social media editor is dead? Not quite yet:

> I think it's a good thing for journalism that it's not just something done by the geeky guy in the corner. I think you'll still have people who are specialists in social media who are driving forward change in journalism, it's a very fast evolving area, but I think you'll see a shift in the way that newsrooms work around social media. It won't be such a specific thing any more, it will be ingrained in the entire operation. I think the big change will come when one of the major news organisations has someone at the very top who was once a specialist in social media. That's when there will be a huge shift. At that point, the social media editor will be dead, because it will be run by an editor who fully understands, who is a social media native and a digital native.

In any event, changes in journalistic practice never happen everywhere at the same time or in the same way, and even within the same newsroom there can be tensions and contradictions. As one editor told *BuzzFeed*: "I both agree that the social media editor is dead and I just hired a social media editor" (Fishman, 2013).

See Chapters 4, 5 and 6 for more on using social media for finding and verifying sources and information, and Chapter 15 for more on what the future of journalism might look like.

SUMMARY

Whether they like it or not (and many embrace it with unbridled enthusiasm) journalists are increasingly expected to engage directly with members of the audience via digital communication technologies such as Twitter, Facebook and online comments' threads. The shift towards a more active audience raises questions about the concept of gatekeeping and about the future role of journalists and journalism in an age of ubiquitous social media and "polyvocal" or multiple-voiced conversations. New forms of reporting have emerged that have audience engagement built into them, including tweeting big trials and live-blogging major political events. As more journalists engage with the audience as an everyday part of their job, they are having to respond to a range of issues, including the blurring of a personal and professional voice, the threat of trolling and a seemingly ever-increasing workload. The extent to which everything has been changed by the latest technology – or not – remains contested in both journalistic and academic circles.

QUESTIONS

Can you be an effective journalist today without using social media?
Is Twitter really better than BBC journalists at reporting?
What's the point of users' below-the-line comments?
Could live-blogging be the future of reporting?
Does the internet undermine or reinforce the mainstream news agenda?

HOW MIGHT YOU TACKLE THIS ISSUE?

WHAT WOULD YOU DO?

As the editor of a news organisation you are required to expand your audience and promote the brand. Towards this end you expect all your journalists to engage with the audience (and potential audience) via Facebook, Twitter, Instagram and so on as well as taking part in conversations in below-the-line comments' threads on the main website. Some journalists complain to you that, although they do not have a problem with most users, a few posters are subjecting them to unwarranted criticism, unfounded allegations, personal abuse and even threats. What do you do?

FURTHER READING

Knight and Cook (2013) is probably the best place to start to see how journalists have taken to social media, even if you don't wish to go all the way with the authors' argument that "in social spaces, the distinction between journalist and audience has vanished completely" (2013: 4). Also worth consulting in relation to social media, user-generated content and journalism are Bradshaw and Rohumaa (2011) and Jones and Salter (2012). Hermida (2013) is a useful round-up of academic research to date into journalists' use of Twitter and the theorising thereof, while Thurman and Walters (2013) offer an illuminating study of live-blogging. Rob Fishman's (2013) article "The social media editor is dead" can be found online at *BuzzFeed*, while evidence that digital technology has not necessarily changed everything or liberated everybody can be found in *Misunderstanding the Internet* by Curran et al (2012) and *New Media, Old News*, edited by Natalie Fenton (2010); also see Freedman (2014).

TOP THREE TO TRY NEXT

James Curran, Natalie Fenton and Des Freedman (2012) *Misunderstanding the Internet*
Janet Jones and Lee Salter (2012) *Digital Journalism*
Megan Knight and Clare Cook (2013) *Social Media for Journalists: Principles and Practice*

SOURCES FOR SOUNDBITES

Mann, Buzasi, Hartley, Kiss, Gibbons, all from interviews with the author; Shea quoted in Fishman, 2013.

CHAPTER 15

THE FUTURE IS UNWRITTEN: CHALLENGES FACING THE JOURNALISTS OF TOMORROW

KEY TERMS

Constraints; Consumers; Curiosity; Informed citizens; Mobile journalism; Multimedia; Public sphere; Reflective practice; Slow journalism; Work experience

As a university student at the dawn of the 21st century Carla Buzasi was lucky – and persistent – enough to get work experience at *Cosmopolitan* magazine. Although it was only a decade and a half ago it already feels like ancient history, as she recalls: "There was only one computer in the office that had the internet on it, and nobody was using it. One computer! And that's not all that long ago." Indeed, in the first few years of the web it was not uncommon to find employers blocking internet access on newsroom computers, on the assumption that if journalists were online they were more likely to be wasting company time than working. "Now if I walk around and people haven't got Facebook and Twitter open I'm slightly concerned," Buzasi says of the *Huffington Post*'s journalists, "because (a) you should be promoting the stories, but (b) you need to know what people are talking about online. It's been a total turnaround."

This turnaround is symbolised by the fact that most of her journalistic career has been spent in jobs that simply had not been invented at the time she did her work experience around the year 2000. Neal Mann has been in a similar position since finishing his postgraduate course in broadcast journalism in 2007:

> When I graduated Facebook was around but nobody was talking about it. The jobs of social media editor and multimedia innovations editor did not exist when I graduated and did not exist for a couple of years after. Who knows what jobs people are going to go into in the future? People can shape their own jobs.
>
> I think it's a really exciting time for journalists to come into the industry right now because they're coming in as digital natives, they're coming in with a lot of skills that, frankly, 50 per cent to 70 per cent of journalists

> "It's handy to have as many skills as you can."
> *Lindsay Eastwood.*

JOURNALISM

Thanks largely to the market forces under which it exists, journalism is little more than "a magic mirror" held up to society that, far from reflecting real life, actually has "the effect of keeping the popular classes, in particular, in a state of ecstasy and to deny them knowledge about the world and knowledge about their position in the world." So writes sociologist Jean Chalaby (1998: 5) in *The Invention of Journalism*. He argues that journalists have little interest in informing or educating people about the society in which we live, and instead "bypass the social dimension of individuals, address their fantasies and reconstruct a world of illusions around their readers' dreams" (Chalaby, 1998: 193). Few critical observers would deny that there is an element of the above going on in journalism, and not only at the more fanciful end of the market exemplified by splashes such as WORLD WAR 2 BOMBER FOUND ON MOON, once brought to you by the *Sunday Sport*, FREDDIE STARR ATE MY HAMSTER by the *Sun*, or 45 MINUTES FROM ATTACK, courtesy of the *Evening Standard*. But is that really the full story? We have heard from many journalists in the preceding 14 chapters of this book and we have seen something of the good and bad of journalism – some of its principles, practices and ethics – at work in the real world. Two things that should have become apparent by now are that journalists are not all the same and that the future of journalism is unwritten. Everything has changed and yet, arguably, little fundamental has changed. Alan Knight, an Australian journalist-turned-academic, spells out some of the challenges facing 21st-century journalism:

> Journalists were once defined by where they worked; in newspapers, or radio and television stations. The internet promises everyone can be a publisher. But

don't have. They need to learn the traditional aspects of journalism but they don't need to play by the rules that the older generation were forced to play by, were bound by. They can create content in a very different way that engages the audience and, moving forward, it's a very different way of thinking that's liberating for a young journalist, I think.

Potentially liberating but also, perhaps, pretty scary; especially after successive rounds of job losses and office closures have hit many news organisations and after some employers have begun talking about "harvesting content" without the need for many journalists.

This is, then, a "moment of promise and peril" for journalism, according to a major report by, and about, the *New York Times*. The internal report, called *Innovation*, caused quite a stir when it was leaked in 2014 because it highlighted the extent to which the "print-centric" news organisation's journalistic strengths and traditions were failing to prevent it losing market share to more nimble and audience-focused digital competitors such as the *Huffington Post* and *BuzzFeed*. The *New York Times* needs to transform the way it organises and distributes its digital output if its journalism is to reach the widest possible audience, but the report warns against thinking this will be a one-off change:

> "I like to come at a story from all angles."
> *Deborah Wain.*

THE INNOVATION REPORT

> Transformation can be a dangerous word in our current environment because it suggests a shift from one solid state to another; it implies there is an end point. Instead, we have watched the dizzying growth of smart phones and tablets, even as we are still figuring out the web. We have watched the massive migration of readers to social media even as we were redesigning our home page. Difficult new questions will arrive with each new shift. In all likelihood, we will spend the rest of our careers wrestling with them. (*New York Times*, 2014: 5)

OLD SKILLS, NEW CONTEXTS

Newsrooms across the media and across the world are wrestling with similar questions, albeit with different specifics, at different speeds and with a range of different proposed solutions to what sometimes feels like a threat to the very existence of **journalism**.

not everyone has the skills or training to be a journalist; defined by their professional practices and codes of ethics. Such journalists will continue to authorise information, providing signposts for discerning audiences. . . . Anyone applying professional practices within recognised codes of ethics will be differentiated from most bloggers as well as our friends at Fox News. . . . Journalists should be trained to produce fair and accurate stories about their communities, and if journalism educators make ethics and professional practices the core of their courses, journalists should still be the best equipped to deliver such information. If they do so, journalists will adapt to the internet, in the same ways they embraced the telephone, the telegraph and the printing press. (Knight, 2008: 123)

As with the impact of the internet and technological convergence, the extent to which individual journalists retain sufficient agency to *make a difference* is an area of disagreement within journalism studies. Some academic theorists and commentators have been criticised for a tendency to downplay the room for agency in the production of journalism. So, for example, the *political economy* model emphasises the determining role played by economic power and material factors in creating media products. In the view of Peter Golding and Philip Elliott: "News changes very little when the individuals that produce it are changed" (quoted in Curran and Seaton, 1997: 277).

For Chalaby, not only does the news not change much when individual journalists change, but much journalism within commercial media is actually doing the opposite of producing an informed and enlightened citizenry:

> Journalists do not venture beyond what they think are the limits of their readers' cognitive abilities and seek to produce a newspaper without a cognitive gap with the average reader's mind. Newspapers, those reaching a popular audience in particular, may try to influence or even manipulate their readers, but they will never attempt to educate them. . . . As a result, journalists rarely challenge readers' preconceived ideas and prejudices or transcend readers' present state of consciousness. Journalists open no new levels of perception for their readers and do not expand their intellectual horizon. . . . [T]he popular media not

The future of journalism might just turn out to be mobile, believes Mann:

I don't think news organisations have that long to make a lot of digital changes, looking at the way the audience is shifting and the way that advertising revenue is shifting. I came into journalism through shooting and editing, photography and video, I saw myself as a broadcast journalist. But then in 2009 I discovered Twitter and I understood where the audience was going and how I could engage with it. At that point I sort of became a digital native. Now I wouldn't just say digital, I'd say a mobile native. Mobile is not the next idea, it's here already. News organisations going forward have to think about mobile ahead of everything else, it's mobile first.

> "It's a daily ritual of moral and intellectual compromise – it is a good job, but it is hard."
>
> *Abul Taher.*

Mobile is a different experience and the key thing around it is time, you're engaging with people who have a variety of distractions they didn't use to have. Newsrooms going forward have to shift very, very quickly to producing content designed for the mobile experience. You might break the article down into an easily digestible format. What you can potentially do is compress long-form journalism and put it in a format that they can engage with in under a minute and give them the option to go deeper when they want.

Traditionally you would just publish content and people could engage with it on different platforms, but it might be the same content. Now, even if you look at making mobile-first content designed specifically for mobile, the tablet experience is very different. People use it at different times of day, often at their leisure at night. That's what journalists and news organisations need to think about, transferring somebody's behaviour across platforms. That's where our thinking needs to go, because that's the only way we're going to engage people with our journalism.

Buzasi agrees that journalism for mobile and tablet is something that today's journalists need to get to grips with by, for example, creating shorter versions of stories for the times of day that see peak mobile use and longer versions for other times. And by

only put limits to their readers' intellectual horizon but, by making readers unaware of their lack of information, undermine the conditions for the appropriation of further knowledge. With such a relation to knowledge, the commercial popular press could only annihilate the promises of the project of enlightenment . . . (Chalaby, 1998: 190–191)

That's quite a claim. That, far from enlightening citizens with information about society, journalists *deny* people the knowledge needed to understand the world. But it represents a strand of academic thought that seems to dismiss the possibility that many journalists *do* indeed seek to inform, to educate and even to stretch intellectual horizons, not just of their audiences but sometimes even of themselves. How much leeway do they have to achieve this? Cultural studies theorist Stuart Hall argues that journalists have "relative autonomy from ruling class power in the narrow sense", within certain ideological limits (Hall, 1977: 345–346). But his emphasis is on the "relative" because he argues that – whatever their personal thoughts and wishes – journalists *tend to* reproduce society's prevailing ideology. This is not because of the "conscious intentions and biases" of individual journalists, but as "a function of the discourse and of the logic of social processes", including sourcing strategies that privilege the powerful (Hall, 1982: 88).

Yet individual journalists *do* retain the power to resist the demands of the market and to insist on acting in an ethical manner (Harcup, 2007). John O'Neill argues that the relationship between the "virtues and vices" of journalism can be more fluid than is portrayed in the simplistic depiction of the journalist as either hero or villain:

> Many, I suspect, find themselves forced to compromise the constitutive values of journalism, while at the same time insisting that some of the standards be enforced. . . . Journalists, like other workers, are not totally passive in their attitude to their own faculties. (O'Neill, 1992: 28)

Put another way, the agency of individuals may be limited by economic and social structures, but it exists; just as ethical journalists exist. Journalists work in a field that is – or claims to be – constituted by a professional commitment to ethics and truth telling, yet at the same time journalists may be expendable employees expected to produce stories to sell in the marketplace (O'Neill, 1992: 27–28; Harcup, 2002b: 103).

thinking across traditional boundaries because there is no such thing as having too many skills, as she explains:

> When I'm interviewing people [for jobs] now I expect them to be able to take pictures, edit video, be happy in front of a camera and behind a camera, create a quiz – all those skills are super-important to be a multimedia journalist. I don't think anybody should be thinking, "I want to be a print journalist or a magazine journalist or a radio journalist". Try to pick up every skill you can. There are very few brands that only exist in one version of themselves. Just as newspapers have to grapple with the rise of digital, we have to grapple with the rise of mobile. There are always these new skills that everybody needs to learn, myself included, so why not start off by learning as many as you can?

But what about the doom and gloom felt by many journalists today? Buzasi is having none of it:

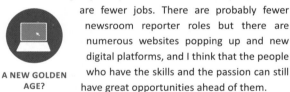

> **"This is the golden age."**
> *Carla Buzasi.*

> This is the golden age. I think it's never been more interesting, there have never been more possibilities. Tweets and short videos don't mean you can't have brilliant long-form investigative journalism, and the best media experience I think brings those two together. Nobody should be deterred from going into journalism because they think there are fewer jobs. There are probably fewer newsroom reporter roles but there are numerous websites popping up and new digital platforms, and I think that the people who have the skills and the passion can still have great opportunities ahead of them.

A NEW GOLDEN AGE?

And some will no doubt start up their own media, just as many of their 18th- and 19th-century predecessors started producing their own newspapers when they spotted a social need, a gap in the market – or both.

History suggests that journalism can often develop in contradictory ways at the same time. So it may be that alongside trends such as always-on "ambient journalism" (Hermida, 2010), speedy bite-sized "McJournalism" (Franklin, 2005b: 148) and journalists becoming 24/7 "output slaves" (White, 2013: 51), we might also see more interest in what

Discussion of the agency of journalists – of their ability to make a difference and/or to act in an ethical manner even when working within a commercial and/or bureaucratic operation – needs to take account of the tension between journalists' different identities. Those different identities include being skilled individuals, socially responsible citizens, factors of production at the whim of management, and workers with at least the potential to share a sense of collective identity and even occasionally to speak or act collectively (Harcup, 2002b: 101–114, and 2007). If journalism matters to society, then surely the actions of journalists matter too.

CONSTRAINTS

In Chapter 2 we came across David Randall's suggested journalistic disclaimer. Having heard a bit more about the principles, practices and ethics of journalism, perhaps we might now rewrite it along the following lines:

> This product has been produced by underpaid and overworked journalists who were recruited from a relatively small section of the population before being socialised into the routines and news values of journalism. Much of the material originated from press officers and public relations professionals, mostly working on behalf of well-resourced organisations. Many news items were selected to meet the perceived interests of audiences thought to be most desirable to advertisers and/or or to promote the brand by being shared or discussed on social media. Stories were produced against the clock and things may have changed since then which may or may not be reflected in updated copy. Stories have been made to fit largely arbitrary word or time limits determined by decisions on format, design and production. In the processes of research, writing and editing, stories may have been simplified and made more dramatic, with certain elements inserted or emphasised largely to improve search engine results. The sources consulted may not have known the full story and/or may have had their own interests to promote, and some of the journalists may have been concerned not to jeopardise relations with some sources. The journalists involved may have their own opinions, and these opinions may or may not have influenced the finished product. The

has been called *slow journalism*. That is, journalism "that takes its time to find things out, notices stories that others miss, and communicates it all to the highest standards", as Susan Greenberg (2007) puts it (see also Harcup, 2007: 142). Is there any money in journalism that puts quality, depth, accuracy and insight above speed and brevity? It would be nice to think so, but since when was journalism only about making money?

"NOBODY ELSE KNOWS ABOUT THIS"

Despite all the uncertainty about the future of journalism, despite all the **constraints** discussed in this book, despite the difficulty of finding new revenue streams to fund labour-intensive journalism, despite the low pay and the even lower public esteem suffered by many journalists, and despite the unethical behaviour that sometimes gives journalism a bad name, many intelligent, questioning, sociable and articulate people are determined that's what they want to be. Why? Partly because of the excitement inherent in finding something out and telling people about it, as Andrew Norfolk explains:

> "The best reporter is somebody who's naturally nosy."
> *Brian Whittle.*

Never in my entire career have I got the buzz I got from my very first bit of investigative journalism, which was on the *Scarborough Evening News*. It was about a further education college, just after they'd all been privatised and income was dependent on the number of students you had. So they had a crèche for babies and toddlers of staff, and some bright spark had decided to enrol them as full-time students with learning difficulties. It was the first story I'd ever done thinking, "Nobody else knows about this and unless it goes in the paper nobody ever will". And it had my name on it. You can't beat that.

Then there are the inspirational people you might meet, sometimes in the unlikeliest of circumstances, as Cathy Newman recalls:

I've interviewed a teenage rape survivor and she was really inspiring, how she'd got her life together at a point when she could have completely crumbled, and actually managed to build something positive out of this

journalists may also have been influenced in story selection and construction by the attitudes of their proprietors, editors, colleagues and by views expressed on social media. They will have been mindful of legal constraints, regulatory rules and maybe even codes of ethical conduct, knowing how far things can be pushed and who is most likely to complain or take legal action. They will also have been aware of what will most impress current and prospective employers. By the time you read this, the journalists may have lost interest in many of these stories and will probably have moved on to fresh ones.

It's become a bit long now, so we could sub it down to:

Don't believe everything you read.

It could go next to the corrections column.

REFLECTIVE PRACTICE

If journalists are not to absolve themselves of all social responsibilities then they must become reflective practitioners, argues Lynette Sheridan Burns. Journalists should reflect critically on what they do, because "a journalist who is conscious of and understands the active decisions that make up daily practice is best prepared to negotiate the challenges involved" (Sheridan Burns, 2002: 11). That does not mean taking time off and sitting back in leisurely contemplation; rather, it means "an active commitment in journalists to scrutinise their own actions, exposing the processes and underlying values in their work *while* they are doing it" (Sheridan Burns, 2002: 41–44, emphasis in original). Such a concept rests upon a belief that journalists have both the individual capacity to reflect upon their own practice and sufficient room to manoeuvre to effect some change in their practice; that "conscience and a personal value system can influence conduct and transcend the limitations of the system and external pressures", as Denis McQuail (2013: 219) puts it.

For Sarah Niblock, a reflective journalist is "one who can make confident editorial judgements that are informed by a strong awareness of their role in society. Consequently, they can anticipate and effectively negotiate a dynamic and evolving context for journalism production and reception" (Niblock, 2007: 26). In this context Pat Aufderheide argues that there is a need to cultivate "a more self-aware journalistic culture" horrendous tragedy. That was very inspiring. That's as memorable to me as meeting the Dalai Lama, who said to my cameraman that he was overweight.

"All jobs entail compromises of some sort," concedes Abul Taher, "and journalism has its share of them too." Yet he feels that journalism still looks attractive to many young people today, just as it did to him:

I was attracted to journalism because I had always wanted to be a writer. Journalism is easily the most widely read type of literature in modern societies, beating novels, books and poetry. There is a huge pleasure from writing a good, well-researched article, and you really do get a unique window into society through journalism. Journalism informs and educates people about the world beyond their own personal experience. It is a good profession, but it is also one where there is very little financial reward unless you are at the top. Money is the biggest problem . . . and it is especially hard if you have moved to London and are having to pay rent as well as student loans. . . . I have a lot of friends who have become sick of finding that elusive break and want to do other things in life.

> "The best journalists go into situations with open and absorbing minds."
> *Martin Wainwright.*

"THE GREAT VIRTUE OF A JOURNALIST IS CURIOSITY"

For those who haven't been put off, then, what words of wisdom do some of the more experienced journalists interviewed for this book have for coming generations? Jane Merrick stresses the importance of learning "the basics" such as shorthand and the law. She points out that a humble attitude is also an attribute:

Never think that you know more than the lowest journalist on the newspaper or agency, or wherever you start. Take *everything* on board. There's a balance between giving your newsdesk the confidence that you can do the job and being level-headed. It's a matter of getting that balance right. Journalists will respect somebody prepared to take it all on board.

Andrew Norfolk also advises young journalists to spend time learning the basics, including learning from experience:

in which journalists have the time, space and imagination "to bring other voices into their coverage" and "to introduce disturbing and conflicting perspectives" (Aufderheide, 2002: 12–14). Reflective practice therefore involves working both sides of the street: reporting conflicting voices and perspectives, offering differing readings, challenging the common sense of audiences and journalists alike, and thinking twice before using words such as "we" and "us".

PUBLIC SPHERE

As introduced in Chapter 1, the concept of a space in which informed citizens can engage in critical discussion and reflection – a public sphere – is an ideal against which journalism has come to be measured and is often found to be wanting: "Analysts and critics may dispute the extent to which Britain *has* a properly functioning 'public sphere' . . . but all agree that such a space *should* exist, and that the media are at its core" (McNair, 2000: 1, first emphasis in original, second is mine). The concept of the public sphere is associated with the writings of Jürgen Habermas, who – from a 20th-century vantage point – looked back on late 17th- and early 18th-century Britain and identified "the advent of a public sphere of reasoned discourses circulating in the political realm independently of both the Crown and Parliament" (Allan, 1997: 298). Although this public sphere was a conceptual space, it also had physical manifestations, for example in the coffee houses of London where this "reasoned discourse" would take place, albeit among a limited section of the (male) population. Habermas also points to the existence of multiple or competing public spheres, including a "plebeian public sphere" with its own radical forms of alternative media (Habermas, 1989: xviii, 425, 430, and 1992: 425–427; see also Downing et al, 2001: 27–33; and Harcup, 2013).

Yet the idea of journalism serving informed citizens is undermined by a tendency to put a commercial value on everything, to regard media output as just another commodity and to treat audiences as mere consumers, argues Granville Williams:

Counterposed to this is a view of the media as a liberating force for human enlightenment and

Don't be in too much of a hurry. Some people get a job on a national newspaper and within a couple of years, if they haven't got a title they're feeling frustrated. And yet they're the luckiest people in the world. I spent 11 years in regional journalism before I joined the *Times*. It doesn't matter how brilliant you are, the grounding you get – admittedly on terrible pay – from two or three years on a regional newspaper is the building block that then allows you in the end to build whatever you want. Learning by making mistakes, learning that it doesn't matter how simple the surname is, you always ask how to spell it – something as simple as that. Going to boring council meetings and magistrates courts is a really useful grounding.

> **"It doesn't matter how simple the surname is, you always ask how to spell it."**
> *Andrew Norfolk.*

One of my strengths is getting people to talk to me, and if I hadn't had those days on the *Scarborough Evening News* when a kid had died and I had to do the doorknock, and somebody takes you into their home – just learning the way to deal with people, from all different walks of life.

Persistence, charm and trust are three key requirements of anybody who wants to be a good journalist, believes Cathy Newman:

Never give up. Keep hammering away at the story. I see people who think, "Oh that's quite interesting", and they put in a call and then that's it. Keep on bashing the phones, don't take no for an answer, get to the top, don't be fobbed off with the PR. Speak to the chief executive rather than the junior on the PR account because you're not going to find out very much from them. Charm your contacts, look after your contacts, don't burn your sources, earn their trust.

Brian Whittle feels that "naturally nosy" people make the best reporters: "You want somebody who's nosy, somebody with enthusiasm, somebody who wants to do it more than anything else." Similarly, for Martin Wainwright, "the best journalists go into situations with open and absorbing minds. The great virtue of a journalist is curiosity – a constant interest in what makes people tick." Jemima Kiss also mentions the value of having an open mind, not

progress, informing, entertaining, nurturing creative talent and being financially and editorially independent from powerful vested commercial or political interests. (Williams, 1996: 3; see also Williams, 2014a)

His words echo those of US broadcast journalist Ed Murrow, who famously told the 1958 convention of the Radio-Television News Directors Association in Chicago:

Our history will be what we make it. And if there are any historians about 50 or 100 years from now, and there should be preserved the kinescopes for one week of all three networks, they will find there recorded in black and white, or colour, evidence of decadence, escapism and insulation from the realities of the world in which we live. . . . In this kind of complex and confusing world, you can't tell very much about the why of the news in broadcasts where only three minutes is available for news. . . . I am frightened by the imbalance, the constant striving to reach the largest possible audience for everything, by the absence of a sustained study of the state of the nation. Heywood Broun once said, "No body politic is healthy until it begins to itch". I would like television to produce some itching pills rather than this endless outpouring of tranquillisers. It can be done. Maybe it won't be, but it could. . . . This instrument can teach, it can illuminate; yes, and it can even inspire. But it can do so only to the extent that humans are determined to use it to those ends. Otherwise it is merely wires and lights in a box. There is a great and perhaps decisive battle to be fought against ignorance, intolerance and indifference. (Murrow, 1958)

ED MURROW ON JOURNALISM

Whatever the media, platform or technology, that battle continues. And our journalism, like our history, will be what we make it.

just towards people and stories but open also to the fast-changing technological possibilities of the digital age:

> The one thing they will need is an open mind, an attitude that they will not be intimidated or immediately dismissive of new technologies but instead approach them with an open mind and innate journalistic curiosity. A competitive edge comes down to being adaptive and fast to explore and understand something, whether a tech platform or a breaking story. Some of the most valued reporters here are those who understand news and the journalistic process but who also have technical skill and a willingness to learn it. Our experts in security and encryption, for example, were invaluable during the [Edward] Snowden stories, for example. Data journalism, the ability to find the story in the data and show it visually, is exploding. There are huge opportunities there.

> **"Meet as many people as possible, always."**
> *Jemima Kiss.*

But making the most of technology and social media does not devalue the importance of meeting people in real life, she adds: "Get out and meet as many people as possible – join the union, go to meetings, go to conferences and talks, meet as many people as possible, always. And the old work experience thing."

The work experience thing is still useful because spending some time in a real newsroom is one way of finding out if journalism is really for you (and vice versa) as well as the start of making contacts within the industry. However, journalism lecturers and the NUJ usually advise students against spending more than a couple of weeks in any workplace unless you are getting paid. While you are on work experience, keep your eyes and ears open and soak it all up, because everybody else there is likely to know far more about the job than you do; even if they don't, it's probably best not to let them know right away. Also, remember that at certain times you might be most helpful (and make the best impression) simply by offering to fetch some teas or coffees; if they notice that you are not

WORK EXPERIENCE GUIDELINES

too precious to do that, then at less frantic moments people might be more likely to chat and/or listen to your own story ideas. As *Independent on Sunday* editor Lisa Markwell advises those who want to break into journalism: "Show initiative, be passionate, and be young" (Markwell, 2013).

"KEEP YOUR SENSE OF INDEPENDENT OBSERVATION"

Journalism may well be more akin to prostitution than it is to the more formally regulated professions, as Louis Heren would have it; and it may well be that, although you don't *have* to be one of Sharon Marshall's mad or immoral drunks to be a journalist, it may help you fit in (Chapter 1). But that is not all that journalism is. For all their flaws journalists play an important role in informing society about itself, and the best journalists engage in **reflective practice** while contributing to the **public sphere**. A chaotic "anti-profession" journalism might be, in Andrew Marr's phrase (Chapter 1), but what an immeasurably poorer place the world would be without it.

For a last word, I turned to Paul Foot – veteran reporter, investigator and columnist – and asked what advice he had for aspiring young journalists in the 21st century. This is what he said:

> **"Look after your contacts, don't burn your sources, earn their trust."**
> *Cathy Newman.*

> I think people should join the NUJ and if there isn't a union where they work they should do their best to try and form one. That's the first thing. The other thing is, don't lose your sense of curiosity or your sense of scepticism.

> Understand the way the industry works and do your best to apply yourself against that. The last thing I mean is young people rushing in and telling their editors how to run the world, that's absolutely fatal. There's nothing worse than the arrogant young person – who knows *everything* – going and telling people what to do. Even if they're right, which often they are, that's not the way to behave. That's the way to get sacked. You've got to keep your head, you've got to bite your lip, and you've got to do what you're told a lot of the time. Nine

times out of 10 it's better to go ahead and do what you are told, but there's a tenth time when it is worth resisting.

The main thing is to keep your sense of independent observation as to what's happening around you, and to try to use what ability you have to get those things into print. Whatever you see,

> "Whatever you see, there's a story behind it."
> *Paul Foot.*

there's a story behind it. There is a truth and there's no doubt there are facts. Facts are facts, you can't bend them.

And that seems to be as good a note as any on which to conclude a book on the principles and practice of journalism. Over to you.

ALTERNATIVE JOURNALISM

SUMMARY

The future of journalism is both uncertain and unwritten, but the social role of journalism in informing citizens, and contributing towards the health of the public sphere, means that journalists have an ethical responsibility to engage in a process of critical reflection on their practice. Despite the structural forces and constraints that bear down on journalists, individuals and groups of journalists retain elements of choice in their work. Recruits to journalism are advised to learn everything they can from more experienced journalists without ever losing their own sense of curiosity and independent observation.

QUESTIONS

Who is journalism for?
What is journalism for?
Where is journalism practised?
When is journalism at its best?
Why are journalists not trusted?
How might journalism develop?

WHAT WOULD YOU DO?

You have learned a range of multimedia journalism skills and you know how to find, investigate and tell an accurate and interesting story. However, none of the media employers you approach are taking on new staff at the moment. What are you going to do?

HOW MIGHT YOU TACKLE THIS ISSUE?

FURTHER READING

You could usefully start by going back through this book once again and looking up the references and suggestions for further reading contained in each chapter. Then read David Randall's (2005) *The Great Reporters*, an enjoyable and inspiring introduction to the work of some, yes, great reporters. *Journalists* by Tim Gopsill and Greg Neal (2007) charts the first century of the NUJ and its members, while some different ways of doing journalism are explored in Susan Forde (2011)'s *Challenging the News* as well as *Alternative Journalism, Alternative Voices* (Harcup, 2013).

Journalism in Context by Angela Phillips (2015) combines journalistic insight with academic analysis to explore the role of journalism in the unfolding digital age. An overview of different academic

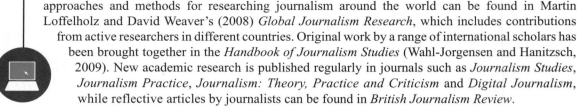

approaches and methods for researching journalism around the world can be found in Martin Loffelholz and David Weaver's (2008) *Global Journalism Research*, which includes contributions from active researchers in different countries. Original work by a range of international scholars has been brought together in the *Handbook of Journalism Studies* (Wahl-Jorgensen and Hanitzsch, 2009). New academic research is published regularly in journals such as *Journalism Studies*, *Journalism Practice, Journalism: Theory, Practice and Criticism* and *Digital Journalism*, while reflective articles by journalists can be found in *British Journalism Review*.

Finally, if you are serious about journalism, don't forget to check relevant websites, follow journalists on Twitter, read a range of papers and magazines, and watch/listen to news and current affairs – every day.

ACADEMIC RESEARCH INTO JOURNALISM

TOP THREE TO TRY NEXT

Tony Harcup (2013) *Alternative Journalism, Alternative Voices*
Angela Phillips (2015) *Journalism in Context: Practice and Theory for the Digital Age*
David Randall (2005) *The Great Reporters*

SOURCES FOR SOUNDBITES

Interviews with the author.

REFERENCES AND BIBLIOGRAPHY

INTERVIEWS

Unless otherwise indicated in the text, comments by the following are taken from interviews conducted by the author between 2001 and 2014:

Carla Buzasi
Lindsay Eastwood
Paul Foot
Trevor Gibbons
Sarah Hartley
David Helliwell
Jemima Kiss
Neal Mann
Jane Merrick
Cathy Newman
Andrew Norfolk
Kevin Peachey
Abul Taher
Deborah Wain
Martin Wainwright
Brian Whittle
Waseem Zakir

BIBLIOGRAPHY

ACPO (2001) *Guide to Meeting the Policing Needs of Asylum Seekers and Refugees.* London: Association of Chief Police Officers.

Adams, Catherine (2001) 'Inside story', *Guardian*, 13 March.

Adams, Sally (1999) 'Writing features', in Wynford Hicks, with Sally Adams and Harriett Gilbert, *Writing for Journalists.* London: Routledge, pp 47–98.

Adams, Sally (2008) 'Writing features', in Wynford Hicks, with Sally Adams, Harriett Gilbert and Tim Holmes, *Writing for Journalists* (second edition). London: Routledge, pp 45–105.

Adams, Sally with Hicks, Wynford (2001) *Interviewing for Journalists.* London: Routledge.

Adams, Sally with Hicks, Wynford (2009) *Interviewing for Journalists* (second edition). London: Routledge.

Addicott, Ruth (2002) 'Magazines warned not to ignore financial watchdog', *Press Gazette*, 17 May.

Aitchison, James (1988) *Writing for the Press.* London: Hutchinson.

Aitchison, Jean (2007) *The Word Weavers: Newshounds and Wordsmiths.* Cambridge: Cambridge University Press.

Allan, Stuart (1997) 'News and the public sphere: towards a history of objectivity and impartiality', in Michael Bromley and Tom O'Malley (eds), *A Journalism Reader.* London: Routledge, pp 296–329.

Allan, Stuart (1998) '(En)gendering the truth politics of news discourse', in Cynthia Carter, Gill Branston and Stuart Allan (eds), *News, Gender and Power*. London: Routledge, pp 121–137.

Allan, Stuart (2004) *News Culture*. Maidenhead: Open University Press.

Allan, Stuart (ed) (2005) *Journalism: Critical Issues*. Maidenhead: Open University Press.

Arlidge, John and Cole, Sandra (2001) 'Jon Snow slams ITV's "crazy" cut in news budget', *Observer*, 2 December.

Armitstead, Claire (2002) 'Write the same thing over and over', *Guardian*, 31 January.

Atton, Chris (2002) *Alternative Media*. London: SAGE.

Aufderheide, Pat (2002) 'All-too-reality TV: challenges for television journalists after September 11', *Journalism: Theory, Practice and Criticism*, Vol. 3, No. 1, pp 7–14.

Austin, Tim (2003) *The Times Style and Usage Guide*. London: Harper Collins.

Bailey, Sally and Williams, Granville (1997) 'Memoirs are made of this: journalists' memoirs in the United Kingdom, 1945–95', in Michael Bromley and Tom O'Malley (eds), *A Journalism Reader*. London: Routledge, pp 351–377.

Bakhtin, Mikhail (1935) 'The Dialogic Imagination', extract printed in Pam Morris (ed) (1994) *The Bakhtin Reader: Selected Writings of Bakhtin, Medvedev and Voloshinov*. London: Edward Arnold, pp 74–80.

Barber, Lynn (1999) 'The art of the interview', in Stephen Glover (ed), *The Penguin Book of Journalism*. London: Penguin, pp 196–205.

Barnett, Steven (2008) 'On the road to self-destruction', *British Journalism Review*, Vol. 19, No. 2, pp 5–13.

Barnett, Steven (2012) *The Rise and Fall of Television Journalism: Just Wires and Lights in a Box?* London: Bloomsbury.

Barnett, Steven and Seymour, Emily (2000) *From Callaghan to Kosovo: Changing Trends in British Television News 1975–1999*. London: University of Westminster.

Barnicoat, Becky (2007) 'The fine art of interrogation', *Guardian*, 8 September.

Bawdon, Fiona (2012) *Seen but Not Heard: How Women Make Front Page News*. London: Women in Journalism.

BBC (2002) *The Message*, BBC Radio Four, 15 February.

BBC (2003) 'WTC attacks death toll falls', *BBC Online*, 29 October, http://news.bbc.co.uk/1/hi/world/americas/3225313.stm.

BBC Trust (2007a) *From Seesaw to Wagon Wheel: Safeguarding Impartiality in the 21st Century*, www.bbc.co.uk/bbctrust/research/impartiality.html.

BBC Trust (2007b) *Report of the Independent Panel for the BBC Trust on Impartiality of BBC Business Coverage*, www.bbc.co.uk/bbctrust/research/business_news_impartiality.html.

Beaman, Jim (2011) *Interviewing for Radio* (second edition). London: Routledge.

Beckett, Andy (2001) 'Mail order', *Guardian*, 22 February.

Beckett, Charlie and Ball, James (2012) *WikiLeaks: News in the Networked Era*. Cambridge: Polity Press.

Behr, Edward (1992) *Anyone Here Been Raped and Speaks English?* London: Penguin.

Bell, Allan (1991) *The Language of News Media*. Oxford: Blackwell.

Bell, Emily (2013) 'Harding's dated approach isn't going to boost BBC's global power', *Guardian*, 9 December.

Bell, Martin (1998) 'The journalism of attachment', in Matthew Kieran (ed), *Media Ethics*. London: Routledge, pp 15–22.

Bell, Martin (2002) 'Glamour is not good news', *Independent*, 19 February.

Berenger, Ralph D (2007) 'Book reviews', *Journalism: Theory, Practice and Criticism*, Vol. 8, No. 4, pp 474–481.

Bernstein, Carl (1992) 'The idiot culture', *New Republic*, 8 June, pp 22–28.

Bernstein, Carl and Woodward, Bob ([1974] 2005) *All the President's Men*. New York: Pocket.

Bivens, Rena Kim (2008) 'The internet, mobile phones and blogging: how new media are transforming traditional journalism', *Journalism Practice*, Vol. 2, No. 1, pp 113–129.

Blastland, Michael and Dilnot, Andrew (2007) *The Tiger That Isn't: Seeing Through a World of Numbers*. London: Profile.

Blumler, Jay (1999) 'Political communication systems all change: a response to Kees Brants', *European Journal of Communication*, Vol. 14, No. 2, pp 241–249.

Boorstin, Daniel (1963) *The Image: Or What Happened to the American Dream*. Harmondsworth: Pelican.

Bourdieu, Pierre (1998) *On Television and Journalism*. London: Pluto.

Boyd, Andrew (2001) *Broadcast Journalism: Techniques of Radio and Television News*. Oxford: Focal.

Boyer, JH (1981) 'How editors view objectivity', *American Journalism Quarterly*, No. 58. Cited in Watson, James (1998) *Media Communication: An Introduction to Theory and Process*. Basingstoke: Macmillan, p 98.

Bradshaw, Paul and Rohumaa, Liisa (2011) *The Online Journalism Handbook*. London: Pearson Longman.

Brandenburg, Heinz (2007) 'Security at the source: embedding journalists as a superior strategy to military censorship', *Journalism Studies*, Vol. 8, No. 6, pp 948–963.

Brants, Kees (1998) 'Who's afraid of infotainment?', *European Journal of Communication*, Vol. 13, No. 3, pp 315–335.

Brants, Kees (1999) 'A rejoinder to Jay G Blumler', *European Journal of Communication*, Vol. 14, No. 3, pp 411–415.

Brennen, Bonnie (2003) 'Sweat not melodrama: reading the structure of feeling in *All the President's Men*', *Journalism: Theory, Practice and Criticism*, Vol. 4, No. 1, pp 113–131.

Briggs, Asa and Burke, Peter (2002) *A Social History of the Media: From Gutenberg to the Internet*. Cambridge: Polity Press.

Bright, Martin (2000) 'I'm handing nothing over', *Journalist*, May/June.

Bromley, Michael (1997) 'The end of journalism? Changes in workplace practices in the press and broadcasting in the 1990s', in Michael Bromley and Tom O'Malley (eds), *A Journalism Reader*. London: Routledge, pp 330–350.

Bromley, Michael (ed) (2001) *No News is Bad News: Radio, Television and the Public*. Harlow: Longman.

Bromley, Michael and O'Malley, Tom (eds) (1997) *A Journalism Reader*. London: Routledge.

Bromley, Michael and Stephenson, Hugh (eds) (1998) *Sex, Lies and Democracy: The Press and the Public*. Harlow: Longman.

Brooke, Heather (2007) *Your Right to Know* (second edition). London: Pluto.

Brown, Andrew (2000) 'Newspapers and the internet', in Stephen Glover (ed), *The Penguin Book of Journalism*. London: Penguin, pp 177–185.

Brown, Maggie (2003) 'Documentary maker's fury at BBC2 revamp of series on Asians', *Guardian*, 30 September.

Brown, Maggie (2005) 'I want to brighten and enlighten', *Guardian*, 24 October.

Cacho, Lydia (2009) 'A life under threat', *CPJ Blog*, 11 August, www.cpj.org/blog/2009/08/cacho-a-top-mexican-reporter-describes-a-life-unde.php.

Calhoun, Craig (ed) (1992) *Habermas and the Public Sphere*. Cambridge, MA and London: MIT Press.

Cameron, Deborah (1996) 'Style policy and style politics: a neglected aspect of the language of the news', *Media, Culture & Society*, Vol. 18, pp 315–333.

Cameron, James (1968) *Point of Departure*. London: Readers Union.

Campbell, Duncan (2011) 'Whistleblowing – from the Xerox machine to WikiLeaks via Ellsberg, Agee and Vanunu', in John Mair and Richard Keeble (eds), *Investigative Journalism: Dead or Alive?* Bury St Edmunds: Abramis, pp 223–229.

Canter, Lily (2013) 'The misconception of online comment threads: content and control on local newspaper websites', *Journalism Practice*, Vol. 7, No. 5, pp 604–619.

Caple, Helen and Bednarek, Monika (2013) *Delving into the Discourse: Approaches to News Values in Journalism Studies and Beyond*. Reuters Institute for the Study of Journalism working paper, https://reutersinstitute.politics.ox.ac.uk/fileadmin/documents/Publications/Working_Papers/Bednarek_and_Caple_-_Delving_into_the_Discourse.pdf.

Carlyle, Thomas (1840) *On Heroes, Hero-worship, and the Heroic in History*. London: Chapman & Hall.

Carroll, Rory (2002) 'Yes, prime minister', *Guardian*, 1 April.

Carroll, Rory (2010) 'Mexican paper asks cartels how to avoid journalists being killed', *Guardian*, 21 September.

Carter, Cynthia, Branston, Gill and Allan, Stuart (eds) (1998) *News, Gender and Power*. London: Routledge.

Castells, Manuel (1997) *The Power of Identity. Volume 2 of The Information Age: Economy, Society and Culture*. Oxford: Blackwell.

Cathcart, Brian (2007) 'Baiting the goody-goody', *New Statesman*, 21 June.

Chalaby, Jean (1998) *The Invention of Journalism*. London: Macmillan.

Chambers, Deborah (2000) 'Critical approaches to the media: the changing context for investigative journalism', in Hugo de Burgh (ed), *Investigative Journalism: Context and Practice*. London: Routledge, pp 89–107.

Chandler, Raymond (1984) *Raymond Chandler Speaking*. London: Alison and Busby.

Channel 4 (1998) *The Real Rupert Murdoch*, broadcast 21 November.

Channel 4 News (2014) 'Al Jazeera journalists handed seven year jail term in Egypt', 23 June, www.channel4.com/news/egypt-al-jazeera-journalists-trial-terrorist-charges-verdict.

Chantler, Paul and Harris, Sim (1997) *Local Radio Journalism*. Oxford: Focal.

Chapman, Jane and Kinsey, Marie (eds) (2009) *Broadcast Journalism: A Critical Introduction*. London: Routledge.

Chesterton, GK (1981) 'The wisdom of Father Brown: the purple wig', in *The Penguin Complete Father Brown*. Harmondsworth: Penguin, pp 244–255.

Chippindale, Peter and Horrie, Chris (1992) *Stick It Up Your Punter! The Rise and Fall of the Sun*. London: Mandarin.

Clement, Barrie and Grice, David (2001) 'Secret ministry email: "use attack to bury bad news"', *Independent*, 9 October.

Cockburn, Claud (1967) *I, Claud*. Harmondsworth: Penguin.

Cohen, Stanley (1972) *Folk Devils and Moral Panics: The Creation of the Mods and Rockers*. London: MacGibbon and Kee.

Cohen, Stanley and Young, Jock (eds) (1973) *The Manufacture of News: Deviance, Social Problems and the Mass Media*. London: Constable.

Cole, Peter and Harcup, Tony (2010) *Newspaper Journalism*. London: SAGE.

Cooper, Glenda and Whittle, Stephen (2009) *Privacy, Probity and Public Interest*. Oxford: Reuters Institute for the Study of Journalism.

Cottle, Simon (2000) 'Rethinking news access', *Journalism Studies*, Vol. 1, No. 3, pp 427–448.

Cottle, Simon (2001) 'Television news and citizenship: packaging the public sphere', in Michael Bromley (ed), *No News is Bad News: Radio, Television and the Public*. Harlow: Longman, pp 61–79.

Coward, Rosalind (2013) *Speaking Personally: The Rise of Subjective and Confessional Journalism*. Basingstoke: Palgrave Macmillan.

Critcher, Chas (2002) 'Media, government and moral panic: the politics of paedophilia in Britain 2000–1', *Journalism Studies*, Vol. 3, No. 4, pp 521–535.

Curran, James (2000) 'Press reformism 1918–98: a study of failure', in Howard Tumber (ed), *Media Power, Professionals and Policies*. London: Routledge, pp 35–55.

Curran, James and Gurevitch, Michael (eds) (1991) *Mass Media and Society*. London: Edward Arnold.

Curran, James and Seaton, Jean (1997) *Power without Responsibility: The Press and Broadcasting in Britain* (fifth edition). London: Routledge.

Curran, James and Seaton, Jean (2003) *Power without Responsibility: The Press, Broadcasting and New Media in Britain* (sixth edition). London: Routledge.

Curran, James, Fenton, Natalie and Freedman, Des (2012) *Misunderstanding the Internet.* London: Routledge.

Cushion, Stephen (2012) *Television Journalism*. London: SAGE.

Dahlgren, Peter and Sparks, Colin (eds) (1992) *Journalism and Popular Culture*. London: SAGE.

Daly, Mark (2011) 'The ethics of going undercover', in John Mair and Richard Keeble (eds), *Investigative Journalism: Dead or Alive?* Bury St Edmunds: Abramis, pp 88–96.

Davies, Nick (2008) *Flat Earth News*. London: Chatto & Windus.

Davies, Nick (2014) *Hack Attack*. London: Chatto & Windus.

Day, Julia (2001) 'Hellier condemns Express "interference"', 6 September, www.mediaguardian.co.uk.

de Burgh, Hugo (ed) (2000) *Investigative Journalism: Context and Practice*. London: Routledge.

de Burgh, Hugo (2003) 'Skills are not enough: the case for journalism as an academic discipline', *Journalism: Theory, Practice and Criticism*, Vol. 4, No. 1, pp 95–112.

de Burgh, Hugo (2008) *Investigative Journalism* (second edition). London: Routledge.

Dejevsky, Mary (2014) 'Who really did kill Russian journalist Anna Politkovskaya?', *Independent*, 13 June, www.independent.co.uk/news/world/europe/who-really-did-kill-russian-journalist-anna-politkovskaya-9535772.html.

Delano, Anthony ([1975] 2008) *Slip Up: How Fleet Street Found Ronnie Biggs and Scotland Yard Lost Him* (revised edition). Gozo: Revel Barker.

Delano, Anthony (2009) *Joyce McKinney and the Case of the Manacled Mormon* (second edition). Gozo: Revel Barker.

Deuze, Mark and Dimoudi, Christina (2002) 'Online journalists in the Netherlands: towards a profile of a new profession', *Journalism: Theory, Practice and Criticism*, Vol. 3, No. 1, pp 85–100.

Dewdney, Andrew and Ride, Peter (2006) *The New Media Handbook*. London: Routledge.

Dick, Murray (2013) *Search: Theory and Practice in Online Journalism*. London: Macmillan.

Dixon, Sara (2002) 'The gentle touch', *Press Gazette*, 5 April.

Dodd, Mike and Hanna, Mark (2014) *McNae's Essential Law for Journalists* (twenty-second edition). Oxford: Oxford University Press.

Dodson, Sean (2001) 'Hacks hit in drugs war', *Guardian*, 25 June.

Doig, Alan (1997) 'The decline of investigatory journalism', in Michael Bromley and Tom O'Malley (eds), *A Journalism Reader*. London: Routledge, pp 189–213.

Dorril, Stephen (2000) 'What is investigative journalism?', *Free Press*, No. 116, May/June.

Dovey, Jon (2000) *Freakshow: First Person Media and Factual Television*. London: Pluto.

Downing, John, with Villarreal Ford, Tamara, Gil, Geneve and Stein, Laura (2001) *Radical Media: Rebellious Communication and Social Movements*. London: SAGE.

Doyle, Gillian (2002) *Understanding Media Economics*. London: SAGE.

Drabble, Margaret and Stringer, Jenny (eds) (1990) *The Concise Oxford Companion to English Literature*. Oxford: Oxford University Press.

DTLR (2001) *News Release 388: Consultation Begins on Council Allowances*. London: Department for Transport, Local Government and the Regions, 11 September.

Eaves, End Violence Against Women Coalition, Equality Now, Object (2012) *Just the Women*. London: Eaves, End Violence Against Women Coalition, Equality Now, Object.

Economist (2008) *Style Guide*. London: Profile Books.

Eliot, George (1859) *Adam Bede*. Edinburgh: Blackwood.

Engel, Matthew (1997) *Tickle the Public: One Hundred Years of the Popular Press*. London: Indigo.

Epstein, Robert (2014) 'Robert Capa ready for his close-up', *Independent on Sunday*, 6 April.

Errigo, Jackie and Franklin, Bob (2004) 'Surviving in the hackademy', *British Journalism Review*, Vol. 15, No. 2, pp 43–48.

Evans, Harold ([1978] 1997) *Pictures on a Page: Photo-journalism, Graphics and Picture Editing*. London: Pimlico.

Evans, Harold (2000) *Essential English for Journalists, Editors and Writers*. London: Pimlico.

Fanon, Frantz ([1967]1970) *The Wretched of the Earth*. London: Penguin.

Fenton, Natalie (ed) (2010) *New Media, Old News: Journalism and Democracy in the Digital Age*. London: SAGE.

Fenton, Natalie (2012) 'The internet and social networking', in James Curran, Natalie Fenton and Des Freedman, *Misunderstanding the Internet*. London: Routledge, pp 123–148.

Figdor, Carrie (2010) 'Is objective news possible?', in Christopher Meyers (ed), *Journalism Ethics: A Philosophical Approach*. New York: Oxford University Press, pp 153–164.

Fishman, Rob (2013) 'The social media editor is dead: every reporter works for Twitter now'. *BuzzFeed*, 29 May, www.buzzfeed.com/robf4/the-rise-and-fall-of-the-social-media-editor.

Fiske, John (1989) *Reading the Popular*. London: Routledge.

Fleming, Carole (2002) *The Radio Handbook*. London: Routledge.

Fletcher, Kim (2014) 'Editorial: give it a chance', *British Journalism Review*, Vol. 25, No. 2, pp 3–4.

Foley, Michael (2000) 'Press regulation', *Administration*, Vol. 48, No. 1, Spring, pp 40–51.

Foot, Paul (1999) 'The slow death of investigative journalism', in Stephen Glover (ed), *The Penguin Book of Journalism: Secrets of the Press*. London: Penguin, pp 79–89.

Foot, Paul (2000) *Articles of Resistance*. London: Bookmarks.

Forde, Eamonn (2001) 'From polyglottism to branding: on the decline of personality journalism in the British music press', *Journalism: Theory, Practice and Criticism*, Vol. 2, No. 1, pp 23–43.

Forde, Susan (2011) *Challenging the News: The Journalism of Alternative and Community Media*. Basingstoke: Palgrave Macmillan.

Fowler, HW (1983) *A Dictionary of Modern English Usage*. Oxford: Oxford University Press.

Fowler, Roger (1991) *Language in the News: Discourse and Ideology in the Press*. London: Routledge.

Franklin, Bob (1994) *Packaging Politics: Political Communications in Britain's Media Democracy*. London: Edward Arnold.

Franklin, Bob (1997) *Newszak and News Media*. London: Arnold.

Franklin, Bob (2005a) 'Framing', in Bob Franklin, Martin Hamer, Mark Hanna, Marie Kinsey and John Richardson, *Key Concepts in Journalism Studies*. London: SAGE, pp 85–86.

Franklin, Bob (2005b) 'McJournalism: the local press and the McDonalization thesis', in Stuart Allan (ed), *Journalism: Critical Issues*. Maidenhead: Open University Press, pp 137–150.

Franklin, Bob, Hamer, Martin, Hanna, Mark, Kinsey, Marie and Richardson, John (2005) *Key Concepts in Journalism Studies*. London: SAGE.

Franklin, Bob and Murphy, David (eds) (1998) *Making the Local News: Local Journalism in Context*. London: Routledge.

Franks, Suzanne (2013) *Women and Journalism*. London: IB Tauris.

Frayn, Michael ([1965] 1995) *The Tin Men*. London: Penguin.

Freedman, Des (2014) 'Power in the digital economy', in Granville Williams (ed), *Big Media & Internet Titans*. London: CPBF, pp 94–105.

Fresco, Adam, Syal, Rajeev and Bird, Steve (2005) 'Suspect shot dead "had no bomb" – London terror', *Times*, 23 July.

Friend, Cecilia and Singer, Jane (2007) *Online Journalism Ethics: Traditions and Transitions*. London: ME Sharpe.

Frith, Simon and Meech, Peter (2007) 'Becoming a journalist: journalism education and journalism culture', *Journalism: Theory, Practice and Criticism*, Vol. 8, No. 2, pp 137–164.

Frost, Chris (2000) *Media Ethics and Self-Regulation*. Harlow: Longman.

Frost, Chris (2002) *Reporting for Journalists*. London: Routledge.

Frost, Chris (2007) *Journalism Ethics and Self-regulation*. Harlow: Pearson.

Frost, Chris (2010) *Reporting for Journalists* (second edition). London: Routledge.

Frost, Chris (2011) *Journalism Ethics and Regulation* (third edition). Harlow: Longman.

Fry, Don (2004) 'Unmuddling middles', *Poynter Online*, 16 June, www.poynter.org.

Fryer, Peter (1998) *Lucid, Vigorous and Brief: Advice to New Writers* (second edition). London: Index.

Galtung, Johan and Ruge, Mari (1965) 'The structure of foreign news: the presentation of the Congo, Cuba and Cyprus crises in four Norwegian newspapers', *Journal of International Peace Research*, Vol. 1, pp 64–91.

Gans, Herbert J (1980) *Deciding What's News: A Study of CBS Evening News, NBC Nightly News, Newsweek and Time*. London: Constable.

Gieber, Walter (1964) 'News is what newspapermen make it', in Howard Tumber (ed) (1999), *News: A Reader*. Oxford: Oxford University Press, pp 218–223.

Gilbert, Harriett (2008) 'Writing reviews', in Wynford Hicks, with Sally Adams, Harriett Gilbert and Tim Holmes, *Writing for Journalists* (second edition). London: Routledge, pp 107–130.

Glover, Mike (1998) 'Looking at the world through the eyes of . . . reporting the "local" in daily, weekly and Sunday local newspapers', in Bob Franklin and David Murphy (eds), *Making the Local News: Local Journalism in Context*. London: Routledge, pp 117–124.

Glover, Stephen (ed) (1999) *The Penguin Book of Journalism: Secrets of the Press*. London: Penguin.

Golding, Peter and Elliott, Philip (1979) *Making the News*. London and New York: Longman.

Golding, Peter and Murdock, Graham (1979) 'Ideology and the mass media: the question of determination', in Michele Barrett, Philip Corrigan, Annette Kuhn and Janet Wolff (eds), *Ideology and Cultural Production*. London: Croom Helm, pp 198–224.

Goodwin, Bill (1996) 'Safe sources', *Journalist*, April/May.

Gopsill, Tim and Neale, Greg (2007) *Journalists: A Hundred Years of the National Union of Journalists*. London: Profile.

Gramsci, Antonio (1971) *Selections from the Prison Notebooks*. London: Lawrence & Wishart.

Green, Nigel (2008) 'Insight', *Press Gazette*, 1 February.

Greenberg, Susan (2007) 'Slow journalism', *Prospect*, 27 February.

Greenslade, Roy (2003a) 'Their master's voice', *Guardian*, 17 February.

Greenslade, Roy (2003b) 'Readers in Ilkley, owners in Virginia', *Guardian*, 1 September.

Greenslade, Roy (2004) *Press Gang: How Newspapers Make Profits from Propaganda*. London: Pan.

Greenslade, Roy (2008) 'The digital challenge', *Guardian*, 7 January.

Griffiths, Dennis (2006) *Fleet Street: Five Hundred Years of the Press*. London: The British Library.

Gurevitch, Michael, Bennett, Tony, Curran, James and Woollacott, Janet (eds) (1982) *Culture, Society and the Media*. London: Methuen.

Guttenplan, DD (2012) *American Radical: The life and Times of IF Stone*. Evanston, IL: Northwestern University Press.

Habermas, Jürgen (1989) *The Structural Transformation of the Public Sphere: An Inquiry into a Category of Bourgeois Society*. Cambridge: Polity Press.

Habermas, Jürgen (1992) 'Further reflections on the public sphere', in Craig Calhoun (ed), *Habermas and the Public Sphere*. Cambridge, MA and London: MIT Press, pp 421–461.

Hahn, Daniel (2004) *The Tower Menagerie: The Amazing True Story of the Royal Collection of Wild Beasts*. London: Pocket.

Hall, Jim (2001) *Online Journalism: A Critical Primer*. London: Pluto.

Hall, Sarah (2006) 'Doctors enjoy the greatest public trust', *Guardian*, 2 November.

Hall, Stuart (1967) 'People, personalities and personalisation', in Richard Hoggart (ed), *Your Sunday Paper*. London: University of London Press.

Hall, Stuart (1973) 'The determinations of news photographs', in Stanley Cohen and Jock Young (eds), *The Manufacture of News: Deviance, Social Problems and the Mass Media*. London: Constable, pp 176–190.

Hall, Stuart (1977) 'Culture, the media and the "ideological effect"', in James Curran, Michael Gurevitch and Janet Woollacott (eds), *Mass Communication and Society*. London: Edward Arnold, pp 315–348.

Hall, Stuart (1982) 'The rediscovery of "ideology": return of the repressed in media studies', in Michael Gurevitch, Tony Bennett, James Curran and Janet Woollacott (eds), *Culture, Society and the Media*. London: Methuen, pp 56–90.

Hall, Stuart (1986) 'Media power and class power', in James Curran, Jake Ecclestone, Giles Oakley and Alan Richardson (eds), *Bending Reality: The State of the Media*. London: Pluto, pp 5–14.

Hall, Stuart, Critcher, Chas, Jefferson, Tony, Clarke, John and Roberts, Brian (1978) *Policing the Crisis*. London: Macmillan.

Hall, Stuart, Critcher, Chas, Jefferson, Tony, Clarke, John and Roberts, Brian (2013) *Policing the Crisis* (second edition). London: Macmillan.

Hanna, Mark (2000) 'British investigative journalism: protecting the continuity of talent through changing times'. Paper presented to the International Association for Media and Communication Research, Singapore, 18 July.

Hanning, James with Mulcaire, Glenn (2014) *The News Machine: Hacking – the Untold Story*. London: Gibson Square.

Harcup, Tony (1994) *A Northern Star: Leeds Other Paper and the Alternative Press 1974–1994*. London and Pontefract: Campaign for Press and Broadcasting Freedom.

Harcup, Tony (1996) 'More news means worse news, conference on media ethics told', *Broadcast*, 27 September.

Harcup, Tony (2002a) 'Conduct unbecoming?', *Press Gazette*, 1 March.

Harcup, Tony (2002b) 'Journalists and ethics: the quest for a collective voice', *Journalism Studies*, Vol. 3, No. 1, pp 101–114.

Harcup, Tony (2003) 'The unspoken – said: the journalism of alternative media', *Journalism: Theory, Practice and Criticism*, Vol. 4, No. 3, pp 356–376.

Harcup, Tony (2005) '"I'm doing this to change the world": journalism in alternative and mainstream media', *Journalism Studies*, Vol. 6, No. 3, pp 361–374.

Harcup, Tony (2007) *The Ethical Journalist*. London: SAGE.

Harcup, Tony (2008) 'Learning some lessons at the school of hard knocks', *Press Gazette*, 11 April.

Harcup, Tony (2013) *Alternative Journalism, Alternative Voices*. London: Routledge.

Harcup, Tony (2014a) *Oxford Dictionary of Journalism*. Oxford: Oxford University Press.

Harcup, Tony (2014b) 'Reporting the next battle: lessons from Orgreave', in Granville Williams (ed), *Settling Scores: The Media, the Police and the Miners' Strike*. London: Campaign for Press and Broadcasting Freedom, pp 95–105.

Harcup, Tony and O'Neill, Deirdre (2001) 'What is news? Galtung and Ruge revisited', *Journalism Studies*, Vol. 2, No. 2, pp 261–280.

Hardt, Hanno (2000) 'Conflicts of interest: newsworkers, media, and patronage journalism', in Howard Tumber (ed), *Media Power, Professionals and Policies*. London: Routledge, pp 209–224.

Harris, Paul (2007) 'Why I said "no" to Paris Hilton mania', *Observer*, 1 July.

Harrison, Jackie (2000) *Terrestrial TV News in Britain: The Culture of Production*. Manchester: Manchester University Press.

Harrison, Jackie (2006) *News*. London: Routledge.

Hart-Davis, Duff (1990) *The House the Berrys Built*. London: Hodder & Stoughton.

Hartley, John (1982) *Understanding News*. London: Methuen.

Hastings, Max (2004) 'Never forget that they lie', *Guardian*, 31 January.

Hattenstone, Simon (2005) 'Looking for trouble', *Guardian*, 5 March.

Hattenstone, Simon (2007) 'Reflections of a professional stalker', *Guardian*, 8 September.

Hecht, Ben and MacArthur, Charles (1974) *The Front Page*. A U-I film.

Hedman, Ulrika and Djerf-Pierre, Monika (2013) 'The social journalist: embracing the social media life or creating a new digital divide?', *Digital Journalism*, Vol. 1, No. 3, pp 368–385.

Helgren, Chris (2014) 'Remembering D-day, 70 years on', *Reuters Photographers' Blog*, 28 May, http://blogs.reuters.com/photographers-blog/2014/05/28/remembering-d-day/.

Helmore, Ed (2001) 'Meet the enforcer', *Observer*, 3 June.

Hencke, David (2001) 'No news is bad news', *Guardian*, 5 March.

Heren, Louis (1973 [1996]) *Growing Up Poor in London*. London: Indigo.

Herman, David (2013) 'Paxo, Katz and the two Kims', *Prospect Blog*, 12 December, www.prospectmagazine.co.uk/blog/10990136531237428994-paxman-beard-newsnight-bbc-ian-katz-editor-revision-5/#.U0lfV1dK33A.

Herman, Edward (2000) 'The propaganda model: a retrospective', *Journalism Studies*, Vol. 1, No. 1, pp 101–112.

Herman, Edward and Chomsky, Noam (1988) *Manufacturing Consent: The Political Economy of the Mass Media*. London: Vintage.

Hermida, Alfred (2010) 'Twittering the news: the emergence of ambient journalism', *Journalism Practice*, Vol. 4, No. 3, pp 297–308.

Hermida, Alfred (2013) '#Journalism: reconfiguring journalism research about Twitter, one tweet at a time', *Digital Journalism*, Vol. 1, No. 3, pp 295–313.

Hetherington, Alastair (1985) *News, Newspapers and Television*. London: Macmillan.

Hicks, Wynford (1998) *English for Journalists*. London: Routledge.

Hicks, Wynford (2007) *English for Journalists* (second edition). London: Routledge.

Hicks, Wynford (2013) *English for Journalists* (fourth edition). London: Routledge.

Hicks, Wynford with Adams, Sally and Gilbert, Harriett (1999) *Writing for Journalists*. London: Routledge.

Hicks, Wynford with Adams, Sally, Gilbert, Harriett and Holmes, Tim (2008) *Writing for Journalists* (second edition). London: Routledge.

Hicks, Wynford and Holmes, Tim (2002) *Subediting for Journalists*. London: Routledge.

Hilton, Phil (2007) 'Show us your bids!', *Guardian*, 26 May.

Hobsbawm, Julia and Lloyd, John (2008) *The Power of the Commentariat*. London: Editorial Intelligence.

Hodge, Robert and Kress, Gunther (1993) *Language as Ideology*. London: Routledge.

Hodgson, FW (1993) *Subediting: A Handbook of Modern Newspaper Editing and Production*. Oxford: Focal Press.

Holland, Patricia (1998) 'The politics of the smile: "soft news" and the sexualisation of the popular press', in Cynthia Carter, Gill Branston and Stuart Allan (eds), *News, Gender and Power*. London: Routledge, pp 17–32.

Holland, Patricia (2000) *The Television Handbook*. London: Routledge.

Hollander, Gavriel (2013) 'Local World's David Montgomery: "we will harvest content and publish it without human interface"', *Press Gazette*, 21 May, www.pressgazette.co.uk/david-montgomery-we-will-harvest-content-and-publish-it-without-human-interface.

Hollingsworth, Mark (1986) *The Press and Political Dissent: A Question of Censorship*. London: Pluto.

Honigsbaum, Mark (2005) 'Brazilian did not wear bulky jacket: Stockwell shoot-to-kill relatives say Met admits that, contrary to reports, electrician did not leap tube station barrier', *Guardian*, 28 July.

Hudson, Gary and Rowlands, Sarah (2007) *The Broadcast Journalism Handbook*. Harlow: Pearson.

Hudson, Gary and Rowlands, Sarah (2012) *The Broadcast Journalism Handbook* (second edition). Harlow: Pearson.

Hutton, Robert (2013) *Romps, Tots and Boffins: The Strange Language of News*. London: Elliott & Thompson.

IFJ (International Federation of Journalists) (2007) '"Tragedy unlimited" says IFJ as killings of journalists in 2007 maintain record levels', 31 December, www.ifj.org/default.asp?lndex=5638&Language=EN.

IFJ (2008) *Deadly Stories 2007: Killings of Journalists Touch Record Levels*. Brussels: International Federation of Journalists.

IFJ (2015) IFJ List of Journalists and Media Staff Killed in 2014. http://ifj-safety.org/assets/docs/078/194/a86304e-7deeac2.pdf.

Ingrams, Richard (2005) *My Friend Footy: A Memoir of Paul Foot*. London: Private Eye.

IPI (2010) 'Lydia Cacho Ribeiro: world press freedom hero', International Press Institute, www.freemedia.at/awards/lydia-cacho-ribeiro.html.

Ipso (2014) *Editors' Code of Practice*, www.ipso.co.uk/IPSO/cop.html

Jack, Ian (2006) 'Things that have interested me', *Guardian*, 5 August.

Jarvis, Jeff (2008) 'Why Twitter is the canary in the news coalmine', *Guardian*, 19 May.

Jeffries, Stuart (2008) 'There's humour in the darkest places', *Guardian*, 18 March.

Jenkins, Simon (2007) 'The British media does not do responsibility. It does stories', *Guardian*, 18 May.

Johnston, Alan (2007) *Kidnapped and Other Dispatches*. London: Profile.

Jones, Janet and Salter, Lee (2012) *Digital Journalism*. London: SAGE.

Journalism Training Forum (2002) *Journalists at Work: Their Views on Training, Recruitment and Conditions*. London: Publishing National Training Organisation/Skillset.

Journalist (2007a) 'Threat came with a bullet', *Journalist*, November.

Journalist (2007b) 'Robin's final triumph as the Lords slam door on NHS Trust', *Journalist*, September/October.

Kampfner, John (2007) 'Less stenography and more reporting, please', *Guardian*, 16 July.

Karim, Karim (2002) 'Making sense of the "Islamic Peril": journalism as cultural practice', in Barbie Zelizer and Stuart Allan (eds), *Journalism after September 11*. London: Routledge, pp 101–116.

Katwala, Sunder (2010) 'Do the manifesto differently', *Next Left*, 14 January, www.nextleft.org/2010/01/do-manifesto-differently.html.

Keeble, Richard (1998) *The Newspapers Handbook* (second edition). London: Routledge.

Keeble, Richard (2001a) *The Newspapers Handbook* (third edition). London: Routledge.

Keeble, Richard (2001b) *Ethics for Journalists*. London: Routledge.

Keeble, Richard (2006) *The Newspapers Handbook* (fourth edition). London: Routledge.

Keeble, Richard and Mair, John (eds) (2012) *The Phone Hacking Scandal: Journalism on Trial* (second edition). Bury St Edmunds: Abramis.

Kelner, Martin (2013) *Sit Down and Cheer: A History of Sport on TV*. London: Bloomsbury.

Kelso, Paul (2001) 'We have known about this for 15 years. The media should have exposed this man a long time ago', *Guardian*, 23 July.

Kieran, Matthew (ed) (1998) *Media Ethics*. London: Routledge.

Kiley, Sam (2001) 'The Middle East's war of words', *Evening Standard*, 5 September.

Kiss, Jemima (2006) 'Changing media summit: citizen media will unlock the secret society, says Jon Snow', 28 March, www.journalism.co.uk/news/story1779.shtml.

Knight, Alan (2008) 'Journalism in the age of blogging', *Journalism Practice*, Vol. 2, No. 1, pp 117–124.

Knight, Megan and Cook, Clare (2013) *Social Media for Journalists: Principles and Practice*. London: SAGE.

Knightley, Phillip (1998) *A Hack's Progress*. London: Vintage.

Knightley, Phillip (2001) 'The disinformation campaign', *Guardian*, 4 October.

Knightley, Phillip (2002) 'The creation of public enemy No. 1', *Evening Standard*, 11 September.

Knightley, Phillip (2004) *The First Casualty: The War Correspondent as Hero and Myth-maker from the Crimea to Iraq* (revised edition). Baltimore, MD: Johns Hopkins University Press.

Knightley, Phillip (2011) 'Mundane reality behind the myth of the dashing, devil-may-care super sleuths', in John Mair and Richard Keeble (eds), *Investigative Journalism: Dead or Alive?* Bury St Edmunds: Abramis, pp 19–25.

Krajicek, David J (1998) 'The bad, the ugly and the worse', *Guardian*, 11 May.

Kroeger, Brooke (1994) *Nellie Bly: Daredevil, Reporter, Feminist.* New York: Random House.

Kuhn, Raymond (2002) 'The first Blair government and political journalism', in Raymond Kuhn and Erik Neveu (eds), *Political Journalism: New Challenges, New Practices.* London: Routledge, pp 47–68.

Lagan, Sarah (2007) 'Duped Cumbria papers slam April fool prank', *Press Gazette*, 4 April.

Larsson, Larsake (2002) 'Journalists and politicians: a relationship requiring manoeuvring space', *Journalism Studies*, Vol. 3, No. 1, pp 21–33.

Lavie, Aliza and Lehman-Wilzig, Sam (2003) 'Whose news? Does gender determine the editorial product?' *European Journal of Communication*, Vol. 18, No. 1, pp 5–29.

Lee, Seow Ting, Maslog, Crispin C. and Kim, Hun Shik (2006) 'Asian conflicts and the Iraq War', *International Communication Gazette*, Vol. 68, pp 499–518.

Leigh, David (2007) 'Anthony Sampson Chair inaugural lecture', City University, 1 November, www.city. ac.uk/journalism/download_files/01_11_07_sampson_lecture.pdf.

Leigh, David and Evans, Rob (2008) 'Sources', 17 February, www.guardian.co.uk/world/2007/jun/07/ bae18.

Leveson, Lord Justice (2012) *An Inquiry into the Culture, Practices, and Ethics of the Press: Report.* London: The Stationery Office. Available online at: http://webarchive.nationalarchives.gov.uk/20140122145147/ http://www.levesoninquiry.org.uk/about/the-report/.

Levy, Steven (2012) 'Can an algorithm write a better news story than a human reporter?', *Wired*, 24 April, www.wired.com/2012/04/can-an-algorithm-write-a-better-news-story-than-a-human-reporter/.

Lewis, Justin (2006) 'News and the empowerment of citizens', *European Journal of Cultural Studies*, Vol. 9, No. 3, pp 303–319.

Lewis, Justin, Williams, Andrew and Franklin, Bob (2008a) 'A compromised fourth estate? UK news journalism, public relations and news sources', *Journalism Studies*, Vol. 9, No. 1, pp 1–20.

Lewis, Justin, Williams, Andrew and Franklin, Bob (2008b) 'Four rumours and an explanation: a political economic account of journalists' changing newsgathering and reporting practices', *Journalism Practice*, Vol. 2, No. 1, pp 27–45.

Lewis, Paul (2011) 'How "citizen journalism" aided two major *Guardian* scoops', in John Mair and Richard Keeble (eds), *Investigative Journalism: Dead or Alive?* Bury St Edmunds: Abramis, pp 31–38. Chapter extract also available online at: http://onlinejournalismblog.com/2011/11/01/paul-lewis-how-citizen-journalism-aided-two-major-guardian-scoops-guest-post/.

Lipton, Eric (2001) 'Toll from attack at Trade Center is down sharply', *New York Times*, 21 November.

Lipton, Eric (2002) 'Death toll is near 3,000, but some uncertainty over count remains', *New York Times*, 11 September.

Loffelholz, Martin and Weaver, David (eds) (2008) *Global Journalism Research: Theories, Methods, Findings, Future.* Oxford: Blackwell.

Lule, Jack (2001) *Daily News, Eternal Stories: The Mythological Role of Journalism.* New York: Guilford Press.

Lynch, Jake (2002) 'Reporting the world: how ethical journalism can seek solutions', 23 January, www. mediachannel.org.

Machin, David and Niblock, Sarah (2008) 'Branding newspapers: visual texts as social practice', *Journalism Studies*, Vol. 9, No. 2, pp 244–259.

Mair, John (ed) (2013) *After Leveson? The Future for British Journalism*. Bury St Edmunds: Abramis.

Mair, John and Keeble, Richard (eds) (2011) *Investigative Journalism: Dead or Alive?* Bury St Edmunds: Abramis.

Mair, John, Tait, Richard and Keeble, Richard (eds) (2014) *Is the BBC in Crisis?* Bury St Edmunds: Abramis.

Malcolm, Janet (2004) *The Journalist and the Murderer*. London: Granta.

Malik, Shiv (2008) 'Stop police seizing reporters' notes', *Press Gazette*, 23 May.

Manning, Paul (2001) *News and News Sources: A Critical Introduction*. London: SAGE.

Mansfield, FJ (1936) *The Complete Journalist: A Study of the Principles and Practice of Newspaper-making*. London: Sir Isaac Pitman and Sons.

Mansfield, FJ (1943) *Gentlemen, the Press! Chronicles of a Crusade: Official History of the National Union of Journalists*. London: WH Allen.

Markwell, Lisa (2013) Guest lecture, 12 November, University of Sheffield.

Marr, Andrew (2005) *My Trade: A Short History of British Journalism*. London: Pan.

Marsh, David (ed) (2007) *Guardian Style*. London: Guardian Books.

Marsh, David (2013) *For Who the Bell Tolls*. London: Guardian Faber.

Marshall, Sharon (2010) *Tabloid Girl*. London: Sphere.

Martinson, Jane (2005) 'It's hello, good evening and welcome to *al-Jazeera* for David Frost', *Guardian*, 7 October.

Marx, Karl and Engels, Friedrich ([1846] 1965) *The German Ideology*. London: Lawrence & Wishart.

Mayes, Ian (2000) *The Guardian Corrections and Clarifications*. London: Guardian Newspapers.

McCafferty, Nell (1981) *In the Eyes of the Law*. Dublin: Ward River Press.

McCafferty, Nell (1984) *The Best of Nell: A Selection of Writings over Fourteen Years*. Dublin: Attic Press.

McChesney, Robert (2000) *Rich Media, Poor Democracy: Communication Politics in Dubious Times*. New York: New Press.

McChesney, Robert (2002) 'The US news media and World War III', *Journalism: Theory, Practice and Criticism*, Vol. 3, No. 1, pp 14–21.

McCombs, Maxwell and Shaw, Donald (1972) 'The agenda setting function of mass media', in Howard Tumber (ed) (1999) *News: A Reader*. Oxford: Oxford University Press, pp 320–328.

McGinty, Lawrence (2014) 'The NUJ and me', *Journalist*, March/April.

McKane, Anna (2006) *News Writing*. London: SAGE.

McKane, Anna (2014) *News Writing* (second edition). London: SAGE.

McKay, Jenny (2006) *The Magazines Handbook*. London: Routledge.

McKay, Peter (1999) 'Gossip', in Stephen Glover (ed), *The Penguin Book on Journalism: Secrets of the Press*. London: Penguin, pp 186–195.

McKnight, David (2013) *Murdoch's Politics: How One Man's Thirst for Wealth and Power Shapes Our World*. London: Pluto.

McLaughlin, Greg (2002a) 'Rules of engagement: television journalism and NATO's "faith in bombing" during the Kosovo crisis, 1999', *Journalism Studies*, Vol. 3, No. 2, pp 257–266.

McLaughlin, Greg (2002b) *The War Correspondent*. London: Pluto.

McMullan, Paul (2011) Transcript of evidence to Leveson, 29 November, http://webarchive.nationalarchives.gov.uk/20140122145147/http://www.levesoninquiry.org.uk/wp-content/uploads/2011/11/Transcript-of-Afternoon-Hearing-29-November-2011.txt.

McNair, Brian (2000) *Journalism and Democracy: An Evaluation of the Political Public Sphere*. London: Routledge.

McQuail, Denis (1992) *Media Performance: Mass Communication and the Public Interest*. London: SAGE.

McQuail, Denis (2000) *McQuail's Mass Communication Theory*. London: SAGE.

McQuail, Denis (2013) *Journalism and Society*. London: SAGE.

Meyers, Christopher (ed) (2010) *Journalism Ethics: A Philosophical Approach*. New York: Oxford University Press.

Millar, Stuart (2001) 'Robot reporter "to write news in future"', *Guardian*, 9 August.

Milton, John ([1644] 2005) 'Areopagitica: a speech for the liberty of unlicensed printing', in John Milton and Granville Williams, *Milton and the Modern Media: A Defence of a Free Press*. Accrington: B&D.

Morgan, Jean (1999) 'Reporter who refused death-knock loses job fight', *Press Gazette*, 17 December.

Morgan, Jean (2002a) '"Lack of humanity" over Soham led to *Herald* sacking', *Press Gazette*, 6 September.

Morgan, Jean (2002b) 'Never ever sign copy deals, says freelance in singer row', *Press Gazette*, 22 March.

Morris, Steven (2007) 'I can't believe the story went so big. I didn't even get any money out of it', *Guardian*, 9 August.

Morse, Felicity (2013) '*Newsnight* marks Ian Katz Twitter gaffe with #fail in credits', *Independent*, 11 September, www.independent.co.uk/news/newsnight-marks-ian-katz-twitter-gaffe-with-fail-in-credits-8808525.html.

Murrow, Ed (1958) 'Speech at the 1958 RTNDA Convention', Chicago, 15 October, http://media.www.mediaethicsmagazine.com/media/storage/paper655/news/2004/12/31/AnalysesCommentary/Ed.Murrows.Speech.At.The.1958.Rtnda.Convention-833533.shtml.

Ndlela, Nkosi (2005) 'The African paradigm: the coverage of the Zimbabwean crisis in the Norwegian media', *Westminster Papers in Communication and Culture*, Special Issue, November, pp 71–90.

Neil, Andrew (1996) *Full Disclosure*. London: Macmillan.

Neveu, Erik (2002) 'The local press and farmers' protests in Brittany: proximity and distance in the local newspaper coverage of a social movement', *Journalism Studies*, Vol. 3, No. 1, pp 53–67.

Newton, Jackie and Duncan, Sallyanne (2012) 'Hacking into tragedy: exploring the ethics of death reporting in the social media age', in Richard Keeble and John Mair (eds), *The Phone Hacking Scandal: Journalism on Trial*. Bury St Edmunds: Abramis, pp 208–219.

New York Times (2014) *Innovation Report*, available at http://mashable.com/2014/05/16/full-new-york-times-innovation-report/

NGO-EC Liaison Committee (1989) *Code of Conduct: Images and Messages Relating to the Third World*, www.globalnews.org.uk/teacher_values.htm.

Niblock, Sarah (2007) 'From "knowing how" to "being able": negotiating the meanings of reflective practice and reflexive research in journalism studies', *Journalism Practice*, Vol. 1, No. 1, pp 20–32.

Niblock, Sarah and Machin, David (2007) 'News values for consumer groups: the case of Independent Radio News, London, UK', *Journalism: Theory, Practice and Criticism*, Vol. 8, No. 2, pp 184–204.

Nielsen, Jakob (2006) *Participation Inequality: Encouraging More Users to Contribute*, www.nngroup.com/articles/participation-inequality/.

Nielsen, Rasmus Kleis and Schroder, Kim Christian (2014) 'The relative importance of social media for accessing, finding, and engaging with news', *Digital Journalism*. DOI:10.1080/21670811.2013.872420

Northmore, David (2001) 'Investigative reporting: why and how', in Richard Keeble, *The Newspapers Handbook* (third edition). London: Routledge, pp 183–193.

Norton-Taylor, Richard (2000) 'Bombing in Iraq an "undeclared war"', *Guardian*, 11 November.

NUJ (2011) *National Union of Journalists Code of Conduct*, www.nuj.org.uk/about/nuj-code/.

Observer (2002) 'Talking about my generation', *Observer*, 21 July.

Ofcom (2013) *The Ofcom Broadcasting Code*, http://stakeholders.ofcom.org.uk/broadcasting/broadcast-codes/broadcast-code/?a=0.

O'Malley, Tom (1997) 'Labour and the 1947–9 Royal Commission on the Press', in Michael Bromley and Tom O'Malley (eds), *A Journalism Reader*. London: Routledge, pp 126–158.

O'Malley, Tom and Soley, Clive (2000) *Regulating the Press*. London: Pluto.

O'Neill, Deirdre and Harcup, Tony (2009) 'News values and selectivity', in Karin Wahl-Jorgensen and Thomas Hanitzsch (eds), *Handbook of Journalism Studies*. Mahwah, NJ: Lawrence Erlbaum Associates, pp 161–174.

O'Neill, Deirdre and O'Connor, Catherine (2008) 'The passive journalist: how sources dominate local news', *Journalism Practice*, Vol. 2, No. 3, pp 487–500.

O'Neill, John (1992) 'Journalism in the market place', in Andrew Belsey and Ruth Chadwick (eds), *Ethical Issues in Journalism and the Media*. London: Routledge, pp 15–32.

Orwell, George (1946a) 'Decline of the English murder', in George Orwell (1965), *Decline of the English Murder and Other Essays*. Harmondsworth: Penguin, pp 9–13.

Orwell, George (1946b) 'Politics and the English language', in George Orwell (1962), *Inside the Whale and Other Essays*. Harmondsworth: Penguin, pp 143–157.

Osborn, Andrew (2007) 'These are the faces of the 20 journalists who have lost their lives in Putin's Russia', *Independent on Sunday*, 11 March.

O'Sullivan, Kevin (2001) 'Kate Winslet disappears up her a***', *Daily Mirror*, 27 November.

Page, Bruce (2011) *The Murdoch Archipelago* (second edition). London: Simon & Schuster.

Palast, Greg (2002) *The Best Democracy Money Can Buy: An Investigative Reporter Exposes the Truth about Globalisation, Corporate Cons, and High Finance Fraudsters*. London: Pluto.

Palmer, Jerry (2000) *Spinning into Control: News Values and Source Strategies*. London: Leicester University Press.

Pape, Susan and Featherstone, Sue (2005) *Newspaper Journalism: A Practical Introduction*. London: SAGE.

Pape, Susan and Featherstone, Sue (2006) *Feature Writing: A Practical Introduction*. London: SAGE.

Parfitt, Tom (2006) 'The only good journalist . . .', *Guardian*, 10 October.

Patterson, Thomas (2012) *Informing the News: The Need for Knowledge-based Reporting*, available at: http://journalistsresource.org/reference/research/knowledge-based-reporting/.

PCC (1992) 'Editorial', *Report No. 7*, March, pp 2–3. London: Press Complaints Commission.

PCC (2008) *The Review 2007*. London: Press Complaints Commission.

PCC (2012) *Editors' Code of Practice*, www.pcc.org.uk/cop/practice.html.

Peppiatt, Richard (2012) 'The story factory: infotainment and the tabloid newsroom', in Richard Keeble and John Mair (eds), *The Phone Hacking Scandal: Journalism on Trial* (second edition). Bury St Edmunds: Abramis, pp 17–25.

Perkins, Anne (2001) 'Hands up who fell off the career ladder as they hit motherhood', *Guardian*, 31 May.

Petley, Julian (1999) 'The regulation of media content', in Jane Stokes and Anna Reading (eds), *The Media in Britain: Current Debates and Developments*. Basingstoke: Palgrave.

Phillips, Angela (2007) *Good Writing for Journalists*. London: SAGE.

Phillips, Angela (2015) *Journalism in Context: Practice and Theory for the Digital Age*. London: Routledge.

Philo, Greg (1991) 'Audience beliefs and the 1984/5 miners' strike', in Greg Philo (ed) (1995), *Glasgow Media Group Reader. Vol. 2: Industry, Economy, War and Politics*. London: Routledge, pp 37–42.

Philo, Greg and McLaughlin, Greg (1993) 'The British media and the Gulf War', in Greg Philo (ed) (1995), *Glasgow Media Group Reader. Vol. 2: Industry, Economy, War and Politics*. London: Routledge, pp 146–156.

Philo, Greg, Briant, Emma and Donald, Pauline (2013) *Bad News for Refugees*. London: Pluto.

Pilger, John (1998) *Hidden Agendas*. London: Vintage.

Pilger, John (2001) 'This war of lies goes on', *Daily Mirror*, 16 November.

Plaisance, Patrick Lee, Skewes, Elizabeth and Hanitzsch, Thomas (2012) 'Ethical orientations of journalists around the globe: implications from a cross-national survey', *Communication Research*, Vol. 39, No. 5, pp 641–661.

Plunkett, John (2003) 'Hello girls', *Guardian*, 22 December.

Politkovskaya, Anna (2008) *A Russian Diary*. London: Vintage.

Ponsford, Dominic (2006) 'Shifting of Sands baffles staff', *Press Gazette*, 10 March.

Porter, Roy (2000) *Enlightenment: Britain and the Creation of the Modern World*. London: Allen Lane.

Powell, James (2001) 'The allure of foreign affairs', 30 October, www.mediaguardian.co.uk.

Press Gazette (2000a) 'PA reporter stops identification ban on dead baby', *Press Gazette*, 28 July.

Press Gazette (2000b) 'On and off the record', *Press Gazette*, 21 January.

Press Gazette (2004) 'PCC rap for Welsh weekly over story of dog eating dead man', *Press Gazette*, 26 March.

Press Gazette (2014) 'Man bites dog (and beats up partner) … headline goes viral', 16 June, www.pressgazette. co.uk/content/man-bites-dog-and-beats-partnerheadline-goes-viral.

Private Eye (2001) 'Hackwatch: the big story', *Private Eye*, 26 January.

Pulford, Cedric (2001) *JournoLISTS: 201 Ways to Improve Your Journalism*. Banbury: Ituri.

Purvis, Stewart and Hulbert, Jeff (2013) *When Reporters Cross the Line*. London: Biteback.

Randall, David (2000) *The Universal Journalist*. London: Pluto.

Randall, David (2005) *The Great Reporters*. London: Pluto.

Randall, David (2007) *The Universal Journalist* (third edition). London: Pluto.

Randall, David (2011) *The Universal Journalist* (fourth edition). London: Pluto.

Reah, Danuta (1998) *The Language of Newspapers*. London: Routledge.

Reece, Peter (2005) 'Brian Whittle dies after suffering heart attack', *Hold The Front Page*, 12 December, www.holdthefrontpage.co.Uk/news/2005/12dec/051212whit2.shtml.

Richardson, John (2001) 'British Muslims in the broadsheet press: a challenge to cultural hegemony?', *Journalism Studies*, Vol. 2, No. 2, pp 221–242.

Richardson, John (2005) 'News values', in Bob Franklin, Martin Hamer, Mark Hanna, Marie Kinsey and John Richardson, *Key Concepts in Journalism Studies*. London: SAGE, pp 173–174.

Richardson, John (2006) *Analysing Newspapers: An Approach from Critical Discourse Analysis*. Basingstoke: Palgrave Macmillan.

Richardson, John (2008) (ed) Special issue on language and journalism, *Journalism Studies*, Vol. 9, No. 2.

Robinson, Nick (2012) *Live from Downing Street*. London: Transworld.

Robinson, Sue (2007) '"Someone's gotta be in control here": the institutionalisation of online news and the creation of a shared journalistic authority', *Journalism Practice*, Vol. 1, No. 3, pp 305–321.

Rocco, Fiammetta (1999) 'Stockholm Syndrome: journalists taken hostage', in Stephen Glover (ed), *The Penguin Book of Journalism*. London: Penguin, pp 48–59.

Rose, David (2003) 'Wake up or face privacy law, warns Rusbridger', *Press Gazette*, 14 March.

Ross, Karen (2001) 'Women at work: journalism as en-gendered practice', *Journalism Studies*, Vol. 2, No. 4, pp 531–544.

Roth, Eric and Mann, Michael (1999) *The Insider*. A Forward Pass film.

Rowland, Jacky (2002) 'Milosevic trial: I saw it as my duty', *Ariel*, 3 September.

Rowson, Martin (2001) 'We are the true outsiders of journalism', *British Journalism Review*, Vol. 12, No. 1, pp 29–37.

Roy, Kenneth (2002) 'One pair of eyes: Jon Snow, presenter of *Channel 4 News*, laments the decline and fall of the broadcasting characters', interview published in *The Journalist's Handbook*, No. 71, Autumn, pp 33–38.

Ruddock, Alan (2001) 'Hello! Have redtops said goodbye to politics?', *Observer*, 26 August.

Rusbridger, Alan (2000) 'Versions of seriousness', *Guardian*, 4 November.

Rusbridger, Alan (2013) 'The Snowden leaks and the public', *New York Review of Books*, 21 November, www.nybooks.com/articles/archives/2013/nov/21/snowden-leaks-and-public/.

Salas, Randy A (2007) 'Wilder's "Ace" is a buried treasure', *Star Tribune*, 16 July, www.startribune.com/459/story/1306175.html.

Sambrook, Richard (2004) 'Tragedy in the fog of war', *British Journalism Review*, Vol. 15, No. 3, pp 7–13.

Sanders, Karen (2003) *Ethics and Journalism*. London: SAGE.

Sands, Sarah (2010) *What the Election Papers Say*, BBC Radio 4, 11 April.

Saner, Emine (2012) 'Mexican journalist Lydia Cacho: "I don't scare easily"', *Guardian*, 1 September, www.theguardian.com/world/2012/sep/01/lydia-cacho-mexican-journalist-interview.

Saunders, Mr Justice (2014) 'Mr Justice Saunders' Phone-Hacking Trial Sentencing Remarks in Full', *Press Gazette*, 4 July, http://www.pressgazette.co.uk/mr-justice-saunders-phone-hacking-trial-sentencing-remarks-full.

Schlesinger, Philip (1987) *Putting 'Reality' Together*. London: Routledge.

Schlesinger, Philip (1990) 'Rethinking the sociology of journalism: source strategies and the limits of media-centrism', in Marjorie Ferguson (ed), *Public Communication the New Imperatives: Future Directions for Media Research*. London: SAGE, pp 61–83.

Schudson, Michael (1978) 'Discovering the news: a social history of American newspapers', in Howard Tumber (ed) (1999), *News: A Reader*. Oxford: Oxford University Press, pp 291–296.

Schudson, Michael (1989) 'The sociology of news production', *Media, Culture and Society*, Vol. 11, No. 3, pp 263–282.

Schudson, Michael (1991) 'The sociology of news production revisited', in James Curran and Michael Gurevitch (eds), *Mass Media and Society*. London: Edward Arnold, pp 141–159.

Schudson, Michael (2001) 'The objectivity norm in American journalism', *Journalism: Theory, Practice and Criticism*, Vol. 2, No. 2, pp 149–170.

Seib, Philip (2002) *The Global Journalist: News and Conscience in a World of Conflict*. Oxford: Rowman & Littlefield.

Sergeant, John (2001) *Give Me Ten Seconds*. London: Macmillan.

Shapiro, Ivor, Brin, Colette, Bedard-Brule, Isabelle and Mychajlowycz, Kasia (2013) 'Verification as a strategic ritual: how journalists retrospectively describe processes for ensuring accuracy', *Journalism Practice*, Vol. 7, No. 6, pp 657–673.

Sheridan Burns, Lynette (2002) *Understanding Journalism*. London: SAGE.

Sheridan Burns, Lynette (2013) *Understanding Journalism* (second edition). London: SAGE.

Shoemaker, Pamela (1991) 'Gatekeeping', in Howard Tumber (ed) (1999), *News: A Reader*. Oxford: Oxford University Press, pp 73–78.

Silver, James (2007) 'Hillary brought to book', *Guardian*, 25 June.

Silvester, Christopher (ed) (1994) *The Penguin Book of Interviews*. London: Penguin.

Singer, Jane (2004) 'Strange bedfellows: diffusion of convergence in four news organisations', *Journalism Studies*, Vol. 5, No. 1, pp 3–18.

Singer, Jane (2005) 'The political blogger: "normalizing a new media form to fit old norms and practice"', *Journalism: Theory, Practice and Criticism*, Vol. 6, No. 2, pp 173–198.

Sissons, Helen (2006) *Practical Journalism: How to Write News*. London: SAGE.

Slattery, Jon (2002) 'Journalism must halt drift into "unintended apartheid"', *Press Gazette*, 12 July.

Slattery, Jon (2005) 'Never mind the corporate bollocks – what about the future?', *Press Gazette*, 2 December.

Smith, Angela and Higgins, Michael (2013) *The Language of Journalism: A Multi-genre Perspective*. London: Bloomsbury.

Spark, David (1999) *Investigative Reporting: A Study in Technique*. Oxford: Focal.

Sparks, Colin (1992) 'Popular journalism: theories and practice', in Peter Dahlgren and Colin Sparks (eds), *Journalism and Popular Culture*. London: SAGE, pp 24–44.

Sparks, Colin (1999) 'The press', in Jane Stokes and Anna Reading (eds), *The Media in Britain: Current Debates and Developments*. Basingstoke: Macmillan, pp 41–60.

Sparrow, Andrew (2014) 'Andrew Sparrow's response in full', *Guardian*, 9 March, www.theguardian.com/commentisfree/2014/mar/09/comment-fact-live-news-blogs.

Specter, Michael (2007) 'Who's killing Putin's enemies?', *Observer*, 25 February.

Staab, Joachim Friedrick (1990) 'The role of news factors in news selection: a theoretical reconsideration', *European Journal of Communication*, Vol. 5, pp 423–443.

Stabe, Martin (2008) '*Times* milks web search benefits', *Press Gazette*, 16 May.

Starkey, Guy and Crisell, Andrew (2009) *Radio Journalism*. London: SAGE.

Stevens, Mary (2001) 'The new doorstep challenge', *Press Gazette*, 15 June.

Stevenson, Nick (2002) *Understanding Media Cultures*. London: SAGE.

Sugden, John and Tomlinson, Alan (2007) 'Stories from planet football and sportsworld: source relations and collusion in sport journalism', *Journalism Practice*, Vol. 1, No. 1, pp 44–61.

Sullivan, Andrew (2002) 'Out of the ashes: a new way of communicating', *Sunday Times*, 24 February.

Susman, Gary (2001) 'Tales of the junket', *Guardian*, 5 October.

Telegraph (2008) *Telegraph Style Book*, www.telegraph.co.uk/news/main.jhtml?xml=/news/exclusions/stylebook/nosplit/SBintrostyle.xml.

Temple, Mick (2006) 'Dumbing down is good for you', *British Politics*, Vol. 1, pp 257–273.

Temple, Mick (2008) *The British Press*. Maidenhead: Open University Press.

Tench, Dan (2001) 'Don't pull the dog's teeth', *Guardian*, 23 July.

Thomas, Lou (2006) '"I was never going to work for the *Telegraph*, put it that way"', *Press Gazette*, 23 June.

Thurman, Neil and Walters, Anna (2013) 'Live blogging: digital journalism's pivotal platform?', *Digital Journalism*, Vol. 1, No. 1, pp 82–101.

Times (2005) 'Questions for the Met – the shoot-to-kill policy must have more safeguards', *Times* leader, 18 August.

Tomasky, Michael (2007) 'Newsreader strikes a blow for journalistic integrity, but Paris packs a stronger punch', *Guardian*, 30 June.

Tuchman, Gaye (1972) 'Objectivity as a strategic ritual: an examination of newsmen's notions of objectivity', *American Journal of Sociology*, Vol. 77, No. 4. Reprinted in Howard Tumber (ed) (1999) *News: A Reader*. Oxford: Oxford University Press, pp 297–307.

Tumber, Howard (ed) (1999) *News: A Reader*. Oxford: Oxford University Press.

Tumber, Howard (ed) (2000) *Media Power, Professionals and Policies*. London: Routledge.

Tumber, Howard and Palmer, Jerry (2004) *Media at War: the Iraq crisis*. London: SAGE.

Tunstall, Jeremy (2002) 'Trends in news media and political journalism', in Raymond Kuhn and Erik Neveu (eds), *Political Journalism: New Challenges, New Practices*. London: Routledge, pp 227–241.

Tutek, Edwin Andres Martinez (2006) 'Undocumented workers uncounted victims of 9/11, *Newsday*, 7 September, www.newsday.com/news/local/newyork/am-gone0907,0,5880980.story.

UK Metric Association (2002) *Measurement Units Style Guide*. Available at: www.metric.org.uk.

Ursell, Gill (2001) 'Dumbing down or shaping up? New technologies, new media, new journalism', *Journalism: Theory, Practice and Criticism*, Vol. 2, No. 2, pp 175–196.

Vasterman, Peter (1995) 'Media hypes', www.journalism.fcj.hvu.nl/mediahype/mchype/hype_article.html (article first published, in Dutch, in magazine *Massacommunicatie*, September 1995).

Wahl-Jorgensen, Karin (2013) 'The strategic ritual of emotionality: a case study of Pulitzer Prize-winning articles', *Journalism: Theory, Practice and Criticism*, Vol. 14, No. 1, pp 129–145.

Wahl-Jorgensen, Karin and Hanitzsch, Thomas (eds) (2009) *Handbook of Journalism Studies*. Mahwah, NJ: Lawrence Erlbaum Associates.

Walker, David (2000) 'Newspaper power: a practitioner's account', in Howard Tumber (ed), *Media Power, Professionals and Policies*. London: Routledge, pp 236–246.

Walker, David (2002) 'Low visibility on the inside track', *Journalism: Theory, Practice and Criticism*, Vol. 3, No. 1, pp 101–110.

Ward, Mike (2002) *Journalism Online*. Oxford: Focal.

Ward, Stephen (2010) 'Inventing objectivity: new philosophical foundations', in Christopher Meyers (ed), *Journalism Ethics: A Philosophical Approach*. New York: Oxford University Press, pp 137–152.

Wasserman, Herman (2013) 'Journalism in a new democracy: the ethics of listening', *Communicatio: South African Journal for Communication Theory and Research*, Vol. 39, No. 1, pp 67–84.

Waterhouse, Keith ([1993] 2010) *Waterhouse on Newspaper Style*. Gozo: Revel Barker.

Waterhouse, Keith (1994) *English Our English (and How to Sing It)*. London: Penguin.

Watkins, Alan (2001) *A Short Walk Down Fleet Street: From Beaverbrook to Boycott*. London: Duckbacks.

Watson, James (1998) *Media Communication: An Introduction to Theory and Process*. Basingstoke: Macmillan.

Watson, Tom and Hickman, Martin (2012) *Dial M for Murdoch*. London: Penguin.

Waugh, Evelyn (1943) *Scoop*. London: Penguin.

Weitz, Katy (2003) 'Why I quit the *Sun*', *Guardian*, 31 March.

Wells, Matt (2001a) 'ITN cuts jobs and shifts towards lifestyle news', *Guardian*, 22 November.

Wells, Matt (2001b) 'BBC's "brighter" news to beat rising rival, *Guardian*, 18 January.

Wells, Matt (2005) 'Paxman answers the questions', *Guardian*, 31 January.

Welsh, Tom and Greenwood, Walter (2001) *Essential Law for Journalists*. London: Butterworths.

Welsh, Tom, Greenwood, Walter and Banks, David (2007) *Essential Law for Journalists* (nineteenth edition). Oxford: Oxford University Press.

Westerstahl, Jorgen and Johansson, Folke (1994) 'Foreign news: news values and ideologies', *European Journal of Communication*, Vol. 9, pp 71–89.

Wheeler, Sharon (2009) *Feature Writing for Journalists*. London: Routledge.

Wheen, Francis (2002) *Hoo-hahs and Passing Frenzies: Collected Journalism 1991–2001*. London: Atlantic Books.

Whitaker, Brian (1981) *News Ltd: Why You Can't Read All About It*. London: Minority Press Group.

White, David Manning (1950) 'The gatekeeper: a case study in the selection of news', in Howard Tumber (ed) (1999), *News: A Reader*. Oxford: Oxford University Press, pp 66–72.

White, Michael (2013) 'Plenty of mischief, less of the malice', *British Journalism Review*, Vol. 24, No. 4, pp 48–53.

Wickrematunge, Lasantha (2009) 'And then they came for me', *Sunday Leader* Editorial, 11 January, www. thesundayleader.lk/20090111/editorial-.htm.

Williams, Andy and Gajevic, Slavko (2013) 'Selling science? Source struggles, public relations, and UK press coverage of animal–human hybrid embryos', *Journalism Studies*, Vol. 14, No. 4, pp 507–522.

Williams, Francis (1959) *Dangerous Estate: The Anatomy of Newspapers*. London: Arrow.

Williams, Granville (1996) *Britain's Media: How They are Related*. London: Campaign for Press and Broadcasting Freedom.

Williams Granville (ed) (2009) *Shafted: The Media, the Miners' Strike and Aftermath*. London: Campaign for Press and Broadcasting Freedom.

Williams, Granville (ed) (2014a) *Big Media & Internet Titans*. London: Campaign for Press and Broadcasting Freedom.

Williams, Granville (ed) (2014b) *Settling Scores: The Media, the Police and the Miners' Strike*. London: Campaign for Press and Broadcasting Freedom.

Williams, Kevin (1992) 'Something more important than truth: ethical issues in war reporting', in Andrew Belsey and Ruth Chadwick (eds), *Ethical Issues in Journalism and the Media*. London: Routledge, pp 154–170.

Williams, Raymond (1980) *Problems in Materialism and Culture*. London: Verso.

Wilson, John (1996) *Understanding Journalism: A Guide to Issues*. London: Routledge.

Winch, Samuel P (1997) *Mapping the Cultural Space of Journalism: How Journalists Distinguish News from Entertainment*. Westport, CT: Praeger.

Winchester, Simon (2001) 'My tainted days', *Guardian*, 22 May.

Wu, H Denis (2000) 'Systemic determinants of international news coverage: a comparison of 38 countries', *Journal of Communication*, Vol. 50, pp 110–130.

Wyatt, Wendy (ed) (2014) *The Ethics of Journalism: Individual, Institutional, and Cultural Influences*. London: I.B. Tauris.

Wykes, Maggie (2001) *News, Crime and Culture*. London: Pluto.

Yelland, David (2013) Leveson Anniversary Lecture, Media Standards Trust, 29 November, http://media-standardstrust.org/mst-news/david-yellands-leveson-anniversary-lecture-29th-november-2013-full-text/.

Younge, Gary (2001) 'Bradford needs hope, not teargas', *Guardian*, 10 July.

Younge, Gary (2002) 'Temples for tomorrow', *Guardian*, 9 December.

Younge, Gary (2006) 'Take a potshot at the powerless, and you too can win a medal of valour', *Guardian*, 6 March.

Zelizer, Barbie (2004) *Taking Journalism Seriously: News and the Academy*. London: SAGE.

Zelizer, Barbie and Allan, Stuart (eds) (2002) *Journalism after September 11*. London: Routledge.

INDEX

death knocks, 29, 130, 135–7, 139
defamation, 21–2
Defence, Press and Broadcasting Advisory Committee, 23–4
Defence Advisory (DA) Notices, 24
delayed drops, 148, 150
democracy, investigative journalism, 96–7, 106
Derbyshire, Victoria, 132
description, 165–6
developing countries, 41
dialogic language, 148
Diana, Princess, 59, 67
Dictionary of Modern English Usage, 201
digital economy, 222–3, 228
digital journalism *see* online journalism
Dillow, Gordon, 79
discourse analysis, 148
Dixon, Sara, 130
dogs, 37–9
Doncaster Education City, 95–8, 106, 107
Doncaster Free Press, 95–8
doorstepping, 135–7
Dorril, Stephen, 93–4
Dovey, Jon, 159
dual product market, 22
dumbing down, 113–14, 116, 121
Duncan, Sallyanne, 130
Duncan-Smith, Iain, 129–30

Eastwood, Lindsay
    broadcast journalism, 28–9, 174–7, 179
    entertainment, 113, 119
    online journalism, 178–9
    profile of, 9
    skills required for journalism, 231
    sources, 71
    statutory regulation, 24
Economist, 186–7
editors' code of practice, 25, 26–7, 209, 212
EDL (English Defence League), 211
education, journalism, 12–14
El Diario de Juarez, 20
elections, 77–8
Eliot, George, 75, 88
elite nations, 38
elitism, 115–16, 120
Elliot, Philip, 39, 174, 232
email
    interviews, 132
    lists, 63
emotionality, 84, 88
encryption, 105, 238
Engel, Matthew, 114, 121, 136
Engels, Friedrich, 10
English Defence League (EDL), 211
entertainment
    dumbing down, 121
    versus elitism, 115–16, 120

entertainment *cont.*
    historical perspective, 114, 121
    industry, 63
    popular views of media output, 115
    stories, 47
    trends in journalism, 113–18, 121
    values, 41, 118–19
ethical journalism, 26, 29, 51, 71, 72, 207–15, 231–4
Ethical Journalism Initiative, 213
ethics, 14, 19–33, 207–15
    see also ethical journalism
ethnicity
    journalists, 25, 31
    language, 188–9
    moral panics, 82
    news access, 57
European Convention on Human Rights, 211
Evans, Harold, 37, 187, 201
Express see Daily Express
eyes and ears, 56, 63

Facebook, 63, 220, 223, 224, 231
    see also social media
face-to-face interviews, 132–3
Factcheck, 11, 102
facts
    checking, 86–7
    features, 165
    investigative journalism, 95–6
    see also accuracy; verification
Fanon, Frantz, 127
features
    guidance on writing, 157–69
    personal voice of journalist, 159–60, 163
    structure, 159, 161–8
    topics, 158–9, 160–1
    types, 157–60
Fenton, Natalie, 223–4
Figdor, Carrie, 85
Financial Times, 29
fire brigade, 60, 64
Fisk, Robert, 32
Fiske, John, 80–1
Flat Earth News, 8, 147
floods, 176–7
Foley, Michael, 20, 29
follow-ups, 41, 48–9
Foot, Paul
    interviews, 132
    investigative journalism, 95, 98, 99–100, 106–7, 108
    Iraq war, 79
    journalistic skills, 238–9
    news sources, 69
    profile of, 9–10
    proprietors, 28
    trade unions, 26, 32